The
Odyssey

of

Homer

ISBN: 1721245197
ISBN-13: 978-1721245192

Odyssey is the second classic poem after Iliad attributed to an Ancient Greek poet Homer. Presumably, it was created in the eighth century BC or a little later. The poem describes the journey of a mythic character Odyssey to his homeland after the end of the Trojan war, and the adventures of his wife Penelope who had been waiting for Odyssey in Ithaca.

Both Odyssey and another famous poem by Homer, Iliad, are full of mythic elements – Odyssey meets Cyclope Polyphemus, the witch-goddess Circe, the god Aeolus etc.

Odyssey describes most of his adventures during the feast with the King Alcinous.

Table of Contents

Book I

In a council of the Gods, Minerva calls their attention to Ulysses, still a wanderer. They resolve to grant him a safe return to Ithaca. Minerva descends to encourage Telemachus, and in the form of Mentes directs him in what manner to proceed. Throughout this book the extravagance and profligacy of the suitors are occasionally suggested.

Muse make the man thy theme, for shrewdness famed
And genius versatile, who far and wide
A Wand'rer, after Ilium overthrown,
Discover'd various cities, and the mind
And manners learn'd of men, in lands remote.
He num'rous woes on Ocean toss'd, endured,
Anxious to save himself, and to conduct
His followers to their home; yet all his care
Preserved them not; they perish'd self-destroy'd
By their own fault; infatuate! who devoured
10 The oxen of the all-o'erseeing Sun,
And, punish'd for that crime, return'd no more.
Daughter divine of Jove, these things record,
As it may please thee, even in our ears.
The rest, all those who had perdition 'scaped
By war or on the Deep, dwelt now at home;
Him only, of his country and his wife
Alike desirous, in her hollow grots
Calypso, Goddess beautiful, detained
Wooing him to her arms. But when, at length,
20 (Many a long year elapsed) the year arrived
Of his return (by the decree of heav'n)
To Ithaca, not even then had he,
Although surrounded by his people, reach'd
The period of his suff'rings and his toils.
Yet all the Gods, with pity moved, beheld
His woes, save Neptune; He alone with wrath
Unceasing and implacable pursued
Godlike Ulysses to his native shores.
But Neptune, now, the Æthiopians fought,
30 (The Æthiopians, utmost of mankind,
These Eastward situate, those toward the West)
Call'd to an hecatomb of bulls and lambs.
There sitting, pleas'd he banqueted; the Gods
In Jove's abode, meantime, assembled all,
'Midst whom the Sire of heav'n and earth began.
For he recall'd to mind Ægisthus slain
By Agamemnon's celebrated son
Orestes, and retracing in his thought
That dread event, the Immortals thus address'd.
40 Alas! how prone are human-kind to blame
The Pow'rs of Heav'n! From us, they say, proceed
The ills which they endure, yet more than Fate
Herself inflicts, by their own crimes incur.
So now Ægisthus, by no force constrained
Of Destiny, Atrides' wedded wife
Took to himself, and him at his return
Slew, not unwarn'd of his own dreadful end
By us: for we commanded Hermes down
The watchful Argicide, who bade him fear
50 Alike, to slay the King, or woo the Queen.

For that Atrides' son Orestes, soon
As grown mature, and eager to assume
His sway imperial, should avenge the deed.
So Hermes spake, but his advice moved not
Ægisthus, on whose head the whole arrear
Of vengeance heap'd, at last, hath therefore fall'n.
Whom answer'd then Pallas cærulean-eyed.
Oh Jove, Saturnian Sire, o'er all supreme!
And well he merited the death he found;
60 So perish all, who shall, like him, offend.
But with a bosom anguish-rent I view
Ulysses, hapless Chief! who from his friends
Remote, affliction hath long time endured
In yonder woodland isle, the central boss
Of Ocean. That retreat a Goddess holds,
Daughter of sapient Atlas, who the abyss
Knows to its bottom, and the pillars high
Himself upbears which sep'rate earth from heav'n.
His daughter, there, the sorrowing Chief detains,
70 And ever with smooth speech insidious seeks
To wean his heart from Ithaca; meantime
Ulysses, happy might he but behold
The smoke ascending from his native land,
Death covets. Canst thou not, Olympian Jove!
At last relent? Hath not Ulysses oft
With victims slain amid Achaia's fleet
Thee gratified, while yet at Troy he fought?
How hath he then so deep incensed thee, Jove?
To whom, the cloud-assembler God replied.
80 What word hath pass'd thy lips, Daughter belov'd?
Can I forget Ulysses? Him forget
So noble, who in wisdom all mankind
Excels, and who hath sacrific'd so oft
To us whose dwelling is the boundless heav'n?
Earth-circling Neptune-He it is whose wrath
Pursues him ceaseless for the Cyclops' sake
Polypheme, strongest of the giant race,
Whom of his eye Ulysses hath deprived.
For Him, Thoösa bore, Nymph of the sea
90 From Phorcys sprung, by Ocean's mighty pow'r
Impregnated in caverns of the Deep.
E'er since that day, the Shaker of the shores,
Although he slay him not, yet devious drives
Ulysses from his native isle afar.
Yet come-in full assembly his return
Contrive we now, both means and prosp'rous end;
So Neptune shall his wrath remit, whose pow'r
In contest with the force of all the Gods
Exerted single, can but strive in vain.
100 To whom Minerva, Goddess azure-eyed.
Oh Jupiter! above all Kings enthroned!

If the Immortals ever-blest ordain
That wise Ulysses to his home return,
Dispatch we then Hermes the Argicide,
Our messenger, hence to Ogygia's isle,
Who shall inform Calypso, nymph divine,
Of this our fixt resolve, that to his home
Ulysses, toil-enduring Chief, repair.
Myself will hence to Ithaca, meantime,
110 His son to animate, and with new force
Inspire, that (the Achaians all convened
In council,) he may, instant, bid depart
The suitors from his home, who, day by day,
His num'rous flocks and fatted herds consume.
And I will send him thence to Sparta forth,
And into sandy Pylus, there to hear
(If hear he may) some tidings of his Sire,
And to procure himself a glorious name.
This said, her golden sandals to her feet
120 She bound, ambrosial, which o'er all the earth
And o'er the moist flood waft her fleet as air,
Then, seizing her strong spear pointed with brass,
In length and bulk, and weight a matchless beam,
With which the Jove-born Goddess levels ranks
Of Heroes, against whom her anger burns,
From the Olympian summit down she flew,
And on the threshold of Ulysses' hall
In Ithaca, and within his vestibule
Apparent stood; there, grasping her bright spear,
130 Mentes[1] she seem'd, the hospitable Chief
Of Taphos' isle-she found the haughty throng
The suitors; they before the palace gate
With iv'ry cubes sported, on num'rous hides
Reclined of oxen which themselves had slain.
The heralds and the busy menials there
Minister'd to them; these their mantling cups
With water slaked; with bibulous sponges those
Made clean the tables, set the banquet on,
And portioned out to each his plenteous share.
140 Long ere the rest Telemachus himself
Mark'd her, for sad amid them all he sat,
Pourtraying in deep thought contemplative
His noble Sire, and questioning if yet
Perchance the Hero might return to chase
From all his palace that imperious herd,
To his own honour lord of his own home.
Amid them musing thus, sudden he saw
The Goddess, and sprang forth, for he abhorr'd
To see a guest's admittance long delay'd;
150 Approaching eager, her right hand he seized,
The brazen spear took from her, and in words
With welcome wing'd Minerva thus address'd.
Stranger, all hail! to share our cordial love
Thou com'st; the banquet finish'd, thou shalt next
Inform me wherefore thou hast here arrived.
So saying, toward the spacious hall he moved,
Follow'd by Pallas, and, arriving soon
Beneath the lofty roof, placed her bright spear

Within a pillar's cavity, long time
160 The armoury where many a spear had stood,
Bright weapons of his own illustrious Sire.
Then, leading her toward a footstool'd throne
Magnificent, which first he overspread
With linen, there he seated her, apart
From that rude throng, and for himself disposed
A throne of various colours at her side,
Lest, stunn'd with clamour of the lawless band,
The new-arrived should loth perchance to eat,
And that more free he might the stranger's ear
170 With questions of his absent Sire address,
And now a maiden charg'd with golden ew'r,
And with an argent laver, pouring first
Pure water on their hands, supplied them, next,
With a resplendent table, which the chaste
Directress of the stores furnish'd with bread
And dainties, remnants of the last regale.

Then, in his turn, the sewer[2] with sav'ry meats,
Dish after dish, served them, of various kinds,
And golden cups beside the chargers placed,
180 Which the attendant herald fill'd with wine.
Ere long, in rush'd the suitors, and the thrones
And couches occupied, on all whose hands
The heralds pour'd pure water; then the maids
Attended them with bread in baskets heap'd,
And eager they assail'd the ready feast.
At length, when neither thirst nor hunger more
They felt unsatisfied, to new delights
Their thoughts they turn'd, to song and sprightly dance,
Enlivening sequel of the banquet's joys.
190 An herald, then, to Phemius' hand consign'd
His beauteous lyre; he through constraint regaled
The suitors with his song, and while the chords
He struck in prelude to his pleasant strains,
Telemachus his head inclining nigh
To Pallas' ear, lest others should his words
Witness, the blue-eyed Goddess thus bespake.
My inmate and my friend! far from my lips
Be ev'ry word that might displease thine ear!
The song-the harp, — what can they less than charm
200 These wantons? who the bread unpurchased eat
Of one whose bones on yonder continent
Lie mould'ring, drench'd by all the show'rs of heaven,
Or roll at random in the billowy deep.
Ah! could they see him once to his own isle
Restored, both gold and raiment they would wish
Far less, and nimbleness of foot instead.
But He, alas! hath by a wretched fate,
Past question perish'd, and what news soe'er
We hear of his return, kindles no hope
210 In us, convinced that he returns no more.
But answer undissembling; tell me true;
Who art thou? whence? where stands thy city? where
Thy father's mansion? In what kind of ship
Cam'st thou? Why steer'd the mariners their course
To Ithaca, and of what land are they?

---

[1] We are told that Homer was under obligations to Mentes, who had frequently given him a passage in his ship to different countries which he wished to see, for which reason he has here immortalised him.

[2] Milton uses the word-Sewers and seneschals.

For that on foot thou found'st us not, is sure.
This also tell me, hast thou now arrived
New to our isle, or wast thou heretofore
My father's guest? Since many to our house
220 Resorted in those happier days, for he
Drew pow'rful to himself the hearts of all.
Then Pallas thus, Goddess cærulean-eyed.
I will with all simplicity of truth
Thy questions satisfy. Behold in me
Mentes, the offspring of a Chief renown'd
In war, Anchialus; and I rule, myself,
An island race, the Taphians oar-expert.
With ship and mariners I now arrive,
Seeking a people of another tongue
230 Athwart the gloomy flood, in quest of brass
For which I barter steel, ploughing the waves
To Temesa. My ship beneath the woods
Of Neïus, at yonder field that skirts
Your city, in the haven Rhethrus rides.
We are hereditary guests; our Sires
Were friends long since; as, when thou seest him next,
The Hero old Laertes will avouch,
Of whom, I learn, that he frequents no more
The city now, but in sequester'd scenes
240 Dwells sorrowful, and by an antient dame
With food and drink supplied oft as he feels
Refreshment needful to him, while he creeps
Between the rows of his luxuriant vines.
But I have come drawn hither by report,
Which spake thy Sire arrived, though still it seems
The adverse Gods his homeward course retard.
For not yet breathless lies the noble Chief,
But in some island of the boundless flood
Resides a prisoner, by barbarous force
250 Of some rude race detained reluctant there.
And I will now foreshow thee what the Gods
Teach me, and what, though neither augur skill'd
Nor prophet, I yet trust shall come to pass.
He shall not, henceforth, live an exile long
From his own shores, no, not although in bands
Of iron held, but will ere long contrive
His own return; for in expedients, framed
With wond'rous ingenuity, he abounds.
But tell me true; art thou, in stature such,
260 Son of himself Ulysses? for thy face
And eyes bright-sparkling, strongly indicate
Ulysses in thee. Frequent have we both
Conversed together thus, thy Sire and I,
Ere yet he went to Troy, the mark to which
So many Princes of Achaia steer'd.
Him since I saw not, nor Ulysses me.
To whom Telemachus, discrete, replied.
Stranger! I tell thee true; my mother's voice
Affirms me his, but since no mortal knows
270 His derivation, I affirm it not.
Would I had been son of some happier Sire,
Ordain'd in calm possession of his own
To reach the verge of life. But now, report
Proclaims me his, whom I of all mankind

Unhappiest deem.-Thy question is resolved.
Then answer thus Pallas blue-eyed return'd.
From no ignoble race, in future days,
The Gods shall prove thee sprung, whom so endow'd
With ev'ry grace Penelope hath borne.
280 But tell me true. What festival is this?
This throng-whence are they? wherefore hast thou need
Of such a multitude? Behold I here
A banquet, or a nuptial? for these
Meet not by contribution[3] to regale,
With such brutality and din they hold
Their riotous banquet! a wise man and good
Arriving, now, among them, at the sight
Of such enormities would much be wroth.
To whom replied Telemachus discrete.
290 Since, stranger! thou hast ask'd, learn also this.
While yet Ulysses, with his people dwelt,
His presence warranted the hope that here
Virtue should dwell and opulence; but heav'n
Hath cast for us, at length, a diff'rent lot,
And he is lost, as never man before.
For I should less lament even his death,
Had he among his friends at Ilium fall'n,
Or in the arms of his companions died,
Troy's siege accomplish'd. Then his tomb the Greeks
300 Of ev'ry tribe had built, and for his son,
He had immortal glory atchieved; but now,
By harpies torn inglorious, beyond reach
Of eye or ear he lies; and hath to me
Grief only, and unceasing sighs bequeath'd.
Nor mourn I for his sake alone; the Gods
Have plann'd for me still many a woe beside;
For all the rulers of the neighbour isles,
Samos, Dulichium, and the forest-crown'd
Zacynthus, others also, rulers here
310 In craggy Ithaca, my mother seek
In marriage, and my household stores consume.
But neither she those nuptial rites abhorr'd,
Refuses absolute, nor yet consents
To end them; they my patrimony waste
Meantime, and will not long spare even me.
To whom, with deep commiseration pang'd,
Pallas replied. Alas! great need hast thou
Of thy long absent father to avenge
These num'rous wrongs; for could he now appear
320 There, at yon portal, arm'd with helmet, shield,
And grasping his two spears, such as when first
I saw him drinking joyous at our board,
From Ilus son of Mermeris, who dwelt
In distant Ephyre, just then return'd,
(For thither also had Ulysses gone
In his swift bark, seeking some pois'nous drug
Wherewith to taint his brazen arrows keen,
Which drug through fear of the eternal Gods
Ilus refused him, and my father free
330 Gave to him, for he loved him past belief)
Could now, Ulysses, clad in arms as then,
Mix with these suitors, short his date of life
To each, and bitter should his nuptials prove.

---

[3] +Eranos+, a convivial meeting, at which every man paid his proportion, at least contributed something; but it seems to have been a meeting at which strict sobriety was observed, else Pallas would not have inferred from the noise and riot of this, that it was not such a one.

But these events, whether he shall return
To take just vengeance under his own roof,
Or whether not, lie all in the Gods lap.
Meantime I counsel thee, thyself to think
By what means likeliest thou shalt expel
These from thy doors. Now mark me: close attend.
340 To-morrow, summoning the Grecian Chiefs
To council, speak to them, and call the Gods
To witness that solemnity. Bid go
The suitors hence, each to his own abode.
Thy mother-if her purpose be resolved
On marriage, let her to the house return
Of her own potent father, who, himself,
Shall furnish forth her matrimonial rites,
And ample dow'r, such as it well becomes
A darling daughter to receive, bestow.
350 But hear me now; thyself I thus advise.
The prime of all thy ships preparing, mann'd
With twenty rowers, voyage hence to seek
Intelligence of thy long-absent Sire.

Some mortal may inform thee, or a word,[4]
Perchance, by Jove directed (safest source
Of notice to mankind) may reach thine ear.
First voyaging to Pylus, there enquire
Of noble Nestor; thence to Sparta tend,
To question Menelaus amber-hair'd,
360 Latest arrived of all the host of Greece.
There should'st thou learn that still thy father lives,
And hope of his return, although
Distress'd, thou wilt be patient yet a year.
But should'st thou there hear tidings that he breathes
No longer, to thy native isle return'd,
First heap his tomb; then with such pomp perform
His funeral rites as his great name demands,
And make thy mother's spousals, next, thy care.
These duties satisfied, delib'rate last
370 Whether thou shalt these troublers of thy house
By stratagem, or by assault, destroy.
For thou art now no child, nor longer may'st
Sport like one. Hast thou not the proud report
Heard, how Orestes hath renown acquired
With all mankind, his father's murtherer
Ægisthus slaying, the deceiver base
Who slaughter'd Agamemnon? Oh my friend!
(For with delight thy vig'rous growth I view,
And just proportion) be thou also bold,
380 And merit praise from ages yet to come.
But I will to my vessel now repair,
And to my mariners, whom, absent long,
I may perchance have troubled. Weigh thou well
My counsel; let not my advice be lost.
To whom Telemachus discrete replied.
Stranger! thy words bespeak thee much my friend,
Who, as a father teaches his own son,
Hast taught me, and I never will forget.
But, though in haste thy voyage to pursue,
390 Yet stay, that in the bath refreshing first
Thy limbs now weary, thou may'st sprightlier seek
Thy gallant bark, charged with some noble gift

Of finish'd workmanship, which thou shalt keep
As my memorial ever; such a boon
As men confer on guests whom much they love.
Then Pallas thus, Goddess cærulean-eyed.
Retard me not, for go I must; the gift
Which liberal thou desirest to bestow,
Give me at my return, that I may bear
400 The treasure home; and, in exchange, thyself
Expect some gift equivalent from me.
She spake, and as with eagle-wings upborne,
Vanish'd incontinent, but him inspired
With daring fortitude, and on his heart
Dearer remembrance of his Sire impress'd
Than ever. Conscious of the wond'rous change,
Amazed he stood, and, in his secret thought
Revolving all, believed his guest a God.
The youthful Hero to the suitors then
410 Repair'd; they silent, listen'd to the song
Of the illustrious Bard: he the return
Deplorable of the Achaian host
From Ilium by command of Pallas, sang.
Penelope, Icarius' daughter, mark'd
Meantime the song celestial, where she sat
In the superior palace; down she came,
By all the num'rous steps of her abode;
Not sole, for two fair handmaids follow'd her.
She then, divinest of her sex, arrived
420 In presence of that lawless throng, beneath
The portal of her stately mansion stood,
Between her maidens, with her lucid veil
Her lovely features mantling. There, profuse
She wept, and thus the sacred bard bespake.
Phemius! for many a sorrow-soothing strain
Thou know'st beside, such as exploits record
Of Gods and men, the poet's frequent theme;
Give them of those a song, and let themselves
Their wine drink noiseless; but this mournful strain
430 Break off, unfriendly to my bosom's peace,
And which of all hearts nearest touches mine,
With such regret my dearest Lord I mourn,
Rememb'ring still an husband praised from side
To side, and in the very heart of Greece.
Then answer thus Telemachus return'd.
My mother! wherefore should it give thee pain
If the delightful bard that theme pursue
To which he feels his mind impell'd? the bard
Blame not, but rather Jove, who, as he wills,
440 Materials for poetic art supplies.
No fault is his, if the disastrous fate
He sing of the Achaians, for the song
Wins ever from the hearers most applause
That has been least in use. Of all who fought
At Troy, Ulysses hath not lost, alone,
His day of glad return; but many a Chief
Hath perish'd also. Seek thou then again
Thy own apartment, spindle ply and loom,
And task thy maidens; management belongs
450 To men of joys convivial, and of men
Especially to me, chief ruler here.

---

[4] +Ossa+-a word spoken, with respect to the speaker, casually; but with reference to the inquirer supposed to be sent for his information by the especial appointment and providential favour of the Gods.

She heard astonish'd; and the prudent speech
Reposing of her son deep in her heart,
Again with her attendant maidens sought
Her upper chamber. There arrived, she wept
Her lost Ulysses, till Minerva bathed
Her weary lids in dewy sleep profound.
Then echoed through the palace dark-bedimm'd
With evening shades the suitors boist'rous roar,
460 For each the royal bed burn'd to partake,
Whom thus Telemachus discrete address'd.
All ye my mother's suitors, though addict
To contumacious wrangling fierce, suspend
Your clamour, for a course to me it seems
More decent far, when such a bard as this,
Godlike, for sweetness, sings, to hear his song.
To-morrow meet we in full council all,
That I may plainly warn you to depart
From this our mansion. Seek ye where ye may
470 Your feasts; consume your own; alternate feed
Each at the other's cost; but if it seem
Wisest in your account and best, to eat
Voracious thus the patrimonial goods

Of one man, rend'ring no account of all,[5]
Bite to the roots; but know that I will cry
Ceaseless to the eternal Gods, in hope
That Jove, for retribution of the wrong,
Shall doom you, where ye have intruded, there
To bleed, and of your blood ask no account.
480 He ended, and each gnaw'd his lip, aghast
At his undaunted hardiness of speech.
Then thus Antinoüs spake, Eupithes' son.
Telemachus! the Gods, methinks, themselves
Teach thee sublimity, and to pronounce
Thy matter fearless. Ah forbid it, Jove!
That one so eloquent should with the weight
Of kingly cares in Ithaca be charged,
A realm, by claim hereditary, thine.
Then prudent thus Telemachus replied.
490 Although my speech Antinoüs may, perchance,
Provoke thee, know that I am not averse
From kingly cares, if Jove appoint me such.
Seems it to thee a burthen to be fear'd
By men above all others? trust me, no,
There is no ill in royalty; the man
So station'd, waits not long ere he obtain
Riches and honour. But I grant that Kings
Of the Achaians may no few be found
In sea-girt Ithaca both young and old,
500 Of whom since great Ulysses is no more,
Reign whoso may; but King, myself, I am
In my own house, and over all my own
Domestics, by Ulysses gained for me.
To whom Eurymachus replied, the son
Of Polybus. What Grecian Chief shall reign
In sea-girt Ithaca, must be referr'd
To the Gods' will, Telemachus! meantime

Thou hast unquestionable right to keep
Thy own, and to command in thy own house.
510 May never that man on her shores arrive,
While an inhabitant shall yet be left
In Ithaca, who shall by violence wrest
Thine from thee. But permit me, noble Sir!
To ask thee of thy guest. Whence came the man?
What country claims him? Where are to be found
His kindred and his patrimonial fields?
Brings he glad tidings of thy Sire's approach
Homeward? or came he to receive a debt
Due to himself? How swift he disappear'd!
520 Nor opportunity to know him gave
To those who wish'd it; for his face and air
Him speak not of Plebeian birth obscure.
Whom answered thus Telemachus discrete.
Eurymachus! my father comes no more.
I can no longer now tidings believe,
If such arrive; nor he'd I more the song
Of sooth-sayers whom my mother may consult.
But this my guest hath known in other days
My father, and he came from Taphos, son
530 Of brave Anchialus, Mentes by name,
And Chief of the sea-practis'd Taphian race.
So spake Telemachus, but in his heart
Knew well his guest a Goddess from the skies.
Then they to dance and heart-enlivening song
Turn'd joyous, waiting the approach of eve,
And dusky evening found them joyous still.
Then each, to his own house retiring, sought
Needful repose. Meantime Telemachus
To his own lofty chamber, built in view
540 Of the wide hall, retired; but with a heart
In various musings occupied intense.
Sage Euryclea, bearing in each hand
A torch, preceded him; her sire was Ops,
Pisenor's son, and, in her early prime,
At his own cost Laertes made her his,
Paying with twenty beeves her purchase-price,
Nor in less honour than his spotless wife
He held her ever, but his consort's wrath
Fearing, at no time call'd her to his bed.
550 She bore the torches, and with truer heart
Loved him than any of the female train,
For she had nurs'd him in his infant years.
He open'd his broad chamber-valves, and sat
On his couch-side: then putting off his vest
Of softest texture, placed it in the hands
Of the attendant dame discrete, who first
Folding it with exactest care, beside
His bed suspended it, and, going forth,
Drew by its silver ring the portal close,
560 And fasten'd it with bolt and brace secure.
There lay Telemachus, on finest wool
Reposed, contemplating all night his course
Prescribed by Pallas to the Pylian shore.

---

[5] There is in the Original an evident stress laid on the word +Nêpoinoi+ which is used in both places. It was a sort of Lex Talionis which Telemachus hoped might be put in force against them; and that Jove would demand no satisfaction for the lives of those who made him none for the waste of his property.

Book II

Telemachus having convened an assembly of the Greecians, publicly calls on the Suitors to relinquish the house of Ulysses. During the continuance of the Council he has much to suffer from the petulance of the Suitors, from whom, having informed them of his design to undertake a voyage in hope to obtain news of Ulysses, he asks a ship, with all things necessary for the purpose. He is refused, but is afterwards furnished with what he wants by Minerva, in the form of Mentor. He embarks in the evening without the privity of his mother, and the Goddess sails with him.

Aurora, rosy daughter of the dawn,
Now ting'd the East, when habited again,
Uprose Ulysses' offspring from his bed.
Athwart his back his faulchion keen he flung,
His sandals bound to his unsullied feet,
And, godlike, issued from his chamber-door.
At once the clear-voic'd heralds he enjoin'd
To call the Greeks to council; they aloud
Gave forth the summons, and the throng began.
When all were gather'd, and the assembly full,
10 Himself, his hand arm'd with a brazen spear,
Went also; nor alone he went; his hounds
Fleet-footed follow'd him, a faithful pair.
O'er all his form Minerva largely shed
Majestic grace divine, and, as he went,
The whole admiring concourse gaz'd on him,
The seniors gave him place, and down he sat
On his paternal Throne. Then grave arose
The Hero, old Ægyptius; bow'd with age
Was he, and by experience deep-inform'd.
20 His son had with Ulysses, godlike Chief,
On board his fleet to steed-fam'd Ilium gone,
The warrior Antiphus, whom in his cave
The savage Cyclops slew, and on his flesh
At ev'ning made obscene his last regale.
Three sons he had beside, a suitor one,
Eurynomus; the other two, employ
Found constant managing their Sire's concerns.
Yet he forgat not, father as he was
Of these, his absent eldest, whom he mourn'd
3 °Ceaseless, and thus his speech, weeping, began.
Hear me, ye men of Ithaca, my friends!
Nor council here nor session hath been held
Since great Ulysses left his native shore.
Who now convenes us? what especial need
Hath urged him, whether of our youth he be,
Or of our senators by age matured?
Have tidings reach'd him of our host's return,
Which here he would divulge? or brings he aught
Of public import on a diff'rent theme?
40 I deem him, whosoe'er he be, a man
Worthy to prosper, and may Jove vouchsafe
The full performance of his chief desire!
He ended, and Telemachus rejoiced
In that good omen. Ardent to begin,
He sat not long, but, moving to the midst,

Received the sceptre from Pisenor's hand,
His prudent herald, and addressing, next,
The hoary Chief Ægyptius, thus began.
Not far remote, as thou shalt soon thyself
50 Perceive, oh venerable Chief! he stands,
Who hath convened this council. I, am He.
I am in chief the suff'rer. Tidings none
Of the returning host I have received,
Which here I would divulge, nor bring I aught
Of public import on a different theme,
But my own trouble, on my own house fall'n,
And twofold fall'n. One is, that I have lost
A noble father, who, as fathers rule
Benign their children, govern'd once yourselves;
60 The other, and the more alarming ill,
With ruin threatens my whole house, and all
My patrimony with immediate waste.
Suitors, (their children who in this our isle
Hold highest rank) importunate besiege
My mother, though desirous not to wed,
And rather than resort to her own Sire
Icarius, who might give his daughter dow'r,
And portion her to whom he most approves,
(A course which, only named, moves their disgust)
70 They chuse, assembling all within my gates
Daily to make my beeves, my sheep, my goats
Their banquet, and to drink without restraint
My wine; whence ruin threatens us and ours;
For I have no Ulysses to relieve
Me and my family from this abuse.
Ourselves are not sufficient; we, alas!
Too feeble should be found, and yet to learn
How best to use the little force we own;
Else, had I pow'r, I would, myself, redress
80 The evil; for it now surpasses far
All suff'rance, now they ravage uncontroul'd,
Nor show of decency vouchsafe me more.

Oh be ashamed[6] yourselves; blush at the thought
Of such reproach as ye shall sure incur
From all our neighbour states, and fear beside
The wrath of the Immortals, lest they call
Yourselves one day to a severe account.
I pray you by Olympian Jove, by her
Whose voice convenes all councils, and again
90 Dissolves them, Themis, that henceforth ye cease,
That ye permit me, oh my friends! to wear

---

[6] The reader is to be reminded that this is not an assembly of the suitors only, but a general one, which affords Telemachus an opportunity to apply himself to the feelings of the Ithacans at large.

My days in solitary grief away,
Unless Ulysses, my illustrious Sire,
Hath in his anger any Greecian wrong'd,
Whose wrongs ye purpose to avenge on me,
Inciting these to plague me. Better far
Were my condition, if yourselves consumed
My substance and my revenue; from you
I might obtain, perchance, righteous amends
100 Hereafter; you I might with vehement suit
O'ercome, from house to house pleading aloud
For recompense, till I at last prevail'd.
But now, with darts of anguish ye transfix
My inmost soul, and I have no redress.
He spake impassion'd, and to earth cast down
His sceptre, weeping. Pity at that sight
Seiz'd all the people; mute the assembly sat
Long time, none dared to greet Telemachus
With answer rough, till of them all, at last,
110 Antinoüs, sole arising, thus replied.
Telemachus, intemp'rate in harangue,
High-sounding orator! it is thy drift
To make us all odious; but the offence
Lies not with us the suitors; she alone
Thy mother, who in subtlety excels,
And deep-wrought subterfuge, deserves the blame.
It is already the third year, and soon
Shall be the fourth, since with delusive art
Practising on their minds, she hath deceived
120 The Greecians; message after message sent
Brings hope to each, by turns, and promise fair,
But she, meantime, far otherwise intends.
Her other arts exhausted all, she framed
This stratagem; a web of amplest size
And subtlest woof beginning, thus she spake.
Princes, my suitors! since the noble Chief
Ulysses is no more, press not as yet
My nuptials, wait till I shall finish, first,
A fun'ral robe (lest all my threads decay)
130 Which for the antient Hero I prepare,
Laertes, looking for the mournful hour
When fate shall snatch him to eternal rest;
Else I the censure dread of all my sex,
Should he, so wealthy, want at last a shroud.
So spake the Queen, and unsuspicious, we
With her request complied. Thenceforth, all day
She wove the ample web, and by the aid
Of torches ravell'd it again at night.
Three years by such contrivance she deceived
140 The Greecians; but when (three whole years elaps'd)
The fourth arriv'd, then, conscious of the fraud,
A damsel of her train told all the truth,
And her we found rav'ling the beauteous work.
Thus, through necessity she hath, at length,
Perform'd the task, and in her own despight.
Now therefore, for the information clear
Of thee thyself, and of the other Greeks,
We answer. Send thy mother hence, with charge
That him she wed on whom her father's choice
150 Shall fall, and whom she shall, herself, approve.
But if by long procrastination still
She persevere wearing our patience out,
Attentive only to display the gifts

By Pallas so profusely dealt to her,
Works of surpassing skill, ingenious thought,
And subtle shifts, such as no beauteous Greek
(For aught that we have heard) in antient times
E'er practised, Tyro, or Alcemena fair,
Or fair Mycene, of whom none in art
160 E'er match'd Penelope, although we yield
To this her last invention little praise,
Then know, that these her suitors will consume
So long thy patrimony and thy goods,
As she her present purpose shall indulge,
With which the Gods inspire her. Great renown
She to herself insures, but equal woe
And devastation of thy wealth to thee;
For neither to our proper works at home
Go we, of that be sure, nor yet elsewhere,
170 Till him she wed, to whom she most inclines.
Him prudent, then, answer'd Telemachus.
Antinoüs! it is not possible
That I should thrust her forth against her will,
Who both produced and reared me. Be he dead,
Or still alive, my Sire is far remote,
And should I, voluntary, hence dismiss
My mother to Icarius, I must much
Refund, which hardship were and loss to me.
So doing, I should also wrath incur
180 From my offended Sire, and from the Gods
Still more; for she, departing, would invoke
Erynnis to avenge her, and reproach
Beside would follow me from all mankind.
That word I, therefore, never will pronounce.
No, if ye judge your treatment at her hands
Injurious to you, go ye forth yourselves,
Forsake my mansion; seek where else ye may
Your feasts; consume your own; alternate feed
Each at the other's cost. But if it seem
190 Wisest in your account and best to eat
Voracious thus the patrimonial goods
Of one man, rend'ring no account of all,
Bite to the roots; but know that I will cry
Ceaseless to the eternal Gods, in hope
That Jove, in retribution of the wrong,
Shall doom you, where ye have intruded, there
To bleed, and of your blood ask no account.
So spake Telemachus, and while he spake,
The Thund'rer from a lofty mountain-top
200 Turn'd off two eagles; on the winds, awhile,
With outspread pinions ample side by side
They floated; but, ere long, hov'ring aloft,
Right o'er the midst of the assembled Chiefs
They wheel'd around, clang'd all their num'rous plumes,
And with a downward look eyeing the throng,
Death boded, ominous; then rending each
The other's face and neck, they sprang at once
Toward the right, and darted through the town.
Amazement universal, at that sight,
210 Seized the assembly, and with anxious thought
Each scann'd the future; amidst whom arose
The Hero Halitherses, antient Seer,
Offspring of Mastor; for in judgment he
Of portents augural, and in forecast
Unerring, his coevals all excell'd,

And prudent thus the multitude bespake.
Ye men of Ithaca, give ear! hear all!
Though chief my speech shall to the suitors look,
For, on their heads devolved, comes down the woe.
220 Ulysses shall not from his friends, henceforth,
Live absent long, but, hasting to his home,
Comes even now, and as he comes, designs
A bloody death for these, whose bitter woes
No few shall share, inhabitants with us
Of pleasant Ithaca; but let us frame
Effectual means maturely to suppress
Their violent deeds, or rather let themselves
Repentant cease; and soonest shall be best.
Not inexpert, but well-inform'd I speak
230 The future, and the accomplishment announce
Of all which when Ulysses with the Greeks
Embark'd for Troy, I to himself foretold.
I said that, after many woes, and loss
Of all his people, in the twentieth year,
Unknown to all, he should regain his home,
And my prediction shall be now fulfill'd.
Him, then, Eurymachus thus answer'd rough
The son of Polybus. Hence to thy house,
Thou hoary dotard! there, prophetic, teach
240 Thy children to escape woes else to come.
Birds num'rous flutter in the beams of day,
Not all predictive. Death, far hence remote
Hath found Ulysses, and I would to heav'n
That, where he died, thyself had perish'd too.
Thou hadst not then run o'er with prophecy
As now, nor provocation to the wrath
Giv'n of Telemachus, in hope to win,
Perchance, for thine some favour at his hands.
But I to *thee* foretell, skilled as thou art
250 In legends old, (nor shall my threat be vain)
That if by artifice thou move to wrath
A younger than thyself, no matter whom,
Woe first the heavier on himself shall fall,
Nor shalt thou profit him by thy attempt,
And we will charge thee also with a mulct,
Which thou shalt pay with difficulty, and bear
The burthen of it with an aching heart.
As for Telemachus, I him advise,
Myself, and press the measure on his choice
260 Earnestly, that he send his mother hence
To her own father's house, who shall, himself,
Set forth her nuptial rites, and shall endow
His daughter sumptuously, and as he ought.
For this expensive wooing, as I judge,
Till then shall never cease; since we regard
No man-no-not Telemachus, although
In words exub'rant; neither fear we aught
Thy vain prognostics, venerable sir!
But only hate thee for their sake the more.
270 Waste will continue and disorder foul
Unremedied, so long as she shall hold
The suitors in suspense, for, day by day,
Our emulation goads us to the strife,
Nor shall we, going hence, seek to espouse
Each his own comfort suitable elsewhere.
To whom, discrete, Telemachus replied.
Eurymachus, and ye the suitor train

Illustrious, I have spoken: ye shall hear
No more this supplication urged by me.
280 The Gods, and all the Greeks, now know the truth.
But give me instantly a gallant bark
With twenty rowers, skill'd their course to win
To whatsoever haven; for I go
To sandy Pylus, and shall hasten thence
To Lacedemon, tidings to obtain
Of my long-absent Sire, or from the lips
Of man, or by a word from Jove vouchsafed
Himself, best source of notice to mankind.
If, there inform'd that still my father lives,
290 I hope conceive of his return, although
Distress'd, I shall be patient yet a year.
But should I learn, haply, that he survives
No longer, then, returning, I will raise
At home his tomb, will with such pomp perform
His fun'ral rites, as his great name demands,
And give my mother's hand to whom I may.
This said, he sat, and after him arose
Mentor, illustrious Ulysses' friend,
To whom, embarking thence, he had consign'd
300 All his concerns, that the old Chief might rule
His family, and keep the whole secure.
Arising, thus the senior, sage, began.
Hear me, ye Ithacans! be never King
Henceforth, benevolent, gracious, humane
Or righteous, but let every sceptred hand
Rule merciless, and deal in wrong alone,
Since none of all his people, whom he sway'd
With such paternal gentleness and love,
Remembers the divine Ulysses more!
310 That the imperious suitors thus should weave
The web of mischief and atrocious wrong,
I grudge not; since at hazard of their heads
They make Ulysses' property a prey,
Persuaded that the Hero comes no more.
But much the people move me; how ye sit
All mute, and though a multitude, yourselves,
Opposed to few, risque not a single word
To check the license of these bold intruders!
Then thus Liocritus, Evenor's son.
320 Injurious Mentor! headlong orator!
How dar'st thou move the populace against
The suitors? Trust me they should find it hard,
Numerous as they are, to cope with us,
A feast the prize. Or should the King himself
Of Ithaca, returning, undertake
T' expell the jovial suitors from his house,
Much as Penelope his absence mourns,
His presence should afford her little joy;
For fighting sole with many, he should meet
330 A dreadful death. Thou, therefore, speak'st amiss.
As for Telemachus, let Mentor him
And Halytherses furnish forth, the friends
Long valued of his Sire, with all dispatch;
Though him I judge far likelier to remain
Long-time contented an enquirer here,
Than to perform the voyage now proposed.
Thus saying, Liocritus dissolved in haste
The council, and the scattered concourse sought
Their sev'ral homes, while all the suitors flock'd

340 Thence to the palace of their absent King.
Meantime, Telemachus from all resort
Retiring, in the surf of the gray Deep
First laved his hands, then, thus to Pallas pray'd.
O Goddess! who wast yesterday a guest
Beneath my roof, and didst enjoin me then
A voyage o'er the sable Deep in quest
Of tidings of my long regretted Sire!
Which voyage, all in Ithaca, but most
The haughty suitors, obstinate impede,
350 Now hear my suit and gracious interpose!
Such pray'r he made; then Pallas, in the form,
And with the voice of Mentor, drawing nigh,
In accents wing'd, him kindly thus bespake.
Telemachus! thou shalt hereafter prove
Nor base, nor poor in talents. If, in truth,
Thou have received from heav'n thy father's force
Instill'd into thee, and resemblest him
In promptness both of action and of speech,
Thy voyage shall not useless be, or vain.
360 But if Penelope produced thee not
His son, I, then, hope not for good effect
Of this design which, ardent, thou pursuest.
Few sons their fathers equal; most appear
Degenerate; but we find, though rare, sometimes
A son superior even to his Sire.
And since thyself shalt neither base be found
Nor spiritless, nor altogether void
Of talents, such as grace thy royal Sire,
I therefore hope success of thy attempt.
370 Heed not the suitors' projects; neither wise
Are they, nor just, nor aught suspect the doom
Which now approaches them, and in one day
Shall overwhelm them all. No long suspense
Shall hold thy purposed enterprise in doubt,
Such help from me, of old thy father's friend,
Thou shalt receive, who with a bark well-oar'd
Will serve thee, and myself attend thee forth.
But haste, join thou the suitors, and provide,
In sep'rate vessels stow'd, all needful stores,
380 Wine in thy jars, and flour, the strength of man,
In skins close-seam'd. I will, meantime, select
Such as shall voluntary share thy toils.
In sea-girt Ithaca new ships and old
Abound, and I will chuse, myself, for thee
The prime of all, which without more delay
We will launch out into the spacious Deep.
Thus Pallas spake, daughter of Jove; nor long,
So greeted by the voice divine, remain'd
Telemachus, but to his palace went
390 Distress'd in heart. He found the suitors there
Goats slaying in the hall, and fatted swine
Roasting; when with a laugh Antinoüs flew
To meet him, fasten'd on his hand, and said,
Telemachus, in eloquence sublime,
And of a spirit not to be controul'd!
Give harbour in thy breast on no account
To after-grudge or enmity, but eat,
Far rather, cheerfully as heretofore,
And freely drink, committing all thy cares
400 To the Achaians, who shall furnish forth
A gallant ship and chosen crew for thee,

That thou may'st hence to Pylus with all speed,
Tidings to learn of thy illustrious Sire.
To whom Telemachus, discrete, replied.
Antinoüs! I have no heart to feast
With guests so insolent, nor can indulge
The pleasures of a mind at ease, with you.
Is't not enough, suitors, that ye have used
My noble patrimony as your own
410 While I was yet a child? now, grown mature,
And competent to understand the speech
Of my instructors, feeling, too, a mind
Within me conscious of augmented pow'rs,
I will attempt your ruin, be assured,
Whether at Pylus, or continuing here.
I go, indeed, (nor shall my voyage prove
Of which I speak, bootless or vain) I go
An humble passenger, who neither bark
Nor rowers have to boast my own, denied
420 That honour (so ye judg'd it best) by you.
He said, and from Antinoüs' hand his own
Drew sudden. Then their delicate repast
The busy suitors on all sides prepar'd,
Still taunting as they toil'd, and with sharp speech
Sarcastic wantoning, of whom a youth,
Arrogant as his fellows, thus began.
I see it plain, Telemachus intends
Our slaughter; either he will aids procure
From sandy Pylus, or will bring them arm'd
430 From Sparta; such is his tremendous drift.
Even to fruitful Ephyre, perchance,
He will proceed, seeking some baneful herb
Which cast into our cup, shall drug us all.
To whom some haughty suitor thus replied.
Who knows but that himself, wand'ring the sea
From all his friends and kindred far remote,
May perish like Ulysses? Whence to us
Should double toil ensue, on whom the charge
To parcel out his wealth would then devolve,
440 And to endow his mother with the house
For his abode whom she should chance to wed.
So sported they; but he, ascending sought
His father's lofty chamber, where his heaps
He kept of brass and gold, garments in chests,
And oils of fragrant scent, a copious store.
There many a cask with season'd nectar fill'd
The grape's pure juice divine, beside the wall
Stood orderly arranged, waiting the hour
(Should e'er such hour arrive) when, after woes
450 Num'rous, Ulysses should regain his home.
Secure that chamber was with folding doors
Of massy planks compact, and night and day,
Within it antient Euryclea dwelt,
Guardian discrete of all the treasures there,
Whom, thither call'd, Telemachus address'd.
Nurse! draw me forth sweet wine into my jars,
Delicious next to that which thou reserv'st
For our poor wand'rer; if escaping death
At last, divine Ulysses e'er return.
460 Fill twelve, and stop them close; pour also meal
Well mill'd (full twenty measures) into skins
Close-seam'd, and mention what thou dost to none.
Place them together; for at even-tide

I will convey them hence, soon as the Queen,
Retiring to her couch, shall seek repose.
For hence to Sparta will I take my course,
And sandy Pylus, tidings there to hear
(If hear I may) of my lov'd Sire's return.
He ceas'd, then wept his gentle nurse that sound
470 Hearing, and in wing'd accents thus replied.
My child! ah, wherefore hath a thought so rash
Possess'd thee? whither, only and belov'd,
Seek'st thou to ramble, travelling, alas!
To distant climes? Ulysses is no more;
Dead lies the Hero in some land unknown,
And thou no sooner shalt depart, than these
Will plot to slay thee, and divide thy wealth.
No, stay with us who love thee. Need is none
That thou should'st on the barren Deep distress
480 Encounter, roaming without hope or end.
Whom, prudent, thus answer'd Telemachus.
Take courage, nurse! for not without consent
Of the Immortals I have thus resolv'd.
But swear, that till eleven days be past,
Or twelve, or, till enquiry made, she learn
Herself my going, thou wilt not impart
Of this my purpose to my mother's ear,
Lest all her beauties fade by grief impair'd.
He ended, and the antient matron swore
490 Solemnly by the Gods; which done, she fill'd
With wine the vessels and the skins with meal,
And he, returning, join'd the throng below.
Then Pallas, Goddess azure-eyed, her thoughts
Elsewhere directing, all the city ranged
In semblance of Telemachus, each man
Exhorting, at the dusk of eve, to seek
The gallant ship, and from Noëmon, son
Renown'd of Phronius, ask'd, herself, a bark,
Which soon as ask'd, he promis'd to supply.
500 Now set the sun, and twilight dimm'd the ways,
When, drawing down his bark into the Deep,
He gave her all her furniture, oars, arms
And tackle, such as well-built galleys bear,
Then moor'd her in the bottom of the bay.
Meantime, his mariners in haste repair'd
Down to the shore, for Pallas urged them on.
And now on other purposes intent,
The Goddess sought the palace, where with dews

Of slumber drenching ev'ry suitor's eye,
510 She fool'd the drunkard multitude, and dash'd
The goblets from their idle hands away.
They through the city reeled, happy to leave
The dull carousal, when the slumb'rous weight
Oppressive on their eye-lids once had fall'n.
Next, Pallas azure-eyed in Mentor's form
And with the voice of Mentor, summoning
Telemachus abroad, him thus bespake.
Telemachus! already at their oars
Sit all thy fellow-voyagers, and wait
520 Thy coming; linger not, but haste away.
This said, Minerva led him thence, whom he
With nimble steps follow'd, and on the shore
Arrived, found all his mariners prepared,
Whom thus the princely voyager address'd.
Haste, my companions! bring we down the stores
Already sorted and set forth; but nought
My mother knows, or any of her train
Of this design, one matron sole except.
He spake, and led them; they, obedient, brought
530 All down, and, as Ulysses' son enjoin'd,
Within the gallant bark the charge bestow'd.
Then, led by Pallas, went the prince on board,
Where down they sat, the Goddess in the stern,
And at her side Telemachus. The crew
Cast loose the hawsers, and embarking, fill'd
The benches. Blue-eyed Pallas from the West
Call'd forth propitious breezes; fresh they curled
The sable Deep, and, sounding, swept the waves.
He loud-exhorting them, his people bade
540 Hand, brisk, the tackle; they, obedient, reared
The pine-tree mast, which in its socket deep
They lodg'd, then strain'd the cordage, and with thongs
Well-twisted, drew the shining sail aloft.
A land-breeze fill'd the canvas, and the flood
Roar'd as she went against the steady bark
That ran with even course her liquid way.
The rigging, thus, of all the galley set,
Their beakers crowning high with wine, they hail'd
The ever-living Gods, but above all
550 Minerva, daughter azure-eyed of Jove.
Thus, all night long the galley, and till dawn
Had brighten'd into day, cleaved swift the flood.

Book III

Telemachus arriving at Pylus, enquires of Nestor concerning Ulysses. Nestor relates to him all that he knows or has heard of the Greecians since their departure from the siege of Troy, but not being able to give him any satisfactory account of Ulysses, refers him to Menelaus. At evening Minerva quits Telemachus, but discovers herself in going. Nestor sacrifices to the Goddess, and the solemnity ended, Telemachus sets forth for Sparta in one of Nestor's chariots, and accompanied by Nestor's son, Pisistratus.

The sun, emerging from the lucid waves,
Ascended now the brazen vault with light
For the inhabitants of earth and heav'n,
When in their bark at Pylus they arrived,
City of Neleus. On the shore they found
The people sacrificing; bulls they slew
Black without spot, to Neptune azure-hair'd.
On ranges nine of seats they sat; each range
Received five hundred, and to each they made
Allotment equal of nine sable bulls.
10 The feast was now begun; these eating sat
The entrails, those stood off'ring to the God
The thighs, his portion, when the Ithacans
Push'd right ashore, and, furling close the sails,
And making fast their moorings, disembark'd.
Forth came Telemachus, by Pallas led,
Whom thus the Goddess azure-eyed address'd.
Telemachus! there is no longer room
For bashful fear, since thou hast cross'd the flood
With purpose to enquire what land conceals
20 Thy father, and what fate hath follow'd him.
Advance at once to the equestrian Chief
Nestor, within whose bosom lies, perhaps,
Advice well worthy of thy search; entreat
Himself, that he will tell thee only truth,
Who will not lye, for he is passing wise.
To whom Telemachus discrete replied.
Ah Mentor! how can I advance, how greet
A Chief like him, unpractis'd as I am
In manag'd phrase? Shame bids the youth beware
30 How he accosts the man of many years.
But him the Goddess answer'd azure-eyed,
Telemachus! Thou wilt, in part, thyself
Fit speech devise, and heav'n will give the rest;
For thou wast neither born, nor hast been train'd
To manhood, under unpropitious Pow'rs.
So saying, Minerva led him thence, whom he
With nimble steps attending, soon arrived
Among the multitude. There Nestor sat,
And Nestor's sons, while, busily the feast
40 Tending, his num'rous followers roasted, some,
The viands, some, transfix'd them with the spits.
They seeing guests arrived, together all
Advanced, and, grasping courteously their hands,
Invited them to sit; but first, the son
Of Nestor, young Pisistratus, approach'd,
Who, fast'ning on the hands of both, beside
The banquet placed them, where the beach was spread
With fleeces, and where Thrasymedes sat
His brother, and the hoary Chief his Sire.
50 To each a portion of the inner parts

He gave, then fill'd a golden cup with wine,
Which, tasted first, he to the daughter bore
Of Jove the Thund'rer, and her thus bespake.
Oh guest! the King of Ocean now adore!
For ye have chanced on Neptune's festival;
And, when thou hast, thyself, libation made
Duly, and pray'r, deliver to thy friend
The gen'rous juice, that he may also make
Libation; for he, doubtless, seeks, in prayer
60 The Immortals, of whose favour all have need.
But, since he younger is, and with myself
Coeval, first I give the cup to thee.
He ceas'd, and to her hand consign'd the cup,
Which Pallas gladly from a youth received
So just and wise, who to herself had first
The golden cup presented, and in pray'r
Fervent the Sov'reign of the Seas adored.
Hear, earth-encircler Neptune! O vouchsafe
To us thy suppliants the desired effect
70 Of this our voyage; glory, first, bestow
On Nestor and his offspring both, then grant
To all the Pylians such a gracious boon
As shall requite their noble off'ring well.
Grant also to Telemachus and me
To voyage hence, possess'd of what we sought
When hither in our sable bark we came.
So Pallas pray'd, and her own pray'r herself
Accomplish'd. To Telemachus she gave
The splendid goblet next, and in his turn
80 Like pray'r Ulysses' son also preferr'd.
And now (the banquet from the spits withdrawn)
They next distributed sufficient share
To each, and all were sumptuously regaled.
At length, (both hunger satisfied and thirst)
Thus Nestor, the Gerenian Chief, began.
Now with more seemliness we may enquire,
After repast, what guests we have received.
Our guests! who are ye? Whence have ye the waves
Plough'd hither? Come ye to transact concerns
90 Commercial, or at random roam the Deep
Like pirates, who with mischief charged and woe
To foreign States, oft hazard life themselves?
Him answer'd, bolder now, but still discrete,
Telemachus. For Pallas had his heart
With manly courage arm'd, that he might ask
From Nestor tidings of his absent Sire,
And win, himself, distinction and renown.
Oh Nestor, Neleus' son, glory of Greece!
Thou askest whence we are. I tell thee whence.
100 From Ithaca, by the umbrageous woods
Of Neritus o'erhung, by private need,

Not public, urged, we come. My errand is
To seek intelligence of the renown'd
Ulysses; of my noble father, prais'd
For dauntless courage, whom report proclaims
Conqueror, with thine aid, of sacred Troy.
We have already learn'd where other Chiefs
Who fought at Ilium, died; but Jove conceals
Even the death of my illustrious Sire
110 In dull obscurity; for none hath heard
Or confident can answer, where he dy'd;
Whether he on the continent hath fall'n
By hostile hands, or by the waves o'erwhelm'd
Of Amphitrite, welters in the Deep.
For this cause, at thy knees suppliant, I beg
That thou would'st tell me his disast'rous end,
If either thou beheld'st that dread event
Thyself, or from some wanderer of the Greeks
Hast heard it: for my father at his birth
120 Was, sure, predestin'd to no common woes.
Neither through pity, or o'erstrain'd respect
Flatter me, but explicit all relate
Which thou hast witness'd. If my noble Sire
E'er gratified thee by performance just
Of word or deed at Ilium, where ye fell
So num'rous slain in fight, oh, recollect
Now his fidelity, and tell me true.
Then Nestor thus Gerenian Hero old.
Young friend! since thou remind'st me, speaking thus,
130 Of all the woes which indefatigable
We sons of the Achaians there sustain'd,
Both those which wand'ring on the Deep we bore
Wherever by Achilles led in quest
Of booty, and the many woes beside
Which under royal Priam's spacious walls
We suffer'd, know, that there our bravest fell.
There warlike Ajax lies, there Peleus' son;
There, too, Patroclus, like the Gods themselves
In council, and my son beloved there,
140 Brave, virtuous, swift of foot, and bold in fight,
Antilochus. Nor are these sorrows all;
What tongue of mortal man could all relate?
Should'st thou, abiding here, five years employ
Or six, enquiring of the woes endured
By the Achaians, ere thou should'st have learn'd
The whole, thou would'st depart, tir'd of the tale.
For we, nine years, stratagems of all kinds
Devised against them, and Saturnian Jove
Scarce crown'd the difficult attempt at last.
150 There, no competitor in wiles well-plann'd
Ulysses found, so far were all surpass'd
In shrewd invention by thy noble Sire,
If thou indeed art his, as sure thou art,
Whose sight breeds wonder in me, and thy speech
His speech resembles more than might be deem'd
Within the scope of years so green as thine.
There, never in opinion, or in voice
Illustrious Ulysses and myself
Divided were, but, one in heart, contrived
160 As best we might, the benefit of all.
But after Priam's lofty city sack'd,
And the departure of the Greeks on board
Their barks, and when the Gods had scatter'd them,

Then Jove imagin'd for the Argive host
A sorrowful return; for neither just
Were all, nor prudent, therefore many found
A fate disast'rous through the vengeful ire
Of Jove-born Pallas, who between the sons
Of Atreus sharp contention interposed.
170 They both, irregularly, and against
Just order, summoning by night the Greeks
To council, of whom many came with wine
Oppress'd, promulgated the cause for which
They had convened the people. Then it was
That Menelaus bade the general host
Their thoughts bend homeward o'er the sacred Deep,
Which Agamemnon in no sort approved.
His counsel was to slay them yet at Troy,
That so he might assuage the dreadful wrath
180 Of Pallas, first, by sacrifice and pray'r.
Vain hope! he little thought how ill should speed
That fond attempt, for, once provok'd, the Gods
Are not with ease conciliated again.
Thus stood the brothers, altercation hot
Maintaining, till at length, uprose the Greeks
With deaf'ning clamours, and with diff'ring minds.
We slept the night, but teeming with disgust
Mutual, for Jove great woe prepar'd for all.
At dawn of day we drew our gallies down
190 Into the sea, and, hasty, put on board
The spoils and female captives. Half the host,
With Agamemnon, son of Atreus, stay'd
Supreme commander, and, embarking, half
Push'd forth. Swift course we made, for Neptune smooth'd
The waves before us of the monstrous Deep.
At Tenedos arriv'd, we there perform'd
Sacrifice to the Gods, ardent to reach
Our native land, but unpropitious Jove,
Not yet designing our arrival there,
200 Involved us in dissension fierce again.
For all the crews, followers of the King,
Thy noble Sire, to gratify our Chief,
The son of Atreus, chose a diff'rent course,
And steer'd their oary barks again to Troy.
But I, assured that evil from the Gods
Impended, gath'ring all my gallant fleet,
Fled thence in haste, and warlike Diomede
Exhorting his attendants, also fled.
At length, the Hero Menelaus join'd
210 Our fleets at Lesbos; there he found us held
In deep deliberation on the length
Of way before us, whether we should steer
Above the craggy Chios to the isle
Psyria, that island holding on our left,
Or under Chios by the wind-swept heights
Of Mimas. Then we ask'd from Jove a sign,
And by a sign vouchsafed he bade us cut
The wide sea to Euboea sheer athwart,
So soonest to escape the threat'ned harm.
220 Shrill sang the rising gale, and with swift prows
Cleaving the fishy flood, we reach'd by night
Geræstus, where arrived, we burn'd the thighs
Of num'rous bulls to Neptune, who had safe
Conducted us through all our perilous course.
The fleet of Diomede in safety moor'd

On the fourth day at Argos, but myself
Held on my course to Pylus, nor the wind
One moment thwarted us, or died away,
When Jove had once commanded it to blow.
230 Thus, uninform'd, I have arrived, my son!
Nor of the Greecians, who are saved have heard,
Or who have perish'd; but what news soe'er
I have obtain'd, since my return, with truth
I will relate, nor aught conceal from thee.
The spear-famed Myrmidons, as rumour speaks,
By Neoptolemus, illustrious son
Of brave Achilles led, have safe arrived;
Safe, Philoctetes, also son renown'd
Of Pæas; and Idomeneus at Crete
240 Hath landed all his followers who survive
The bloody war, the waves have swallow'd none.
Ye have yourselves doubtless, although remote,
Of Agamemnon heard, how he return'd,
And how Ægisthus cruelly contrived
For him a bloody welcome, but himself
Hath with his own life paid the murth'rous deed.
Good is it, therefore, if a son survive
The slain, since Agamemnon's son hath well
Avenged his father's death, slaying, himself,
250 Ægisthus, foul assassin of his Sire.
Young friend! (for pleas'd thy vig'rous youth I view,
And just proportion) be thou also bold,
That thine like his may be a deathless name.
Then, prudent, him answer'd Telemachus.
Oh Nestor, Neleus' son, glory of Greece!
And righteous was that vengeance; *his* renown
Achaia's sons shall far and wide diffuse,
To future times transmitting it in song.
Ah! would that such ability the Gods
260 Would grant to me, that I, as well, the deeds
Might punish of our suitors, whose excess
Enormous, and whose bitter taunts I feel
Continual, object of their subtle hate.
But not for me such happiness the Gods
Have twined into my thread; no, not for me
Or for my father. Patience is our part.
To whom Gerenian Nestor thus replied.
Young friend! (since thou remind'st me of that theme)
Fame here reports that num'rous suitors haunt
270 Thy palace for thy mother's sake, and there
Much evil perpetrate in thy despight.
But say, endur'st thou willing their controul
Imperious, or because the people, sway'd
By some response oracular, incline
Against thee? But who knows? the time may come
When to his home restored, either alone,
Or aided by the force of all the Greeks,
Ulysses may avenge the wrong; at least,
Should Pallas azure-eyed thee love, as erst
280 At Troy, the scene of our unnumber'd woes,
She lov'd Ulysses (for I have not known
The Gods assisting so apparently
A mortal man, as him Minerva there)

Should Pallas view thee also with like love
And kind solicitude, some few of those
Should dream, perchance, of wedlock never more.
Then answer thus Telemachus return'd.
That word's accomplishment I cannot hope;
It promises too much; the thought alone
290 O'erwhelms me; an event so fortunate
Would, unexpected on my part, arrive,
Although the Gods themselves should purpose it.
But Pallas him answer'd cærulean-eyed.
Telemachus! what word was that which leap'd
The iv'ry guard[7] that should have fenced it in?
A God, so willing, could with utmost ease
Save any man, howe'er remote. Myself,
I had much rather, many woes endured,
Revisit home, at last, happy and safe,
300 Than, sooner coming, die in my own house,
As Agamemnon perish'd by the arts
Of base Ægisthus and the subtle Queen.
Yet not the Gods themselves can save from death
All-levelling, the man whom most they love,
When Fate ordains him once to his last sleep.
To whom Telemachus, discrete, replied.
Howe'er it interest us, let us leave
This question, Mentor! He, I am assured,
Returns no more, but hath already found
310 A sad, sad fate by the decree of heav'n.
But I would now interrogate again
Nestor, and on a different theme, for him
In human rights I judge, and laws expert,
And in all knowledge beyond other men;
For he hath govern'd, as report proclaims,
Three generations; therefore in my eyes
He wears the awful impress of a God.
Oh Nestor, son of Neleus, tell me true;
What was the manner of Atrides' death,
320 Wide-ruling Agamemnon? Tell me where
Was Menelaus? By what means contrived
Ægisthus to inflict the fatal blow,
Slaying so much a nobler than himself?
Had not the brother of the Monarch reach'd
Achaian Argos yet, but, wand'ring still
In other climes, his long absence gave
Ægisthus courage for that bloody deed?
Whom answer'd the Gerenian Chief renown'd.
My son! I will inform thee true; meantime
330 Thy own suspicions border on the fact.
Had Menelaus, Hero, amber hair'd,
Ægisthus found living at his return
From Ilium, never on *his* bones the Greeks
Had heap'd a tomb, but dogs and rav'ning fowls
Had torn him lying in the open field
Far from the town, nor him had woman wept
Of all in Greece, for he had foul transgress'd.
But we, in many an arduous task engaged,
Lay before Ilium; he, the while, secure
340 Within the green retreats of Argos, found
Occasion apt by flatt'ry to delude

---

[7] +Erkos odontôn+. Prior, alluding to this expression, ludicrously renders it-
"When words like these in vocal breath
Burst from his twofold hedge of teeth."

The spouse of Agamemnon; she, at first,
(The royal Clytemnestra) firm refused
The deed dishonourable (for she bore
A virtuous mind, and at her side a bard
Attended ever, whom the King, to Troy
Departing, had appointed to the charge.)
But when the Gods had purposed to ensnare
Ægisthus, then dismissing far remote
350 The bard into a desert isle, he there
Abandon'd him to rav'ning fowls a prey,
And to his own home, willing as himself,
Led Clytemnestra. Num'rous thighs he burn'd
On all their hallow'd altars to the Gods,
And hung with tap'stry, images, and gold
Their shrines, his great exploit past hope atchiev'd.
We (Menelaus and myself) had sailed
From Troy together, but when we approach'd
Sunium, headland of th' Athenian shore,
360 There Phoebus, sudden, with his gentle shafts
Slew Menelaus' pilot while he steer'd
The volant bark, Phrontis, Onetor's son,
A mariner past all expert, whom none
In steerage match'd, what time the tempest roar'd.
Here, therefore, Menelaus was detained,
Giving his friend due burial, and his rites
Funereal celebrating, though in haste
Still to proceed. But when, with all his fleet
The wide sea traversing, he reach'd at length
370 Malea's lofty foreland in his course,
Rough passage, then, and perilous he found.
Shrill blasts the Thund'rer pour'd into his sails,
And wild waves sent him mountainous. His ships
There scatter'd, some to the Cydonian coast
Of Crete he push'd, near where the Jardan flows.
Beside the confines of Gortyna stands,
Amid the gloomy flood, a smooth rock, steep
Toward the sea, against whose leftward point
Phæstus by name, the South wind rolls the surge
380 Amain, which yet the rock, though small, repells.
Hither with part he came, and scarce the crews
Themselves escaped, while the huge billows broke
Their ships against the rocks; yet five he saved,
Which winds and waves drove to the Ægyptian shore.
Thus he, provision gath'ring as he went
And gold abundant, roam'd to distant lands
And nations of another tongue. Meantime,
Ægisthus these enormities at home
Devising, slew Atrides, and supreme
390 Rul'd the subjected land; sev'n years he reign'd
In opulent Mycenæ, but the eighth
From Athens brought renown'd Orestes home
For his destruction, who of life bereaved
Ægisthus base assassin of his Sire.
Orestes, therefore, the funereal rites
Performing to his shameless mother's shade
And to her lustful paramour, a feast
Gave to the Argives; on which self-same day
The warlike Menelaus, with his ships
400 All treasure-laden to the brink, arrived.

And thou, young friend! from thy forsaken home
Rove not long time remote, thy treasures left
At mercy of those proud, lest they divide
And waste the whole, rend'ring thy voyage vain.
But hence to Menelaus is the course
To which I counsel thee; for he hath come
Of late from distant lands, whence to escape
No man could hope, whom tempests first had driv'n
Devious into so wide a sea, from which
410 Themselves the birds of heaven could not arrive
In a whole year, so vast is the expanse.
Go, then, with ship and shipmates, or if more
The land delight thee, steeds thou shalt not want
Nor chariot, and my sons shall be thy guides
To noble Lacedemon, the abode
Of Menelaus; ask from him the truth,
Who will not lye, for he is passing wise.
While thus he spake, the sun declined, and night
Approaching, blue-eyed Pallas interposed.
420 O antient King! well hast thou spoken all.

But now delay not. Cut ye forth the tongues,[8]
And mingle wine, that (Neptune first invoked
With due libation, and the other Gods)
We may repair to rest; for even now
The sun is sunk, and it becomes us not
Long to protract a banquet to the Gods
Devote, but in fit season to depart.
So spake Jove's daughter; they obedient heard.
The heralds, then, pour'd water on their hands,
430 And the attendant youths, filling the cups,
Served them from left to right. Next all the tongues
They cast into the fire, and ev'ry guest
Arising, pour'd libation to the Gods.
Libation made, and all with wine sufficed,
Godlike Telemachus and Pallas both
Would have return'd, incontinent, on board,
But Nestor urged them still to be his guests.
Forbid it, Jove, and all the Pow'rs of heav'n!
That ye should leave me to repair on board
440 Your vessel, as I were some needy wretch
Cloakless and destitute of fleecy stores
Wherewith to spread the couch soft for myself,
Or for my guests. No. I have garments warm
An ample store, and rugs of richest dye;
And never shall Ulysses' son belov'd,
My frend's own son, sleep on a galley's plank
While I draw vital air; grant also, heav'n,
That, dying, I may leave behind me sons
Glad to accommodate whatever guest!
450 Him answer'd then Pallas cærulean-eyed.
Old Chief! thou hast well said, and reason bids
Telemachus thy kind commands obey.
Let *him* attend thee hence, that he may sleep
Beneath thy roof, but I return on board
Myself, to instruct my people, and to give
All needful orders; for among them none
Is old as I, but they are youths alike,
Coevals of Telemachus, with whom
They have embark'd for friendship's sake alone.

---

[8] It is said to have been customary in the days of Homer, when the Greeks retired from a banquet to their beds, to cut out the tongues of the victims, and offer them to the Gods in particular who presided over conversation.

460 I therefore will repose myself on board
This night, and to the Caucons bold in arms
Will sail to-morrow, to demand arrears
Long time unpaid, and of no small amount.
But, since he is become thy guest, afford
My friend a chariot, and a son of thine
Who shall direct his way, nor let him want
Of all thy steeds the swiftest and the best.
So saying, the blue-eyed Goddess as upborne
On eagle's wings, vanish'd; amazement seized
470 The whole assembly, and the antient King
O'erwhelmed with wonder at that sight, the hand
Grasp'd of Telemachus, whom he thus bespake.
My friend! I prophesy that thou shalt prove
Nor base nor dastard, whom, so young, the Gods
Already take in charge; for of the Pow'rs
Inhabitants of heav'n, none else was this
Than Jove's own daughter Pallas, who among
The Greecians honour'd most thy gen'rous Sire.
But thou, O Queen! compassionate us all,
480 Myself, my sons, my comfort; give to each
A glorious name, and I to thee will give
For sacrifice an heifer of the year,
Broad-fronted, one that never yet hath borne
The yoke, and will incase her horns with gold.
So Nestor pray'd, whom Pallas gracious heard.
Then the Gerenian warrior old, before
His sons and sons in law, to his abode
Magnificent proceeded: they (arrived
Within the splendid palace of the King)
490 On thrones and couches sat in order ranged,
Whom Nestor welcom'd, charging high the cup
With wine of richest sort, which she who kept
That treasure, now in the eleventh year
First broach'd, unsealing the delicious juice.
With this the hoary Senior fill'd a cup,
And to the daughter of Jove Ægis-arm'd
Pouring libation, offer'd fervent pray'r.
When all had made libation, and no wish
Remain'd of more, then each to rest retired,
500 And Nestor the Gerenian warrior old
Led thence Telemachus to a carved couch
Beneath the sounding portico prepared.
Beside him he bade sleep the spearman bold,
Pisistratus, a gallant youth, the sole
Unwedded in his house of all his sons.
Himself in the interior palace lay,
Where couch and cov'ring for her antient spouse
The consort Queen had diligent prepar'd.
But when Aurora, daughter of the dawn,
510 Had tinged the East, arising from his bed,
Gerenian Nestor issued forth, and sat
Before his palace-gate on the white stones
Resplendent as with oil, on which of old
His father Neleus had been wont to sit,
In council like a God; but he had sought,
By destiny dismiss'd long since, the shades.
On those stones therefore now, Nestor himself,
Achaia's guardian, sat, sceptre in hand,
Where soon his num'rous sons, leaving betimes
520 The place of their repose, also appeared,
Echephron, Stratius, Perseus, Thrasymedes,

Aretus and Pisistratus. They placed
Godlike Telemachus at Nestor's side,
And the Gerenian Hero thus began.
Sons be ye quick-execute with dispatch
My purpose, that I may propitiate first
Of all the Gods Minerva, who herself
Hath honour'd manifest our hallow'd feast.
Haste, one, into the field, to order thence
530 An ox, and let the herdsman drive it home.
Another, hasting to the sable bark
Of brave Telemachus, bring hither all
His friends, save two, and let a third command
Laerceus, that he come to enwrap with gold
The victim's horns. Abide ye here, the rest,
And bid my female train (for I intend
A banquet) with all diligence provide
Seats, stores of wood, and water from the rock.
He said, whom instant all obey'd. The ox
54 °Came from the field, and from the gallant ship
The shipmates of the brave Telemachus;
Next, charged with all his implements of art,
His mallet, anvil, pincers, came the smith
To give the horns their gilding; also came
Pallas herself to her own sacred rites.
Then Nestor, hoary warrior, furnish'd gold,
Which, hammer'd thin, the artist wrapp'd around
The victim's horns, that seeing him attired
So costly, Pallas might the more be pleased.
550 Stratius and brave Echephron introduced
The victim by his horns; Aretus brought
A laver in one hand, with flow'rs emboss'd,
And in his other hand a basket stored
With cakes, while warlike Thrasymedes, arm'd
With his long-hafted ax, prepared to smite
The ox, and Perseus to receive the blood.
The hoary Nestor consecrated first
Both cakes and water, and with earnest pray'r
To Pallas, gave the forelock to the flames.
560 When all had worshipp'd, and the broken cakes
Sprinkled, then godlike Thrasymedes drew
Close to the ox, and smote him. Deep the edge
Enter'd, and senseless on the floor he fell.
Then Nestor's daughters, and the consorts all
Of Nestor's sons, with his own consort, chaste
Eurydice, the daughter eldest-born
Of Clymenus, in one shrill orison
Vocif'rous join'd, while they, lifting the ox,
Held him supported firmly, and the prince
570 Of men, Pisistratus, his gullet pierced.
Soon as the sable blood had ceased, and life
Had left the victim, spreading him abroad,
With nice address they parted at the joint
His thighs, and wrapp'd them in the double cawl,
Which with crude slices thin they overspread.
Nestor burn'd incense, and libation pour'd
Large on the hissing brands, while him beside,
Busy with spit and prong, stood many a youth
Train'd to the task. The thighs consumed, each took
His portion of the maw, then, slashing well
581 The remnant, they transpierced it with the spits
Neatly, and held it reeking at the fire.
Meantime the youngest of the daughters fair

Of Nestor, beauteous Polycaste, laved,
Anointed, and in vest and tunic cloathed
Telemachus, who, so refresh'd, stepp'd forth
From the bright laver graceful as a God,
And took his seat at antient Nestor's side.
The viands dress'd, and from the spits withdrawn,
590 They sat to share the feast, and princely youths
Arising, gave them wine in cups of gold.
When neither hunger now nor thirst remain'd
Unsated, thus Gerenian Nestor spake.
My sons, arise, lead forth the sprightly steeds,
And yoke them, that Telemachus may go.
So spake the Chief, to whose commands his sons,
Obedient, yoked in haste the rapid steeds,
And the intendant matron of the stores
Disposed meantime within the chariot, bread
600 And wine, and dainties, such as princes eat.
Telemachus into the chariot first
Ascended, and beside him, next, his place
Pisistratus the son of Nestor took,

Then seiz'd the reins, and lash'd the coursers on.
They, nothing loth, into the open plain
Flew, leaving lofty Pylus soon afar.
Thus, journeying, they shook on either side
The yoke all day, and now the setting sun
To dusky evening had resign'd the roads,
610 When they to Pheræ came, and the abode
Reach'd of Diocles, whose illustrious Sire
Orsilochus from Alpheus drew his birth,
And there, with kindness entertain'd, they slept.
But when Aurora, daughter of the dawn,
Look'd rosy from the East, yoking the steeds,
They in their sumptuous chariot sat again.
The son of Nestor plied the lash, and forth
Through vestibule and sounding portico
The royal coursers, not unwilling, flew.
620 A corn-invested land receiv'd them next,
And there they brought their journey to a close,
So rapidly they moved; and now the sun
Went down, and even-tide dimm'd all the ways.

Book IV

Telemachus, with Pisistratus, arrives at the palace of Menelaus, from whom he receives some fresh information concerning the return of the Greecians, and is in particular told on the authority of Proteus, that his father is detained by Calypso. The suitors, plotting against the life of Telemachus, lie in wait to intercept him in his return to Ithaca. Penelope being informed of his departure, and of their designs to slay him, becomes inconsolable, but is relieved by a dream sent to her from Minerva.

In hollow Lacedæmon's spacious vale
Arriving, to the house they drove direct
Of royal Menelaus; him they found
In his own palace, all his num'rous friends
Regaling at a nuptial banquet giv'n
Both for his daughter and the prince his son.
His daughter to renown'd Achilles' heir
He sent, to whom he had at Troy engaged
To give her, and the Gods now made her his.
With chariots and with steeds he sent her forth
10 To the illustrious city where the prince,
Achilles' offspring, ruled the Myrmidons.
But to his son he gave a Spartan fair,
Alector's daughter; from an handmaid sprang
That son to Menelaus in his age,
Brave Megapenthes; for the Gods no child
To Helen gave, made mother, once, of her
Who vied in perfect loveliness of form
With golden Venus' self, Hermione.
Thus all the neighbour princes and the friends
20 Of noble Menelaus, feasting sat
Within his spacious palace, among whom
A sacred bard sang sweetly to his harp,
While, in the midst, two dancers smote the ground
With measur'd steps responsive to his song.
And now the Heroes, Nestor's noble son
And young Telemachus arrived within
The vestibule, whom, issuing from the hall,
The noble Eteoneus of the train
Of Menelaus, saw; at once he ran
30 Across the palace to report the news
To his Lord's ear, and, standing at his side,
In accents wing'd with haste thus greeted him.
Oh Menelaus! Heav'n descended Chief!
Two guests arrive, both strangers, but the race
Of Jove supreme resembling each in form.
Say, shall we loose, ourselves, their rapid steeds,
Or hence dismiss them to some other host?
But Menelaus, Hero golden-hair'd,
Indignant answer'd him. Boethe's son!
40 Thou wast not, Eteoneus, heretofore,
A babbler, who now pratest as a child.
We have ourselves arrived indebted much
To hospitality of other men,
If Jove shall, even here, some pause at last
Of woe afford us. Therefore loose, at once,
Their steeds, and introduce them to the feast.
He said, and, issuing, Eteoneus call'd
The brisk attendants to his aid, with whom

He loos'd their foaming coursers from the yoke.
50 Them first they bound to mangers, which with oats
And mingled barley they supplied, then thrust
The chariot sidelong to the splendid wall.[9]
Themselves he, next, into the royal house
Conducted, who survey'd, wond'ring, the abode
Of the heav'n-favour'd King; for on all sides
As with the splendour of the sun or moon
The lofty dome of Menelaus blazed.
Satiate, at length, with wonder at that sight,
They enter'd each a bath, and by the hands
60 Of maidens laved, and oil'd, and cloath'd again
With shaggy mantles and resplendent vests,
Sat both enthroned at Menelaus' side.
And now a maiden charged with golden ew'r,
And with an argent laver, pouring first
Pure water on their hands, supplied them next
With a bright table, which the maiden, chief
In office, furnish'd plenteously with bread
And dainties, remnants of the last regale.
Then came the sew'r, who with delicious meats
70 Dish after dish, served them, and placed beside
The chargers cups magnificent of gold,
When Menelaus grasp'd their hands, and said.
Eat and rejoice, and when ye shall have shared
Our nuptial banquet, we will then inquire
Who are ye both, for, certain, not from those
Whose generation perishes are ye,
But rather of some race of sceptred Chiefs
Heav'n-born; the base have never sons like you.
So saying, he from the board lifted his own
80 Distinguish'd portion, and the fatted chine
Gave to his guests; the sav'ry viands they
With outstretch'd hands assail'd, and when the force
No longer now of appetite they felt,
Telemachus, inclining close his head
To Nestor's son, lest others should his speech
Witness, in whisper'd words him thus address'd.
Dearest Pisistratus, observe, my friend!
How all the echoing palace with the light
Of beaming brass, of gold and amber shines
90 Silver and ivory! for radiance such
Th' interior mansion of Olympian Jove
I deem. What wealth, how various, how immense
Is here! astonish'd I survey the sight!
But Menelaus, golden-hair'd, his speech
O'erhearing, thus in accents wing'd replied
My children! let no mortal man pretend

---

[9] Hesychius tells us, that the Greecians ornamented with much attention the front wall of their courts for the admiration of passengers.

Comparison with Jove; for Jove's abode
And all his stores are incorruptible.
But whether mortal man with me may vie
100 In the display of wealth, or whether not,
This know, that after many toils endured,
And perilous wand'rings wide, in the eighth year
I brought my treasures home. Remote I roved
To Cyprus, to Phoenice, to the shores
Of Ægypt; Æthiopia's land I reach'd,
Th' Erembi, the Sidonians, and the coasts
Of Lybia, where the lambs their foreheads shew
At once with horns defended, soon as yean'd.
There, thrice within the year the flocks produce,
110 Nor master, there, nor shepherd ever feels
A dearth of cheese, of flesh, or of sweet milk
Delicious, drawn from udders never dry.
While, thus, commodities on various coasts
Gath'ring I roam'd, another, by the arts
Of his pernicious spouse aided, of life
Bereav'd my brother privily, and when least
He fear'd to lose it. Therefore little joy
To me results from all that I possess.
Your fathers (be those fathers who they may)
120 These things have doubtless told you; for immense
Have been my suff'rings, and I have destroy'd
A palace well inhabited and stored
With precious furniture in ev'ry kind;
Such, that I would to heav'n! I own'd at home
Though but the third of it, and that the Greeks
Who perish'd then, beneath the walls of Troy
Far from steed-pastured Argos, still survived.
Yet while, sequester'd here, I frequent mourn
My slaughter'd friends, by turns I sooth my soul
130 With tears shed for them, and by turns again
I cease; for grief soon satiates free indulged.
But of them all, although I all bewail,
None mourn I so as one, whom calling back
To memory, I both sleep and food abhor.
For, of Achaia's sons none ever toiled
Strenuous as Ulysses; but his lot
Was woe, and unremitting sorrow mine
For his long absence, who, if still he live,
We know not aught, or be already dead.
140 Him doubtless, old Laertes mourns, and him
Discrete Penelope, nor less his son
Telemachus, born newly when he sail'd.
So saying, he kindled in him strong desire
To mourn his father; at his father's name
Fast fell his tears to ground, and with both hands
He spread his purple cloak before his eyes;
Which Menelaus marking, doubtful sat
If he should leave him leisure for his tears,
Or question him, and tell him all at large.
150 While thus he doubted, Helen (as it chanced)
Leaving her fragrant chamber, came, august
As Dian, goddess of the golden bow.
Adrasta, for her use, set forth a throne,
Alcippe with soft arras cover'd it,
And Philo brought her silver basket, gift
Of fair Alcandra, wife of Polybus,

Whose mansion in Ægyptian Thebes is rich
In untold treasure, and who gave, himself,
Ten golden talents, and two silver baths
160 To Menelaus, with two splendid tripods
Beside the noble gifts which, at the hand
Of his illustrious spouse, Helen receiv'd;
A golden spindle, and a basket wheel'd,
Itself of silver, and its lip of gold.
That basket Philo, her own handmaid, placed
At beauteous Helen's side, charged to the brim
With slender threads, on which the spindle lay
With wool of purple lustre wrapp'd around.
Approaching, on her footstool'd throne she sat,
170 And, instant, of her royal spouse enquired.
Know we, my Menelaus, dear to Jove!
These guests of ours, and whence they have arrived?
Erroneous I may speak, yet speak I must;
In man or woman never have I seen
Such likeness to another (wonder-fixt
I gaze) as in this stranger to the son
Of brave Ulysses, whom that Hero left
New-born at home, when (shameless as I was)
For my unworthy sake the Greecians sailed
180 To Ilium, with fierce rage of battle fir'd.
Then Menelaus, thus, the golden-hair'd.
I also such resemblance find in him

As thou; such feet, such hands, the cast of eye[10]
Similar, and the head and flowing locks.
And even now, when I Ulysses named,
And his great sufferings mention'd, in my cause,
The bitter tear dropp'd from his lids, while broad
Before his eyes his purple cloak he spread.
To whom the son of Nestor thus replied.
190 Atrides! Menelaus! Chief renown'd!
He is in truth his son, as thou hast said,
But he is modest, and would much himself
Condemn, if, at his first arrival here,
He should loquacious seem and bold to thee,
To whom we listen, captived by thy voice,
As if some God had spoken. As for me,
Nestor, my father, the Gerenian Chief
Bade me conduct him hither, for he wish'd
To see thee, promising himself from thee
200 The benefit of some kind word or deed.
For, destitute of other aid, he much
His father's tedious absence mourns at home.
So fares Telemachus; his father strays
Remote, and, in his stead, no friend hath he
Who might avert the mischiefs that he feels.
To whom the Hero amber-hair'd replied.
Ye Gods! the offspring of indeed a friend
Hath reach'd my house, of one who hath endured
Arduous conflicts num'rous for my sake;
210 And much I purpos'd, had Olympian Jove
Vouchsaf'd us prosp'rous passage o'er the Deep,
To have receiv'd him with such friendship here
As none beside. In Argos I had then
Founded a city for him, and had rais'd
A palace for himself; I would have brought
The Hero hither, and his son, with all

---

10 +Ophthalmôn te bolai+.

His people, and with all his wealth, some town
Evacuating for his sake, of those
Ruled by myself, and neighb'ring close my own.
220 Thus situate, we had often interchanged
Sweet converse, nor had other cause at last
Our friendship terminated or our joys,
Than death's black cloud o'ershadowing him or me.
But such delights could only envy move
Ev'n in the Gods, who have, of all the Greeks,
Amerc'd *him* only of his wish'd return.
So saying, he kindled the desire to weep
In ev'ry bosom. Argive Helen wept
Abundant, Jove's own daughter; wept as fast
230 Telemachus and Menelaus both;
Nor Nestor's son with tearless eyes remain'd,
Calling to mind Antilochus[11] by the son[12]
Illustrious of the bright Aurora slain,
Rememb'ring whom, in accents wing'd he said.
Atrides! antient Nestor, when of late
Conversing with him, we remember'd thee,
Pronounced thee wise beyond all human-kind.
Now therefore, let not even my advice
Displease thee. It affords me no delight
240 To intermingle tears with my repast,
And soon, Aurora, daughter of the dawn,
Will tinge the orient. Not that I account
Due lamentation of a friend deceased
Blameworthy, since, to sheer the locks and weep,
Is all we can for the unhappy dead.
I also have my grief, call'd to lament
One, not the meanest of Achaia's sons,
My brother; him I cannot but suppose
To thee well-known, although unknown to me
250 Who saw him never;[13] but report proclaims
Antilochus superior to the most,
In speed superior, and in feats of arms.
To whom, the Hero of the yellow locks.
O friend belov'd! since nought which thou hast said
Or recommended now, would have disgraced
A man of years maturer far than thine,
(For wise thy father is, and such art thou,
And easy is it to discern the son
Of such a father, whom Saturnian Jove
260 In marriage both and at his birth ordain'd
To great felicity; for he hath giv'n
To Nestor gradually to sink at home
Into old age, and, while he lives, to see
His sons past others wise, and skill'd in arms)
The sorrow into which we sudden fell
Shall pause. Come-now remember we the feast;
Pour water on our hands, for we shall find,
(Telemachus and I) no dearth of themes
For mutual converse when the day shall dawn.
270 He ended; then, Asphalion, at his word,
Servant of glorious Menelaus, poured
Pure water on their hands, and they the feast
Before them with keen appetite assail'd.

But Jove-born Helen otherwise, meantime,
Employ'd, into the wine of which they drank
A drug infused, antidote to the pains
Of grief and anger, a most potent charm
For ills of ev'ry name. Whoe'er his wine
So medicated drinks, he shall not pour
280 All day the tears down his wan cheek, although
His father and his mother both were dead,
Nor even though his brother or his son
Had fall'n in battle, and before his eyes.
Such drugs Jove's daughter own'd, with skill prepar'd,
And of prime virtue, by the wife of Thone,
Ægyptian Polydamna, giv'n her.
For Ægypt teems with drugs, yielding no few
Which, mingled with the drink, are good, and many
Of baneful juice, and enemies to life.
290 There ev'ry man in skill medicinal
Excels, for they are sons of Pæon all.
That drug infused, she bade her servant pour
The bev'rage forth, and thus her speech resumed.
Atrides! Menelaus! dear to Jove!
These also are the sons of Chiefs renown'd,
(For Jove, as pleases him, to each assigns
Or good or evil, whom all things obey)
Now therefore, feasting at your ease reclin'd,
Listen with pleasure, for myself, the while,
300 Will matter seasonable interpose.
I cannot all rehearse, nor even name,
(Omitting none) the conflicts and exploits
Of brave Ulysses; but with what address
Successful, one atchievement he perform'd
At Ilium, where Achaia's sons endured
Such hardship, will I speak. Inflicting wounds
Dishonourable on himself, he took
A tatter'd garb, and like a serving-man
Enter'd the spacious city of your foes.
310 So veil'd, some mendicant he seem'd, although
No Greecian less deserved that name than he.
In such disguise he enter'd; all alike
Misdeem'd him; me alone he not deceived
Who challeng'd him, but, shrewd, he turn'd away.
At length, however, when I had myself
Bathed him, anointed, cloath'd him, and had sworn
Not to declare him openly in Troy
Till he should reach again the camp and fleet,
He told me the whole purpose of the Greeks.
320 Then, (many a Trojan slaughter'd,) he regain'd
The camp, and much intelligence he bore
To the Achaians. Oh what wailing then
Was heard of Trojan women! but my heart
Exulted, alter'd now, and wishing home;
For now my crime committed under force
Of Venus' influence I deplored, what time
She led me to a country far remote,
A wand'rer from the matrimonial bed,
From my own child, and from my rightful Lord
330 Alike unblemish'd both in form and mind.

---

[11] Antilochus was his brother.

[12] The son of Aurora, who slew Antilochus, was Memnon.

[13] Because Pisistratus was born after Antilochus had sailed to Troy.

Her answer'd then the Hero golden-hair'd.
Helen! thou hast well spoken. All is true.
I have the talents fathom'd and the minds
Of num'rous Heroes, and have travell'd far
Yet never saw I with these eyes in man
Such firmness as the calm Ulysses own'd;
None such as in the wooden horse he proved,
Where all our bravest sat, designing woe
And bloody havoc for the sons of Troy.
340 Thou thither cam'st, impell'd, as it should seem,
By some divinity inclin'd to give
Victory to our foes, and with thee came
Godlike Deiphobus. Thrice round about
The hollow ambush, striking with thy hand
Its sides thou went'st, and by his name didst call
Each prince of Greece feigning his consort's voice.
Myself with Diomede, and with divine
Ulysses, seated in the midst, the call
Heard plain and loud; we (Diomede and I)
350 With ardour burn'd either to quit the horse
So summon'd, or to answer from within.
But, all impatient as we were, Ulysses
Controul'd the rash design; so there the sons
Of the Achaians silent sat and mute,
And of us all Anticlus would alone
Have answer'd; but Ulysses with both hands
Compressing close his lips, saved us, nor ceased
Till Pallas thence conducted thee again.
Then thus, discrete, Telemachus replied.
360 Atrides! Menelaus! prince renown'd!
Hard was his lot whom these rare qualities
Preserved not, neither had his dauntless heart
Been iron, had he scaped his cruel doom.
But haste, dismiss us hence, that on our beds
Reposed, we may enjoy sleep, needful now.
He ceas'd; then Argive Helen gave command
To her attendant maidens to prepare
Beds in the portico with purple rugs
Resplendent, and with arras, overspread,
370 And cover'd warm with cloaks of shaggy pile.
Forth went the maidens, bearing each a torch,
And spread the couches; next, the herald them
Led forth, and in the vestibule the son
Of Nestor and the youthful Hero slept,
Telemachus; but in the interior house
Atrides, with the loveliest of her sex
Beside him, Helen of the sweeping stole.
But when Aurora, daughter of the dawn,
Glow'd in the East, then from his couch arose
380 The warlike Menelaus, fresh attir'd;
His faulchion o'er his shoulders slung, he bound
His sandals fair to his unsullied feet,
And like a God issuing, at the side
Sat of Telemachus, to whom he spake.
Hero! Telemachus! what urgent cause
Hath hither led thee, to the land far-famed
Of Lacedæmon o'er the spacious Deep?
Public concern or private? Tell me true.
To whom Telemachus discrete replied.
390 Atrides! Menelaus! prince renown'd!

News seeking of my Sire, I have arrived.
My household is devour'd, my fruitful fields
Are desolated, and my palace fill'd
With enemies, who while they mutual wage
Proud competition for my mother's love,
My flocks continual slaughter, and my beeves.
For this cause, at thy knees suppliant, I beg
That thou wouldst tell me his disastrous end,
If either thou beheld'st with thine own eyes
400 His death, or from some wand'rer of the Greeks
Hast heard it; for no common woes, alas!
Was he ordain'd to share ev'n from the womb.
Neither through pity or o'erstrain'd respect
Flatter me, but explicit all relate
Which thou hast witness'd. If my noble Sire
E'er gratified thee by performance just
Of word or deed at Ilium, where ye fell
So num'rous slain in fight, oh recollect
Now his fidelity, and tell me true!
410 Then Menelaus, sighing deep, replied.
Gods! their ambition is to reach the bed
Of a brave man, however base themselves.
But as it chances, when the hart hath lay'd
Her fawns new-yean'd and sucklings yet, to rest
Within some dreadful lion's gloomy den,
She roams the hills, and in the grassy vales
Feeds heedless, till the lion, to his lair
Return'd, destroys her and her little-ones,
So them thy Sire shall terribly destroy.
420 Jove, Pallas and Apollo! oh that such
As erst in well-built Lesbos, where he strove
With Philomelides, and threw him flat,
A sight at which Achaia's sons rejoic'd,
Such, now, Ulysses might assail them all!
Short life and bitter nuptials should be theirs.
But thy enquiries neither indirect
Will I evade, nor give thee false reply,
But all that from the Antient of the Deep[14]
I have receiv'd will utter, hiding nought.
430 As yet the Gods on Ægypt's shore detained
Me wishing home, angry at my neglect
To heap their altars with slain hecatombs.
For they exacted from us evermore
Strict rev'rence of their laws. There is an isle
Amid the billowy flood, Pharos by name,
In front of Ægypt, distant from her shore
Far as a vessel by a sprightly gale
Impell'd, may push her voyage in a day.
The haven there is good, and many a ship
440 Finds wat'ring there from riv'lets on the coast.
There me the Gods kept twenty days, no breeze
Propitious granting, that might sweep the waves,
And usher to her home the flying bark.
And now had our provision, all consumed,
Left us exhausted, but a certain nymph
Pitying saved me. Daughter fair was she
Of mighty Proteus, Antient of the Deep,
Idothea named; her most my sorrows moved;
She found me from my followers all apart
450 Wand'ring (for they around the isle, with hooks

_____

[14] Proteus.

24

The fishes snaring roamed, by famine urged)
And standing at my side, me thus bespake.
Stranger! thou must be ideot born, or weak
At least in intellect, or thy delight
Is in distress and mis'ry, who delay'st
To leave this island, and no egress hence
Canst find, although thy famish'd people faint.
So spake the Goddess, and I thus replied.
I tell thee, whosoever of the Pow'rs
460 Divine thou art, that I am prison'd here
Not willingly, but must have, doubtless, sinn'd
Against the deathless tenants of the skies.
Yet say (for the Immortals all things know)
What God detains me, and my course forbids
Hence to my country o'er the fishy Deep?
So I; to whom the Goddess all-divine.
Stranger! I will inform thee true. A seer
Oracular, the Antient of the Deep,
Immortal Proteus, the Ægyptian, haunts
470 These shores, familiar with all Ocean's gulphs,
And Neptune's subject. He is by report
My father; him if thou art able once
To seize and bind, he will prescribe the course
With all its measured distances, by which
Thou shalt regain secure thy native shores.
He will, moreover, at thy suit declare,
Thou favour'd of the skies! what good, what ill
Hath in thine house befall'n, while absent thou
Thy voyage difficult perform'st and long.
480 She spake, and I replied-Thyself reveal
By what effectual bands I may secure
The antient Deity marine, lest, warn'd
Of my approach, he shun me and escape.
Hard task for mortal hands to bind a God!
Then thus Idothea answer'd all-divine.
I will inform thee true. Soon as the sun
Hath climb'd the middle heav'ns, the prophet old,
Emerging while the breezy zephyr blows,
And cover'd with the scum of ocean, seeks
490 His spacious cove, in which outstretch'd he lies.

The phocæ[15] also, rising from the waves,
Offspring of beauteous Halosydna, sleep
Around him, num'rous, and the fishy scent
Exhaling rank of the unfathom'd flood.
Thither conducting thee at peep of day
I will dispose thee in some safe recess,
But from among thy followers thou shalt chuse
The bravest three in all thy gallant fleet.
And now the artifices understand
500 Of the old prophet of the sea. The sum
Of all his phocæ numb'ring duly first,
He will pass through them, and when all by fives
He counted hath, will in the midst repose
Content, as sleeps the shepherd with his flock.
When ye shall see him stretch'd, then call to mind
That moment all your prowess, and prevent,
Howe'er he strive impatient, his escape.
All changes trying, he will take the form
Of ev'ry reptile on the earth, will seem
510 A river now, and now devouring fire;

---

15 Seals, or sea-calves.

But hold him ye, and grasp him still the more.
And when himself shall question you, restored
To his own form in which ye found him first
Reposing, then from farther force abstain;
Then, Hero! loose the Antient of the Deep,
And ask him, of the Gods who checks thy course
Hence to thy country o'er the fishy flood.
So saying, she plunged into the billowy waste.
I then, in various musings lost, my ships
520 Along the sea-beach station'd sought again,
And when I reach'd my galley on the shore
We supp'd, and sacred night falling from heav'n,
Slept all extended on the ocean-side.
But when Aurora, daughter of the dawn,
Look'd rosy forth, pensive beside the shore
I walk'd of Ocean, frequent to the Gods
Praying devout, then chose the fittest three
For bold assault, and worthiest of my trust.
Meantime the Goddess from the bosom wide
530 Of Ocean rising, brought us thence four skins
Of phocæ, and all newly stript, a snare
Contriving subtle to deceive her Sire.
Four cradles in the sand she scoop'd, then sat
Expecting us, who in due time approach'd;
She lodg'd us side by side, and over each
A raw skin cast. Horrible to ourselves
Proved that disguise whom the pernicious scent
Of the sea-nourish'd phocæ sore annoy'd;
For who would lay him down at a whale's side?
540 But she a potent remedy devised
Herself to save us, who the nostrils sooth'd
Of each with pure ambrosia thither brought
Odorous, which the fishy scent subdued.
All morning, patient watchers, there we lay;
And now the num'rous phocæ from the Deep
Emerging, slept along the shore, and he
At noon came also, and perceiving there
His fatted monsters, through the flock his course
Took regular, and summ'd them; with the first
550 He number'd us, suspicion none of fraud
Conceiving, then couch'd also. We, at once,
Loud-shouting flew on him, and in our arms
Constrain'd him fast; nor the sea-prophet old
Call'd not incontinent his shifts to mind.
First he became a long-maned lion grim,
Then dragon, panther then, a savage boar,
A limpid stream, and an o'ershadowing tree.
We persevering held him, till at length
The Antient of the Deep, skill'd as he is
560 In wiles, yet weary, question'd me, and said.
Oh Atreus' son, by what confed'rate God
Instructed liest thou in wait for me,
To seize and hold me? what is thy desire?
So He; to whom thus answer I return'd.
Old Seer! thou know'st; why, fraudful, should'st thou ask?
It is because I have been prison'd long
Within this isle, whence I have sought in vain
Deliv'rance, till my wonted courage fails.
Yet say (for the Immortals all things know)
570 What God detains me, and my course forbids

Hence to my country o'er the fishy Deep?
So I; when thus the old one of the waves.

But thy plain duty[16] was to have adored
Jove, first, in sacrifice, and all the Gods,
That then embarking, by propitious gales
Impell'd, thou might'st have reach'd thy country soon.
For thou art doom'd ne'er to behold again
Thy friends, thy palace, or thy native shores,
Till thou have seen once more the hallow'd flood
580 Of Ægypt, and with hecatombs adored
Devout, the deathless tenants of the skies.
Then will they speed thee whither thou desir'st.
He ended, and my heart broke at his words,
Which bade me pass again the gloomy gulph
To Ægypt; tedious course, and hard to atchieve!
Yet, though in sorrow whelm'd, I thus replied.
Old prophet! I will all thy will perform.
But tell me, and the truth simply reveal;
Have the Achaians with their ships arrived
590 All safe, whom Nestor left and I, at Troy?
Or of the Chiefs have any in their barks,
Or in their followers' arms found a dire death
Unlook'd for, since that city's siege we closed?
I spake, when answer thus the God return'd.
Atrides, why these questions? Need is none
That thou should'st all my secrets learn, which once
Reveal'd, thou would'st not long dry-eyed remain.
Of those no few have died, and many live;
But leaders, two alone, in their return
600 Have died (thou also hast had war to wage)
And one, still living, roams the boundless sea.

Ajax,[17] surrounded by his galleys, died.
Him Neptune, first, against the bulky rocks
The Gyræ drove, but saved him from the Deep;
Nor had he perish'd, hated as he was
By Pallas, but for his own impious boast
In frenzy utter'd that he would escape
The billows, even in the Gods' despight.
Neptune that speech vain-glorious hearing, grasp'd
610 His trident, and the huge Gyræan rock
Smiting indignant, dash'd it half away;
Part stood, and part, on which the boaster sat
When, first, the brainsick fury seiz'd him, fell,
Bearing him with it down into the gulphs
Of Ocean, where he drank the brine, and died.
But thy own brother in his barks escaped
That fate, by Juno saved; yet when, at length,
He should have gain'd Malea's craggy shore,
Then, by a sudden tempest caught, he flew
620 With many a groan far o'er the fishy Deep
To the land's utmost point, where once his home
Thyestes had, but where Thyestes' son
Dwelt then, Ægisthus. Easy lay his course
And open thence, and, as it pleased the Gods,
The shifted wind soon bore them to their home.
He, high in exultation, trod the shore
That gave him birth, kiss'd it, and, at the sight,
The welcome sight of Greece, shed many a tear.
Yet not unseen he landed; for a spy,
630 One whom the shrewd Ægisthus had seduced
By promise of two golden talents, mark'd
His coming from a rock where he had watch'd
The year complete, lest, passing unperceived,
The King should reassert his right in arms.
Swift flew the spy with tidings to this Lord,
And He, incontinent, this project framed
Insidious. Twenty men, the boldest hearts
Of all the people, from the rest he chose,
Whom he in ambush placed, and others charged
640 Diligent to prepare the festal board.
With horses, then, and chariots forth he drove
Full-fraught with mischief, and conducting home
The unsuspicious King, amid the feast
Slew him, as at his crib men slay an ox.
Nor of thy brother's train, nor of his train
Who slew thy brother, one survived, but all,
Welt'ring in blood together, there expired.
He ended, and his words beat on my heart
As they would break it. On the sands I sat
650 Weeping, nor life nor light desiring more.
But when I had in dust roll'd me, and wept
To full satiety, mine ear again
The oracle of Ocean thus address'd.
Sit not, O son of Atreus! weeping here
Longer, for remedy can none be found;
But quick arising, trial make, how best
Thou shalt, and soonest, reach thy home again.
For either him still living thou shalt find,
Or ere thou come, Orestes shall have slain
660 The traytor, and thine eyes shall see his tomb.
He ceas'd, and I, afflicted as I was,
Yet felt my spirit at that word refresh'd,
And in wing'd accents answer thus return'd.
Of these I am inform'd; but name the third
Who, dead or living, on the boundless Deep
Is still detain'd; I dread, yet wish to hear.
So I; to whom thus Proteus in return.
Laertes' son, the Lord of Ithaca-
Him in an island weeping I beheld,
670 Guest of the nymph Calypso, by constraint
Her guest, and from his native land withheld
By sad necessity; for ships well-oar'd,
Or faithful followers hath he none, whose aid
Might speed him safely o'er the spacious flood.
But, Menelaus dear to Jove! thy fate
Ordains not thee the stroke of death to meet
In steed-fam'd Argos, but far hence the Gods
Will send thee to Elysium, and the earth's
Extremest bounds; (there Rhadamanthus dwells,
680 The golden-hair'd, and there the human kind
Enjoy the easiest life; no snow is there,
No biting winter, and no drenching show'r,
But zephyr always gently from the sea

---

[16] From the abruptness of this beginning, Virgil, probably, who has copied the story, took the hint of his admired exordium.
Nam quis te, juvenum confidentissime, nostras.
Egit adire domos.

[17] Son of Oïleus.

Breathes on them to refresh the happy race)
For that fair Helen is by nuptial bands
Thy own, and thou art son-in-law of Jove.
So saying, he plunged into the billowy waste,
I then, with my brave comrades to the fleet
Return'd, deep-musing as I went, and sad.
690 No sooner had I reach'd my ship beside
The ocean, and we all had supp'd, than night
From heav'n fell on us, and, at ease reposed
Along the margin of the sea, we slept.
But when Aurora, daughter of the dawn,
Look'd rosy forth, drawing our galleys down
Into the sacred Deep, we rear'd again
The mast, unfurl'd the sail, and to our seats
On board returning, thresh'd the foamy flood.
Once more, at length, within the hallow'd stream
700 Of Ægypt mooring, on the shore I slew
Whole hecatombs, and (the displeasure thus
Of the immortal Gods appeased) I reared
To Agamemnon's never-dying fame
A tomb, and finishing it, sail'd again
With such a gale from heaven vouchsafed, as sent
My ships swift-scudding to the shores of Greece.
But come-eleven days wait here, or twelve
A guest with me, when I will send thee hence
Nobly, and honour'd with illustrious gifts,
710 With polish'd chariot, with three princely steeds,
And with a gorgeous cup, that to the Gods
Libation pouring ever while thou liv'st
From that same cup, thou may'st remember me.
Him, prudent, then answer'd Telemachus.
Atrides, seek not to detain me here
Long time; for though contented I could sit
The year beside thee, nor regret my home
Or parents, (so delightful thy discourse
Sounds in my ear) yet, even now, I know,
720 That my attendants to the Pylian shore
Wish my return, whom thou thus long detain'st.
What boon soe'er thou giv'st me, be it such
As I may treasur'd keep; but horses none
Take I to Ithaca; them rather far
Keep thou, for thy own glory. Thou art Lord
Of an extended plain, where copious springs
The lotus, herbage of all savours, wheat,
Pulse, and white barley of luxuriant growth.
But Ithaca no level champaign owns,
730 A nursery of goats, and yet a land
Fairer than even pastures to the eye.
No sea-encircled isle of ours affords
Smooth course commodious and expanse of meads,
But my own Ithaca transcends them all!
He said; the Hero Menelaus smiled,
And stroaking tenderly his cheek, replied.
Dear youth! thy speech proclaims thy noble blood.
I can with ease supply thee from within
With what shall suit thee better, and the gift
740 Of all that I possess which most excels
In beauty, and the noblest shall be thine.
I give thee, wrought elaborate, a cup

Itself all silver, bound with lip of gold.
It is the work of Vulcan, which to me
The Hero Phædimus imparted, King
Of the Sidonians, when on my return
His house received me. That shall be thy own.
Thus they conferr'd; and now the busy train
Of menials culinary,[18] at the gate
750 Enter'd of Menelaus, Chief renown'd;
They brought him sheep, with heart-ennobling wine,
While all their wives, their brows with frontlets bound,
Came charg'd with bread. Thus busy they prepared
A banquet in the mansion of the King.
Meantime, before Ulysses' palace gate
The suitors sported with the quoit and spear
On the smooth area, customary scene
Of all their strife and angry clamour loud.
There sat Antinoüs, and the godlike youth
760 Eurymachus, superior to the rest
And Chiefs among them, to whom Phronius' son
Noëmon drawing nigh, with anxious mien
Question'd Antinoüs, and thus began.
Know we, Antinoüs! or know we not,
When to expect Telemachus at home
Again from Pylus? in my ship he went,
Which now I need, that I may cross the sea
To Elis, on whose spacious plain I feed
Twelve mares, each suckling a mule-colt as yet
770 Unbroken, but of which I purpose one
To ferry thence, and break him into use.
He spake, whom they astonish'd heard; for him
They deem'd not to Nelëian Pylus gone,
But haply into his own fields, his flocks
To visit, or the steward of his swine.
Then thus, Eupithes' son, Antinoüs, spake.
Say true. When sail'd he forth? of all our youth,
Whom chose he for his followers? his own train
Of slaves and hirelings? hath he pow'r to effect
780 This also? Tell me too, for I would learn-
Took he perforce thy sable bark away,
Or gav'st it to him at his first demand?
To whom Noëmon, Phronius' son, replied.
I gave it voluntary; what could'st thou,
Should such a prince petition for thy bark
In such distress? Hard were it to refuse.
Brave youths (our bravest youths except yourselves)
Attend him forth; and with them I observed
Mentor embarking, ruler o'er them all,
790 Or, if not him, a God; for such he seem'd.
But this much moves my wonder. Yester-morn
I saw, at day-break, noble Mentor here,
Whom shipp'd for Pylus I had seen before.
He ceas'd; and to his father's house return'd;
They, hearing, sat aghast. Their games meantime
Finish'd, the suitors on their seats reposed,
To whom Eupithes' son, Antinoüs, next,
Much troubled spake; a black storm overcharged
His bosom, and his vivid eyes flash'd fire.
800 Ye Gods, a proud exploit is here atchieved,
This voyage of Telemachus, by us

---

[18] +Daitymôn+-generally signifies the founder of a feast; but we are taught by Eustathius to understand by it, in this place, the persons employed in preparing it.

Pronounced impracticable; yet the boy
In downright opposition to us all,
Hath headlong launched a ship, and, with a band
Selected from our bravest youth, is gone.
He soon will prove more mischievous, whose pow'r
Jove wither, ere we suffer its effects!
But give me a swift bark with twenty rowers,
That, watching his return within the streights
810 Of rocky Samos and of Ithaca,
I may surprise him; so shall he have sail'd
To seek his Sire, fatally for himself.
He ceased and loud applause heard in reply,
With warm encouragement. Then, rising all,
Into Ulysses' house at once they throng'd.
Nor was Penelope left uninformed
Long time of their clandestine plottings deep,
For herald Medon told her all, whose ear
Their councils caught while in the outer-court
820 He stood, and they that project framed within.
Swift to Penelope the tale he bore,
Who as he pass'd the gate, him thus address'd.
For what cause, herald! have the suitors sent
Thee foremost? Wou'd they that my maidens lay
Their tasks aside, and dress the board for them?
Here end their wooing! may they hence depart
Never, and may the banquet now prepared,

This banquet prove your last![19] who in such throngs
Here meeting, waste the patrimony fair
830 Of brave Telemachus; ye never, sure,
When children, heard how gracious and how good
Ulysses dwelt among your parents, none
Of all his people, or in word or deed
Injuring, as great princes oft are wont,
By favour influenc'd now, now by disgust.
He no man wrong'd at any time; but plain
Your wicked purpose in your deeds appears,
Who sense have none of benefits conferr'd.
Then Medon answer'd thus, prudent, return'd.
840 Oh Queen! may the Gods grant this prove the worst.
But greater far and heavier ills than this
The suitors plan, whose counsels Jove confound!
Their base desire and purpose are to slay
Telemachus on his return; for he,
To gather tidings of his Sire is gone
To Pylus, or to Sparta's land divine.
He said; and where she stood, her trembling knees
Fail'd under her, and all her spirits went.
Speechless she long remain'd, tears filled her eyes,
850 And inarticulate in its passage died
Her utt'rance, till at last with pain she spake.
Herald! why went my son? he hath no need
On board swift ships to ride, which are to man
His steeds that bear him over seas remote.
Went he, that, with himself, his very name
Might perish from among mankind for ever?
Then answer, thus, Medon the wise return'd.
I know not whether him some God impell'd
Or his own heart to Pylus, there to hear
860 News of his Sire's return, or by what fate

At least he died, if he return no more.
He said, and traversing Ulysses' courts,
Departed; she with heart consuming woe
O'erwhelm'd, no longer could endure to take
Repose on any of her num'rous seats,
But on the threshold of her chamber-door
Lamenting sat, while all her female train
Around her moan'd, the antient and the young,
Whom, sobbing, thus Penelope bespake.
870 Hear me, ye maidens! for of women born
Coeval with me, none hath e'er received
Such plenteous sorrow from the Gods as I,
Who first my noble husband lost, endued
With courage lion-like, of all the Greeks
The Chief with ev'ry virtue most adorn'd,
A prince all-excellent, whose glorious praise
Through Hellas and all Argos flew diffused.
And now, my darling son, — him storms have snatch'd
Far hence inglorious, and I knew it not.
880 Ah treach'rous servants! conscious as ye were
Of his design, not one of you the thought
Conceived to wake me when he went on board.
For had but the report once reach'd my ear,
He either had not gone (how much soe'er
He wish'd to leave me) or had left me dead.
But haste ye, — bid my antient servant come,
Dolion, whom (when I left my father's house
He gave me, and whose office is to attend
My num'rous garden-plants) that he may seek
890 At once Laertes, and may tell him all,
Who may contrive some remedy, perchance,
Or fit expedient, and shall come abroad
To weep before the men who wish to slay
Even the prince, godlike Ulysses' son.
Then thus the gentle Euryclea spake,
Nurse of Telemachus. Alas! my Queen!
Slay me, or spare, deal with me as thou wilt,
I will confess the truth. I knew it all.
I gave him all that he required from me.
900 Both wine and bread, and, at his bidding, swore
To tell thee nought in twelve whole days to come,
Or till, enquiry made, thou should'st thyself
Learn his departure, lest thou should'st impair
Thy lovely features with excess of grief.
But lave thyself, and, fresh attired, ascend
To thy own chamber, there, with all thy train,
To worship Pallas, who shall save, thenceforth,
Thy son from death, what ills soe'er he meet.
Add not fresh sorrows to the present woes
910 Of the old King, for I believe not yet
Arcesias' race entirely by the Gods
Renounced, but trust that there shall still be found
Among them, who shall dwell in royal state,
And reap the fruits of fertile fields remote.
So saying, she hush'd her sorrow, and her eyes
No longer stream'd. Then, bathed and fresh attired,
Penelope ascended with her train
The upper palace, and a basket stored
With hallow'd cakes off'ring, to Pallas pray'd.

---

[19] This transition from the third to the second person belongs to the original, and is considered as a fine stroke of art in the poet, who represents Penelope in the warmth of her resentment, forgetting where she is, and addressing the suitors as if present.

920 Hear matchless daughter of Jove Ægis-arm'd!
If ever wise Ulysses offer'd here
The thighs of fatted kine or sheep to thee,
Now mindful of his piety, preserve
His darling son, and frustrate with a frown
The cruelty of these imperious guests!
She said, and wept aloud, whose earnest suit
Pallas received. And now the spacious hall
And gloomy passages with tumult rang
And clamour of that throng, when thus, a youth,
930 Insolent as his fellows, dared to speak.
Much woo'd and long, the Queen at length prepares
To chuse another mate,[20] and nought suspects
The bloody death to which her son is doom'd.
So he; but they, meantime, themselves remain'd
Untaught, what course the dread concern elsewhere
Had taken, whom Antinoüs thus address'd.
Sirs! one and all, I counsel you, beware
Of such bold boasting unadvised; lest one
O'erhearing you, report your words within.
940 No-rather thus, in silence, let us move
To an exploit so pleasant to us all.
He said, and twenty chose, the bravest there,
With whom he sought the galley on the shore,
Which drawing down into the deep, they placed
The mast and sails on board, and, sitting, next,
Each oar in order to its proper groove,
Unfurl'd and spread their canvas to the gale.
Their bold attendants, then, brought them their arms,
And soon as in deep water they had moor'd
950 The ship, themselves embarking, supp'd on board,
And watch'd impatient for the dusk of eve.
But when Penelope, the palace stairs
Remounting, had her upper chamber reach'd,
There, unrefresh'd with either food or wine,
She lay'd her down, her noble son the theme
Of all her thoughts, whether he should escape
His haughty foes, or perish by their hands.
Num'rous as are the lion's thoughts, who sees,
Not without fear, a multitude with toils
960 Encircling him around, such num'rous thoughts
Her bosom occupied, till sleep at length
Invading her, she sank in soft repose.
Then Pallas, teeming with a new design,
Set forth an airy phantom in the form
Of fair Iphthima, daughter of the brave
Icarius, and Eumelus' wedded wife
In Pheræ. Shaped like her the dream she sent
Into the mansion of the godlike Chief
Ulysses, with kind purpose to abate
970 The sighs and tears of sad Penelope.
Ent'ring the chamber-portal, where the bolt
Secured it, at her head the image stood,
And thus, in terms compassionate, began.

Sleep'st thou, distress'd Penelope? The Gods,
Happy in everlasting rest themselves,
Forbid thy sorrows. Thou shalt yet behold
Thy son again, who hath by no offence
Incurr'd at any time the wrath of heav'n.
To whom, sweet-slumb'ring in the shadowy gate
980 By which dreams pass, Penelope replied.
What cause, my sister, brings thee, who art seen
Unfrequent here, for that thou dwell'st remote?
And thou enjoin'st me a cessation too
From sorrows num'rous, and which, fretting, wear
My heart continual; first, my spouse I lost
With courage lion-like endow'd, a prince
All-excellent, whose never-dying praise
Through Hellas and all Argos flew diffused;
And now my only son, new to the toils
990 And hazards of the sea, nor less untaught
The arts of traffic, in a ship is gone
Far hence, for whose dear cause I sorrow more
Than for his Sire himself, and even shake
With terror, lest he perish by their hands
To whom he goes, or in the stormy Deep;
For num'rous are his foes, and all intent
To slay him, ere he reach his home again.
Then answer thus the shadowy form return'd.
Take courage; suffer not excessive dread
1000 To overwhelm thee, such a guide he hath
And guardian, one whom many wish their friend,
And ever at their side, knowing her pow'r,
Minerva; she compassionates thy griefs,
And I am here her harbinger, who speak
As thou hast heard by her own kind command.
Then thus Penelope the wise replied.
Oh! if thou art a goddess, and hast heard
A Goddess' voice, rehearse to me the lot
Of that unhappy one, if yet he live
1010 Spectator of the cheerful beams of day,
Or if, already dead, he dwell below.
Whom answer'd thus the fleeting shadow vain.
I will not now inform thee if thy Lord
Live, or live not. Vain words are best unspoken.
So saying, her egress swift beside the bolt
She made, and melted into air. Upsprang
From sleep Icarius' daughter, and her heart
Felt heal'd within her, by that dream distinct
Visited in the noiseless night serene.
1020 Meantime the suitors urged their wat'ry way,
To instant death devoting in their hearts
Telemachus. There is a rocky isle
In the mid sea, Samos the rude between
And Ithaca, not large, named Asteris.
It hath commodious havens, into which
A passage clear opens on either side,
And there the ambush'd Greeks his coming watch'd.

---

[20] Mistaking, perhaps, the sound of her voice, and imagining that she sang.-Vide Barnes in loco.

Book V

Mercury bears to Calypso a command from Jupiter that she dismiss Ulysses. She, after some remonstrances, promises obedience, and furnishes him with instruments and materials, with which he constructs a raft. He quits Calypso's island; is persecuted by Neptune with dreadful tempests, but by the assistance of a sea nymph, after having lost his raft, is enabled to swim to Phæacia.

Aurora from beside her glorious mate
Tithonus now arose, light to dispense
Through earth and heav'n, when the assembled Gods
In council sat, o'er whom high-thund'ring Jove
Presided, mightiest of the Pow'rs above.
Amid them, Pallas on the num'rous woes
Descanted of Ulysses, whom she saw
With grief, still prison'd in Calypso's isle.
Jove, Father, hear me, and ye other Pow'rs
Who live for ever, hear! Be never King
10 Henceforth to gracious acts inclined, humane,
Or righteous, but let ev'ry sceptred hand
Rule merciless, and deal in wrong alone,
Since none of all his people whom he sway'd
With such paternal gentleness and love
Remembers, now, divine Ulysses more.
He, in yon distant isle a suff'rer lies
Of hopeless sorrow, through constraint the guest
Still of the nymph Calypso, without means
Or pow'r to reach his native shores again,
20 Alike of gallant barks and friends depriv'd,
Who might conduct him o'er the spacious Deep.
Nor is this all, but enemies combine
To slay his son ere yet he can return
From Pylus, whither he hath gone to learn
There, or in Sparta, tidings of his Sire.
To whom the cloud-assembler God replied.
What word hath pass'd thy lips, daughter belov'd?
Hast thou not purpos'd that arriving soon
At home, Ulysses shall destroy his foes?
30 Guide thou, Telemachus, (for well thou canst)
That he may reach secure his native coast,
And that the suitors baffled may return.
He ceas'd, and thus to Hermes spake, his son.
Hermes! (for thou art herald of our will
At all times) to yon bright-hair'd nymph convey
Our fix'd resolve, that brave Ulysses thence
Depart, uncompanied by God or man.
Borne on a corded raft, and suff'ring woe
Extreme, he on the twentieth day shall reach,
40 Not sooner, Scherie the deep-soil'd, possess'd
By the Phæacians, kinsmen of the Gods.
They, as a God shall reverence the Chief,
And in a bark of theirs shall send him thence
To his own home, much treasure, brass and gold
And raiment giving him, to an amount
Surpassing all that, had he safe return'd,
He should by lot have shared of Ilium's spoil.
Thus Fate appoints Ulysses to regain
His country, his own palace, and his friends.
50 He ended, nor the Argicide refused,
Messenger of the skies; his sandals fair,

Ambrosial, golden, to his feet he bound,
Which o'er the moist wave, rapid as the wind,
Bear him, and o'er th' illimitable earth,
Then took his rod with which, at will, all eyes
He closes soft, or opes them wide again.
So arm'd, forth flew the valiant Argicide.
Alighting on Pieria, down he stoop'd
To Ocean, and the billows lightly skimm'd
60 In form a sew-mew, such as in the bays
Tremendous of the barren Deep her food
Seeking, dips oft in brine her ample wing.
In such disguise o'er many a wave he rode,
But reaching, now, that isle remote, forsook
The azure Deep, and at the spacious grot,
Where dwelt the amber-tressed nymph arrived,
Found her within. A fire on all the hearth
Blazed sprightly, and, afar-diffused, the scent
Of smooth-split cedar and of cypress-wood
70 Odorous, burning, cheer'd the happy isle.
She, busied at the loom, and plying fast
Her golden shuttle, with melodious voice
Sat chaunting there; a grove on either side,
Alder and poplar, and the redolent branch
Wide-spread of Cypress, skirted dark the cave.
There many a bird of broadest pinion built
Secure her nest, the owl, the kite, and daw
Long-tongued, frequenter of the sandy shores.
A garden-vine luxuriant on all sides
80 Mantled the spacious cavern, cluster-hung
Profuse; four fountains of serenest lymph
Their sinuous course pursuing side by side,
Stray'd all around, and ev'ry where appear'd
Meadows of softest verdure, purpled o'er
With violets; it was a scene to fill
A God from heav'n with wonder and delight.
Hermes, Heav'n's messenger, admiring stood
That sight, and having all survey'd, at length
Enter'd the grotto; nor the lovely nymph
90 Him knew not soon as seen, for not unknown
Each to the other the Immortals are,
How far soever sep'rate their abodes.
Yet found he not within the mighty Chief
Ulysses; he sat weeping on the shore,
Forlorn, for there his custom was with groans
Of sad regret t' afflict his breaking heart.
Looking continual o'er the barren Deep.
Then thus Calypso, nymph divine, the God
Question'd, from her resplendent throne august.
100 Hermes! possessor of the potent rod!
Who, though by me much reverenc'd and belov'd,
So seldom com'st, say, wherefore comest now?
Speak thy desire; I grant it, if thou ask

Things possible, and possible to me.
Stay not, but ent'ring farther, at my board
Due rites of hospitality receive.
So saying, the Goddess with ambrosial food
Her table cover'd, and with rosy juice
Nectareous charged the cup. Then ate and drank
110 The argicide and herald of the skies,
And in his soul with that repast divine
Refresh'd, his message to the nymph declared.
Questionest thou, O Goddess, me a God?
I tell thee truth, since such is thy demand.
Not willing, but by Jove constrain'd, I come.
For who would, voluntary, such a breadth
Enormous measure of the salt expanse,
Where city none is seen in which the Gods
Are served with chosen hecatombs and pray'r?
120 But no divinity may the designs
Elude, or controvert, of Jove supreme.
He saith, that here thou hold'st the most distrest
Of all those warriors who nine years assail'd
The city of Priam, and, (that city sack'd)
Departed in the tenth; but, going thence,
Offended Pallas, who with adverse winds
Opposed their voyage, and with boist'rous waves.
Then perish'd all his gallant friends, but him
Billows and storms drove hither; Jove commands
130 That thou dismiss him hence without delay,
For fate ordains him not to perish here
From all his friends remote, but he is doom'd
To see them yet again, and to arrive
At his own palace in his native land.
He said; divine Calypso at the sound
Shudder'd, and in wing'd accents thus replied.
Ye are unjust, ye Gods, and envious past
All others, grudging if a Goddess take
A mortal man openly to her arms!
140 So, when the rosy-finger'd Morning chose
Orion, though ye live yourselves at ease,
Yet ye all envied her, until the chaste
Diana from her golden throne dispatch'd
A silent shaft, which slew him in Ortygia.
So, when the golden-tressed Ceres, urged
By passion, took Iäsion to her arms
In a thrice-labour'd fallow, not untaught
Was Jove that secret long, and, hearing it,
Indignant, slew him with his candent bolt.
150 So also, O ye Gods, ye envy me
The mortal man, my comfort. Him I saved
Myself, while solitary on his keel
He rode, for with his sulph'rous arrow Jove
Had cleft his bark amid the sable Deep.
Then perish'd all his gallant friends, but him
Billows and storms drove hither, whom I lov'd
Sincere, and fondly destin'd to a life
Immortal, unobnoxious to decay.
But since no Deity may the designs
160 Elude or controvert of Jove supreme,
Hence with him o'er the barren Deep, if such
The Sov'reign's will, and such his stern command.
But undismiss'd he goes by me, who ships
Myself well-oar'd and mariners have none
To send with him athwart the spacious flood;
Yet freely, readily, my best advice

I will afford him, that, escaping all
Danger, he may regain his native shore.
Then Hermes thus, the messenger of heav'n.
170 Act as thou say'st, fearing the frown of Jove,
Lest, if provoked, he spare not even thee.
So saying, the dauntless Argicide withdrew,
And she (Jove's mandate heard) all-graceful went,
Seeking the brave Ulysses; on the shore
She found him seated; tears succeeding tears
Delug'd his eyes, while, hopeless of return,
Life's precious hours to eating cares he gave
Continual, with the nymph now charm'd no more.
Yet, cold as she was am'rous, still he pass'd
180 His nights beside her in the hollow grot,
Constrain'd, and day by day the rocks among
Which lined the shore heart-broken sat, and oft
While wistfully he eyed the barren Deep,
Wept, groaned, desponded, sigh'd, and wept again.
Then, drawing near, thus spake the nymph divine.
Unhappy! weep not here, nor life consume
In anguish; go; thou hast my glad consent.
Arise to labour; hewing down the trunks
Of lofty trees, fashion them with the ax
190 To a broad raft, which closely floor'd above,
Shall hence convey thee o'er the gloomy Deep.
Bread, water, and the red grape's cheering juice
Myself will put on board, which shall preserve
Thy life from famine; I will also give
New raiment for thy limbs, and will dispatch
Winds after thee to waft thee home unharm'd,
If such the pleasure of the Gods who dwell
In yonder boundless heav'n, superior far
To me, in knowledge and in skill to judge.
200 She ceas'd; but horror at that sound the heart
Chill'd of Ulysses, and in accents wing'd
With wonder, thus the noble Chief replied.
Ah! other thoughts than of my safe return
Employ thee, Goddess, now, who bid'st me pass
The perilous gulph of Ocean on a raft,
That wild expanse terrible, which even ships
Pass not, though form'd to cleave their way with ease,
And joyful in propitious winds from Jove.
No-let me never, in despight of thee,
210 Embark on board a raft, nor till thou swear,
O Goddess! the inviolable oath,
That future mischief thou intend'st me none.
He said; Calypso, beauteous Goddess, smiled,
And, while she spake, stroaking his cheek, replied.
Thou dost asperse me rudely, and excuse
Of ignorance hast none, far better taught;
What words were these? How could'st thou thus reply?
Now hear me Earth, and the wide Heav'n above!
Hear, too, ye waters of the Stygian stream
220 Under the earth (by which the blessed Gods
Swear trembling, and revere the awful oath!)
That future mischief I intend thee none.
No, my designs concerning thee are such
As, in an exigence resembling thine,
Myself, most sure, should for myself conceive.
I have a mind more equal, not of steel
My heart is form'd, but much to pity inclined.
So saying, the lovely Goddess with swift pace
Led on, whose footsteps he as swift pursued.

230 Within the vaulted cavern they arrived,
The Goddess and the man; on the same throne
Ulysses sat, whence Hermes had aris'n,
And viands of all kinds, such as sustain
The life of mortal man, Calypso placed
Before him, both for bev'rage and for food.
She opposite to the illustrious Chief
Reposed, by her attendant maidens served
With nectar and ambrosia. They their hands
Stretch'd forth together to the ready feast,
240 And when nor hunger more nor thirst remain'd
Unsated, thus the beauteous nymph began.
Laertes' noble son, for wisdom famed
And artifice! oh canst thou thus resolve
To seek, incontinent, thy native shores?
I pardon thee. Farewell! but could'st thou guess
The woes which fate ordains thee to endure
Ere yet thou reach thy country, well-content
Here to inhabit, thou would'st keep my grot
And be immortal, howsoe'er thy wife
250 Engage thy ev'ry wish day after day.
Yet can I not in stature or in form
Myself suspect inferior aught to her,
Since competition cannot be between
Mere mortal beauties, and a form divine.
To whom Ulysses, ever-wise, replied.
Awful Divinity! be not incensed.
I know that my Penelope in form
And stature altogether yields to thee,
For she is mortal, and immortal thou,
260 From age exempt; yet not the less I wish
My home, and languish daily to return.
But should some God amid the sable Deep
Dash me again into a wreck, my soul
Shall bear *that* also; for, by practice taught,
I have learned patience, having much endured
By tempest and in battle both. Come then
This evil also! I am well prepared.
He ended, and the sun sinking, resign'd
The earth to darkness. Then in a recess
270 Interior of the cavern, side by side
Reposed, they took their amorous delight.
But when Aurora, daughter of the dawn,
Look'd rosy forth, Ulysses then in haste
Put on his vest and mantle, and, the nymph
Her snowy vesture of transparent woof,
Graceful, redundant; to her waist she bound
Her golden zone, and veil'd her beauteous head,
Then, musing, plann'd the noble Chief's return.
She gave him, fitted to the grasp, an ax
280 Of iron, pond'rous, double-edg'd, with haft
Of olive-wood, inserted firm, and wrought
With curious art. Then, placing in his hand
A polish'd adze, she led, herself, the way
To her isles' utmost verge, where tallest trees
But dry long since and sapless stood, which best
Might serve his purposes, as buoyant most,
The alder, poplar, and cloud-piercing fir.
To that tall grove she led and left him there,
Seeking her grot again. Then slept not He,
290 But, swinging with both hands the ax, his task

Soon finish'd; trees full twenty to the ground
He cast, which, dext'rous, with his adze he smooth'd,
The knotted surface chipping by a line.
Meantime the lovely Goddess to his aid
Sharp augres brought, with which he bored the beams,
Then, side by side placing them, fitted each
To other, and with long cramps join'd them all.
Broad as an artist, skill'd in naval works,
The bottom of a ship of burthen spreads,
300 Such breadth Ulysses to his raft assign'd.
He deck'd her over with long planks, upborne
On massy beams; He made the mast, to which
He added suitable the yard;-he framed
Rudder and helm to regulate her course,
With wicker-work he border'd all her length
For safety, and much ballast stow'd within.
Meantime, Calypso brought him for a sail
Fittest materials, which he also shaped,
And to his sail due furniture annex'd
310 Of cordage strong, foot-ropes, and ropes aloft,
Then heav'd her down with levers to the Deep.
He finish'd all his work on the fourth day,
And on the fifth, Calypso, nymph divine,
Dismiss'd him from her isle, but laved him first,
And cloath'd him in sweet-scented garments new.
Two skins the Goddess also placed on board,
One charg'd with crimson wine, and ampler one
With water, nor a bag with food replete
Forgot, nutritious, grateful to the taste,
320 Nor yet, her latest gift, a gentle gale
And manageable, which Ulysses spread,
Exulting, all his canvas to receive.
Beside the helm he sat, steering expert,
Nor sleep fell ever on his eyes that watch'd
Intent the Pleiads, tardy in decline
Bootes, and the Bear, call'd else the Wain,
Which, in his polar prison circling, looks
Direct toward Orion, and alone
Of these sinks never to the briny Deep.
330 That star the lovely Goddess bade him hold
Continual on his left through all his course.
Ten days and sev'n, he, navigating, cleav'd
The brine, and on the eighteenth day, at length,
The shadowy mountains of Phæacia's land
Descried, where nearest to his course it lay
Like a broad buckler on the waves afloat.
But Neptune, now returning from the land
Of Ethiopia, mark'd him on his raft
Skimming the billows, from the mountain-tops
340 Of distant Solyma.[21] With tenfold wrath
Inflamed that sight he view'd, his brows he shook,
And thus within himself, indignant, spake.
So then-new counsels in the skies, it seems,
Propitious to Ulysses, have prevail'd
Since Æthiopia hath been my abode.
He sees Phæacia nigh, where he must leap
The bound'ry of his woes; but ere that hour
Arrive, I will ensure him many a groan.
So saying, he grasp'd his trident, gather'd dense
350 The clouds and troubled ocean; ev'ry storm
From ev'ry point he summon'd, earth and sea

---

21 The Solymi were the ancient inhabitants of Pisidia in Asia-Minor.

Darkening, and the night fell black from heav'n.
The East, the South, the heavy-blowing West,
And the cold North-wind clear, assail'd at once
His raft, and heaved on high the billowy flood.
All hope, all courage, in that moment, lost,
The Hero thus within himself complain'd.
Wretch that I am, what destiny at last
Attends me! much I fear the Goddess' words
360 All true, which threaten'd me with num'rous ills
On the wide sea, ere I should reach my home.
Behold them all fulfill'd! with what a storm
Jove hangs the heav'ns, and agitates the Deep!
The winds combined beat on me. Now I sink!
Thrice blest, and more than thrice, Achaia's sons
At Ilium slain for the Atridæ' sake!
Ah, would to heav'n that, dying, I had felt
That day the stroke of fate, when me the dead
Achilles guarding, with a thousand spears
370 Troy's furious host assail'd! Funereal rites
I then had shared, and praise from ev'ry Greek,
Whom now the most inglorious death awaits.
While thus he spake, a billow on his head
Bursting impetuous, whirl'd the raft around,
And, dashing from his grasp the helm, himself
Plunged far remote. Then came a sudden gust
Of mingling winds, that in the middle snapp'd
His mast, and, hurried o'er the waves afar,
Both sail and sail-yard fell into the flood.
380 Long time submerged he lay, nor could with ease
The violence of that dread shock surmount,
Or rise to air again, so burthensome
His drench'd apparel proved; but, at the last,
He rose, and, rising, sputter'd from his lips
The brine that trickled copious from his brows.
Nor, harass'd as he was, resign'd he yet
His raft, but buffetting the waves aside
With desp'rate efforts, seized it, and again
Fast seated on the middle deck, escaped.
390 Then roll'd the raft at random in the flood,
Wallowing unwieldy, toss'd from wave to wave.
As when in autumn, Boreas o'er the plain
Conglomerated thorns before him drives,
They, tangled, to each other close adhere,
So her the winds drove wild about the Deep.
By turns the South consign'd her to be sport
For the rude North-wind, and, by turns, the East
Yielded her to the worrying West a prey.
But Cadmus' beauteous daughter (Ino once,
400 Now named Leucothea) saw him; mortal erst
Was she, and trod the earth,[22] but nymph become
Of Ocean since, in honours shares divine.
She mark'd his anguish, and, while toss'd he roam'd,
Pitied Ulysses; from the flood, in form
A cormorant, she flew, and on the raft
Close-corded perching, thus the Chief address'd.
Alas! unhappy! how hast thou incensed
So terribly the Shaker of the shores,
That he pursues thee with such num'rous ills?
410 Sink thee he cannot, wish it as he may.
Thus do (for I account thee not unwise)
Thy garments putting off, let drive thy raft

As the winds will, then, swimming, strive to reach
Phæacia, where thy doom is to escape.
Take this. This ribbon bind beneath thy breast,
Celestial texture. Thenceforth ev'ry fear
Of death dismiss, and, laying once thy hands
On the firm continent, unbind the zone,
Which thou shalt cast far distant from the shore
420 Into the Deep, turning thy face away.
So saying, the Goddess gave into his hand
The wond'rous zone, and, cormorant in form,
Plunging herself into the waves again
Headlong, was hidden by the closing flood.
But still Ulysses sat perplex'd, and thus
The toil-enduring Hero reason'd sad.
Alas! I tremble lest some God design
T' ensnare me yet, bidding me quit the raft.
But let me well beware how I obey
430 Too soon that precept, for I saw the land
Of my foretold deliv'rance far remote.
Thus, therefore, will I do, for such appears
My wiser course. So long as yet the planks
Mutual adhere, continuing on board
My raft, I will endure whatever woes,
But when the waves shall shatter it, I will swim,
My sole resource then left. While thus he mused,
Neptune a billow of enormous bulk
Hollow'd into an overwhelming arch
440 On high up-heaving, smote him. As the wind
Tempestuous, falling on some stubble-heap,
The arid straws dissipates ev'ry way,
So flew the timbers. He, a single beam
Bestriding, oar'd it onward with his feet,
As he had urged an horse. His raiment, then,
Gift of Calypso, putting off, he bound
His girdle on, and prone into the sea
With wide-spread palms prepar'd for swimming, fell.
Shore-shaker Neptune noted him; he shook
450 His awful brows, and in his heart he said,
Thus, suff'ring many mis'ries roam the flood,
Till thou shalt mingle with a race of men
Heav'n's special favourites; yet even there
Fear not that thou shalt feel thy sorrows light.
He said, and scourging his bright steeds, arrived
At Ægæ, where his glorious palace stands.
But other thoughts Minerva's mind employ'd
Jove's daughter; ev'ry wind binding beside,
She lull'd them, and enjoin'd them all to sleep,
460 But roused swift Boreas, and the billows broke
Before Ulysses, that, deliver'd safe
From a dire death, the noble Chief might mix
With maritime Phæacia's sons renown'd.
Two nights he wander'd, and two days, the flood
Tempestuous, death expecting ev'ry hour;
But when Aurora, radiant-hair'd, had brought
The third day to a close, then ceas'd the wind,
And breathless came a calm; he, nigh at hand
The shore beheld, darting acute his sight
470 Toward it, from a billow's tow'ring top.
Precious as to his children seems the life
Of some fond father through disease long time
And pain stretch'd languid on his couch, the prey

---

[22] The Translator finding himself free to chuse between +audêessa+ and +êdêessa+, has preferred the latter.

Of some vindictive Pow'r, but now, at last,
By gracious heav'n to ease and health restored,
So grateful to Ulysses' sight appear'd
Forests and hills. Impatient with his feet
To press the shore, he swam; but when within
Such distance as a shout may fly, he came,
480 The thunder of the sea against the rocks
Then smote his ear; for hoarse the billows roar'd
On the firm land, belch'd horrible abroad,
And the salt spray dimm'd all things to his view.
For neither port for ships nor shelt'ring cove
Was there, but the rude coast a headland bluff
Presented, rocks and craggy masses huge.
Then, hope and strength exhausted both, deep-groan'd
The Chief, and in his noble heart complain'd.
Alas! though Jove hath given me to behold,
490 Unhoped, the land again, and I have pass'd,
Furrowing my way, these num'rous waves, there seems
No egress from the hoary flood for me.
Sharp stones hem in the waters; wild the surge
Raves ev'ry where; and smooth the rocks arise;
Deep also is the shore, on which my feet
No standing gain, or chance of safe escape.
What if some billow catch me from the Deep
Emerging, and against the pointed rocks
Dash me conflicting with its force in vain?
500 But should I, swimming, trace the coast in search
Of sloping beach, haven or shelter'd creek,
I fear lest, groaning, I be snatch'd again
By stormy gusts into the fishy Deep,
Or lest some monster of the flood receive
Command to seize me, of the many such
By the illustrious Amphitrite bred;
For that the mighty Shaker of the shores
Hates me implacable, too well I know.
While such discourse within himself he held,
510 A huge wave heav'd him on the rugged coast,
Where flay'd his flesh had been, and all his bones
Broken together, but for the infused
Good counsel of Minerva azure-eyed.
With both hands suddenly he seized the rock,
And, groaning, clench'd it till the billow pass'd.
So baffled he that wave; but yet again
The refluent flood rush'd on him, and with force
Resistless dash'd him far into the sea.
As pebbles to the hollow polypus
520 Extracted from his stony bed, adhere,
So he, the rough rocks clasping, stripp'd his hands
Raw, and the billows now whelm'd him again.
Then had the hapless Hero premature
Perish'd, but for sagacity inspired
By Pallas azure-eyed. Forth from the waves
Emerging, where the surf burst on the rocks,
He coasted (looking landward as he swam)
The shore, with hope of port or level beach.
But when, still swimming, to the mouth he came
530 Of a smooth-sliding river, there he deem'd
Safest th' ascent, for it was undeform'd
By rocks, and shelter'd close from ev'ry wind.
He felt the current, and thus, ardent, pray'd.
O hear, whate'er thy name, Sov'reign, who rul'st
This river! at whose mouth, from all the threats

Of Neptune 'scap'd, with rapture I arrive.
Even the Immortal Gods the wand'rer's pray'r
Respect, and such am I, who reach, at length,
Thy stream, and clasp thy knees, after long toil.
540 I am thy suppliant. Oh King! pity me.
He said; the river God at once repress'd
His current, and it ceas'd; smooth he prepared
The way before Ulysses, and the land
Vouchsafed him easy at his channel's mouth.
There, once again he bent for ease his limbs
Both arms and knees, in conflict with the floods
Exhausted; swoln his body was all o'er,
And from his mouth and nostrils stream'd the brine.
Breathless and speechless, and of life well nigh
550 Bereft he lay, through dreadful toil immense.
But when, revived, his dissipated pow'rs
He recollected, loosing from beneath
His breast the zone divine, he cast it far
Into the brackish stream, and a huge wave
Returning bore it downward to the sea,
Where Ino caught it. Then, the river's brink
Abandoning, among the rushes prone
He lay, kiss'd oft the soil, and sighing, said,
Ah me! what suff'rings must I now sustain,
560 What doom, at last, awaits me? If I watch
This woeful night, here, at the river's side,
What hope but that the frost and copious dews,
Weak as I am, my remnant small of life
Shall quite extinguish, and the chilly air
Breath'd from the river at the dawn of day?
But if, ascending this declivity
I gain the woods, and in some thicket sleep,
(If sleep indeed can find me overtoil'd
And cold-benumb'd) then I have cause to fear
570 Lest I be torn by wild beasts, and devour'd.
Long time he mused, but, at the last, his course
Bent to the woods, which not remote he saw
From the sea-brink, conspicuous on a hill.
Arrived, between two neighbour shrubs he crept,
Both olives, this the fruitful, that the wild;
A covert, which nor rough winds blowing moist
Could penetrate, nor could the noon-day sun
Smite through it, or unceasing show'rs pervade,
So thick a roof the ample branches form'd
58 °Close interwoven; under these the Chief
Retiring, with industrious hands a bed
Collected broad of leaves, which there he found
Abundant strew'd, such store as had sufficed
Two travellers or three for cov'ring warm,
Though winter's roughest blasts had rag'd the while.
That bed with joy the suff'ring Chief renown'd
Contemplated, and occupying soon
The middle space, hillock'd it high with leaves.
As when some swain hath hidden deep his torch
590 Beneath the embers, at the verge extreme
Of all his farm, where, having neighbours none,
He saves a seed or two of future flame
Alive, doom'd else to fetch it from afar,
So with dry leaves Ulysses overspread
His body, on whose eyes Minerva pour'd
The balm of sleep copious, that he might taste
Repose again, after long toil severe.

Book VI

Minerva designing an interview between the daughter of Alcinoüs and Ulysses, admonishes her in a dream to carry down her clothes to the river, that she may wash them, and make them ready for her approaching nuptials. That task performed, the Princess and her train amuse themselves with play; by accident they awake Ulysses; he comes forth from the wood, and applies himself with much address to Nausicaa, who compassionating his distressed condition, and being much affected by the dignity of his appearance, interests himself in his favour, and conducts him to the city.

There then the noble suff'rer lay, by sleep
Oppress'd and labour; meantime, Pallas sought
The populous city of Phæacia's sons.
They, in old time, in Hypereia dwelt
The spacious, neighbours of a giant race
The haughty Cyclops, who, endued with pow'r
Superior, troubled them with frequent wrongs.
Godlike Nausithoüs then arose, who thence
To Scheria led them, from all nations versed
In arts of cultivated life, remote;
10 With bulwarks strong their city he enclosed,
Built houses for them, temples to the Gods,
And gave to each a portion of the soil.
But he, already by decree of fate
Had journey'd to the shades, and in his stead
Alcinoüs, by the Gods instructed, reign'd.
To his abode Minerva azure-eyed
Repair'd, neglecting nought which might advance
Magnanimous Ulysses' safe return.
She sought the sumptuous chamber where, in form
20 And feature perfect as the Gods, the young
Nausicaa, daughter of the King, reposed.
Fast by the pillars of the portal lay
Two damsels, one on either side, adorn'd
By all the Graces, and the doors were shut.
Soft as a breathing air, she stole toward
The royal virgin's couch, and at her head
Standing, address'd her. Daughter she appear'd
Of Dymas, famed for maritime exploits,
Her friend and her coeval; so disguised
3 °Cærulean-eyed Minerva thus began.
Nausicaa! wherefore hath thy mother borne
A child so negligent? Thy garments share,
Thy most magnificent, no thought of thine.
Yet thou must marry soon, and must provide
Robes for thyself, and for thy nuptial train.
Thy fame, on these concerns, and honour stand;
These managed well, thy parents shall rejoice.
The dawn appearing, let us to the place
Of washing, where thy work-mate I will be
40 For speedier riddance of thy task, since soon
The days of thy virginity shall end;
For thou art woo'd already by the prime
Of all Phæacia, country of thy birth.
Come then-solicit at the dawn of day
Thy royal father, that he send thee forth
With mules and carriage for conveyance hence

Of thy best robes, thy mantles and thy zones.
Thus, more commodiously thou shalt perform
The journey, for the cisterns lie remote.
50 So saying, Minerva, Goddess azure-eyed,
Rose to Olympus, the reputed seat
Eternal of the Gods, which never storms
Disturb, rains drench, or snow invades, but calm
The expanse and cloudless shines with purest day.
There the inhabitants divine rejoice
For ever, (and her admonition giv'n)
Cærulean-eyed Minerva thither flew.
Now came Aurora bright-enthroned, whose rays
Awaken'd fair Nausicaa; she her dream
60 Remember'd wond'ring, and her parents sought
Anxious to tell them. Them she found within.
Beside the hearth her royal mother sat,
Spinning soft fleeces with sea-purple dyed
Among her menial maidens, but she met
Her father, whom the Nobles of the land
Had summon'd, issuing abroad to join
The illustrious Chiefs in council. At his side
She stood, and thus her filial suit preferr'd.
Sir![23] wilt thou lend me of the royal wains
70 A sumpter-carriage? for I wish to bear
My costly cloaths but sullied and unfit
For use, at present, to the river side.
It is but seemly that thou should'st repair
Thyself to consultation with the Chiefs
Of all Phæacia, clad in pure attire;
And my own brothers five, who dwell at home,
Two wedded, and the rest of age to wed,
Are all desirous, when they dance, to wear
Raiment new bleach'd; all which is my concern.
80 So spake Nausicaa; for she dared not name
Her own glad nuptials to her father's ear,
Who, conscious yet of all her drift, replied.
I grudge thee neither mules, my child, nor aught
That thou canst ask beside. Go, and my train
Shall furnish thee a sumpter-carriage forth
High-built, strong-wheel'd, and of capacious size.
So saying, he issued his command, whom quick
His grooms obey'd. They in the court prepared
The sumpter-carriage, and adjoin'd the mules.
90 And now the virgin from her chamber, charged
With raiment, came, which on the car she placed,
And in the carriage-chest, meantime, the Queen,
Her mother, viands of all kinds disposed,

---

[23] In the Original, she calls him, pappa! a more natural stile of address and more endearing. But ancient as this appellative is, it is also so familiar in modern use, that the Translator feared to hazard it.

And fill'd a skin with wine. Nausicaa rose
Into her seat; but, ere she went, received
A golden cruse of oil from the Queen's hand
For unction of herself, and of her maids.
Then, seizing scourge and reins, she lash'd the mules.
They trampled loud the soil, straining to draw
100 Herself with all her vesture; nor alone
She went, but follow'd by her virgin train.
At the delightful rivulet arrived
Where those perennial cisterns were prepared
With purest crystal of the fountain fed
Profuse, sufficient for the deepest stains,
Loosing the mules, they drove them forth to browze
On the sweet herb beside the dimpled flood.
The carriage, next, light'ning, they bore in hand
The garments down to the unsullied wave,
110 And thrust them heap'd into the pools, their task
Dispatching brisk, and with an emulous haste.
When they had all purified, and no spot
Could now be seen, or blemish more, they spread
The raiment orderly along the beach
Where dashing tides had cleansed the pebbles most,
And laving, next, and smoothing o'er with oil
Their limbs, all seated on the river's bank,
They took repast, leaving the garments, stretch'd
In noon-day fervour of the sun, to dry.
120 Their hunger satisfied, at once arose
The mistress and her train, and putting off
Their head-attire, play'd wanton with the ball,
The princess singing to her maids the while.
Such as shaft-arm'd Diana roams the hills,
Täygetus sky-capt, or Erymanth,
The wild boar chasing, or fleet-footed hind,
All joy; the rural nymphs, daughters of Jove,
Sport with her, and Latona's heart exults;
She high her graceful head above the rest
130 And features lifts divine, though all be fair,
With ease distinguishable from them all;
So, all her train, she, virgin pure, surpass'd.
But when the hour of her departure thence
Approach'd (the mules now yoked again, and all
Her elegant apparel folded neat)
Minerva azure-eyed mused how to wake
Ulysses, that he might behold the fair
Virgin, his destin'd guide into the town.
The Princess, then, casting the ball toward
140 A maiden of her train, erroneous threw
And plunged it deep into the dimpling stream.
All shriek'd; Ulysses at the sound awoke,
And, sitting, meditated thus the cause.
Ah me! what mortal race inhabit here?
Rude are they, contumacious and unjust?
Or hospitable, and who fear the Gods?
So shrill the cry and feminine of nymphs
Fills all the air around, such as frequent
The hills, clear fountains, and herbaceous meads.
150 Is this a neighbourhood of men endued
With voice articulate? But what avails
To ask; I will myself go forth and see.
So saying, divine Ulysses from beneath
His thicket crept, and from the leafy wood
A spreading branch pluck'd forcibly, design'd

A decent skreen effectual, held before.
So forth he went, as goes the lion forth,
The mountain-lion, conscious of his strength,
Whom winds have vex'd and rains; fire fills his eyes,
160 And whether herds or flocks, or woodland deer
He find, he rends them, and, adust for blood,
Abstains not even from the guarded fold,
Such sure to seem in virgin eyes, the Chief,
All naked as he was, left his retreat,
Reluctant, by necessity constrain'd.
Him foul with sea foam horror-struck they view'd,
And o'er the jutting shores fled all dispersed.
Nausicaa alone fled not; for her
Pallas courageous made, and from her limbs,
170 By pow'r divine, all tremour took away.
Firm she expected him; he doubtful stood,
Or to implore the lovely maid, her knees
Embracing, or aloof standing, to ask
In gentle terms discrete the gift of cloaths,
And guidance to the city where she dwelt.
Him so deliberating, most, at length,
This counsel pleas'd; in suppliant terms aloof
To sue to her, lest if he clasp'd her knees,
The virgin should that bolder course resent.
180 Then gentle, thus, and well-advised he spake.
Oh Queen! thy earnest suppliant I approach.
Art thou some Goddess, or of mortal race?
For if some Goddess, and from heaven arrived,
Diana, then, daughter of mighty Jove
I deem thee most, for such as hers appear
Thy form, thy stature, and thy air divine.
But if, of mortal race, thou dwell below,
Thrice happy then, thy parents I account,
And happy thrice thy brethren. Ah! the joy
190 Which always for thy sake, their bosoms fill,
When thee they view, all lovely as thou art,
Ent'ring majestic on the graceful dance.
But him beyond all others blest I deem,
The youth, who, wealthier than his rich compeers,
Shall win and lead thee to his honour'd home.
For never with these eyes a mortal form
Beheld I comparable aught to thine,
In man or woman. Wonder-wrapt I gaze.
Such erst, in Delos, I beheld a palm
200 Beside the altar of Apollo, tall,
And growing still; (for thither too I sail'd,
And num'rous were my followers in a voyage
Ordain'd my ruin) and as then I view'd
That palm long time amazed, for never grew
So strait a shaft, so lovely from the ground,
So, Princess! thee with wonder I behold,
Charm'd into fixt astonishment, by awe
Alone forbidden to embrace thy knees,
For I am one on whom much woe hath fall'n.
210 Yesterday I escaped (the twentieth day
Of my distress by sea) the dreary Deep;
For, all those days, the waves and rapid storms
Bore me along, impetuous from the isle
Ogygia; till at length the will of heav'n
Cast me, that I might also here sustain
Affliction on your shore; for rest, I think,
Is not for me. No. The Immortal Gods

Have much to accomplish ere that day arrive.
But, oh Queen, pity me! who after long
22 °Calamities endured, of all who live
Thee first approach, nor mortal know beside
Of the inhabitants of all the land.
Shew me your city; give me, although coarse,
Some cov'ring (if coarse cov'ring *thou* canst give)
And may the Gods thy largest wishes grant,
House, husband, concord! for of all the gifts
Of heav'n, more precious none I deem, than peace
'Twixt wedded pair, and union undissolved;
Envy torments their enemies, but joy
230 Fills ev'ry virtuous breast, and most their own.
To whom Nausicaa the fair replied.
Since, stranger! neither base by birth thou seem'st,
Nor unintelligent, (but Jove, the King
Olympian, gives to good and bad alike
Prosperity according to his will,
And grief to thee, which thou must patient bear,)
Now, therefore, at our land and city arrived,
Nor garment thou shalt want, nor aught beside
Due to a suppliant guest like thee forlorn.
240 I will both show thee where our city stands,
And who dwell here. Phæacia's sons possess
This land; but I am daughter of their King
The brave Alcinoüs, on whose sway depends
For strength and wealth the whole Phæacian race.
She said, and to her beauteous maidens gave
Instant commandment-My attendants, stay!
Why flee ye thus, and whither, from the sight
Of a mere mortal? Seems he in your eyes
Some enemy of ours? The heart beats not,
250 Nor shall it beat hereafter, which shall come
An enemy to the Phæacian shores,
So dear to the immortal Gods are we.
Remote, amid the billowy Deep, we hold
Our dwelling, utmost of all human-kind,
And free from mixture with a foreign race.
This man, a miserable wand'rer comes,
Whom we are bound to cherish, for the poor
And stranger are from Jove, and trivial gifts
To such are welcome. Bring ye therefore food
260 And wine, my maidens, for the guest's regale,
And lave him where the stream is shelter'd most.
She spake; they stood, and by each other's words
Encouraged, placed Ulysses where the bank
O'erhung the stream, as fair Nausicaa bade,
Daughter of King Alcinoüs the renown'd.
Apparel also at his side they spread,
Mantle and vest, and, next, the limpid oil
Presenting to him in the golden cruse,
Exhorted him to bathe in the clear stream.
270 Ulysses then the maidens thus bespake.
Ye maidens, stand apart, that I may cleanse,
Myself, my shoulders from the briny surf,
And give them oil which they have wanted long.
But in your presence I bathe not, ashamed
To show myself uncloath'd to female eyes.
He said; they went, and to Nausicaa told
His answer; then the Hero in the stream
His shoulders laved, and loins incrusted rough
With the salt spray, and with his hands the scum

280 Of the wild ocean from his locks express'd.
Thus wash'd all over, and refresh'd with oil,
He put the garments on, Nausicaa's gift.
Then Pallas, progeny of Jove, his form
Dilated more, and from his head diffused
His curling locks like hyacinthine flowers.
As when some artist, by Minerva made
And Vulcan wise to execute all tasks
Ingenious, binding with a golden verge
Bright silver, finishes a graceful work,
290 Such grace the Goddess o'er his ample chest
Copious diffused, and o'er his manly brows.
Retiring, on the beach he sat, with grace
And dignity illumed, where, viewing him,
The virgin Princess, with amazement mark'd
His beauty, and her damsels thus bespake.
My white-arm'd maidens, listen to my voice!
Not hated, sure, by all above, this man
Among Phæacia's godlike sons arrives.
At first I deem'd him of plebeian sort
300 Dishonourable, but he now assumes
A near resemblance to the Gods above.
Ah! would to heaven it were my lot to call
Husband, some native of our land like him
Accomplish'd, and content to inhabit here!
Give him, my maidens, food, and give him wine.
She ended; they obedient to her will,
Both wine and food, dispatchful, placed, and glad,
Before Ulysses; he rapacious ate,
Toil-suff'ring Chief, and drank, for he had lived
310 From taste of aliment long time estranged.
On other thoughts meantime intent, her charge
Of folded vestments neat the Princess placed
Within the royal wain, then yoked the mules,
And to her seat herself ascending, call'd
Ulysses to depart, and thus she spake.
Up, stranger! seek the city. I will lead
Thy steps toward my royal Father's house,
Where all Phæacia's Nobles thou shalt see.
But thou (for I account thee not unwise)
320 This course pursue. While through the fields we pass,
And labours of the rural hind, so long
With my attendants follow fast the mules
And sumpter-carriage. I will be thy guide.
But, once the summit gain'd, on which is built
Our city with proud bulwarks fenced around,
And laved on both sides by its pleasant port
Of narrow entrance, where our gallant barks
Line all the road, each station'd in her place,
And where, adjoining close the splendid fane
330 Of Neptune, stands the forum with huge stones
From quarries thither drawn, constructed strong,
In which the rigging of their barks they keep,
Sail-cloth and cordage, and make smooth their oars;
(For bow and quiver the Phæacian race
Heed not, but masts and oars, and ships well-poised,
With which exulting they divide the flood)
Then, cautious, I would shun their bitter taunts
Disgustful, lest they mock me as I pass;
For of the meaner people some are coarse
340 In the extreme, and it may chance that one,
The basest there seeing us shall exclaim-

What handsome stranger of athletic form
Attends the Princess? Where had she the chance
To find him? We shall see them wedded soon.
Either she hath received some vagrant guest
From distant lands, (for no land neighbours ours)
Or by her pray'rs incessant won, some God
Hath left the heav'ns to be for ever hers.
'Tis well if she have found, by her own search,
350 An husband for herself, since she accounts
The Nobles of Phæacia, who her hand
Solicit num'rous, worthy to be scorn'd-
Thus will they speak, injurious. I should blame
A virgin guilty of such conduct much,
Myself, who reckless of her parents' will,
Should so familiar with a man consort,
Ere celebration of her spousal rites.
But mark me, stranger! following my advice,
Thou shalt the sooner at my father's hands
360 Obtain safe conduct and conveyance home.
Sacred to Pallas a delightful grove
Of poplars skirts the road, which we shall reach
Ere long; within that grove a fountain flows,
And meads encircle it; my father's farm
Is there, and his luxuriant garden plot;
A shout might reach it from the city-walls.
There wait, till in the town arrived, we gain
My father's palace, and when reason bids
Suppose us there, then ent'ring thou the town,
370 Ask where Alcinoüs dwells, my valiant Sire.
Well known is his abode, so that with ease
A child might lead thee to it, for in nought
The other houses of our land the house
Resemble, in which dwells the Hero, King
Alcinoüs. Once within the court received

Pause not, but, with swift pace advancing, seek
My mother; she beside a column sits
In the hearth's blaze, twirling her fleecy threads
Tinged with sea-purple, bright, magnificent!
380 With all her maidens orderly behind.
There also stands my father's throne, on which
Seated, he drinks and banquets like a God.
Pass that; then suppliant clasp my mother's knees,
So shalt thou quickly win a glad return
To thy own home, however far remote.
Her favour, once, and her kind aid secured,
Thenceforth thou may'st expect thy friends to see,
Thy dwelling, and thy native soil again.
So saying, she with her splendid scourge the mules
390 Lash'd onward. They (the stream soon left behind)
With even footsteps graceful smote the ground;
But so she ruled them, managing with art
The scourge, as not to leave afar, although
Following on foot, Ulysses and her train.
The sun had now declined, when in that grove
Renown'd, to Pallas sacred, they arrived,
In which Ulysses sat, and fervent thus
Sued to the daughter of Jove Ægis-arm'd.
Daughter invincible of Jove supreme!
400 Oh, hear me! Hear me now, because when erst
The mighty Shaker of the shores incensed
Toss'd me from wave to wave, thou heard'st me not.
Grant me, among Phæacia's sons, to find
Benevolence and pity of my woes!
He spake, whose pray'r well-pleas'd the Goddess heard,

But, rev'rencing the brother of her sire,[24]
Appear'd not to Ulysses yet, whom he
Pursued with fury to his native shores.

---

[24] Neptune.

Book VII

Nausicaa returns from the river, whom Ulysses follows. He halts, by her direction, at a small distance from the palace, which at a convenient time he enters. He is well received by Alcinoüs and his Queen; and having related to them the manner of his being cast on the shore of Scheria, and received from Alcinoüs the promise of safe conduct home, retires to rest.

Such pray'r Ulysses, toil-worn Chief renown'd,
To Pallas made, meantime the virgin, drawn
By her stout mules, Phæacia's city reach'd,
And, at her father's house arrived, the car
Stay'd in the vestibule; her brothers five,
All godlike youths, assembling quick around,
Released the mules, and bore the raiment in.
Meantime, to her own chamber she return'd,
Where, soon as she arrived, an antient dame
Eurymedusa, by peculiar charge
10 Attendant on that service, kindled fire.
Sea-rovers her had from Epirus brought
Long since, and to Alcinoüs she had fall'n
By public gift, for that he ruled, supreme,
Phæacia, and as oft as he harangued
The multitude, was rev'renced as a God.
She waited on the fair Nausicaa, she
Her fuel kindled, and her food prepared.
And now Ulysses from his seat arose
To seek the city, around whom, his guard
20 Benevolent, Minerva, cast a cloud,
Lest, haply, some Phæacian should presume
T' insult the Chief, and question whence he came.
But ere he enter'd yet the pleasant town,
Minerva azure-eyed met him, in form
A blooming maid, bearing her pitcher forth.
She stood before him, and the noble Chief
Ulysses, of the Goddess thus enquired.
Daughter! wilt thou direct me to the house
Of brave Alcinoüs, whom this land obeys?
30 For I have here arrived, after long toil,
And from a country far remote, a guest
To all who in Phæacia dwell, unknown.
To whom the Goddess of the azure-eyes.
The mansion of thy search, stranger revered!
Myself will shew thee; for not distant dwells
Alcinoüs from my father's own abode:
But hush! be silent-I will lead the way;
Mark no man; question no man; for the sight
Of strangers is unusual here, and cold
40 The welcome by this people shown to such.
They, trusting in swift ships, by the free grant
Of Neptune traverse his wide waters, borne
As if on wings, or with the speed of thought.
So spake the Goddess, and with nimble pace
Led on, whose footsteps he, as quick, pursued.
But still the seaman-throng through whom he pass'd
Perceiv'd him not; Minerva, Goddess dread,
That sight forbidding them, whose eyes she dimm'd
With darkness shed miraculous around
50 Her fav'rite Chief. Ulysses, wond'ring, mark'd
Their port, their ships, their forum, the resort

Of Heroes, and their battlements sublime
Fenced with sharp stakes around, a glorious show!
But when the King's august abode he reach'd,
Minerva azure-eyed, then, thus began.
My father! thou behold'st the house to which
Thou bad'st me lead thee. Thou shalt find our Chiefs
And high-born Princes banqueting within.
But enter fearing nought, for boldest men
60 Speed ever best, come whencesoe'er they may.
First thou shalt find the Queen, known by her name
Areta; lineal in descent from those
Who gave Alcinoüs birth, her royal spouse.
Neptune begat Nausithoüs, at the first,
On Peribæa, loveliest of her sex,
Latest-born daughter of Eurymedon,
Heroic King of the proud giant race,
Who, losing all his impious people, shared
The same dread fate himself. Her Neptune lov'd,
70 To whom she bore a son, the mighty prince
Nausithoüs, in his day King of the land.
Nausithoüs himself two sons begat,
Rhexenor and Alcinoüs. Phoebus slew
Rhexenor at his home, a bridegroom yet,
Who, father of no son, one daughter left,
Areta, wedded to Alcinoüs now,
And whom the Sov'reign in such honour holds,
As woman none enjoys of all on earth
Existing, subjects of an husband's pow'r.
80 Like veneration she from all receives
Unfeign'd, from her own children, from himself
Alcinoüs, and from all Phæacia's race,
Who, gazing on her as she were divine,
Shout when she moves in progress through the town.
For she no wisdom wants, but sits, herself,
Arbitress of such contests as arise
Between her fav'rites, and decides aright.
Her count'nance once and her kind aid secured,
Thou may'st thenceforth expect thy friends to see,
90 Thy dwelling, and thy native soil again.
So Pallas spake, Goddess cærulean-eyed,
And o'er the untillable and barren Deep
Departing, Scheria left, land of delight,
Whence reaching Marathon, and Athens next,
She pass'd into Erectheus' fair abode.
Ulysses, then, toward the palace moved
Of King Alcinoüs, but immers'd in thought
Stood, first, and paused, ere with his foot he press'd
The brazen threshold; for a light he saw
100 As of the sun or moon illuming clear
The palace of Phæacia's mighty King.
Walls plated bright with brass, on either side
Stretch'd from the portal to th' interior house,

With azure cornice crown'd; the doors were gold
Which shut the palace fast; silver the posts
Rear'd on a brazen threshold, and above,
The lintels, silver, architraved with gold.
Mastiffs, in gold and silver, lined the approach
On either side, by art celestial framed
110 Of Vulcan, guardians of Alcinoüs' gate
For ever, unobnoxious to decay.
Sheer from the threshold to the inner house
Fixt thrones the walls, through all their length, adorn'd,
With mantles overspread of subtlest warp
Transparent, work of many a female hand.
On these the princes of Phæacia sat,
Holding perpetual feasts, while golden youths
On all the sumptuous altars stood, their hands
With burning torches charged, which, night by night,
120 Shed radiance over all the festive throng.
Full fifty female menials serv'd the King
In household offices; the rapid mills
These turning, pulverize the mellow'd grain,
Those, seated orderly, the purple fleece
Wind off, or ply the loom, restless as leaves
Of lofty poplars fluttering in the breeze;
Bright as with oil the new-wrought texture shone.25
Far as Phæacian mariners all else
Surpass, the swift ship urging through the floods,
130 So far in tissue-work the women pass
All others, by Minerva's self endow'd
With richest fancy and superior skill.
Without the court, and to the gates adjoin'd
A spacious garden lay, fenced all around
Secure, four acres measuring complete.
There grew luxuriant many a lofty tree,
Pomegranate, pear, the apple blushing bright,
The honied fig, and unctuous olive smooth.
Those fruits, nor winter's cold nor summer's heat
140 Fear ever, fail not, wither not, but hang
Perennial, whose unceasing zephyr breathes
Gently on all, enlarging these, and those
Maturing genial; in an endless course
Pears after pears to full dimensions swell,
Figs follow figs, grapes clust'ring grow again
Where clusters grew, and (ev'ry apple stript)
The boughs soon tempt the gath'rer as before.
There too, well-rooted, and of fruit profuse,
His vineyard grows; part, wide-extended, basks,
150 In the sun's beams; the arid level glows;
In part they gather, and in part they tread
The wine-press, while, before the eye, the grapes
Here put their blossom forth, there, gather fast
Their blackness. On the garden's verge extreme
Flow'rs of all hues smile all the year, arranged
With neatest art judicious, and amid
The lovely scene two fountains welling forth,
One visits, into ev'ry part diffus'd,
The garden-ground, the other soft beneath
160 The threshold steals into the palace-court,
Whence ev'ry citizen his vase supplies.

Such were the ample blessings on the house
Of King Alcinoüs by the Gods bestow'd.
Ulysses wond'ring stood, and when, at length,
Silent he had the whole fair scene admired,
With rapid step enter'd the royal gate.
The Chiefs he found and Senators within
Libation pouring to the vigilant spy
Mercurius, whom with wine they worshipp'd last
170 Of all the Gods, and at the hour of rest.
Ulysses, toil-worn Hero, through the house
Pass'd undelaying, by Minerva thick
With darkness circumfus'd, till he arrived
Where King Alcinoüs and Areta sat.
Around Areta's knees his arms he cast,
And, in that moment, broken clear away
The cloud all went, shed on him from above.
Dumb sat the guests, seeing the unknown Chief,
And wond'ring gazed. He thus his suit preferr'd.
180 Areta, daughter of the Godlike Prince
Rhexenor! suppliant at thy knees I fall,
Thy royal spouse imploring, and thyself,
(After ten thousand toils) and these your guests,
To whom heav'n grant felicity, and to leave
Their treasures to their babes, with all the rights
And honours, by the people's suffrage, theirs!
But oh vouchsafe me, who have wanted long
And ardent wish'd my home, without delay
Safe conduct to my native shores again!
190 Such suit he made, and in the ashes sat
At the hearth-side; they mute long time remain'd,
Till, at the last, the antient Hero spake
Echeneus, eldest of Phæacia's sons,
With eloquence beyond the rest endow'd,
Rich in traditionary lore, and wise
In all, who thus, benevolent, began.
Not honourable to thyself, O King!
Is such a sight, a stranger on the ground
At the hearth-side seated, and in the dust.
200 Meantime, thy guests, expecting thy command,
Move not; thou therefore raising by his hand
The stranger, lead him to a throne, and bid
The heralds mingle wine, that we may pour
To thunder-bearing Jove, the suppliant's friend.
Then let the cat'ress for thy guest produce
Supply, a supper from the last regale.
Soon as those words Alcinoüs heard, the King,
Upraising by his hand the prudent Chief
Ulysses from the hearth, he made him sit,
210 On a bright throne, displacing for his sake
Laodamas his son, the virtuous youth
Who sat beside him, and whom most he lov'd.
And now, a maiden charg'd with golden ew'r
And with an argent laver, pouring, first,
Pure water on his hands, supply'd him, next,
With a resplendent table, which the chaste
Directress of the stores furnish'd with bread
And dainties, remnants of the last regale.
Then ate the Hero toil-inured, and drank,

---

25 +Kairoseôn d' othoneôn apoleibetai hygron elaion+.
    Pope has given no translation of this line in the text of his work, but has translated it in a note. It is variously interpreted by commentators; the sense which is here given of it is that recommended by Eustathius.

220 And to his herald thus Alcinoüs spake.
Pontonoüs! mingling wine, bear it around
To ev'ry guest in turn, that we may pour
To thunder-bearer Jove, the stranger's friend,
And guardian of the suppliant's sacred rights.
He said; Pontonoüs, as he bade, the wine
Mingled delicious, and the cups dispensed
With distribution regular to all.
When each had made libation, and had drunk
Sufficient, then, Alcinoüs thus began.
230 Phæacian Chiefs and Senators, I speak
The dictates of my mind, therefore attend!
Ye all have feasted-To your homes and sleep.
We will assemble at the dawn of day
More senior Chiefs, that we may entertain
The stranger here, and to the Gods perform
Due sacrifice; the convoy that he asks
Shall next engage our thoughts, that free from pain
And from vexation, by our friendly aid
He may revisit, joyful and with speed,
240 His native shore, however far remote.
No inconvenience let him feel or harm,
Ere his arrival; but, arrived, thenceforth
He must endure whatever lot the Fates
Spun for him in the moment of his birth.
But should he prove some Deity from heav'n
Descended, then the Immortals have in view
Designs not yet apparent; for the Gods
Have ever from of old reveal'd themselves
At our solemnities, have on our seats
250 Sat with us evident, and shared the feast;
And even if a single traveller
Of the Phæacians meet them, all reserve
They lay aside; for with the Gods we boast
As near affinity as do themselves
The Cyclops, or the Giant race profane.[26]
To whom Ulysses, ever-wise, replied.
Alcinoüs! think not so. Resemblance none
In figure or in lineaments I bear
To the immortal tenants of the skies,
260 But to the sons of earth; if ye have known
A man afflicted with a weight of woe
Peculiar, let me be with him compared;
Woes even passing his could I relate,
And all inflicted on me by the Gods.
But let me eat, comfortless as I am,
Uninterrupted; for no call is loud
As that of hunger in the ears of man;
Importunate, unreas'nable, it constrains
His notice, more than all his woes beside.
270 So, I much sorrow feel, yet not the less
Hear I the blatant appetite demand
Due sustenance, and with a voice that drowns
E'en all my suff'rings, till itself be fill'd.
But expedite ye at the dawn of day
My safe return into my native land,
After much mis'ry; and let life itself
Forsake me, may I but once more behold

All that is mine, in my own lofty abode.
He spake, whom all applauded, and advised,
280 Unanimous, the guest's conveyance home,
Who had so fitly spoken. When, at length,
All had libation made, and were sufficed,
Departing to his house, each sought repose.
But still Ulysses in the hall remain'd,
Where, godlike King, Alcinoüs at his side
Sat, and Areta; the attendants clear'd
Meantime the board, and thus the Queen white-arm'd,
(Marking the vest and mantle, which he wore
And which her maidens and herself had made)
290 In accents wing'd with eager haste began.
Stranger! the first enquiry shall be mine;
Who art, and whence? From whom receiv'dst thou these?
Saidst not-I came a wand'rer o'er the Deep?
To whom Ulysses, ever-wise, replied.
Oh Queen! the task were difficult to unfold
In all its length the story of my woes,
For I have num'rous from the Gods receiv'd;
But I will answer thee as best I may.
There is a certain isle, Ogygia, placed
300 Far distant in the Deep; there dwells, by man
Alike unvisited, and by the Gods,
Calypso, beauteous nymph, but deeply skill'd
In artifice, and terrible in pow'r,
Daughter of Atlas. Me alone my fate
Her miserable inmate made, when Jove
Had riv'n asunder with his candent bolt
My bark in the mid-sea. There perish'd all
The valiant partners of my toils, and I
My vessel's keel embracing day and night
310 With folded arms, nine days was borne along.
But on the tenth dark night, as pleas'd the Gods,
They drove me to Ogygia, where resides
Calypso, beauteous nymph, dreadful in pow'r;
She rescued, cherish'd, fed me, and her wish
Was to confer on me immortal life,
Exempt for ever from the sap of age.
But me her offer'd boon sway'd not. Sev'n years
I there abode continual, with my tears
Bedewing ceaseless my ambrosial robes,
320 Calypso's gift divine; but when, at length,
(Sev'n years elaps'd) the circling eighth arrived,
She then, herself, my quick departure thence
Advised, by Jove's own mandate overaw'd,
Which even her had influenced to a change.
On a well-corded raft she sent me forth
With num'rous presents; bread she put and wine
On board, and cloath'd me in immortal robes;
She sent before me also a fair wind
Fresh-blowing, but not dang'rous. Sev'nteen days
330 I sail'd the flood continual, and descried,
On the eighteenth, your shadowy mountains tall
When my exulting heart sprang at the sight,
All wretched as I was, and still ordain'd
To strive with difficulties many and hard
From adverse Neptune; he the stormy winds

---

[26] The Scholiast explains the passage thus-We resemble the Gods in righteousness as much as the Cyclops and Giants resembled each other in impiety. But in this sense of it there is something intricate and contrary to Homer's manner. We have seen that they derived themselves from Neptune, which sufficiently justifies the above interpretation.

Exciting opposite, my wat'ry way
Impeded, and the waves heav'd to a bulk
Immeasurable, such as robb'd me soon
Deep-groaning, of the raft, my only hope;
340 For her the tempest scatter'd, and myself
This ocean measur'd swimming, till the winds
And mighty waters cast me on your shore.
Me there emerging, the huge waves had dash'd
Full on the land, where, incommodious most,
The shore presented only roughest rocks,
But, leaving it, I swam the Deep again,
Till now, at last, a river's gentle stream
Receiv'd me, by no rocks deform'd, and where
No violent winds the shelter'd bank annoy'd.
350 I flung myself on shore, exhausted, weak,
Needing repose; ambrosial night came on,
When from the Jove-descended stream withdrawn,
I in a thicket lay'd me down on leaves
Which I had heap'd together, and the Gods
O'erwhelm'd my eye-lids with a flood of sleep.
There under wither'd leaves, forlorn, I slept
All the long night, the morning and the noon,
But balmy sleep, at the decline of day,
Broke from me; then, your daughter's train I heard
360 Sporting, with whom she also sported, fair
And graceful as the Gods. To her I kneel'd.
She, following the dictates of a mind
Ingenuous, pass'd in her behaviour all
Which even ye could from an age like hers
Have hoped; for youth is ever indiscrete.
She gave me plenteous food, with richest wine
Refresh'd my spirit, taught me where to bathe,
And cloath'd me as thou seest; thus, though a prey
To many sorrows, I have told thee truth.
370 To whom Alcinoüs answer thus return'd.
My daughter's conduct, I perceive, hath been
In this erroneous, that she led thee not
Hither, at once, with her attendant train,
For thy first suit was to herself alone.
Thus then Ulysses, wary Chief, replied.
Blame not, O Hero, for so slight a cause
Thy faultless child; she bade me follow them,
But I refused, by fear and awe restrain'd,
Lest thou should'st feel displeasure at that sight
380 Thyself; for we are all, in ev'ry clime,
Suspicious, and to worst constructions prone.
So spake Ulysses, to whom thus the King.
I bear not, stranger! in my breast an heart

Causeless irascible; for at all times
A temp'rate equanimity is best.
And oh, I would to heav'n, that, being such
As now thou art, and of one mind with me,
Thou would'st accept my daughter, would'st become
My son-in-law, and dwell contented here!
390 House would I give thee, and possessions too,
Were such thy choice; else, if thou chuse it not,
No man in all Phæacia shall by force
Detain thee. Jupiter himself forbid!
For proof, I will appoint thee convoy hence
To-morrow; and while thou by sleep subdued
Shalt on thy bed repose, they with their oars
Shall brush the placid flood, till thou arrive
At home, or at what place soe'er thou would'st,
Though far more distant than Euboea lies,
400 Remotest isle from us, by the report
Of ours, who saw it when they thither bore
Golden-hair'd Rhadamanthus o'er the Deep,
To visit earth-born Tityus. To that isle
They went; they reach'd it, and they brought him thence
Back to Phæacia, in one day, with ease.
Thou also shalt be taught what ships I boast
Unmatch'd in swiftness, and how far my crews
Excel, upturning with their oars the brine.
He ceas'd; Ulysses toil-inur'd his words
410 Exulting heard, and, praying, thus replied.
Eternal Father! may the King perform
His whole kind promise! grant him in all lands
A never-dying name, and grant to me
To visit safe my native shores again!
Thus they conferr'd; and now Areta bade
Her fair attendants dress a fleecy couch
Under the portico, with purple rugs
Resplendent, and with arras spread beneath,
And over all with cloaks of shaggy pile.
420 Forth went the maidens, bearing each a torch,
And, as she bade, prepared in haste a couch
Of depth commodious, then, returning, gave
Ulysses welcome summons to repose.
Stranger! thy couch is spread. Hence to thy rest.
So they-Thrice grateful to his soul the thought
Seem'd of repose. There slept Ulysses, then,
On his carv'd couch, beneath the portico,
But in the inner-house Alcinoüs found
His place of rest, and hers with royal state
430 Prepared, the Queen his consort, at his side.

Book VIII

The Phæacians consult on the subject of Ulysses. Preparation is made for his departure. Antinoüs entertains them at his table. Games follow the entertainment. Demodocus the bard sings, first the loves of Mars and Venus, then the introduction of the wooden horse into Troy. Ulysses, much affected by his song, is questioned by Alcinoüs, whence, and who he is, and what is the cause of his sorrow.

But when Aurora, daughter of the dawn,
Blush'd in the East, then from his bed arose
The sacred might of the Phæacian King.
Then uprose also, city-waster Chief,
Ulysses, whom the King Alcinoüs
Led forth to council at the ships convened.
There, side by side, on polish'd stones they sat
Frequent; meantime, Minerva in the form
Of King Alcinoüs' herald ranged the town,
With purpose to accelerate the return
10 Of brave Ulysses to his native home,
And thus to ev'ry Chief the Goddess spake.
Phæacian Chiefs and Senators, away!
Haste all to council on the stranger held,
Who hath of late beneath Alcinoüs' roof
Our King arrived, a wand'rer o'er the Deep,
But, in his form, majestic as a God.
So saying, she roused the people, and at once
The seats of all the senate-court were fill'd
With fast-assembling throngs, no few of whom
20 Had mark'd Ulysses with admiring eyes.
Then, Pallas o'er his head and shoulders broad
Diffusing grace celestial, his whole form
Dilated, and to the statelier height advanced,
That worthier of all rev'rence he might seem
To the Phæacians, and might many a feat
Atchieve, with which they should assay his force.
When, therefore, the assembly now was full,
Alcinoüs, them addressing, thus began.
Phæacian Chiefs and Senators! I speak
30 The dictates of my mind, therefore attend.
This guest, unknown to me, hath, wand'ring, found
My palace, either from the East arrived,
Or from some nation on our western side.
Safe conduct home he asks, and our consent
Here wishes ratified, whose quick return
Be it our part, as usual, to promote;
For at no time the stranger, from what coast
Soe'er, who hath resorted to our doors,
Hath long complain'd of his detention here.
40 Haste-draw ye down into the sacred Deep
A vessel of prime speed, and, from among
The people, fifty and two youths select,
Approved the best; then, lashing fast the oars,
Leave her, that at my palace ye may make
Short feast, for which myself will all provide.
Thus I enjoin the crew; but as for those
Of sceptred rank, I bid them all alike

To my own board, that here we may regale
The stranger nobly, and let none refuse.
5 °Call, too, Demodocus, the bard divine,
To share my banquet, whom the Gods have blest
With pow'rs of song delectable, unmatch'd
By any, when his genius once is fired.
He ceas'd, and led the way, whom follow'd all
The sceptred senators, while to the house
An herald hasted of the bard divine.
Then, fifty mariners and two, from all
The rest selected, to the coast repair'd,
And, from her station on the sea-bank, launched
60 The galley down into the sacred Deep.
They placed the canvas and the mast on board,
Arranged the oars, unfurl'd the shining sail,
And, leaving her in depth of water moor'd,
All sought the palace of Alcinoüs.
There, soon, the portico, the court, the hall
Were fill'd with multitudes of young and old,
For whose regale the mighty monarch slew
Two beeves, twelve sheep, and twice four fatted brawns.
They slay'd them first, then busily their task
70 Administ'ring, prepared the joyous feast.
And now the herald came, leading with care
The tuneful bard; dear to the muse was he,
Who yet appointed him both good and ill;
Took from him sight, but gave him strains divine.
For him, Pontonoüs in the midst disposed
An argent-studded throne, thrusting it close
To a tall column, where he hung his lyre
Above his head, and taught him where it hung.
He set before him, next, a polish'd board
80 And basket, and a goblet fill'd with wine
For his own use, and at his own command.
Then, all assail'd at once the ready feast,
And when nor hunger more nor thirst they felt,
Then came the muse, and roused the bard to sing
Exploits of men renown'd; it was a song,
In that day, to the highest heav'n extoll'd.
He sang of a dispute kindled between

The son of Peleus, and Laertes'[27] son,
Both seated at a feast held to the Gods.
90 That contest Agamemnon, King of men,
Between the noblest of Achaia's host
Hearing, rejoiced; for when in Pytho erst
He pass'd the marble threshold to consult
The oracle of Apollo, such dispute

---

[27] Agamemnon having inquired at Delphos, at what time the Trojan war would end, was answered that the conclusion of it should happen at a time when a dispute should arise between two of his principal commanders. That dispute occurred at the time here alluded to, Achilles recommending force as most likely to reduce the city, and Ulysses stratagem.

The voice divine had to his ear announced;
For then it was that, first, the storm of war
Came rolling on, ordain'd long time to afflict
Troy and the Greecians, by the will of Jove.
So sang the bard illustrious; then his robe
100 Of purple dye with both hands o'er his head
Ulysses drew, behind its ample folds
Veiling his face, through fear to be observed
By the Phæacians weeping at the song;
And ever as the bard harmonious ceased,
He wiped his tears, and, drawing from his brows
The mantle, pour'd libation to the Gods.
But when the Chiefs (for they delighted heard
Those sounds) solicited again the bard,
And he renew'd the strain, then cov'ring close
110 His count'nance, as before, Ulysses wept.
Thus, unperceiv'd by all, the Hero mourn'd,
Save by Alcinoüs; he alone his tears,
(Beside him seated) mark'd, and his deep sighs
O'erhearing, the Phæacians thus bespake.
Phæacia's Chiefs and Senators, attend!
We have regaled sufficient, and the harp
Heard to satiety, companion sweet
And seasonable of the festive hour.
Now go we forth for honourable proof
120 Of our address in games of ev'ry kind,
That this our guest may to his friends report,
At home arriv'd, that none like us have learn'd
To leap, to box, to wrestle, and to run.
So saying, he led them forth, whose steps the guests
All follow'd, and the herald hanging high
The sprightly lyre, took by his hand the bard
Demodocus, whom he the self-same way
Conducted forth, by which the Chiefs had gone
Themselves, for that great spectacle prepared.
130 They sought the forum; countless swarm'd the throng
Behind them as they went, and many a youth
Strong and courageous to the strife arose.
Upstood Acroneus and Ocyalus,
Elatreus, Nauteus, Prymneus, after whom
Anchialus with Anabeesineus
Arose, Eretmeus, Ponteus, Proreus bold,
Amphialus and Thöon. Then arose,
In aspect dread as homicidal Mars,
Euryalus, and for his graceful form
140 (After Laodamas) distinguish'd most
Of all Phæacia's sons, Naubolides.
Three also from Alcinoüs sprung, arose,
Laodamas, his eldest; Halius, next,
His second-born; and godlike Clytoneus.
Of these, some started for the runner's prize.
They gave the race its limits.[28] All at once
Along the dusty champaign swift they flew.
But Clytoneus, illustrious youth, outstripp'd
All competition; far as mules surpass
150 Slow oxen furrowing the fallow ground,
So far before all others he arrived

Victorious, where the throng'd spectators stood.
Some tried the wrestler's toil severe, in which
Euryalus superior proved to all.
In the long leap Amphialus prevail'd;
Elatreus most successful hurled the quoit,
And at the cestus,[29] last, the noble son
Of Scheria's King, Laodamas excell'd.
When thus with contemplation of the games
160 All had been gratified, Alcinoüs' son
Laodamas, arising, then address'd.
Friends! ask we now the stranger, if he boast
Proficiency in aught. His figure seems
Not ill; in thighs, and legs, and arms he shews
Much strength, and in his brawny neck; nor youth
Hath left him yet, though batter'd he appears
With num'rous troubles, and misfortune-flaw'd.
Nor know I hardships in the world so sure
To break the strongest down, as those by sea.
170 Then answer thus Euryalus return'd.
Thou hast well said, Laodamas; thyself
Approaching, speak to him, and call him forth.
Which when Alcinoüs' noble offspring heard,
Advancing from his seat, amid them all
He stood, and to Ulysses thus began.
Stand forth, oh guest, thou also; prove thy skill
(If any such thou hast) in games like ours,
Which, likeliest, thou hast learn'd; for greater praise
Hath no man, while he lives, than that he know
180 His feet to exercise and hands aright.
Come then; make trial; scatter wide thy cares,
We will not hold thee long; the ship is launch'd
Already, and the crew stand all prepared.
To whom replied the wily Chief renown'd
Wherefore, as in derision, have ye call'd
Me forth, Laodamas, to these exploits?
No games have I, but many a grief, at heart,
And with far other struggles worn, here sit
Desirous only of conveyance home,
190 For which both King and people I implore.
Then him Euryalus aloud reproach'd.
I well believ'd it, friend! in thee the guise
I see not of a man expert in feats
Athletic, of which various are perform'd
In ev'ry land; thou rather seem'st with ships
Familiar; one, accustom'd to controul
Some crew of trading mariners; well-learn'd
In stowage, pilotage, and wealth acquired
By rapine, but of no gymnastic pow'rs.
200 To whom Ulysses, frowning dark, replied.
Thou hast ill spoken, sir, and like a man
Regardless whom he wrongs. Therefore the Gods
Give not endowments graceful in each kind,
Of body, mind, and utt'rance, all to one.
This man in figure less excels, yet Jove
Crowns him with eloquence; his hearers charm'd
Behold him, while with modest confidence
He bears the prize of fluent speech from all,

---

[28] +Toisi d' apo nysoês tetato dromos+-This expression is by the commentators generally understood to be significant of the effort which they made at starting, but it is not improbable that it relates merely to the measurement of the course, otherwise, +karpalimôs epetonto+ will be tautologous.

[29] In boxing.

And in the streets is gazed on as a God!
210 Another, in his form the Pow'rs above
Resembles, but no grace around his words
Twines itself elegant. So, thou in form
Hast excellence to boast; a God, employ'd
To make a master-piece in human shape,
Could but produce proportions such as thine;
Yet hast thou an untutor'd intellect.
Thou much hast moved me; thy unhandsome phrase
Hath roused my wrath; I am not, as thou say'st,
A novice in these sports, but took the lead
220 In all, while youth and strength were on my side.
But I am now in bands of sorrow held,
And of misfortune, having much endured
In war, and buffeting the boist'rous waves.
Yet, though with mis'ry worn, I will essay
My strength among you; for thy words had teeth
Whose bite hath pinch'd and pain'd me to the proof.
He said; and mantled as he was, a quoit
Upstarting, seized, in bulk and weight all those
Transcending far, by the Phæacians used.
230 Swiftly he swung, and from his vig'rous hand
Sent it. Loud sang the stone, and as it flew
The maritime Phæacians low inclined
Their heads beneath it; over all the marks,
And far beyond them, sped the flying rock.
Minerva, in a human form, the cast
Prodigious measur'd, and aloud exclaim'd.
Stranger! the blind himself might with his hands
Feel out the 'vantage here. Thy quoit disdains
Fellowship with a crowd, borne far beyond.
240 Fear not a losing game; Phæacian none
Will reach thy measure, much less overcast.
She ceased; Ulysses, hardy Chief, rejoiced
That in the circus he had found a judge
So favorable, and with brisker tone,
As less in wrath, the multitude address'd.
Young men, reach this, and I will quickly heave
Another such, or yet a heavier quoit.
Then, come the man whose courage prompts him forth
To box, to wrestle with me, or to run;
250 For ye have chafed me much, and I decline
No strife with any here, but challenge all
Phæacia, save Laodamas alone.
He is mine host. Who combats with his friend?
To call to proof of hardiment the man
Who entertains him in a foreign land,
Would but evince the challenger a fool,
Who, so, would cripple his own interest there.
As for the rest, I none refuse, scorn none,
But wish for trial of you, and to match
260 In opposition fair my force with yours.
There is no game athletic in the use
Of all mankind, too difficult for me;
I handle well the polish'd bow, and first
Amid a thousand foes strike whom I mark,
Although a throng of warriors at my side
Imbattled, speed their shafts at the same time.

Of all Achaia's sons who erst at Troy
Drew bow, the sole who bore the prize from me
Was Philoctetes; I resign it else
270 To none now nourish'd with the fruits of earth.
Yet mean I no comparison of myself
With men of antient times, with Hercules,
Or with Oechalian Eurytus, who, both,
The Gods themselves in archery defied.
Soon, therefore, died huge Eurytus, ere yet
Old age he reach'd; him, angry to be call'd
To proof of archership, Apollo slew.
But if ye name the spear, mine flies a length
By no man's arrow reach'd; I fear no foil
280 From the Phæacians, save in speed alone;
For I have suffer'd hardships, dash'd and drench'd
By many a wave, nor had I food on board
At all times, therefore I am much unstrung.
He spake; and silent the Phæacians sat,
Of whom alone Alcinoüs thus replied.
Since, stranger, not ungraceful is thy speech,
Who hast but vindicated in our ears
Thy question'd prowess, angry that this youth
Reproach'd thee in the presence of us all,
290 That no man qualified to give his voice
In public, might affront thy courage more;
Now mark me, therefore, that in time to come,
While feasting with thy children and thy spouse,
Thou may'st inform the Heroes of thy land
Even of our proficiency in arts
By Jove enjoin'd us in our father's days.
We boast not much the boxer's skill, nor yet
The wrestler's; but light-footed in the race
Are we, and navigators well-inform'd.
300 Our pleasures are the feast, the harp, the dance,
Garments for change; the tepid bath; the bed.
Come, ye Phæacians, beyond others skill'd
To tread the circus with harmonious steps,
Come, play before us; that our guest, arrived
In his own country, may inform his friends
How far in seamanship we all excel,
In running, in the dance, and in the song.
Haste! bring ye to Demodocus his lyre
Clear-toned, left somewhere in our hall at home.
310 So spake the godlike King, at whose command
The herald to the palace quick return'd
To seek the charming lyre. Meantime arose
Nine arbiters, appointed to intend
The whole arrangement of the public games,
To smooth the circus floor, and give the ring
Its compass, widening the attentive throng.
Ere long the herald came, bearing the harp,
With which Demodocus supplied, advanced
Into the middle area, around whom
320 Stood blooming youths, all skilful in the dance.
With footsteps justly timed all smote at once
The sacred floor; Ulysses wonder-fixt,

The ceaseless play of twinkling[30] feet admired.

---

[30] The Translator is indebted to Mr Grey for an epithet more expressive of the original (+Marmarygas+) than any other, perhaps, in all our language. See the Ode on the Progress of Poetry.
"To brisk notes in cadence beating,

Then, tuning his sweet chords, Demodocus
A jocund strain began, his theme, the loves
Of Mars and Cytherea chaplet-crown'd;
How first, clandestine, they embraced beneath
The roof of Vulcan, her, by many a gift
Seduced, Mars won, and with adult'rous lust
330 The bed dishonour'd of the King of fire.
The sun, a witness of their amorous sport,
Bore swift the tale to Vulcan; he, apprized
Of that foul deed, at once his smithy sought,
In secret darkness of his inmost soul
Contriving vengeance; to the stock he heav'd
His anvil huge, on which he forged a snare
Of bands indissoluble, by no art
To be untied, durance for ever firm.
The net prepared, he bore it, fiery-wroth,
340 To his own chamber and his nuptial couch,
Where, stretching them from post to post, he wrapp'd
With those fine meshes all his bed around,
And hung them num'rous from the roof, diffused
Like spiders' filaments, which not the Gods
Themselves could see, so subtle were the toils.
When thus he had encircled all his bed
On ev'ry side, he feign'd a journey thence
To Lemnos, of all cities that adorn
The earth, the city that he favours most.
350 Nor kept the God of the resplendent reins
Mars, drowsy watch, but seeing that the famed
Artificer of heav'n had left his home,
Flew to the house of Vulcan, hot to enjoy
The Goddess with the wreath-encircled brows.
She, newly from her potent Sire return'd
The son of Saturn, sat. Mars, ent'ring, seiz'd
Her hand, hung on it, and thus urg'd his suit.
To bed, my fair, and let us love! for lo!
Thine husband is from home, to Lemnos gone,
360 And to the Sintians, men of barb'rous speech.
He spake, nor she was loth, but bedward too
Like him inclined; so then, to bed they went,
And as they lay'd them down, down stream'd the net
Around them, labour exquisite of hands
By ingenuity divine inform'd.
Small room they found, so prison'd; not a limb
Could either lift, or move, but felt at once
Entanglement from which was no escape.
And now the glorious artist, ere he yet
370 Had reach'd the Lemnian isle, limping, return'd
From his feign'd journey, for his spy the sun
Had told him all. With aching heart he sought
His home, and, standing in the vestibule,
Frantic with indignation roar'd to heav'n,
And roar'd again, summoning all the Gods.-
Oh Jove! and all ye Pow'rs for ever blest!
Here; hither look, that ye may view a sight
Ludicrous, yet too monstrous to be borne,
How Venus always with dishonour loads
380 Her cripple spouse, doating on fiery Mars!

And wherefore? for that he is fair in form
And sound of foot, I ricket-boned and weak.
Whose fault is this? Their fault, and theirs alone
Who gave me being; ill-employ'd were they
Begetting me, one, better far unborn.
See where they couch together on my bed
Lascivious! ah, sight hateful to my eyes!
Yet cooler wishes will they feel, I ween,
To press my bed hereafter; here to sleep
390 Will little please them, fondly as they love.
But these my toils and tangles will suffice
To hold them here, till Jove shall yield me back
Complete, the sum of all my nuptial gifts
Paid to him for the shameless strumpet's sake
His daughter, as incontinent as fair.
He said, and in the brazen-floor'd abode
Of Jove the Gods assembled. Neptune came
Earth-circling Pow'r; came Hermes friend of man,
And, regent of the far-commanding bow,
400 Apollo also came; but chaste reserve
Bashful kept all the Goddesses at home.
The Gods, by whose beneficence all live,
Stood in the portal; infinite arose
The laugh of heav'n, all looking down intent
On that shrewd project of the smith divine,
And, turning to each other, thus they said.
Bad works speed ill. The slow o'ertakes the swift.
So Vulcan, tardy as he is, by craft
Hath outstript Mars, although the fleetest far
410 Of all who dwell in heav'n, and the light-heel'd
Must pay the adult'rer's forfeit to the lame.
So spake the Pow'rs immortal; then the King
Of radiant shafts thus question'd Mercury.
Jove's son, heaven's herald, Hermes, bounteous God!
Would'st *thou* such stricture close of bands endure
For golden Venus lying at thy side?
Whom answer'd thus the messenger of heav'n
Archer divine! yea, and with all my heart;
And be the bands which wind us round about
420 Thrice these innumerable, and let all
The Gods and Goddesses in heav'n look on,
So I may clasp Vulcan's fair spouse the while.
He spake; then laugh'd the Immortal Pow'rs again.
But not so Neptune; he with earnest suit
The glorious artist urged to the release
Of Mars, and thus in accents wing'd he said.
Loose him; accept my promise; he shall pay
Full recompense in presence of us all.
Then thus the limping smith far-famed replied.
430 Earth-circler Neptune, spare me that request.

Lame suitor, lame security.[31] What bands
Could I devise for thee among the Gods,
Should Mars, emancipated once, escape,
Leaving both debt and durance, far behind?
Him answer'd then the Shaker of the shores.
I tell thee, Vulcan, that if Mars by flight
Shun payment, I will pay, myself, the fine.

Glance their *many-twinkling* feet"

[31] The original line has received such a variety of interpretations, that a Translator seems free to choose. It has, however, a proverbial turn, which I have endeavoured to preserve, and have adopted the sense of the words which appears best to accord with what immediately follows. Vulcan pleads his own inability to enforce the demand, as a circumstance that made Neptune's promise unacceptable.

To whom the glorious artist of the skies.
Thou must not, canst not, shalt not be refused.
440 So saying, the might of Vulcan loos'd the snare,
And they, detain'd by those coercive bands
No longer, from the couch upstarting, flew,
Mars into Thrace, and to her Paphian home
The Queen of smiles, where deep in myrtle groves
Her incense-breathing altar stands embow'r'd.
Her there, the Graces laved, and oils diffused
O'er all her form, ambrosial, such as add
Fresh beauty to the Gods for ever young,
And cloath'd her in the loveliest robes of heav'n.
450 Such was the theme of the illustrious bard.
Ulysses with delight that song, and all
The maritime Phæacian concourse heard.
Alcinoüs, then, (for in the dance they pass'd
All others) call'd his sons to dance alone,
Halius and Laodamas; they gave
The purple ball into their hands, the work
Exact of Polybus; one, resupine,
Upcast it high toward the dusky clouds,
The other, springing into air, with ease
460 Received it, ere he sank to earth again.
When thus they oft had sported with the ball
Thrown upward, next, with nimble interchange
They pass'd it to each other many a time,
Footing the plain, while ev'ry youth of all
The circus clapp'd his hands, and from beneath
The din of stamping feet fill'd all the air.
Then, turning to Alcinoüs, thus the wise
Ulysses spake: Alcinoüs! mighty King!
Illustrious above all Phæacia's sons!
470 Incomparable are ye in the dance,
Ev'n as thou said'st. Amazement-fixt I stand!
So he, whom hearing, the imperial might
Exulted of Alcinoüs, and aloud
To his oar-skill'd Phæacians thus he spake.
Phæacian Chiefs and Senators, attend!
Wisdom beyond the common stint I mark
In this our guest; good cause in my account,
For which we should present him with a pledge
Of hospitality and love. The Chiefs
480 Are twelve, who, highest in command, controul
The people, and the thirteenth Chief am I.
Bring each a golden talent, with a vest
Well-bleach'd, and tunic; gratified with these,
The stranger to our banquet shall repair
Exulting; bring them all without delay;
And let Euryalus by word and gift
Appease him, for his speech was unadvised.
He ceas'd, whom all applauded, and at once
Each sent his herald forth to bring the gifts,
490 When thus Euryalus his Sire address'd.
Alcinoüs! o'er Phæacia's sons supreme!
I will appease our guest, as thou command'st.
This sword shall be his own, the blade all steel.
The hilt of silver, and the unsullied sheath
Of iv'ry recent from the carver's hand,
A gift like this he shall not need despise.
So saying, his silver-studded sword he gave
Into his grasp, and, courteous, thus began.
Hail, honour'd stranger! and if word of mine

500 Have harm'd thee, rashly spoken, let the winds
Bear all remembrance of it swift away!
May the Gods give thee to behold again
Thy wife, and to attain thy native shore,
Whence absent long, thou hast so much endured!
To whom Ulysses, ever-wise, replied.
Hail also thou, and may the Gods, my friend,
Grant thee felicity, and may never want
Of this thy sword touch thee in time to come,
By whose kind phrase appeas'd my wrath subsides!
510 He ended, and athwart his shoulders threw
The weapon bright emboss'd. Now sank the sun,
And those rich gifts arrived, which to the house
Of King Alcinoüs the heralds bore.
Alcinoüs' sons receiv'd them, and beside
Their royal mother placed the precious charge.
The King then led the way, at whose abode
Arrived, again they press'd their lofty thrones,
And to Areta thus the monarch spake.
Haste, bring a coffer; bring thy best, and store
520 A mantle and a sumptuous vest within;
Warm for him, next, a brazen bath, by which
Refresh'd, and viewing in fair order placed
The noble gifts by the Phæacian Lords
Conferr'd on him, he may the more enjoy
Our banquet, and the bard's harmonious song.
I give him also this my golden cup
Splendid, elaborate; that, while he lives
What time he pours libation forth to Jove
And all the Gods, he may remember me.
530 He ended, at whose words Areta bade
Her maidens with dispatch place o'er the fire
A tripod ample-womb'd; obedient they
Advanced a laver to the glowing hearth,
Water infused, and kindled wood beneath
The flames encircling bright the bellied vase,
Warm'd soon the flood within. Meantime, the Queen
Producing from her chamber-stores a chest
All-elegant, within it placed the gold,
And raiment, gifts of the Phæacian Chiefs,
540 With her own gifts, the mantle and the vest,
And in wing'd accents to Ulysses said.
Now take, thyself, the coffer's lid in charge;
Girdle it quickly with a cord, lest loss
Befall thee on thy way, while thou perchance
Shalt sleep secure on board the sable bark.
Which when Ulysses heard, Hero renown'd,
Adjusting close the lid, he cast a cord
Around it which with many a mazy knot
He tied, by Circe taught him long before.
550 And now, the mistress of the household charge
Summon'd him to his bath; glad he beheld
The steaming vase, uncustom'd to its use
E'er since his voyage from the isle of fair
Calypso, although, while a guest with her,
Ever familiar with it, as a God.
Laved by attendant damsels, and with oil
Refresh'd, he put his sumptuous tunic on
And mantle, and proceeding from the bath
To the symposium, join'd the num'rous guests;
560 But, as he pass'd, the Princess all divine
Beside the pillars of the portal, lost

In admiration of his graceful form,
Stood, and in accents wing'd him thus address'd.
Hail, stranger! at thy native home arrived
Remember me, thy first deliv'rer here.
To whom Ulysses, ever-wise, replied.
Nausicaa! daughter of the noble King
Alcinoüs! So may Jove, high-thund'ring mate
Of Juno, grant me to behold again
570 My native land, and my delightful home,
As, even there, I will present my vows
To thee, adoring thee as I adore
The Gods themselves, virgin, by whom I live!
He said, and on his throne beside the King
Alcinoüs sat. And now they portion'd out
The feast to all, and charg'd the cups with wine,
And introducing by his hand the bard
Phæacia's glory, at the column's side
The herald placed Demodocus again.
580 Then, carving forth a portion from the loins
Of a huge brawn, of which uneaten still
Large part and delicate remain'd, thus spake
Ulysses-Herald! bear it to the bard
For his regale, whom I will soon embrace
In spite of sorrow; for respect is due
And veneration to the sacred bard
From all mankind, for that the muse inspires
Herself his song, and loves the tuneful tribe.
He ended, and the herald bore his charge
590 To the old hero who with joy received
That meed of honour at the bearer's hand.
Then, all, at once, assail'd the ready feast,
And hunger now, and thirst both satisfied,
Thus to Demodocus Ulysses spake.
Demodocus! I give thee praise above
All mortals, for that either thee the muse
Jove's daughter teaches, or the King, himself,
Apollo; since thou so record'st the fate,
With such clear method, of Achaia's host,
600 Their deeds heroic, and their num'rous toils,
As thou hadst present been thyself, or learnt
From others present there, the glorious tale.
Come, then, proceed; that rare invention sing,
The horse of wood, which by Minerva's aid
Epeus framed, and which Ulysses erst
Convey'd into the citadel of Troy
With warriors fill'd, who lay'd all Ilium waste.
These things rehearse regular, and myself
Will, instant, publish in the ears of all
610 Thy fame, reporting thee a bard to whom
Apollo free imparts celestial song.
He ended; then Apollo with full force
Rush'd on Demodocus, and he began
What time the Greeks, first firing their own camp
Steer'd all their galleys from the shore of Troy.
Already, in the horse conceal'd, his band
Around Ulysses sat; for Ilium's sons
Themselves had drawn it to the citadel.
And there the mischief stood. Then, strife arose
620 Among the Trojans compassing the horse,
And threefold was the doubt; whether to cleave
The hollow trunk asunder, or updrawn
Aloft, to cast it headlong from the rocks,

Or to permit the enormous image, kept
Entire, to stand an off'ring to the Gods,
Which was their destined course; for Fate had fix'd
Their ruin sure, when once they had received
Within their walls that engine huge, in which
Sat all the bravest Greecians with the fate
630 Of Ilium charged, and slaughter of her sons.
He sang, how, from the horse effused, the Greeks
Left their capacious ambush, and the town
Made desolate. To others, in his song,
He gave the praise of wasting all beside,
But told how, fierce as Mars, Ulysses join'd
With godlike Menelaus, to the house
Flew of Deiphobus; him there engaged
In direst fight he sang, and through the aid
Of glorious Pallas, conqu'ror over all.
640 So sang the bard illustrious, at whose song
Ulysses melted, and tear after tear
Fell on his cheeks. As when a woman weeps,
Her husband, who hath fallen in defence
Of his own city and his babes before
The gates; she, sinking, folds him in her arms
And, gazing on him as he pants and dies,
Shrieks at the sight; meantime, the enemy
Smiting her shoulders with the spear to toil
Command her and to bondage far away,
650 And her cheek fades with horror at the sound;
Ulysses, so, from his moist lids let fall,
The frequent tear. Unnoticed by the rest
Those drops, but not by King Alcinoüs, fell
Who, seated at his side, his heavy sighs
Remark'd, and the Phæacians thus bespake.
Phæacian Chiefs and Senators attend!
Now let Demodocus enjoin his harp
Silence, for not alike grateful to all
His music sounds; during our feast, and since
660 The bard divine began, continual flow
The stranger's sorrows, by remembrance caused
Of some great woe which wraps his soul around.
Then, let the bard suspend his song, that all
(As most befits th' occasion) may rejoice,
Both guest and hosts together; since we make
This voyage, and these gifts confer, in proof
Of hospitality and unfeign'd love,
Judging, with all wise men, the stranger-guest
And suppliant worthy of a brother's place.
670 And thou conceal not, artfully reserv'd,
What I shall ask, far better plain declared
Than smother'd close; who art thou? speak thy name,
The name by which thy father, mother, friends
And fellow-citizens, with all who dwell
Around thy native city, in times past
Have known thee; for of all things human none
Lives altogether nameless, whether good
Or whether bad, but ev'ry man receives
Ev'n in the moment of his birth, a name.
680 Thy country, people, city, tell; the mark
At which my ships, intelligent, shall aim,
That they may bear thee thither; for our ships
No pilot need or helm, as ships are wont,
But know, themselves, our purpose; know beside
All cities, and all fruitful regions well

Of all the earth, and with dark clouds involv'd
Plough rapid the rough Deep, fearless of harm,
(Whate'er betide) and of disast'rous wreck.
Yet thus, long since, my father I have heard
690 Nausithoüs speaking; Neptune, he would say,
Is angry with us, for that safe we bear
Strangers of ev'ry nation to their home;
And he foretold a time when he would smite
In vengeance some Phæacian gallant bark
Returning after convoy of her charge,
And fix her in the sable flood, transform'd
Into a mountain, right before the town.
So spake my hoary Sire, which let the God
At his own pleasure do, or leave undone.
700 But tell me truth, and plainly. Where have been
Thy wand'rings? in what regions of the earth
Hast thou arrived? what nations hast thou seen,
What cities? say, how many hast thou found

Harsh, savage and unjust? how many, kind
To strangers, and disposed to fear the Gods?
Say also, from what secret grief of heart
Thy sorrows flow, oft as thou hear'st the fate
Of the Achaians, or of Ilium sung?
That fate the Gods prepared; they spin the thread
710 Of man's destruction, that in after days
The bard may make the sad event his theme.
Perish'd thy father or thy brother there?
Or hast thou at the siege of Ilium lost
Father-in-law, or son-in-law? for such
Are next and dearest to us after those
Who share our own descent; or was the dead
Thy bosom-friend, whose heart was as thy own?
For worthy as a brother of our love
The constant friend and the discrete I deem.
720

Book IX

Ulysses discovers himself to the Phœacians, and begins the history of his adventures. He destroys Ismarus, city of the Ciconians; arrives among the Lotophagi; and afterwards at the land of the Cyclops. He is imprisoned by Polypheme in his cave, who devours six of his companions; intoxicates the monster with wine, blinds him while he sleeps, and escapes from him.

Then answer, thus, Ulysses wise return'd.
Alcinoüs! King! illustrious above all
Phæacia's sons, pleasant it is to hear
A bard like this, sweet as the Gods in song.
The world, in my account, no sight affords
More gratifying than a people blest
With cheerfulness and peace, a palace throng'd
With guests in order ranged, list'ning to sounds
Melodious, and the steaming tables spread
With plenteous viands, while the cups, with wine
10 From brimming beakers fill'd, pass brisk around.
No lovelier sight know I. But thou, it seems,
Thy thoughts hast turn'd to ask me whence my groans
And tears, that I may sorrow still the more.
What first, what next, what last shall I rehearse,
On whom the Gods have show'r'd such various woes?
Learn first my name, that even in this land
Remote I may be known, and that escaped
From all adversity, I may requite
Hereafter, this your hospitable care
20 At my own home, however distant hence.
I am Ulysses, fear'd in all the earth
For subtlest wisdom, and renown'd to heaven,
The offspring of Laertes; my abode
Is sun-burnt Ithaca; there waving stands
The mountain Neritus his num'rous boughs,
And it is neighbour'd close by clust'ring isles
All populous; thence Samos is beheld,
Dulichium, and Zacynthus forest-clad.
Flat on the Deep she lies, farthest removed
30 Toward the West, while, situate apart,
Her sister islands face the rising day;
Rugged she is, but fruitful nurse of sons
Magnanimous; nor shall these eyes behold,
Elsewhere, an object dear and sweet as she.
Calypso, beauteous Goddess, in her grot
Detain'd me, wishing me her own espoused;
Ææan Circe also, skill'd profound
In potent arts, within her palace long
Detain'd me, wishing me her own espoused;
40 But never could they warp my constant mind.
So much our parents and our native soil
Attract us most, even although our lot
Be fair and plenteous in a foreign land.
But come-my painful voyage, such as Jove
Gave me from Ilium, I will now relate.
From Troy the winds bore me to Ismarus,
City of the Ciconians; them I slew,
And laid their city waste; whence bringing forth
Much spoil with all their wives, I portion'd it
50 With equal hand, and each received a share.
Next, I exhorted to immediate flight

My people; but in vain; they madly scorn'd
My sober counsel, and much wine they drank,
And sheep and beeves slew num'rous on the shore.
Meantime, Ciconians to Ciconians call'd,
Their neighbours summoning, a mightier host
And braver, natives of the continent,
Expert, on horses mounted, to maintain
Fierce fight, or if occasion bade, on foot.
60 Num'rous they came as leaves, or vernal flow'rs
At day-spring. Then, by the decree of Jove,
Misfortune found us. At the ships we stood
Piercing each other with the brazen spear,
And till the morning brighten'd into noon,
Few as we were, we yet withstood them all;
But, when the sun verged westward, then the Greeks
Fell back, and the Ciconian host prevail'd.
Six warlike Greecians from each galley's crew
Perish'd in that dread field; the rest escaped.
70 Thus, after loss of many, we pursued
Our course, yet, difficult as was our flight,
Went not till first we had invoked by name
Our friends, whom the Ciconians had destroy'd.
But cloud-assembler Jove assail'd us soon
With a tempestuous North-wind; earth alike
And sea with storms he overhung, and night
Fell fast from heav'n. Their heads deep-plunging oft
Our gallies flew, and rent, and rent again
Our tatter'd sail-cloth crackled in the wind.
80 We, fearing instant death, within the barks
Our canvas lodg'd, and, toiling strenuous, reach'd
At length the continent. Two nights we lay
Continual there, and two long days, consumed
With toil and grief; but when the beauteous morn
Bright-hair'd, had brought the third day to a close,
(Our masts erected, and white sails unfurl'd)
Again we sat on board; meantime, the winds
Well managed by the steersman, urged us on.
And now, all danger pass'd, I had attain'd
90 My native shore, but, doubling in my course
Malea, waves and currents and North-winds
Constrain'd me devious to Cythera's isle.
Nine days by cruel storms thence was I borne
Athwart the fishy Deep, but on the tenth
Reach'd the Lotophagi, a race sustain'd
On sweetest fruit alone. There quitting ship,
We landed and drew water, and the crews
Beside the vessels took their ev'ning cheer.
When, hasty, we had thus our strength renew'd,
100 I order'd forth my people to inquire
(Two I selected from the rest, with whom
I join'd an herald, third) what race of men
Might there inhabit. They, departing, mix'd

With the Lotophagi; nor hostile aught
Or savage the Lotophagi devised
Against our friends, but offer'd to their taste
The lotus; of which fruit what man soe'er
Once tasted, no desire felt he to come
With tidings back, or seek his country more,
110 But rather wish'd to feed on lotus still
With the Lotophagi, and to renounce
All thoughts of home. Them, therefore, I constrain'd
Weeping on board, and dragging each beneath
The benches, bound him there. Then, all in haste,
I urged my people to ascend again
Their hollow barks, lest others also, fed
With fruit of lotus, should forget their home.
They quick embark'd, and on the benches ranged
In order, thresh'd with oars the foamy flood.
120 Thence, o'er the Deep proceeding sad, we reach'd

The land at length, where, giant-sized[32] and free
From all constraint of law, the Cyclops dwell.
They, trusting to the Gods, plant not, or plough,
But earth unsow'd, untill'd, brings forth for them
All fruits, wheat, barley, and the vinous grape
Large cluster'd, nourish'd by the show'rs of Jove.
No councils they convene, no laws contrive,
But in deep caverns dwell, found on the heads
Of lofty mountains, judging each supreme
130 His wife and children, heedless of the rest.
In front of the Cyclopean haven lies
A level island, not adjoining close
Their land, nor yet remote, woody and rude.
There, wild goats breed numberless, by no foot
Of man molested; never huntsman there,
Inured to winter's cold and hunger, roams
The dreary woods, or mountain-tops sublime;
No fleecy flocks dwell there, nor plough is known,
But the unseeded and unfurrow'd soil,
140 Year after year a wilderness by man
Untrodden, food for blatant goats supplies.
For no ships crimson-prow'd the Cyclops own,
Nor naval artizan is there, whose toil
Might furnish them with oary barks, by which
Subsists all distant commerce, and which bear
Man o'er the Deep to cities far remote
Who might improve the peopled isle, that seems
Not steril in itself, but apt to yield,
In their due season, fruits of ev'ry kind.
150 For stretch'd beside the hoary ocean lie
Green meadows moist, where vines would never fail;
Light is the land, and they might yearly reap
The tallest crops, so unctuous is the glebe.
Safe is its haven also, where no need
Of cable is or anchor, or to lash
The hawser fast ashore, but pushing in
His bark, the mariner might there abide
Till rising gales should tempt him forth again.
At bottom of the bay runs a clear stream
160 Issuing from a cove hemm'd all around
With poplars; down into that bay we steer'd
Amid the darkness of the night, some God
Conducting us; for all unseen it lay,

Such gloom involved the fleet, nor shone the moon
From heav'n to light us, veil'd by pitchy clouds.
Hence, none the isle descried, nor any saw
The lofty surge roll'd on the strand, or ere
Our vessels struck the ground; but when they struck,
Then, low'ring all our sails, we disembark'd,
170 And on the sea-beach slept till dawn appear'd.
Soon as Aurora, daughter of the dawn,
Look'd rosy forth, we with admiring eyes
The isle survey'd, roaming it wide around.
Meantime, the nymphs, Jove's daughters, roused the goats
Bred on the mountains, to supply with food
The partners of my toils; then, bringing forth
Bows and long-pointed javelins from the ships,
Divided all into three sep'rate bands
We struck them, and the Gods gave us much prey.
180 Twelve ships attended me, and ev'ry ship
Nine goats received by lot; myself alone
Selected ten. All day, till set of sun,
We eating sat goat's flesh, and drinking wine
Delicious, without stint; for dearth was none
Of ruddy wine on board, but much remain'd,
With which my people had their jars supplied
What time we sack'd Ciconian Ismarus.
Thence looking forth toward the neighbour-land
Where dwell the Cyclops, rising smoke we saw,
190 And voices heard, their own, and of their flocks.
Now sank the sun, and (night o'ershadowing all)
We slept along the shore; but when again
The rosy-finger'd daughter of the dawn
Look'd forth, my crews convened, I thus began.
Companions of my course! here rest ye all,
Save my own crew, with whom I will explore
This people, whether wild, they be, unjust,
And to contention giv'n, or well-disposed
To strangers, and a race who fear the Gods.
200 So speaking, I embark'd, and bade embark
My followers, throwing, quick, the hawsers loose.
They, ent'ring at my word, the benches fill'd
Well-ranged, and thresh'd with oars the foamy flood.
Attaining soon that neighbour-land, we found
At its extremity, fast by the sea,
A cavern, lofty, and dark-brow'd above
With laurels; in that cavern slumb'ring lay
Much cattle, sheep and goats, and a broad court
Enclosed it, fenced with stones from quarries hewn,
210 With spiry firs, and oaks of ample bough.
Here dwelt a giant vast, who far remote
His flocks fed solitary, converse none
Desiring, sullen, savage, and unjust.
Monster, in truth, he was, hideous in form,
Resembling less a man by Ceres' gift
Sustain'd, than some aspiring mountain-crag
Tufted with wood, and standing all alone.
Enjoining, then, my people to abide
Fast by the ship which they should closely guard,
220 I went, but not without a goat-skin fill'd
With sable wine which I had erst received
From Maron, offspring of Evanthes, priest
Of Phoebus guardian god of Ismarus,

---

[32] So the Scholium interprets in this place, the word +hyperthialos+.

Because, through rev'rence of him, we had saved
Himself, his wife and children; for he dwelt
Amid the grove umbrageous of his God.
He gave me, therefore, noble gifts; from him
Sev'n talents I received of beaten gold,
A beaker, argent all, and after these
230 No fewer than twelve jars with wine replete,
Rich, unadult'rate, drink for Gods; nor knew
One servant, male or female, of that wine
In all his house; none knew it, save himself,
His wife, and the intendant of his stores.
Oft as they drank that luscious juice, he slaked
A single cup with twenty from the stream,
And, even then, the beaker breath'd abroad
A scent celestial, which whoever smelt,
Thenceforth no pleasure found it to abstain.
24 °Charged with an ample goat-skin of this wine
I went, and with a wallet well supplied,
But felt a sudden presage in my soul
That, haply, with terrific force endued,
Some savage would appear, strange to the laws
And privileges of the human race.
Few steps convey'd us to his den, but him
We found not; he his flocks pastur'd abroad.
His cavern ent'ring, we with wonder gazed
Around on all; his strainers hung with cheese
250 Distended wide; with lambs and kids his penns
Close-throng'd we saw, and folded separate
The various charge; the eldest all apart,
Apart the middle-aged, and the new-yean'd
Also apart. His pails and bowls with whey
Swam all, neat vessels into which he milk'd.
Me then my friends first importuned to take
A portion of his cheeses, then to drive
Forth from the sheep-cotes to the rapid bark
His kids and lambs, and plow the brine again.
260 But me they moved not, happier had they moved!
I wish'd to see him, and to gain, perchance,
Some pledge of hospitality at his hands,
Whose form was such, as should not much bespeak
When he appear'd, our confidence or love.
Then, kindling fire, we offer'd to the Gods,
And of his cheeses eating, patient sat
Till home he trudged from pasture. Charged he came
With dry wood bundled, an enormous load
Fuel by which to sup. Loud crash'd the thorns
270 Which down he cast before the cavern's mouth,
To whose interior nooks we trembling flew.
At once he drove into his spacious cave
His batten'd flock, all those which gave him milk,
But all the males, both rams and goats, he left
Abroad, excluded from the cavern-yard.
Upheaving, next, a rocky barrier huge
To his cave's mouth, he thrust it home. That weight
Not all the oxen from its place had moved
Of twenty and two wains; with such a rock
280 Immense his den he closed. Then down he sat,
And as he milk'd his ewes and bleating goats
All in their turns, her yeanling gave to each;
Coagulating, then, with brisk dispatch,
The half of his new milk, he thrust the curd
Into his wicker sieves, but stored the rest

In pans and bowls-his customary drink.
His labours thus perform'd, he kindled, last,
His fuel, and discerning *us* , enquired,
Who are ye, strangers? from what distant shore
290 Roam ye the waters? traffic ye? or bound
To no one port, wander, as pirates use,
At large the Deep, exposing life themselves,
And enemies of all mankind beside?
He ceased; we, dash'd with terrour, heard the growl
Of his big voice, and view'd his form uncouth,
To whom, though sore appall'd, I thus replied.
Of Greece are we, and, bound from Ilium home,
Have wander'd wide the expanse of ocean, sport
For ev'ry wind, and driven from our course,
300 Have here arrived; so stood the will of Jove.
We boast ourselves of Agamemnon's train,
The son of Atreus, at this hour the Chief
Beyond all others under heav'n renown'd,
So great a city he hath sack'd and slain
Such num'rous foes; but since we reach, at last,
Thy knees, we beg such hospitable fare,
Or other gift, as guests are wont to obtain.
Illustrious lord! respect the Gods, and us
Thy suitors; suppliants are the care of Jove
310 The hospitable; he their wrongs resents
And where the stranger sojourns, there is he.
I ceas'd, when answer thus he, fierce, return'd.
Friend! either thou art fool, or hast arrived
Indeed from far, who bidd'st me fear the Gods
Lest they be wroth. The Cyclops little heeds
Jove Ægis-arm'd, or all the Pow'rs of heav'n.
Our race is mightier far; nor shall myself,
Through fear of Jove's hostility, abstain
From thee or thine, unless my choice be such.
320 But tell me now. Where touch'd thy gallant bark
Our country, on thy first arrival here?
Remote or nigh? for I would learn the truth.
So spake he, tempting me; but, artful, thus
I answer'd, penetrating his intent.
My vessel, Neptune, Shaker of the shores,
At yonder utmost promontory dash'd
In pieces, hurling her against the rocks
With winds that blew right thither from the sea,
And I, with these alone, escaped alive.
330 So I, to whom, relentless, answer none
He deign'd, but, with his arms extended, sprang
Toward my people, of whom seizing two
At once, like whelps against his cavern-floor
He dash'd them, and their brains spread on the ground.
These, piece-meal hewn, for supper he prepared,
And, like a mountain-lion, neither flesh
Nor entrails left, nor yet their marrowy bones.
We, viewing that tremendous sight, upraised
Our hands to Jove, all hope and courage lost.
340 When thus the Cyclops had with human flesh
Fill'd his capacious belly, and had quaff'd
Much undiluted milk, among his flocks
Outstretch'd immense, he press'd his cavern-floor.
Me, then, my courage prompted to approach
The monster with my sword drawn from the sheath,
And to transfix him where the vitals wrap
The liver; but maturer thoughts forbad.

For so, we also had incurred a death
Tremendous, wanting pow'r to thrust aside
350 The rocky mass that closed his cavern-mouth
By force of hand alone. Thus many a sigh
Heaving, we watch'd the dawn. But when, at length,
Aurora, day-spring's daughter rosy-palm'd
Look'd forth, then, kindling fire, his flocks he milk'd
In order, and her yeanling kid or lamb
Thrust under each. When thus he had perform'd
His wonted task, two seizing, as before,
He slew them for his next obscene regale.
His dinner ended, from the cave he drove
360 His fatted flocks abroad, moving with ease
That pond'rous barrier, and replacing it
As he had only closed a quiver's lid.
Then, hissing them along, he drove his flocks
Toward the mountain, and me left, the while,
Deep ruminating how I best might take
Vengeance, and by the aid of Pallas win
Deathless renown. This counsel pleas'd me most.
Beside the sheep-cote lay a massy club
Hewn by the Cyclops from an olive stock,
370 Green, but which dried, should serve him for a staff.
To us consid'ring it, that staff appear'd
Tall as the mast of a huge trading bark,
Impell'd by twenty rowers o'er the Deep.
Such seem'd its length to us, and such its bulk.
Part amputating, (an whole fathom's length)
I gave my men that portion, with command
To shave it smooth. They smooth'd it, and myself,
Shaping its blunt extremity to a point,
Season'd it in the fire; then cov'ring close
380 The weapon, hid it under litter'd straw,
For much lay scatter'd on the cavern-floor.
And now I bade my people cast the lot
Who of us all should take the pointed brand,
And grind it in his eye when next he slept.
The lots were cast, and four were chosen, those
Whom most I wish'd, and I was chosen fifth.
At even-tide he came, his fleecy flocks
Pasturing homeward, and compell'd them all
Into his cavern, leaving none abroad,
390 Either through some surmise, or so inclined
By influence, haply, of the Gods themselves.
The huge rock pull'd into its place again
At the cave's mouth, he, sitting, milk'd his sheep
And goats in order, and her kid or lamb
Thrust under each; thus, all his work dispatch'd,
Two more he seiz'd, and to his supper fell.
I then, approaching to him, thus address'd
The Cyclops, holding in my hands a cup
Of ivy-wood, well-charg'd with ruddy wine.
400 Lo, Cyclops! this is wine. Take this and drink
After thy meal of man's flesh. Taste and learn
What precious liquor our lost vessel bore.

I brought it hither, purposing to make
Libation to thee, if to pity inclined
Thou would'st dismiss us home. But, ah, thy rage
Is insupportable! thou cruel one!
Who, thinkest thou, of all mankind, henceforth
Will visit *thee* , guilty of such excess?
I ceas'd. He took and drank, and hugely pleas'd[33]
410 With that delicious bev'rage, thus enquir'd.
Give me again, and spare not. Tell me, too,
Thy name, incontinent, that I may make
Requital, gratifying also thee
With somewhat to thy taste. We Cyclops own
A bounteous soil, which yields *us* also wine
From clusters large, nourish'd by show'rs from Jove;
But this-this is from above-a stream
Of nectar and ambrosia, all divine!
He ended, and received a second draught,
420 Like measure. Thrice I bore it to his hand,
And, foolish, thrice he drank. But when the fumes
Began to play around the Cyclops' brain,
With show of amity I thus replied.
Cyclops! thou hast my noble name enquired,
Which I will tell thee. Give me, in return,
The promised boon, some hospitable pledge.
My name is Outis,[34] Outis I am call'd
At home, abroad; wherever I am known.
So I; to whom he, savage, thus replied.
430 Outis, when I have eaten all his friends,
Shall be my last regale. Be that thy boon.
He spake, and, downward sway'd, fell resupine,
With his huge neck aslant. All-conqu'ring sleep
Soon seized him. From his gullet gush'd the wine
With human morsels mingled, many a blast
Sonorous issuing from his glutted maw.
Then, thrusting far the spike of olive-wood
Into the embers glowing on the hearth,
I heated it, and cheer'd my friends, the while,
440 Lest any should, through fear, shrink from his part.
But when that stake of olive-wood, though green,
Should soon have flamed, for it was glowing hot,
I bore it to his side. Then all my aids
Around me gather'd, and the Gods infused
Heroic fortitude into our hearts.
They, seizing the hot stake rasp'd to a point,
Bored his eye with it, and myself, advanced
To a superior stand, twirled it about.
As when a shipwright with his wimble bores
450 Tough oaken timber, placed on either side
Below, his fellow-artists strain the thong
Alternate, and the restless iron spins,
So, grasping hard the stake pointed with fire,
We twirl'd it in his eye; the bubbling blood
Boil'd round about the brand; his pupil sent
A scalding vapour forth that sing'd his brow,
And all his eye-roots crackled in the flame.

---

[33] +Linôs+

[34] Clarke, who has preserved this name in his marginal version, contends strenuously, and with great reason, that Outis ought not to be translated, and in a passage which he quotes from the *Acta eruditorum*, we see much fault found with Giphanius and other interpreters of Homer for having translated it. It is certain that in Homer the word is declined not as +outis-tinos+ which signifies no man, but as +outis-tidos+ making +outin+ in the accusative, consequently as a proper name. It is sufficient that the ambiguity was such as to deceive the friends of the Cyclops. Outis is said by some (perhaps absurdly) to have been a name given to Ulysses on account of his having larger ears than common.

As when the smith an hatchet or large axe
Temp'ring with skill, plunges the hissing blade
460 Deep in cold water, (whence the strength of steel)
So hiss'd his eye around the olive-wood.
The howling monster with his outcry fill'd
The hollow rock, and I, with all my aids,
Fled terrified. He, plucking forth the spike
From his burnt socket, mad with anguish, cast
The implement all bloody far away.
Then, bellowing, he sounded forth the name
Of ev'ry Cyclops dwelling in the caves
Around him, on the wind-swept mountain-tops;
470 They, at his cry flocking from ev'ry part,
Circled his den, and of his ail enquired.
What grievous hurt hath caused thee, Polypheme!
Thus yelling to alarm the peaceful ear
Of night, and break our slumbers? Fear'st thou lest
Some mortal man drive off thy flocks? or fear'st
Thyself to die by cunning or by force?
Them answer'd, then, Polypheme from his cave.
Oh, friends! I die! and Outis gives the blow.
To whom with accents wing'd his friends without.
480 If no man[35] harm thee, but thou art alone,
And sickness feel'st, it is the stroke of Jove,
And thou must bear it; yet invoke for aid
Thy father Neptune, Sovereign of the floods.
So saying, they went, and in my heart I laugh'd
That by the fiction only of a name,
Slight stratagem! I had deceived them all.
Then groan'd the Cyclops wrung with pain and grief,
And, fumbling, with stretch'd hands, removed the rock
From his cave's mouth, which done, he sat him down
490 Spreading his arms athwart the pass, to stop
Our egress with his flocks abroad; so dull,
It seems, he held me, and so ill-advised.
I, pondering what means might fittest prove
To save from instant death, (if save I might)
My people and myself, to ev'ry shift
Inclined, and various counsels framed, as one
Who strove for life, conscious of woe at hand.
To me, thus meditating, this appear'd
The likeliest course. The rams well-thriven were,
500 Thick-fleeced, full-sized, with wool of sable hue.
These, silently, with osier twigs on which
The Cyclops, hideous monster, slept, I bound,
Three in one leash; the intermediate rams
Bore each a man, whom the exterior two
Preserved, concealing him on either side.
Thus each was borne by three, and I, at last,
The curl'd back seizing of a ram, (for one
I had reserv'd far stateliest of them all)
Slipp'd underneath his belly, and both hands
510 Enfolding fast in his exub'rant fleece,
Clung ceaseless to him as I lay supine.
We, thus disposed, waited with many a sigh
The sacred dawn; but when, at length, aris'n,
Aurora, day-spring's daughter rosy-palm'd
Again appear'd, the males of all his flocks
Rush'd forth to pasture, and, meantime, unmilk'd,

The wethers bleated, by the load distress'd
Of udders overcharged. Their master, rack'd
With pain intolerable, handled yet
520 The backs of all, inquisitive, as they stood,
But, gross of intellect, suspicion none
Conceiv'd of men beneath their bodies bound.
And now (none left beside) the ram approach'd
With his own wool burthen'd, and with myself,
Whom many a fear molested. Polypheme
The giant stroak'd him as he sat, and said,
My darling ram! why latest of the flock
Com'st thou, whom never, heretofore, my sheep
Could leave behind, but stalking at their head,
530 Thou first was wont to crop the tender grass,
First to arrive at the clear stream, and first
With ready will to seek my sheep-cote here
At evening; but, thy practice chang'd, thou com'st,
Now last of all. Feel'st thou regret, my ram!
Of thy poor master's eye, by a vile wretch
Bored out, who overcame me first with wine,
And by a crew of vagabonds accurs'd,
Followers of Outis, whose escape from death
Shall not be made to-day? Ah! that thy heart
540 Were as my own, and that distinct as I
Thou could'st articulate, so should'st thou tell,
Where hidden, he eludes my furious wrath.
Then, dash'd against the floor his spatter'd brain
Should fly, and I should lighter feel my harm
From Outis, wretch base-named and nothing-worth.
So saying, he left him to pursue the flock.
When, thus drawn forth, we had, at length, escaped
Few paces from the cavern and the court,
First, quitting my own ram, I loos'd my friends,
550 Then, turning seaward many a thriven ewe
Sharp-hoof'd, we drove them swiftly to the ship.
Thrice welcome to our faithful friends we came
From death escaped, but much they mourn'd the dead.
I suffer'd not their tears, but silent shook
My brows, by signs commanding them to lift
The sheep on board, and instant plow the main.
They, quick embarking, on the benches sat
Well ranged, and thresh'd with oars the foamy flood;
But distant now such length as a loud voice
560 May reach, I hail'd with taunts the Cyclops' ear.
Cyclops! when thou devouredst in thy cave
With brutal force my followers, thou devour'dst
The followers of no timid Chief, or base,
Vengeance was sure to recompense that deed
Atrocious. Monster! who wast not afraid
To eat the guest shelter'd beneath thy roof!
Therefore the Gods have well requited thee.
I ended; he, exasp'rate, raged the more,
And rending from its hold a mountain-top,
570 Hurl'd it toward us; at our vessel's stern
Down came the mass, nigh sweeping in its fall
The rudder's head. The ocean at the plunge
Of that huge rock, high on its refluent flood
Heav'd, irresistible, the ship to land.
I seizing, quick, our longest pole on board,

---

[35] Outis, as a *name* could only denote him who bore it; but as a *noun*, it signifies *no man*, which accounts sufficiently for the ludicrous mistake of his brethren.

Back thrust her from the coast and by a nod
In silence given, bade my companions ply
Strenuous their oars, that so we might escape.
Procumbent,[36] each obey'd, and when, the flood
58 °Cleaving, we twice that distance had obtain'd,[37]
Again I hail'd the Cyclops; but my friends
Earnest dissuaded me on ev'ry side.
Ah, rash Ulysses! why with taunts provoke
The savage more, who hath this moment hurl'd
A weapon, such as heav'd the ship again
To land, where death seem'd certain to us all?
For had he heard a cry, or but the voice
Of one man speaking, he had all our heads
With some sharp rock, and all our timbers crush'd
590 Together, such vast force is in his arm.
So they, but my courageous heart remain'd
Unmoved, and thus again, incensed, I spake.
Cyclops! should any mortal man inquire
To whom thy shameful loss of sight thou ow'st,
Say, to Ulysses, city-waster Chief,
Laertes' son, native of Ithaca.
I ceas'd, and with a groan thus he replied.
Ah me! an antient oracle I feel
Accomplish'd. Here abode a prophet erst,
600 A man of noblest form, and in his art
Unrivall'd, Telemus Eurymedes.
He, prophesying to the Cyclops-race,
Grew old among us, and presaged my loss
Of sight, in future, by Ulysses' hand.
I therefore watch'd for the arrival here,
Always, of some great Chief, for stature, bulk
And beauty prais'd, and cloath'd with wond'rous might.
But now-a dwarf, a thing impalpable,
A shadow, overcame me first by wine,
610 Then quench'd my sight. Come hither, O my guest!
Return, Ulysses! hospitable cheer
Awaits thee, and my pray'rs I will prefer
To glorious Neptune for thy prosp'rous course;
For I am Neptune's offspring, and the God
Is proud to be my Sire; he, if he please,
And he alone can heal me; none beside
Of Pow'rs immortal, or of men below.
He spake, to whom I answer thus return'd.
I would that of thy life and soul amerced,
620 I could as sure dismiss thee down to Hell,
As none shall heal thine eye-not even He.

So I; then pray'd the Cyclops to his Sire
With hands uprais'd towards the starry heav'n.
Hear, Earth-encircler Neptune, azure-hair'd!
If I indeed am thine, and if thou boast
Thyself my father, grant that never more
Ulysses, leveller of hostile tow'rs,
Laertes' son, of Ithaca the fair,
Behold his native home! but if his fate
630 Decree him yet to see his friends, his house,
His native country, let him deep distress'd
Return and late, all his companions lost,
Indebted for a ship to foreign aid,
And let affliction meet him at his door.
He spake, and Ocean's sov'reign heard his pray'r.
Then lifting from the shore a stone of size
Far more enormous, o'er his head he whirl'd
The rock, and his immeasurable force
Exerting all, dismiss'd it. Close behind
640 The ship, nor distant from the rudder's head,
Down came the mass. The ocean at the plunge
Of such a weight, high on its refluent flood
Tumultuous, heaved the bark well nigh to land.
But when we reach'd the isle where we had left
Our num'rous barks, and where my people sat
Watching with ceaseless sorrow our return,
We thrust our vessel to the sandy shore,
Then disembark'd, and of the Cyclops' sheep
Gave equal share to all. To me alone
650 My fellow-voyagers the ram consign'd
In distribution, my peculiar meed.
Him, therefore, to cloud-girt Saturnian Jove
I offer'd on the shore, burning his thighs
In sacrifice; but Jove my hallow'd rites
Reck'd not, destruction purposing to all
My barks, and all my followers o'er the Deep.
Thus, feasting largely, on the shore we sat
Till even-tide, and quaffing gen'rous wine;
But when day fail'd, and night o'ershadow'd all,
660 Then, on the shore we slept; and when again
Aurora rosy daughter of the Dawn,
Look'd forth, my people, anxious, I enjoin'd
To climb their barks, and cast the hawsers loose.
They all obedient, took their seats on board
Well-ranged, and thresh'd with oars the foamy flood.
Thus, 'scaping narrowly, we roam'd the Deep
With aching hearts and with diminish'd crews.

---

[36] +propesontes+
---Olli certamine summo
Procumbunt.
VIRGIL
[37] The seeming incongruity of this line with line
560, is reconciled by supposing that Ulysses exerted his voice, naturally loud, in an extraordinary manner on this second occasion. See Clarke.

Book X

Ulysses, in pursuit of his narrative, relates his arrival at the island of Æolus, his departure thence, and the unhappy occasion of his return thither. The monarch of the winds dismisses him at last with much asperity. He next tells of his arrival among the Læstrygonians, by whom his whole fleet, together with their crews, are destroyed, his own ship and crew excepted. Thence he is driven to the island of Circe. By her the half of his people are transformed into swine. Assisted by Mercury, he resists her enchantments himself, and prevails with the Goddess to recover them to their former shape. In consequence of Circe's instructions, after having spent a complete year in her palace, he prepares for a voyage to the infernal regions.

We came to the Æolian isle; there dwells
Æolus, son of Hippotas, belov'd
By the Immortals, in an isle afloat.
A brazen wall impregnable on all sides
Girds it, and smooth its rocky coast ascends.
His children, in his own fair palace born,
Are twelve; six daughters, and six blooming sons.
He gave his daughters to his sons to wife;
They with their father hold perpetual feast
And with their royal mother, still supplied
10 With dainties numberless; the sounding dome
Is fill'd with sav'ry odours all the day,
And with their consorts chaste at night they sleep
On stateliest couches with rich arras spread.
Their city and their splendid courts we reach'd.
A month complete he, friendly, at his board
Regaled me, and enquiry made minute
Of Ilium's fall, of the Achaian fleet,
And of our voyage thence. I told him all.
But now, desirous to embark again,
20 I ask'd dismission home, which he approved,
And well provided for my prosp'rous course.
He gave me, furnish'd by a bullock slay'd
In his ninth year, a bag; ev'ry rude blast
Which from its bottom turns the Deep, that bag
Imprison'd held; for him Saturnian Jove
Hath officed arbiter of all the winds,
To rouse their force or calm them, at his will.
He gave me them on board my bark, so bound
With silver twine that not a breath escaped,
30 Then order'd gentle Zephyrus to fill
Our sails propitious. Order vain, alas!
So fatal proved the folly of my friends.
Nine days continual, night and day we sail'd,
And on the tenth my native land appear'd.
Not far remote my Ithacans I saw
Fires kindling on the coast; but me with toil
Worn, and with watching, gentle sleep subdued;
For constant I had ruled the helm, nor giv'n
That charge to any, fearful of delay.
40 Then, in close conference combined, my crew
Each other thus bespake-He carries home
Silver and gold from Æolus received,
Offspring of Hippotas, illustrious Chief-
And thus a mariner the rest harangued.
Ye Gods! what city or what land soe'er
Ulysses visits, how is he belov'd
By all, and honour'd! many precious spoils
He homeward bears from Troy; but we return,

(We who the self-same voyage have perform'd)
50 With empty hands. Now also he hath gain'd
This pledge of friendship from the King of winds.
But come-be quick-search we the bag, and learn
What stores of gold and silver it contains.
So he, whose mischievous advice prevailed.
They loos'd the bag; forth issued all the winds,
And, caught by tempests o'er the billowy waste,
Weeping they flew, far, far from Ithaca.
I then, awaking, in my noble mind
Stood doubtful, whether from my vessel's side
60 Immersed to perish in the flood, or calm
To endure my sorrows, and content to live.
I calm endured them; but around my head
Winding my mantle, lay'd me down below,
While adverse blasts bore all my fleet again
To the Æolian isle; then groan'd my people.
We disembark'd and drew fresh water there,
And my companions, at their galley's sides
All seated, took repast; short meal we made,
When, with an herald and a chosen friend,
70 I sought once more the hall of Æolus.
Him banqueting with all his sons we found,
And with his spouse; we ent'ring, on the floor
Of his wide portal sat, whom they amazed
Beheld, and of our coming thus enquired.
Return'd? Ulysses! by what adverse Pow'r
Repuls'd hast thou arrived? we sent thee hence
Well-fitted forth to reach thy native isle,
Thy palace, or what place soe'er thou would'st.
So they-to whom, heart-broken, I replied.
80 My worthless crew have wrong'd me, nor alone
My worthless crew, but sleep ill-timed, as much.
Yet heal, O friends, my hurt; the pow'r is yours!
So I their favour woo'd. Mute sat the sons,
But thus their father answer'd. Hence-be gone-
Leave this our isle, thou most obnoxious wretch
Of all mankind. I should, myself, transgress,
Receiving here, and giving conduct hence
To one detested by the Gods as thou.
Away-for hated by the Gods thou com'st.
90 So saying, he sent me from his palace forth,
Groaning profound; thence, therefore, o'er the Deep
We still proceeded sorrowful, our force
Exhausting ceaseless at the toilsome oar,
And, through our own imprudence, hopeless now
Of other furth'rance to our native isle.
Six days we navigated, day and night,
The briny flood, and on the seventh reach'd

The city erst by Lamus built sublime,
Proud Læstrygonia, with the distant gates.

100 The herdsman, there, driving his cattle home,[38]
Summons the shepherd with his flocks abroad.
The sleepless there might double wages earn,
Attending, now, the herds, now, tending sheep,
For the night-pastures, and the pastures grazed
By day, close border, both, the city-walls.
To that illustrious port we came, by rocks
Uninterrupted flank'd on either side
Of tow'ring height, while prominent the shores
And bold, converging at the haven's mouth
110 Leave narrow pass. We push'd our galleys in,
Then moor'd them side by side; for never surge
There lifts its head, or great or small, but clear
We found, and motionless, the shelter'd flood.
Myself alone, staying my bark without,
Secured her well with hawsers to a rock
At the land's point, then climb'd the rugged steep,
And spying stood the country. Labours none
Of men or oxen in the land appear'd,
Nor aught beside saw we, but from the earth
120 Smoke rising; therefore of my friends I sent
Before me two, adding an herald third,
To learn what race of men that country fed.
Departing, they an even track pursued
Made by the waggons bringing timber down
From the high mountains to the town below.
Before the town a virgin bearing forth
Her ew'r they met, daughter of him who ruled
The Læstrygonian race, Antiphatas.
Descending from the gate, she sought the fount
130 Artacia; for their custom was to draw
From that pure fountain for the city's use.
Approaching they accosted her, and ask'd
What King reign'd there, and over whom he reign'd.
She gave them soon to know where stood sublime
The palace of her Sire; no sooner they
The palace enter'd, than within they found,
In size resembling an huge mountain-top,
A woman, whom they shudder'd to behold.
She forth from council summon'd quick her spouse
140 Antiphatas, who teeming came with thoughts
Of carnage, and, arriving, seized at once
A Greecian, whom, next moment, he devoured.
With headlong terrour the surviving two
Fled to the ships. Then sent Antiphatas
His voice through all the town, and on all sides,
Hearing that cry, the Læstrygonians flock'd
Numberless, and in size resembling more
The giants than mankind. They from the rocks
Cast down into our fleet enormous stones,
150 A strong man's burthen each; dire din arose
Of shatter'd galleys and of dying men,
Whom spear'd like fishes to their home they bore,
A loathsome prey. While them within the port
They slaughter'd, I, (the faulchion at my side

Drawn forth) cut loose the hawser of my ship,
And all my crew enjoin'd with bosoms laid
Prone on their oars, to fly the threaten'd woe.
They, dreading instant death tugg'd resupine
Together, and the galley from beneath
160 Those beetling[39] rocks into the open sea
Shot gladly; but the rest all perish'd there.
Proceeding thence, we sigh'd, and roamed the waves,
Glad that we lived, but sorrowing for the slain.
We came to the Ææan isle; there dwelt
The awful Circe, Goddess amber-hair'd,
Deep-skill'd in magic song, sister by birth
Of the all-wise Æætes; them the Sun,
Bright luminary of the world, begat
On Perse, daughter of Oceanus.
170 Our vessel there, noiseless, we push'd to land
Within a spacious haven, thither led
By some celestial Pow'r. We disembark'd,
And on the coast two days and nights entire
Extended lay, worn with long toil, and each
The victim of his heart-devouring woes.
Then, with my spear and with my faulchion arm'd,
I left the ship to climb with hasty steps
An airy height, thence, hoping to espie
Some works of man, or hear, perchance, a voice.
180 Exalted on a rough rock's craggy point
I stood, and on the distant plain, beheld
Smoke which from Circe's palace through the gloom
Of trees and thickets rose. That smoke discern'd,
I ponder'd next if thither I should haste,
Seeking intelligence. Long time I mused,
But chose at last, as my discreter course,
To seek the sea-beach and my bark again,
And, when my crew had eaten, to dispatch
Before me, others, who should first enquire.
190 But, ere I yet had reach'd my gallant bark,
Some God with pity viewing me alone
In that untrodden solitude, sent forth
An antler'd stag, full-sized, into my path.
His woodland pastures left, he sought the stream,
For he was thirsty, and already parch'd
By the sun's heat. Him issuing from his haunt,
Sheer through the back beneath his middle spine,
I wounded, and the lance sprang forth beyond.
Moaning he fell, and in the dust expired.
200 Then, treading on his breathless trunk, I pluck'd
My weapon forth, which leaving there reclined,
I tore away the osiers with my hands
And fallows green, and to a fathom's length
Twisting the gather'd twigs into a band,
Bound fast the feet of my enormous prey,
And, flinging him athwart my neck, repair'd
Toward my sable bark, propp'd on my lance,
Which now to carry shoulder'd as before
Surpass'd my pow'r, so bulky was the load.
210 Arriving at the ship, there I let fall
My burthen, and with pleasant speech and kind,

---

[38] It is supposed by Eustathius that the pastures being infested by gad flies and other noxious insects in the day-time, they drove their sheep a-field in the morning, which by their wool were defended from them, and their cattle in the evening, when the insects had withdrawn. It is one of the few passages in Homer that must lie at the mercy of conjecture.

[39] The word has the authority of Shakspeare, and signifies overhanging.

Man after man addressing, cheer'd my crew.
My friends! we suffer much, but shall not seek
The shades, ere yet our destined hour arrive.
Behold a feast! and we have wine on board-
Pine not with needless famine! rise and eat.
I spake; they readily obey'd, and each
Issuing at my word abroad, beside
The galley stood, admiring, as he lay,
220 The stag, for of no common bulk was he.
At length, their eyes gratified to the full
With that glad spectacle, they laved their hands,
And preparation made of noble cheer.
That day complete, till set of sun, we spent
Feasting deliciously without restraint,
And quaffing generous wine; but when the sun
Went down, and darkness overshadow'd all,
Extended, then, on Ocean's bank we lay;
And when Aurora, daughter of the dawn,
230 Look'd rosy forth, convening all my crew
To council, I arose, and thus began.
My fellow-voyagers, however worn
With num'rous hardships, hear! for neither West
Know ye, nor East, where rises, or where sets
The all-enlight'ning sun. But let us think,
If thought perchance may profit us, of which
Small hope I see; for when I lately climb'd
Yon craggy rock, plainly I could discern
The land encompass'd by the boundless Deep.
240 The isle is flat, and in the midst I saw
Dun smoke ascending from an oaken bow'r.
So I, whom hearing, they all courage lost,
And at remembrance of Antiphatas
The Læstrygonian, and the Cyclops' deeds,
Ferocious feeder on the flesh of man,
Mourn'd loud and wept, but tears could nought avail.
Then numb'ring man by man, I parted them
In equal portions, and assign'd a Chief
To either band, myself to these, to those
250 Godlike Eurylochus. This done, we cast
The lots into the helmet, and at once
Forth sprang the lot of bold Eurylochus.
He went, and with him of my people march'd
Twenty and two, all weeping; nor ourselves
Wept less, at separation from our friends.
Low in a vale, but on an open spot,
They found the splendid house of Circe, built
With hewn and polish'd stones; compass'd she dwelt
By lions on all sides and mountain-wolves
260 Tamed by herself with drugs of noxious pow'rs.
Nor were they mischievous, but as my friends
Approach'd, arising on their hinder feet,
Paw'd them in blandishment, and wagg'd the tail.
As, when from feast he rises, dogs around
Their master fawn, accustom'd to receive
The sop conciliatory from his hand,
Around my people, so, those talon'd wolves
And lions fawn'd. They, terrified, that troop
Of savage monsters horrible beheld.
270 And now, before the Goddess' gates arrived,
They heard the voice of Circe singing sweet
Within, while, busied at the loom, she wove
An ample web immortal, such a work

Transparent, graceful, and of bright design
As hands of Goddesses alone produce.
Thus then Polites, Prince of men, the friend
Highest in my esteem, the rest bespake.
Ye hear the voice, comrades, of one who weaves
An ample web within, and at her task
280 So sweetly chaunts that all the marble floor
Re-echoes; human be she or divine
I doubt, but let us call, that we may learn.
He ceas'd; they call'd; soon issuing at the sound,
The Goddess open'd wide her splendid gates,
And bade them in; they, heedless, all complied,
All save Eurylochus, who fear'd a snare.
She, introducing them, conducted each
To a bright throne, then gave them Pramnian wine,
With grated cheese, pure meal, and honey new,
290 But medicated with her pois'nous drugs
Their food, that in oblivion they might lose
The wish of home. She gave them, and they drank,-
When, smiting each with her enchanting wand,
She shut them in her sties. In head, in voice,
In body, and in bristles they became
All swine, yet intellected as before,
And at her hand were dieted alone
With acorns, chestnuts, and the cornel-fruit,
Food grateful ever to the grovelling swine.
300 Back flew Eurylochus toward the ship,
To tell the woeful tale; struggling to speak,
Yet speechless, there he stood, his heart transfixt
With anguish, and his eyes deluged with tears.
Me boding terrours occupied. At length,
When, gazing on him, all had oft enquired,
He thus rehearsed to us the dreadful change.
Renown'd Ulysses! as thou bad'st, we went
Through yonder oaks; there, bosom'd in a vale,
But built conspicuous on a swelling knoll
310 With polish'd rock, we found a stately dome.
Within, some Goddess or some woman wove
An ample web, carolling sweet the while.
They call'd aloud; she, issuing at the voice,
Unfolded, soon, her splendid portals wide,
And bade them in. Heedless they enter'd, all,
But I remain'd, suspicious of a snare.
Ere long the whole band vanish'd, none I saw
Thenceforth, though, seated there, long time I watch'd.
He ended; I my studded faulchion huge
320 Athwart my shoulder cast, and seized my bow,
Then bade him lead me thither by the way
Himself had gone; but with both hands my knees
He clasp'd, and in wing'd accents sad exclaim'd.
My King! ah lead me not unwilling back,
But leave me here; for confident I judge
That neither thou wilt bring another thence,
Nor come thyself again. Haste-fly we swift
With these, for we, at least, may yet escape.
So he, to whom this answer I return'd.
330 Eurylochus! abiding here, eat thou
And drink thy fill beside the sable bark;
I go; necessity forbids my stay.
So saying, I left the galley and the shore.
But ere that awful vale ent'ring, I reach'd
The palace of the sorceress, a God

Met me, the bearer of the golden wand,
Hermes. He seem'd a stripling in his prime,
His cheeks cloath'd only with their earliest down,
For youth is then most graceful; fast he lock'd
340 His hand in mine, and thus, familiar, spake.
Unhappy! whither, wand'ring o'er the hills,
Stranger to all this region, and alone,
Go'st thou? Thy people-they within the walls
Are shut of Circe, where as swine close-pent
She keeps them. Comest thou to set them free?
I tell thee, never wilt thou thence return
Thyself, but wilt be prison'd with the rest.
Yet hearken-I will disappoint her wiles,
And will preserve thee. Take this precious drug;
350 Possessing this, enter the Goddess' house
Boldly, for it shall save thy life from harm.
Lo! I reveal to thee the cruel arts
Of Circe; learn them. She will mix for thee
A potion, and will also drug thy food
With noxious herbs; but she shall not prevail
By all her pow'r to change thee; for the force
Superior of this noble plant, my gift,
Shall baffle her. Hear still what I advise.
When she shall smite thee with her slender rod,
360 With faulchion drawn and with death-threat'ning looks
Rush on her; she will bid thee to her bed
Affrighted; then beware. Decline not thou
Her love, that she may both release thy friends,
And may with kindness entertain thyself.
But force her swear the dreaded oath of heav'n
That she will other mischief none devise
Against thee, lest she strip thee of thy might,
And, quenching all thy virtue, make thee vile.
So spake the Argicide, and from the earth
370 That plant extracting, placed it in my hand,
Then taught me all its pow'rs. Black was the root,
Milk-white the blossom; Moly is its name
In heav'n; not easily by mortal man
Dug forth, but all is easy to the Gods.
Then, Hermes through the island-woods repair'd
To heav'n, and I to Circe's dread abode,
In gloomy musings busied as I went.
Within the vestibule arrived, where dwelt
The beauteous Goddess, staying there my steps,
380 I call'd aloud; she heard me, and at once
Issuing, threw her splendid portals wide,
And bade me in. I follow'd, heart-distress'd.
Leading me by the hand to a bright throne
With argent studs embellish'd, and beneath
Footstool'd magnificent, she made me sit.
Then mingling for me in a golden cup
My bev'rage, she infused a drug, intent
On mischief; but when I had drunk the draught
Unchanged, she smote me with her wand, and said.
390 Hence-seek the sty. There wallow with thy friends.
She spake; I drawing from beside my thigh
My faulchion keen, with death-denouncing looks
Rush'd on her; she with a shrill scream of fear
Ran under my rais'd arm, seized fast my knees,
And in wing'd accents plaintive thus began.
Who? whence? thy city and thy birth declare.
Amazed I see thee with that potion drench'd,

Yet uninchanted; never man before
Once pass'd it through his lips, and liv'd the same;
400 But in thy breast a mind inhabits, proof
Against all charms. Come then-I know thee well.
Thou art Ulysses artifice-renown'd,
Of whose arrival here in his return
From Ilium, Hermes of the golden wand
Was ever wont to tell me. Sheath again
Thy sword, and let us, on my bed reclined,
Mutual embrace, that we may trust thenceforth
Each other, without jealousy or fear.
The Goddess spake, to whom I thus replied.
410 O Circe! canst thou bid me meek become
And gentle, who beneath thy roof detain'st
My fellow-voyagers transform'd to swine?
And, fearing my escape, invit'st thou me
Into thy bed, with fraudulent pretext
Of love, that there, enfeebling by thy arts
My noble spirit, thou may'st make me vile?
No-trust me-never will I share thy bed
Till first, O Goddess, thou consent to swear
The dread all-binding oath, that other harm
420 Against myself thou wilt imagine none.
I spake. She swearing as I bade, renounced
All evil purpose, and (her solemn oath
Concluded) I ascended, next, her bed
Magnificent. Meantime, four graceful nymphs
Attended on the service of the house,
Her menials, from the fountains sprung and groves,
And from the sacred streams that seek the sea.
Of these, one cast fine linen on the thrones,
Which, next, with purple arras rich she spread;
430 Another placed before the gorgeous seats
Bright tables, and set on baskets of gold.
The third, an argent beaker fill'd with wine
Delicious, which in golden cups she served;
The fourth brought water, which she warm'd within
An ample vase, and when the simm'ring flood
Sang in the tripod, led me to a bath,
And laved me with the pleasant stream profuse
Pour'd o'er my neck and body, till my limbs
Refresh'd, all sense of lassitude resign'd.
440 When she had bathed me, and with limpid oil
Anointed me, and cloathed me in a vest
And mantle, next, she led me to a throne
Of royal state, with silver studs emboss'd,
And footstool'd soft beneath; then came a nymph
With golden ewer charged and silver bowl,
Who pour'd pure water on my hands, and placed
The polish'd board before me, which with food
Various, selected from her present stores,
The cat'ress spread, then, courteous, bade me eat.
450 But me it pleas'd not; with far other thoughts
My spirit teem'd, on vengeance more intent.
Soon, then, as Circe mark'd me on my seat
Fast-rooted, sullen, nor with outstretch'd hands
Deigning to touch the banquet, she approach'd,
And in wing'd accents suasive thus began.
Why sits Ulysses like the Dumb, dark thoughts
His only food? loaths he the touch of meat,
And taste of wine? Thou fear'st, as I perceive,
Some other snare, but idle is that fear,

460 For I have sworn the inviolable oath.
She ceas'd, to whom this answer I return'd.
How can I eat? what virtuous man and just,
O Circe! could endure the taste of wine
Or food, till he should see his prison'd friends
Once more at liberty? If then thy wish
That I should eat and drink be true, produce
My captive people; let us meet again.
So I; then Circe, bearing in her hand
Her potent rod, went forth, and op'ning wide
470 The door, drove out my people from the sty,
In bulk resembling brawns of the ninth year.
They stood before me; she through all the herd
Proceeding, with an unctuous antidote
Anointed each, and at the wholesome touch
All shed the swinish bristles by the drug
Dread Circe's former magic gift, produced.
Restored at once to manhood, they appear'd
More vig'rous far, and sightlier than before.
They knew me, and with grasp affectionate
480 Hung on my hand. Tears follow'd, but of joy,
And with loud cries the vaulted palace rang.
Even the awful Goddess felt, herself,
Compassion, and, approaching me, began.
Laertes' noble son, for wiles renown'd!
Hence to the shore, and to thy gallant bark;
First, hale her safe aground, then, hiding all
Your arms and treasures in the caverns, come
Thyself again, and hither lead thy friends.
So spake the Goddess, and my gen'rous mind
490 Persuaded; thence repairing to the beach,
I sought my ship; arrived, I found my crew
Lamenting miserably, and their cheeks
With tears bedewing ceaseless at her side.
As when the calves within some village rear'd
Behold, at eve, the herd returning home
From fruitful meads where they have grazed their fill,
No longer in the stalls contain'd, they rush
With many a frisk abroad, and, blaring oft,
With one consent, all dance their dams around,
500 So they, at sight of me, dissolved in tears
Of rapt'rous joy, and each his spirit felt
With like affections warm'd as he had reach'd
Just then his country, and his city seen,
Fair Ithaca, where he was born and rear'd.
Then in wing'd accents tender thus they spake.
Noble Ulysses! thy appearance fills
Our soul with transports, such as we should feel
Arrived in safety on our native shore.
Speak-say how perish'd our unhappy friends?
510 So they; to whom this answer mild I gave.
Hale we our vessel first ashore, and hide
In caverns all our treasures and our arms,
Then, hasting hence, follow me, and ere long
Ye shall behold your friends, beneath the roof
Of Circe banqueting and drinking wine
Abundant, for no dearth attends them there.
So I; whom all with readiness obey'd,
All save Eurylochus; he sought alone
To stay the rest, and, eager, interposed.
520 Ah whither tend we, miserable men?
Why covet ye this evil, to go down

To Circe's palace? she will change us all
To lions, wolves or swine, that we may guard
Her palace, by necessity constrain'd.
So some were pris'ners of the Cyclops erst,
When, led by rash Ulysses, our lost friends
Intruded needlessly into his cave,
And perish'd by the folly of their Chief.
He spake, whom hearing, occupied I stood
530 In self-debate, whether, my faulchion keen
Forth-drawing from beside my sturdy thigh,
To tumble his lopp'd head into the dust,
Although he were my kinsman in the bonds
Of close affinity; but all my friends
As with one voice, thus gently interposed.
Noble Ulysses! we will leave him here
Our vessel's guard, if such be thy command,
But us lead thou to Circe's dread abode.
So saying, they left the galley, and set forth
54 °Climbing the coast; nor would Eurylochus
Beside the hollow bark remain, but join'd
His comrades by my dreadful menace awed.
Meantime the Goddess, busily employ'd,
Bathed and refresh'd my friends with limpid oil,
And clothed them. We, arriving, found them all
Banqueting in the palace; there they met;
These ask'd, and those rehearsed the wond'rous tale,
And, the recital made, all wept aloud
Till the wide dome resounded. Then approach'd
550 The graceful Goddess, and address'd me thus.
Laertes' noble son, for wiles renown'd!
Provoke ye not each other, now, to tears.
I am not ignorant, myself, how dread
Have been your woes both on the fishy Deep,
And on the land by force of hostile pow'rs.
But come-Eat now, and drink ye wine, that so
Your freshen'd spirit may revive, and ye
Courageous grow again, as when ye left
The rugged shores of Ithaca, your home.
560 For now, through recollection, day by day,
Of all your pains and toils, ye are become
Spiritless, strengthless, and the taste forget
Of pleasure, such have been your num'rous woes.
She spake, whose invitation kind prevail'd,
And won us to her will. There, then, we dwelt
The year complete, fed with delicious fare
Day after day, and quaffing gen'rous wine.
But when (the year fulfill'd) the circling hours
Their course resumed, and the successive months
570 With all their tedious days were spent, my friends,
Summoning me abroad, thus greeted me.
Sir! recollect thy country, if indeed
The fates ordain thee to revisit safe
That country, and thy own glorious abode.
So they; whose admonition I receiv'd
Well-pleas'd. Then, all the day, regaled we sat
At Circe's board with sav'ry viands rare,
And quaffing richest wine; but when, the sun
Declining, darkness overshadow'd all,
580 Then, each within the dusky palace took
Custom'd repose, and to the Goddess' bed
Magnificent ascending, there I urged
My earnest suit, which gracious she receiv'd,

And in wing'd accents earnest thus I spake.
O Circe! let us prove thy promise true;
Dismiss us hence. My own desires, at length,
Tend homeward vehement, and the desires
No less of all my friends, who with complaints
Unheard by thee, wear my sad heart away.
590 So I; to whom the Goddess in return.
Laertes' noble son, Ulysses famed
For deepest wisdom! dwell not longer here,
Thou and thy followers, in my abode
Reluctant; but your next must be a course
Far diff'rent; hence departing, ye must seek
The dreary house of Ades and of dread
Persephone there to consult the Seer
Theban Tiresias, prophet blind, but blest
With faculties which death itself hath spared.
600 To him alone, of all the dead, Hell's Queen
Gives still to prophesy, while others flit
Mere forms, the shadows of what once they were.
She spake, and by her words dash'd from my soul
All courage; weeping on the bed I sat,
Reckless of life and of the light of day.
But when, with tears and rolling to and fro
Satiate, I felt relief, thus I replied.
O Circe! with what guide shall I perform
This voyage, unperform'd by living man?
610 I spake, to whom the Goddess quick replied.
Brave Laertiades! let not the fear
To want a guide distress thee. Once on board,
Your mast erected, and your canvas white
Unfurl'd, sit thou; the breathing North shall waft
Thy vessel on. But when ye shall have cross'd
The broad expanse of Ocean, and shall reach
The oozy shore, where grow the poplar groves
And fruitless willows wan of Proserpine,
Push thither through the gulphy Deep thy bark,
620 And, landing, haste to Pluto's murky abode.
There, into Acheron runs not alone
Dread Pyriphlegethon, but Cocytus loud,
From Styx derived; there also stands a rock,
At whose broad base the roaring rivers meet.
There, thrusting, as I bid, thy bark ashore,
O Hero! scoop the soil, op'ning a trench
Ell-broad on ev'ry side; then pour around
Libation consecrate to all the dead,
First, milk with honey mixt, then luscious wine,
630 Then water, sprinkling, last, meal over all.
Next, supplicate the unsubstantial forms
Fervently of the dead, vowing to slay,
(Return'd to Ithaca) in thy own house,
An heifer barren yet, fairest and best
Of all thy herds, and to enrich the pile
With delicacies such as please the shades;
But, in peculiar, to Tiresias vow
A sable ram, noblest of all thy flocks.
When thus thou hast propitiated with pray'r
640 All the illustrious nations of the dead,

Next, thou shalt sacrifice to them a ram
And sable ewe, turning the face of each
Right toward Erebus, and look thyself,
Meantime, askance toward the river's course.
Souls num'rous, soon, of the departed dead
Will thither flock; then, strenuous urge thy friends,
Flaying the victims which thy ruthless steel
Hath slain, to burn them, and to sooth by pray'r
Illustrious Pluto and dread Proserpine.
650 While thus is done, thou seated at the foss,
Faulchion in hand, chace thence the airy forms
Afar, nor suffer them to approach the blood,
Till with Tiresias thou have first conferr'd.
Then, glorious Chief! the Prophet shall himself
Appear, who will instruct thee, and thy course
Delineate, measuring from place to place
Thy whole return athwart the fishy flood.
While thus she spake, the golden dawn arose,
When, putting on me my attire, the nymph
660 Next, cloath'd herself, and girding to her waist
With an embroider'd zone her snowy robe
Graceful, redundant, veil'd her beauteous head.
Then, ranging the wide palace, I aroused
My followers, standing at the side of each-
Up! sleep no longer! let us quick depart,
For thus the Goddess hath, herself, advised.
So I, whose early summons my brave friends
With readiness obey'd. Yet even thence
I brought not all my crew. There was a youth,
670 Youngest of all my train, Elpenor; one
Not much in estimation for desert
In arms, nor prompt in understanding more,
Who overcharged with wine, and covetous
Of cooler air, high on the palace-roof
Of Circe slept, apart from all the rest.
Awaken'd by the clamour of his friends
Newly arisen, he also sprang to rise,
And in his haste, forgetful where to find
The deep-descending stairs, plunged through the roof.
680 With neck-bone broken from the vertebræ
Outstretch'd he lay; his spirit sought the shades.
Then, thus to my assembling friends I spake.
Ye think, I doubt not, of an homeward course,
But Circe points me to the drear abode
Of Proserpine and Pluto, to consult
The spirit of Tiresias, Theban seer.
I ended, and the hearts of all alike
Felt consternation; on the earth they sat
Disconsolate, and plucking each his hair,
690 Yet profit none of all their sorrow found.
But while we sought my galley on the beach
With tepid tears bedewing, as we went,
Our cheeks, meantime the Goddess to the shore
Descending, bound within the bark a ram
And sable ewe, passing us unperceived.
For who hath eyes that can discern a God
Going or coming, if he shun the view?

Book XI

Ulysses relates to Alcinoüs his voyage to the infernal regions, his conference there with the prophet Tiresias concerning his return to Ithaca, and gives him an account of the heroes, heroines, and others whom he saw there.

Arriving on the shore, and launching, first,
Our bark into the sacred Deep, we set
Our mast and sails, and stow'd secure on board
The ram and ewe, then, weeping, and with hearts
Sad and disconsolate, embark'd ourselves.
And now, melodious Circe, nymph divine,
Sent after us a canvas-stretching breeze,
Pleasant companion of our course, and we
(The decks and benches clear'd) untoiling sat,
While managed gales sped swift the bark along.
10 All day, with sails distended, e'er the Deep
She flew, and when the sun, at length, declined,
And twilight dim had shadow'd all the ways,
Approach'd the bourn of Ocean's vast profound.
The city, there, of the Cimmerians stands
With clouds and darkness veil'd, on whom the sun
Deigns not to look with his beam-darting eye,
Or when he climbs the starry arch, or when

Earthward he slopes again his west'ring wheels,[40]
But sad night canopies the woeful race.
20 We haled the bark aground, and, landing there
The ram and sable ewe, journey'd beside
The Deep, till we arrived where Circe bade.
Here, Perimedes' son Eurylochus
Held fast the destined sacrifice, while I
Scoop'd with my sword the soil, op'ning a trench
Ell-broad on ev'ry side, then pour'd around
Libation consecrate to all the dead,
First, milk with honey mixt, then luscious wine,
Then water, sprinkling, last, meal over all.
30 This done, adoring the unreal forms
And shadows of the dead, I vow'd to slay,
(Return'd to Ithaca) in my own abode,
An heifer barren yet, fairest and best
Of all my herds, and to enrich the pile
With delicacies, such as please the shades.
But, in peculiar, to the Theban seer
I vow'd a sable ram, largest and best
Of all my flocks. When thus I had implored
With vows and pray'r, the nations of the dead,
40 Piercing the victims next, I turn'd them both
To bleed into the trench; then swarming came
From Erebus the shades of the deceased,
Brides, youths unwedded, seniors long with woe
Oppress'd, and tender girls yet new to grief.
Came also many a warrior by the spear
In battle pierced, with armour gore-distain'd,
And all the multitude around the foss
Stalk'd shrieking dreadful; me pale horror seized.
I next, importunate, my people urged,

50 Flaying the victims which myself had slain,
To burn them, and to supplicate in pray'r
Illustrious Pluto and dread Proserpine.
Then down I sat, and with drawn faulchion chased
The ghosts, nor suffer'd them to approach the blood,
Till with Tiresias I should first confer.
The spirit, first, of my companion came,
Elpenor; for no burial honours yet
Had he received, but we had left his corse
In Circe's palace, tombless, undeplored,
60 Ourselves by pressure urged of other cares.
Touch'd with compassion seeing him, I wept,
And in wing'd accents brief him thus bespake.
Elpenor! how cam'st thou into the realms
Of darkness? Hast thou, though on foot, so far
Outstripp'd my speed, who in my bark arrived?
So I, to whom with tears he thus replied.
Laertes' noble son, for wiles renown'd!
Fool'd by some dæmon and the intemp'rate bowl,
I perish'd in the house of Circe; there
70 The deep-descending steps heedless I miss'd,
And fell precipitated from the roof.
With neck-bone broken from the vertebræ
Outstretch'd I lay; my spirit sought the shades.
But now, by those whom thou hast left at home,
By thy Penelope, and by thy fire,
The gentle nourisher of thy infant growth,
And by thy only son Telemachus
I make my suit to thee. For, sure, I know
That from the house of Pluto safe return'd,
80 Thou shalt ere long thy gallant vessel moor
At the Ææan isle. Ah! there arrived
Remember me. Leave me not undeplored
Nor uninhumed, lest, for my sake, the Gods
In vengeance visit thee; but with my arms
(What arms soe'er I left) burn me, and raise
A kind memorial of me on the coast,
Heap'd high with earth; that an unhappy man
May yet enjoy an unforgotten name.
Thus do at my request, and on my hill
90 Funereal, plant the oar with which I row'd,
While yet I lived a mariner of thine.
He spake, to whom thus answer I return'd.
Poor youth! I will perform thy whole desire.
Thus we, there sitting, doleful converse held,
With outstretch'd faulchion, I, guarding the blood,
And my companion's shadowy semblance sad
Meantime discoursing me on various themes.
The soul of my departed mother, next,
Of Anticleia came, daughter of brave

---

[40] Milton.

62

100 Autolycus; whom, when I sought the shores
Of Ilium, I had living left at home.
Seeing her, with compassion touch'd, I wept,
Yet even her, (although it pain'd my soul)
Forbad, relentless, to approach the blood,
Till with Tiresias I should first confer.
Then came the spirit of the Theban seer
Himself, his golden sceptre in his hand,
Who knew me, and, enquiring, thus began.
Why, hapless Chief! leaving the cheerful day,
110 Arriv'st thou to behold the dead, and this
Unpleasant land? but, from the trench awhile
Receding, turn thy faulchion keen away,
That I may drink the blood, and tell thee truth.
He spake; I thence receding, deep infix'd
My sword bright-studded in the sheath again.
The noble prophet then, approaching, drank
The blood, and, satisfied, address'd me thus.
Thou seek'st a pleasant voyage home again,
Renown'd Ulysses! but a God will make
120 That voyage difficult; for, as I judge,
Thou wilt not pass by Neptune unperceiv'd,
Whose anger follows thee, for that thou hast
Deprived his son Cyclops of his eye.
At length, however, after num'rous woes
Endur'd, thou may'st attain thy native isle,
If thy own appetite thou wilt controul
And theirs who follow thee, what time thy bark
Well-built, shall at Thrinacia's shore arrive,[41]
Escaped from perils of the gloomy Deep.
130 There shall ye find grazing the flocks and herds
Of the all-seeing and all-hearing Sun,
Which, if attentive to thy safe return,
Thou leave unharm'd, though after num'rous woes,
Ye may at length arrive in Ithaca.
But if thou violate them, I denounce
Destruction on thy ship and all thy band,
And though thyself escape, late shalt thou reach
Thy home and hard-bested,[42] in a strange bark,
All thy companions lost; trouble beside
140 Awaits thee there, for thou shalt find within
Proud suitors of thy noble wife, who waste
Thy substance, and with promis'd spousal gifts
Ceaseless solicit her to wed; yet well
Shalt thou avenge all their injurious deeds.
That once perform'd, and ev'ry suitor slain
Either by stratagem, or face to face,
In thy own palace, bearing, as thou go'st,
A shapely oar, journey, till thou hast found
A people who the sea know not, nor eat
150 Food salted; they trim galley crimson prow'd
Have ne'er beheld, nor yet smooth-shaven oar,
With which the vessel wing'd scuds o'er the waves.
Well thou shalt know them; this shall be the sign-
When thou shalt meet a trav'ler, who shall name
The oar on thy broad shoulder borne, a van,[43]
There, deep infixing it within the soil,

Worship the King of Ocean with a bull,
A ram, and a lascivious boar, then seek
Thy home again, and sacrifice at home
160 An hecatomb to the Immortal Gods,
Adoring each duly, and in his course.
So shalt thou die in peace a gentle death,
Remote from Ocean; it shall find thee late,
In soft serenity of age, the Chief
Of a blest people.-I have told thee truth.
He spake, to whom I answer thus return'd.
Tiresias! thou, I doubt not, hast reveal'd
The ordinance of heav'n. But tell me, Seer!
And truly. I behold my mother's shade;
170 Silent she sits beside the blood, nor word
Nor even look vouchsafes to her own son.
How shall she learn, prophet, that I am her's?
So I, to whom Tiresias quick replied.
The course is easy. Learn it, taught by me.
What shade soe'er, by leave of thee obtain'd,
Shall taste the blood, that shade will tell thee truth;
The rest, prohibited, will all retire.
When thus the spirit of the royal Seer
Had his prophetic mind reveal'd, again
180 He enter'd Pluto's gates; but I unmoved
Still waited till my mother's shade approach'd;
She drank the blood, then knew me, and in words
Wing'd with affection, plaintive, thus began.
My son! how hast thou enter'd, still alive,
This darksome region? Difficult it is
For living man to view the realms of death.
Broad rivers roll, and awful floods between,
But chief, the Ocean, which to pass on foot,
Or without ship, impossible is found.
190 Hast thou, long wand'ring in thy voyage home
From Ilium, with thy ship and crew arrived,
Ithaca and thy consort yet unseen?
She spake, to whom this answer I return'd.
My mother! me necessity constrain'd
To Pluto's dwelling, anxious to consult
Theban Tiresias; for I have not yet
Approach'd Achaia, nor have touch'd the shore
Of Ithaca, but suff'ring ceaseless woe
Have roam'd, since first in Agamemnon's train
200 I went to combat with the sons of Troy.
But speak, my mother, and the truth alone;
What stroke of fate slew *thee*? Fell'st thou a prey
To some slow malady? or by the shafts
Of gentle Dian suddenly subdued?
Speak to me also of my ancient Sire,
And of Telemachus, whom I left at home;
Possess I still unalienate and safe
My property, or hath some happier Chief
Admittance free into my fortunes gain'd,
210 No hope subsisting more of my return?
The mind and purpose of my wedded wife
Declare thou also. Dwells she with our son
Faithful to my domestic interests,

---

[41] The shore of Scilly commonly called Trinacria, but *Euphonicè* by Homer, Thrinacia.

[42] The expression is used by Milton, and signifies-Beset with many difficulties.

[43] Mistaking the oar for a corn-van. A sure indication of his ignorance of maritime concerns.

Or is she wedded to some Chief of Greece?
I ceas'd, when thus the venerable shade.
Not so; she faithful still and patient dwells
Thy roof beneath; but all her days and nights
Devoting sad to anguish and to tears.
Thy fortunes still are thine; Telemachus
22 °Cultivates, undisturb'd, thy land, and sits
At many a noble banquet, such as well
Beseems the splendour of his princely state,
For all invite him; at his farm retired
Thy father dwells, nor to the city comes,
For aught; nor bed, nor furniture of bed,
Furr'd cloaks or splendid arras he enjoys,
But, with his servile hinds all winter sleeps
In ashes and in dust at the hearth-side,
Coarsely attired; again, when summer comes,
230 Or genial autumn, on the fallen leaves
In any nook, not curious where, he finds
There, stretch'd forlorn, nourishing grief, he weeps
Thy lot, enfeebled now by num'rous years.
So perish'd I; such fate I also found;
Me, neither the right-aiming arch'ress struck,
Diana, with her gentle shafts, nor me
Distemper slew, my limbs by slow degrees
But sure, bereaving of their little life,
240 But long regret, tender solicitude,
And recollection of thy kindness past,
These, my Ulysses! fatal proved to me.
She said; I, ardent wish'd to clasp the shade
Of my departed mother; thrice I sprang
Toward her, by desire impetuous urged,
And thrice she flitted from between my arms,
Light as a passing shadow or a dream.
Then, pierced by keener grief, in accents wing'd
With filial earnestness I thus replied.
250 My mother, why elud'st thou my attempt
To clasp thee, that ev'n here, in Pluto's realm,
We might to full satiety indulge
Our grief, enfolded in each other's arms?
Hath Proserpine, alas! only dispatch'd
A shadow to me, to augment my woe?
Then, instant, thus the venerable form.
Ah, son! thou most afflicted of mankind!
On thee, Jove's daughter, Proserpine, obtrudes
No airy semblance vain; but such the state
260 And nature is of mortals once deceased.
For they nor muscle have, nor flesh, nor bone;
All those (the spirit from the body once
Divorced) the violence of fire consumes,
And, like a dream, the soul flies swift away.
But haste thou back to light, and, taught thyself
These sacred truths, hereafter teach thy spouse.
Thus mutual we conferr'd. Then, thither came,
Encouraged forth by royal Proserpine,
Shades female num'rous, all who consorts, erst,
270 Or daughters were of mighty Chiefs renown'd.
About the sable blood frequent they swarm'd.
But I, consid'ring sat, how I might each
Interrogate, and thus resolv'd. My sword
Forth drawing from beside my sturdy thigh,

Firm I prohibited the ghosts to drink
The blood together; they successive came;
Each told her own distress; I question'd all.
There, first, the high-born Tyro I beheld;
She claim'd Salmoneus as her sire, and wife
280 Was once of Cretheus, son of Æolus.
Enamour'd of Enipeus, stream divine,
Loveliest of all that water earth, beside
His limpid current she was wont to stray,
When Ocean's God, (Enipeus' form assumed)
Within the eddy-whirling river's mouth
Embraced her; there, while the o'er-arching flood,
Uplifted mountainous, conceal'd the God
And his fair human bride, her virgin zone
He loos'd, and o'er her eyes sweet sleep diffused.
290 His am'rous purpose satisfied, he grasp'd
Her hand, affectionate, and thus he said.
Rejoice in this my love, and when the year
Shall tend to consummation of its course,
Thou shalt produce illustrious twins, for love
Immortal never is unfruitful love.
Rear them with all a mother's care; meantime,
Hence to thy home. Be silent. Name it not.
For I am Neptune, Shaker of the shores.
So saying, he plunged into the billowy Deep.
300 She pregnant grown, Pelias and Neleus bore,
Both, valiant ministers of mighty Jove.
In wide-spread Iäolchus Pelias dwelt,
Of num'rous flocks possess'd; but his abode
Amid the sands of Pylus Neleus chose.
To Cretheus wedded next, the lovely nymph
Yet other sons, Æson and Pheres bore,
And Amythaon of equestrian fame.
I, next, the daughter of Asopus saw,
Antiope; she gloried to have known
310 Th' embrace of Jove himself, to whom she brought
A double progeny, Amphion named
And Zethus; they the seven-gated Thebes
Founded and girded with strong tow'rs, because,
Though puissant Heroes both, in spacious Thebes
Unfenced by tow'rs, they could not dwell secure.
Alcmena, next, wife of Amphitryon
I saw; she in the arms of sov'reign Jove
The lion-hearted Hercules conceiv'd,
And, after, bore to Creon brave in fight
320 His daughter Megara, by the noble son
Unconquer'd of Amphitryon espoused.

The beauteous Epicaste[44] saw I then,
Mother of Oedipus, who guilt incurr'd
Prodigious, wedded, unintentional,
To her own son; his father first he slew,
Then wedded her, which soon the Gods divulged.
He, under vengeance of offended heav'n,
In pleasant Thebes dwelt miserable, King
Of the Cadmean race; she to the gates
330 Of Ades brazen-barr'd despairing went,
Self-strangled by a cord fasten'd aloft
To her own palace-roof, and woes bequeath'd
(Such as the Fury sisters execute
Innumerable) to her guilty son.

---

[44] By the Tragedians called-Jocasta.

There also saw I Chloris, loveliest fair,
Whom Neleus woo'd and won with spousal gifts
Inestimable, by her beauty charm'd
She youngest daughter was of Iasus' son,
Amphion, in old time a sov'reign prince
340 In Minuëian Orchomenus,
And King of Pylus. Three illustrious sons
She bore to Neleus, Nestor, Chromius,
And Periclymenus the wide-renown'd,
And, last, produced a wonder of the earth,
Pero, by ev'ry neighbour prince around
In marriage sought; but Neleus her on none
Deign'd to bestow, save only on the Chief
Who should from Phylace drive off the beeves
(Broad-fronted, and with jealous care secured)
350 Of valiant Iphicles. One undertook
That task alone, a prophet high in fame,
Melampus; but the Fates fast bound him there
In rig'rous bonds by rustic hands imposed.
At length (the year, with all its months and days
Concluded, and the new-born year begun)
Illustrious Iphicles releas'd the seer,

Grateful for all the oracles resolved,[45]
Till then obscure. So stood the will of Jove.
Next, Leda, wife of Tyndarus I saw,
360 Who bore to Tyndarus a noble pair,
Castor the bold, and Pollux cestus-famed.
They pris'ners in the fertile womb of earth,
Though living, dwell, and even there from Jove
High priv'lege gain; alternate they revive
And die, and dignity partake divine.
The comfort of Aloëus, next, I view'd,
Iphimedeia; she th' embrace profess'd
Of Neptune to have shared, to whom she bore
Two sons; short-lived they were, but godlike both,
370 Otus and Ephialtes far-renown'd.
Orion sole except, all-bounteous Earth
Ne'er nourish'd forms for beauty or for size
To be admired as theirs; in his ninth year
Each measur'd, broad, nine cubits, and the height
Was found nine ells of each. Against the Gods
Themselves they threaten'd war, and to excite
The din of battle in the realms above.
To the Olympian summit they essay'd
To heave up Ossa, and to Ossa's crown
380 Branch-waving Pelion; so to climb the heav'ns.
Nor had they failed, maturer grown in might,

To accomplish that emprize, but them the son[46]
Of radiant-hair'd Latona and of Jove
Slew both, ere yet the down of blooming youth
Thick-sprung, their cheeks or chins had tufted o'er.
Phædra I also there, and Procris saw,
And Ariadne for her beauty praised,
Whose sire was all-wise Minos. Theseus her
From Crete toward the fruitful region bore
390 Of sacred Athens, but enjoy'd not there,
For, first, she perish'd by Diana's shafts

In Dia, Bacchus witnessing her crime.[47]
Mæra and Clymene I saw beside,
And odious Eriphyle, who received
The price in gold of her own husband's life.
But all the wives of Heroes whom I saw,
And all their daughters can I not relate;
Night, first, would fail; and even now the hour
Calls me to rest either on board my bark,
400 Or here; meantime, I in yourselves confide,
And in the Gods to shape my conduct home.
He ceased; the whole assembly silent sat,
Charm'd into ecstacy by his discourse
Throughout the twilight hall, till, at the last,
Areta iv'ry arm'd them thus bespake.
Phæacians! how appears he in your eyes
This stranger, graceful as he is in port,
In stature noble, and in mind discrete?
My guest he is, but ye all share with me
410 That honour; him dismiss not, therefore, hence
With haste, nor from such indigence withhold
Supplies gratuitous; for ye are rich,
And by kind heav'n with rare possessions blest.
The Hero, next, Echeneus spake, a Chief
Now ancient, eldest of Phæacia's sons.
Your prudent Queen, my friends, speaks not beside
Her proper scope, but as beseems her well.
Her voice obey; yet the effect of all
Must on Alcinoüs himself depend.
420 To whom Alcinoüs, thus, the King, replied.
I ratify the word. So shall be done,
As surely as myself shall live supreme
O'er all Phæacia's maritime domain.
Then let the guest, though anxious to depart,
Wait till the morrow, that I may complete
The whole donation. His safe conduct home
Shall be the gen'ral care, but mine in Chief,
To whom dominion o'er the rest belongs.
Him answer'd, then, Ulysses ever-wise.
430 Alcinoüs! Prince! exalted high o'er all
Phæacia's sons! should ye solicit, kind,
My stay throughout the year, preparing still
My conduct home, and with illustrious gifts
Enriching me the while, ev'n that request
Should please me well; the wealthier I return'd,
The happier my condition; welcome more
And more respectable I should appear
In ev'ry eye to Ithaca restored.
To whom Alcinoüs answer thus return'd.
440 Ulysses! viewing thee, no fears we feel
Lest thou, at length, some false pretender prove,
Or subtle hypocrite, of whom no few
Disseminated o'er its face the earth
Sustains, adepts in fiction, and who frame
Fables, where fables could be least surmised.
Thy phrase well turn'd, and thy ingenuous mind
Proclaim *thee* diff'rent far, who hast in strains
Musical as a poet's voice, the woes
Rehears'd of all thy Greecians, and thy own.

---

[45] Iphicles had been informed by the Oracles that he should have no children till instructed by a prophet how to obtain them; a service which Melampus had the good fortune to render him.

[46] Apollo.

[47] Bacchus accused her to Diana of having lain with Theseus in his temple, and the Goddess punished her with death.

450 But say, and tell me true. Beheld'st thou there
None of thy followers to the walls of Troy
Slain in that warfare? Lo! the night is long-
A night of utmost length; nor yet the hour
Invites to sleep. Tell me thy wond'rous deeds,
For I could watch till sacred dawn, could'st thou
So long endure to tell me of thy toils.
Then thus Ulysses, ever-wise, replied.
Alcinoüs! high exalted over all
Phæacia's sons! the time suffices yet
460 For converse both and sleep, and if thou wish
To hear still more, I shall not spare to unfold
More pitiable woes than these, sustain'd
By my companions, in the end destroy'd;
Who, saved from perils of disast'rous war
At Ilium, perish'd yet in their return,
Victims of a pernicious woman's crime.[48]
Now, when chaste Proserpine had wide dispers'd
Those female shades, the spirit sore distress'd
Of Agamemnon, Atreus' son, appear'd;
470 Encircled by a throng, he came; by all
Who with himself beneath Ægisthus' roof
Their fate fulfill'd, perishing by the sword.
He drank the blood, and knew me; shrill he wail'd
And querulous; tears trickling bathed his cheeks,
And with spread palms, through ardour of desire
He sought to enfold me fast, but vigour none,
Or force, as erst, his agile limbs inform'd.
I, pity-moved, wept at the sight, and him,
In accents wing'd by friendship, thus address'd.
480 Ah glorious son of Atreus, King of men!
What hand inflicted the all-numbing stroke
Of death on thee? Say, didst thou perish sunk
By howling tempests irresistible
Which Neptune raised, or on dry land by force
Of hostile multitudes, while cutting off
Beeves from the herd, or driving flocks away,
Or fighting for Achaia's daughters, shut
Within some city's bulwarks close besieged?
I ceased, when Agamemnon thus replied.
490 Ulysses, noble Chief, Laertes' son
For wisdom famed! I neither perish'd sunk
By howling tempests irresistible
Which Neptune raised, nor on dry land received
From hostile multitudes the fatal blow,
But me Ægisthus slew; my woeful death
Confed'rate with my own pernicious wife
He plotted, with a show of love sincere
Bidding me to his board, where as the ox
Is slaughter'd at his crib, he slaughter'd *me* .
500 Such was my dreadful death; carnage ensued
Continual of my friends slain all around,
Num'rous as boars bright-tusk'd at nuptial feast,
Or feast convivial of some wealthy Chief.
Thou hast already witness'd many a field
With warriors overspread, slain one by one,
But that dire scene had most thy pity moved,
For we, with brimming beakers at our side,
And underneath full tables bleeding lay.

Blood floated all the pavement. Then the cries
510 Of Priam's daughter sounded in my ears
Most pitiable of all. Cassandra's cries,
Whom Clytemnestra close beside me slew.
Expiring as I lay, I yet essay'd
To grasp my faulchion, but the trayt'ress quick
Withdrew herself, nor would vouchsafe to close
My languid eyes, or prop my drooping chin
Ev'n in the moment when I sought the shades.
So that the thing breathes not, ruthless and fell
As woman once resolv'd on such a deed
520 Detestable, as my base wife contrived,
The murther of the husband of her youth.
I thought to have return'd welcome to all,
To my own children and domestic train;
But she, past measure profligate, hath poured
Shame on herself, on women yet unborn,
And even on the virtuous of her sex.
He ceas'd, to whom, thus, answer I return'd.
Gods! how severely hath the thund'rer plagued
The house of Atreus even from the first,
530 By female counsels! we for Helen's sake
Have num'rous died, and Clytemnestra framed,
While thou wast far remote, this snare for thee!
So I, to whom Atrides thus replied.
Thou, therefore, be not pliant overmuch
To woman; trust her not with all thy mind,
But half disclose to her, and half conceal.
Yet, from thy consort's hand no bloody death,
My friend, hast thou to fear; for passing wise
Icarius' daughter is, far other thoughts,
540 Intelligent, and other plans, to frame.
Her, going to the wars we left a bride
New-wedded, and thy boy hung at her breast,
Who, man himself, consorts ere now with men
A prosp'rous youth; his father, safe restored
To his own Ithaca, shall see him soon,
And *he* shall clasp his father in his arms
As nature bids; but me, my cruel one
Indulged not with the dear delight to gaze
On my Orestes, for she slew me first.
550 But listen; treasure what I now impart.[49]
Steer secret to thy native isle; avoid
Notice; for woman merits trust no more.
Now tell me truth. Hear ye in whose abode
My son resides? dwells he in Pylus, say,
Or in Orchomenos, or else beneath
My brother's roof in Sparta's wide domain?
For my Orestes is not yet a shade.
So he, to whom I answer thus return'd.
Atrides, ask not me. Whether he live,
560 Or have already died, I nothing know;
Mere words are vanity, and better spared.
Thus we discoursing mutual stood, and tears
Shedding disconsolate. The shade, meantime,
Came of Achilles, Peleus' mighty son;
Patroclus also, and Antilochus
Appear'd, with Ajax, for proportion just
And stature tall, (Pelides sole except)

---

[48] Probably meaning Helen.

[49] This is surely one of the most natural strokes to be found in any Poet. Convinced, for a moment, by the virtues of Penelope, he mentioned her with respect; but recollecting himself suddenly, involves even her in his general ill opinion of the sex, begotten in him by the crimes of Clytemnestra.

Distinguish'd above all Achaia's sons.
The soul of swift Æacides at once
570 Knew me, and in wing'd accents thus began.
Brave Laertiades, for wiles renown'd!
What mightier enterprise than all the past
Hath made thee here a guest? rash as thou art!
How hast thou dared to penetrate the gloom
Of Ades, dwelling of the shadowy dead,
Semblances only of what once they were?
He spake, to whom I, answ'ring, thus replied.
O Peleus' son! Achilles! bravest far
Of all Achaia's race! I here arrived
580 Seeking Tiresias, from his lips to learn,
Perchance, how I might safe regain the coast
Of craggy Ithaca; for tempest-toss'd
Perpetual, I have neither yet approach'd
Achaia's shore, or landed on my own.
But as for thee, Achilles! never man
Hath known felicity like thine, or shall,
Whom living we all honour'd as a God,
And who maintain'st, here resident, supreme
Controul among the dead; indulge not then,
590 Achilles, causeless grief that thou hast died.
I ceased, and answer thus instant received.
Renown'd Ulysses! think not death a theme
Of consolation; I had rather live
The servile hind for hire, and eat the bread
Of some man scantily himself sustain'd,
Than sov'reign empire hold o'er all the shades.
But come-speak to me of my noble boy;
Proceeds he, as he promis'd, brave in arms,
Or shuns he war? Say also, hast thou heard
600 Of royal Peleus? shares he still respect
Among his num'rous Myrmidons, or scorn
In Hellas and in Phthia, for that age
Predominates in his enfeebled limbs?
For help is none in me; the glorious sun
No longer sees me such, as when in aid
Of the Achaians I o'erspread the field
Of spacious Troy with all their bravest slain.
Oh might I, vigorous as then, repair[50]
For one short moment to my father's house,
610 They all should tremble; I would shew an arm,
Such as should daunt the fiercest who presumes
To injure *him* , or to despise his age.
Achilles spake, to whom I thus replied.
Of noble Peleus have I nothing heard;
But I will tell thee, as thou bidd'st, the truth
Unfeign'd of Neoptolemus thy son;
For him, myself, on board my hollow bark
From Scyros to Achaia's host convey'd.
Oft as in council under Ilium's walls
620 We met, he ever foremost was in speech,
Nor spake erroneous; Nestor and myself
Except, no Greecian could with him compare.

Oft, too, as we with battle hemm'd around
Troy's bulwarks, from among the mingled crowd
Thy son sprang foremost into martial act,
Inferior in heroic worth to none.
Beneath him num'rous fell the sons of Troy
In dreadful fight, nor have I pow'r to name
Distinctly all, who by his glorious arm
630 Exerted in the cause of Greece, expired.
Yet will I name Eurypylus, the son
Of Telephus, an Hero whom his sword
Of life bereaved, and all around him strew'd
The plain with his Cetean warriors, won
To Ilium's side by bribes to women giv'n.[51]
Save noble Memnon only, I beheld
No Chief at Ilium beautiful as he.
Again, when we within the horse of wood
Framed by Epeüs sat, an ambush chos'n
640 Of all the bravest Greeks, and I in trust
Was placed to open or to keep fast-closed
The hollow fraud; then, ev'ry Chieftain there
And Senator of Greece wiped from his cheeks
The tears, and tremors felt in ev'ry limb;
But never saw I changed to terror's hue
His ruddy cheek, no tears wiped *he* away,
But oft he press'd me to go forth, his suit
With pray'rs enforcing, griping hard his hilt
And his brass-burthen'd spear, and dire revenge
650 Denouncing, ardent, on the race of Troy.
At length, when we had sack'd the lofty town
Of Priam, laden with abundant spoils
He safe embark'd, neither by spear or shaft
Aught hurt, or in close fight by faulchion's edge,
As oft in war befalls, where wounds are dealt
Promiscuous at the will of fiery Mars.
So I; then striding large, the spirit thence
Withdrew of swift Æacides, along
The hoary mead pacing,[52] with joy elate
660 That I had blazon'd bright his son's renown.
The other souls of men by death dismiss'd
Stood mournful by, sad uttering each his woes;
The soul alone I saw standing remote
Of Telamonian Ajax, still incensed
That in our public contest for the arms
Worn by Achilles, and by Thetis thrown
Into dispute, my claim had strongest proved,
Troy and Minerva judges of the cause.
Disastrous victory! which I could wish
670 Not to have won, since for that armour's sake
The earth hath cover'd Ajax, in his form
And martial deeds superior far to all
The Greecians, Peleus' matchless son except.
I, seeking to appease him, thus began.
O Ajax, son of glorious Telamon!
Canst thou remember, even after death,

---

[50] Another most beautiful stroke of nature. Ere yet Ulysses has had opportunity to answer, the very thought that Peleus may possibly be insulted, fires him, and he takes the whole for granted. Thus is the impetuous character of Achilles sustained to the last moment!

[51] +Gynaiôn eineka dôrôn+-Priam is said to have influenced by gifts the wife and mother of Eurypylus, to persuade him to the assistance of Troy, he being himself unwilling to engage. The passage through defect of history has long been dark, and commentators have adapted different senses to it, all conjectural. The Ceteans are said to have been a people of Mysia, of which Eurypylus was King.

[52] +Kat' asphodelon leimôna+-Asphodel was planted on the graves and around the tombs of the deceased, and hence the supposition that the Stygian plain was clothed with asphodel. F.

Thy wrath against me, kindled for the sake
Of those pernicious arms? arms which the Gods
Ordain'd of such dire consequence to Greece,
680 Which caused thy death, our bulwark! Thee we mourn
With grief perpetual, nor the death lament
Of Peleus' son, Achilles, more than thine.
Yet none is blameable; Jove evermore
With bitt'rest hate pursued Achaia's host,
And he ordain'd thy death. Hero! approach,
That thou may'st hear the words with which I seek
To sooth thee; let thy long displeasure cease!
Quell all resentment in thy gen'rous breast!
I spake; nought answer'd he, but sullen join'd
690 His fellow-ghosts; yet, angry as he was,
I had prevail'd even on him to speak,
Or had, at least, accosted him again,
But that my bosom teem'd with strong desire
Urgent, to see yet others of the dead.
There saw I Minos, offspring famed of Jove;
His golden sceptre in his hand, he sat
Judge of the dead; they, pleading each in turn,
His cause, some stood, some sat, filling the house
Whose spacious folding-gates are never closed.
700 Orion next, huge ghost, engaged my view,
Droves urging o'er the grassy mead, of beasts
Which he had slain, himself, on the wild hills,
With strong club arm'd of ever-during brass.
There also Tityus on the ground I saw
Extended, offspring of the glorious earth;
Nine acres he o'erspread, and, at his side
Station'd, two vultures on his liver prey'd,
Scooping his entrails; nor sufficed his hands
To fray them thence; for he had sought to force
710 Latona, illustrious concubine of Jove,
What time the Goddess journey'd o'er the rocks
Of Pytho into pleasant Panopeus.
Next, suff'ring grievous torments, I beheld
Tantalus; in a pool he stood, his chin
Wash'd by the wave; thirst-parch'd he seem'd, but found
Nought to assuage his thirst; for when he bow'd
His hoary head, ardent to quaff, the flood
Vanish'd absorb'd, and, at his feet, adust
The soil appear'd, dried, instant, by the Gods.
720 Tall trees, fruit-laden, with inflected heads
Stoop'd to him, pomegranates, apples bright,
The luscious fig, and unctuous olive smooth;
Which when with sudden grasp he would have seized,
Winds hurl'd them high into the dusky clouds.
There, too, the hard-task'd Sisyphus I saw,

Thrusting before him, strenuous, a vast rock.[53]
With hands and feet struggling, he shoved the stone
Up to a hill-top; but the steep well-nigh

Vanquish'd, by some great force repulsed,[54] the mass
730 Rush'd again, obstinate, down to the plain.
Again, stretch'd prone, severe he toiled, the sweat
Bathed all his weary limbs, and his head reek'd.
The might of Hercules I, next, survey'd;
His semblance; for himself their banquet shares
With the Immortal Gods, and in his arms
Enfolds neat-footed Hebe, daughter fair
Of Jove, and of his golden-sandal'd spouse.
Around him, clamorous as birds, the dead
Swarm'd turbulent; he, gloomy-brow'd as night,
740 With uncased bow and arrow on the string
Peer'd terrible from side to side, as one
Ever in act to shoot; a dreadful belt
He bore athwart his bosom, thong'd with gold.
There, broider'd shone many a stupendous form,
Bears, wild boars, lions with fire-flashing eyes,
Fierce combats, battles, bloodshed, homicide.
The artist, author of that belt, none such
Before, produced, or after. Me his eye
No sooner mark'd, than knowing me, in words
750 By sorrow quick suggested, he began.
Laertes' noble son, for wiles renown'd!
Ah, hapless Hero! thou art, doubtless, charged,
Thou also, with some arduous labour, such
As in the realms of day I once endured.
Son was I of Saturnian Jove, yet woes
Immense sustain'd, subjected to a King
Inferior far to me, whose harsh commands
Enjoin'd me many a terrible exploit.
He even bade me on a time lead hence
760 The dog, that task believing above all
Impracticable; yet from Ades him
I dragg'd reluctant into light, by aid
Of Hermes, and of Pallas azure-eyed.
So saying, he penetrated deep again
The abode of Pluto; but I still unmoved
There stood expecting, curious, other shades
To see of Heroes in old time deceased.
And now, more ancient worthies still, and whom
I wish'd, I had beheld, Pirithoüs
770 And Theseus, glorious progeny of Gods,
But nations, first, numberless of the dead
Came shrieking hideous; me pale horror seized,
Lest awful Proserpine should thither send
The Gorgon-head from Ades, sight abhorr'd!
I, therefore, hasting to the vessel, bade
My crew embark, and cast the hawsers loose.
They, quick embarking, on the benches sat.

Down the Oceanus[55] the current bore
My galley, winning, at the first, her way
780 With oars, then, wafted by propitious gales.

---

[53] +Basazonta+ must have this sense interpreted by what follows. To attempt to make the English numbers expressive as the Greek is a labour like that of Sisyphus. The Translator has done what he could.

[54] It is now, perhaps, impossible to ascertain with precision what Homer meant by the word +krataiis+, which he uses only here, and in the next book, where it is the name of Scylla's dam.-+Anaidês+-is also of very doubtful explication.

[55] The two first lines of the following book seem to ascertain the true meaning of the conclusion of this, and to prove sufficiently that by +Ôkeanos+ here Homer could not possibly intend any other than a river. In those lines he tells us in the plainest terms that *the ship left the stream of the river Oceanus, and arrived in the open sea.* Diodorus Siculus informs us that +Ôkeanos+ had been a name anciently given to the Nile. See Clarke.

Book XII

Ulysses, pursuing his narrative, relates his return from the shades to Circe's island, the precautions given him by that Goddess, his escape from the Sirens, and from Scylla and Charybdis; his arrival in Sicily, where his companions, having slain and eaten the oxen of the Sun, are afterward shipwrecked and lost; and concludes the whole with an account of his arrival, alone, on the mast of his vessel, at the island of Calypso.

And now, borne seaward from the river-stream
Of the Oceanus, we plow'd again
The spacious Deep, and reach'd th' Ææan isle,
Where, daughter of the dawn, Aurora takes
Her choral sports, and whence the sun ascends.
We, there arriving, thrust our bark aground
On the smooth beach, then landed, and on shore
Reposed, expectant of the sacred dawn.
But soon as day-spring's daughter rosy-palm'd
10 Look'd forth again, sending my friends before,
I bade them bring Elpenor's body down
From the abode of Circe to the beach.
Then, on the utmost headland of the coast
We timber fell'd, and, sorrowing o'er the dead,
His fun'ral rites water'd with tears profuse.
The dead consumed, and with the dead his arms,
We heap'd his tomb, and the sepulchral post
Erecting, fix'd his shapely oar aloft.
Thus, punctual, we perform'd; nor our return
From Ades knew not Circe, but attired
20 In haste, ere long arrived, with whom appear'd
Her female train with plenteous viands charged,
And bright wine rosy-red. Amidst us all
Standing, the beauteous Goddess thus began.
Ah miserable! who have sought the shades
Alive! while others of the human race
Die only once, appointed twice to die!
Come-take ye food; drink wine; and on the shore
All day regale, for ye shall hence again
At day-spring o'er the Deep; but I will mark
30 Myself your future course, nor uninform'd
Leave you in aught, lest, through some dire mistake,
By sea or land new mis'ries ye incur.
The Goddess spake, whose invitation kind
We glad accepted; thus we feasting sat
Till set of sun, and quaffing richest wine;
But when the sun went down and darkness fell,
My crew beside the hawsers slept, while me
The Goddess by the hand leading apart,
First bade me sit, then, seated opposite,
40 Enquired, minute, of all that I had seen,
And I, from first to last, recounted all.
Then, thus the awful Goddess in return.
Thus far thy toils are finish'd. Now attend!
Mark well my words, of which the Gods will sure
Themselves remind thee in the needful hour.
First shalt thou reach the Sirens; they the hearts
Enchant of all who on their coast arrive.
The wretch, who unforewarn'd approaching, hears
The Sirens' voice, his wife and little-ones
50 Ne'er fly to gratulate his glad return,

But him the Sirens sitting in the meads
Charm with mellifluous song, while all around
The bones accumulated lie of men
Now putrid, and the skins mould'ring away.
But, pass them thou, and, lest thy people hear
Those warblings, ere thou yet approach, fill all
Their ears with wax moulded between thy palms;
But as for thee-thou hear them if thou wilt.
Yet let thy people bind thee to the mast
60 Erect, encompassing thy feet and arms
With cordage well-secured to the mast-foot,
So shalt thou, raptur'd, hear the Sirens' song.
But if thou supplicate to be released,
Or give such order, then, with added cords
Let thy companions bind thee still the more.
When thus thy people shall have safely pass'd
The Sirens by, think not from me to learn
What course thou next shalt steer; two will occur;
Delib'rate chuse; I shall describe them both.
70 Here vaulted rocks impend, dash'd by the waves
Immense of Amphitrite azure-eyed;
The blessed Gods those rocks, Erratic, call.
Birds cannot pass them safe; no, not the doves
Which his ambrosia bear to Father Jove,
But even of those doves the slipp'ry rock
Proves fatal still to one, for which the God
Supplies another, lest the number fail.
No ship, what ship soever there arrives,
Escapes them, but both mariners and planks
80 Whelm'd under billows of the Deep, or, caught
By fiery tempests, sudden disappear.
Those rocks the billow-cleaving bark alone
The Argo, further'd by the vows of all,
Pass'd safely, sailing from Ææta's isle;
Nor she had pass'd, but surely dash'd had been
On those huge rocks, but that, propitious still
To Jason, Juno sped her safe along.
These rocks are two; one lifts his summit sharp
High as the spacious heav'ns, wrapt in dun clouds
90 Perpetual, which nor autumn sees dispers'd
Nor summer, for the sun shines never there;
No mortal man might climb it or descend,
Though twice ten hands and twice ten feet he own'd,
For it is levigated as by art.
Down scoop'd to Erebus, a cavern drear
Yawns in the centre of its western side;
Pass it, renown'd Ulysses! but aloof
So far, that a keen arrow smartly sent
Forth from thy bark should fail to reach the cave.
100 There Scylla dwells, and thence her howl is heard
Tremendous; shrill her voice is as the note

Of hound new-whelp'd, but hideous her aspect,
Such as no mortal man, nor ev'n a God
Encount'ring her, should with delight survey.
Her feet are twelve, all fore-feet; six her necks
Of hideous length, each clubb'd into a head
Terrific, and each head with fangs is arm'd
In triple row, thick planted, stored with death.
Plunged to her middle in the hollow den
110 She lurks, protruding from the black abyss
Her heads, with which the rav'ning monster dives
In quest of dolphins, dog-fish, or of prey
More bulky, such as in the roaring gulphs
Of Amphitrite without end abounds.
It is no seaman's boast that e'er he slipp'd
Her cavern by, unharm'd. In ev'ry mouth
She bears upcaught a mariner away.
The other rock, Ulysses, thou shalt find
Humbler, a bow-shot only from the first;
120 On this a wild fig grows broad-leav'd, and here
Charybdis dire ingulphs the sable flood.
Each day she thrice disgorges, and each day
Thrice swallows it. Ah! well forewarn'd, beware
What time she swallows, that thou come not nigh,
For not himself, Neptune, could snatch thee thence.
Close passing Scylla's rock, shoot swift thy bark
Beyond it, since the loss of six alone
Is better far than shipwreck made of all.
So Circe spake, to whom I thus replied.
130 Tell me, O Goddess, next, and tell me true!
If, chance, from fell Charybdis I escape,
May I not also save from Scylla's force
My people; should the monster threaten them?
I said, and quick the Goddess in return.
Unhappy! can exploits and toils of war
Still please thee? yield'st not to the Gods themselves?
She is no mortal, but a deathless pest,
Impracticable, savage, battle-proof.
Defence is vain; flight is thy sole resource.
140 For should'st thou linger putting on thy arms
Beside the rock, beware, lest darting forth
Her num'rous heads, she seize with ev'ry mouth
A Greecian, and with others, even thee.
Pass therefore swift, and passing, loud invoke
Cratais, mother of this plague of man,
Who will forbid her to assail thee more.
Thou, next, shalt reach Thrinacia; there, the beeves
And fatted flocks graze num'rous of the Sun;
Sev'n herds; as many flocks of snowy fleece;
150 Fifty in each; they breed not, neither die,
Nor are they kept by less than Goddesses,
Lampetia fair, and Phäethusa, both
By nymph Neæra to Hyperion borne.
Them, soon as she had train'd them to an age
Proportion'd to that charge, their mother sent
Into Thrinacia, there to dwell and keep
Inviolate their father's flocks and herds.
If, anxious for a safe return, thou spare
Those herds and flocks, though after much endured,
160 Ye may at last your Ithaca regain;
But should'st thou violate them, I foretell
Destruction of thy ship and of thy crew,
And though thyself escape, thou shalt return

Late, in ill plight, and all thy friends destroy'd.
She ended, and the golden morning dawn'd.
Then, all-divine, her graceful steps she turn'd
Back through the isle, and, at the beach arrived,
I summon'd all my followers to ascend
The bark again, and cast the hawsers loose.
170 They, at my voice, embarking, fill'd in ranks
The seats, and rowing, thresh'd the hoary flood.
And now, melodious Circe, nymph divine,
Sent after us a canvas-stretching breeze,
Pleasant companion of our course, and we
(The decks and benches clear'd) untoiling sat,
While managed gales sped swift the bark along.
Then, with dejected heart, thus I began.
Oh friends! (for it is needful that not one
Or two alone the admonition hear
180 Of Circe, beauteous prophetess divine)
To all I speak, that whether we escape
Or perish, all may be, at least, forewarn'd.
She bids us, first, avoid the dang'rous song
Of the sweet Sirens and their flow'ry meads.
Me only she permits those strains to hear;
But ye shall bind me with coercion strong
Of cordage well-secured to the mast-foot,
And by no struggles to be loos'd of mine.
But should I supplicate to be released
190 Or give such order, then, with added cords
Be it your part to bind me still the more.
Thus with distinct precaution I prepared
My people; rapid in her course, meantime,
My gallant bark approach'd the Sirens' isle,
For brisk and favourable blew the wind.
Then fell the wind suddenly, and serene
A breathless calm ensued, while all around
The billows slumber'd, lull'd by pow'r divine.
Up-sprang my people, and the folded sails
200 Bestowing in the hold, sat to their oars,
Which with their polish'd blades whiten'd the Deep.
I, then, with edge of steel sev'ring minute
A waxen cake, chafed it and moulded it
Between my palms; ere long the ductile mass
Grew warm, obedient to that ceaseless force,
And to Hyperion's all-pervading beams.
With that soft liniment I fill'd the ears
Of my companions, man by man, and they
My feet and arms with strong coercion bound
210 Of cordage to the mast-foot well secured.
Then down they sat, and, rowing, thresh'd the brine.
But when with rapid course we had arrived
Within such distance as a voice may reach,
Not unperceived by them the gliding bark
Approach'd, and, thus, harmonious they began.
Ulysses, Chief by ev'ry tongue extoll'd,
Achaia's boast, oh hither steer thy bark!
Here stay thy course, and listen to our lay!
These shores none passes in his sable ship
220 Till, first, the warblings of our voice he hear,
Then, happier hence and wiser he departs.
All that the Greeks endured, and all the ills
Inflicted by the Gods on Troy, we know,
Know all that passes on the boundless earth.
So they with voices sweet their music poured

Melodious on my ear, winning with ease
My heart's desire to listen, and by signs
I bade my people, instant, set me free.
But they incumbent row'd, and from their seats
230 Eurylochus and Perimedes sprang
With added cords to bind me still the more.
This danger past, and when the Sirens' voice,
Now left remote, had lost its pow'r to charm,
Then, my companions freeing from the wax
Their ears, deliver'd me from my restraint.
The island left afar, soon I discern'd
Huge waves, and smoke, and horrid thund'rings heard.
All sat aghast; forth flew at once the oars
From ev'ry hand, and with a clash the waves
240 Smote all together; check'd, the galley stood,
By billow-sweeping oars no longer urged,
And I, throughout the bark, man after man
Encouraged all, addressing thus my crew.
We meet not, now, my friends, our first distress.
This evil is not greater than we found
When the huge Cyclops in his hollow den
Imprison'd us, yet even thence we 'scaped,
My intrepidity and fertile thought
Opening the way; and we shall recollect
250 These dangers also, in due time, with joy.
Come, then-pursue my counsel. Ye your seats
Still occupying, smite the furrow'd flood
With well-timed strokes, that by the will of Jove
We may escape, perchance, this death, secure.
To thee the pilot thus I speak, (my words
Mark thou, for at thy touch the rudder moves)
This smoke, and these tumultuous waves avoid;
Steer wide of both; yet with an eye intent
On yonder rock, lest unaware thou hold
260 Too near a course, and plunge us into harm.
So I; with whose advice all, quick, complied.
But Scylla I as yet named not, (that woe
Without a cure) lest, terrified, my crew
Should all renounce their oars, and crowd below.
Just then, forgetful of the strict command
Of Circe not to arm, I cloath'd me all
In radiant armour, grasp'd two quiv'ring spears,
And to the deck ascended at the prow,
Expecting earliest notice there, what time
270 The rock-bred Scylla should annoy my friends.
But I discern'd her not, nor could, although
To weariness of sight the dusky rock
I vigilant explored. Thus, many a groan
Heaving, we navigated sad the streight,
For here stood Scylla, while Charybdis there
With hoarse throat deep absorb'd the briny flood.
Oft as she vomited the deluge forth,
Like water cauldron'd o'er a furious fire
The whirling Deep all murmur'd, and the spray
280 On both those rocky summits fell in show'rs.
But when she suck'd the salt wave down again,
Then, all the pool appear'd wheeling about
Within, the rock rebellow'd, and the sea
Drawn off into that gulph disclosed to view
The oozy bottom. Us pale horror seized.

Thus, dreading death, with fast-set eyes we watch'd
Charybdis; meantime, Scylla from the bark
Caught six away, the bravest of my friends.
With eyes, that moment, on my ship and crew
290 Retorted, I beheld the legs and arms
Of those whom she uplifted in the air;
On me they call'd, my name, the last, last time
Pronouncing then, in agony of heart.
As when from some bold point among the rocks
The angler, with his taper rod in hand,
Casts forth his bait to snare the smaller fry,

He swings away remote his guarded line,[56]
Then jerks his gasping prey forth from the Deep,
So Scylla them raised gasping to the rock,
300 And at her cavern's mouth devour'd them loudShrieking,
and stretching forth to me their arms
In sign of hopeless mis'ry. Ne'er beheld
These eyes in all the seas that I have roam'd,
A sight so piteous, nor in all my toils.
From Scylla and Charybdis dire escaped,
We reach'd the noble island of the Sun
Ere long, where bright Hyperion's beauteous herds
Broad-fronted grazed, and his well-batten'd flocks.
I, in the bark and on the sea, the voice
310 Of oxen bellowing in hovels heard,
And of loud-bleating sheep; then dropp'd the word
Into my memory of the sightless Seer,
Theban Tiresias, and the caution strict
Of Circe, my Ææan monitress,
Who with such force had caution'd me to avoid
The island of the Sun, joy of mankind.
Thus then to my companions, sad, I spake.
Hear ye, my friends! although long time distress'd,
The words prophetic of the Theban seer
320 And of Ææan Circe, whose advice
Was oft repeated to me to avoid
This island of the Sun, joy of mankind.
There, said the Goddess, dread your heaviest woes,
Pass the isle, therefore, scudding swift away.
I ceased; they me with consternation heard,
And harshly thus Eurylochus replied.
Ulysses, ruthless Chief! no toils impair
Thy strength, of senseless iron thou art form'd,
Who thy companions weary and o'erwatch'd
330 Forbidd'st to disembark on this fair isle,
Where now, at last, we might with ease regale.
Thou, rash, command'st us, leaving it afar,
To roam all night the Ocean's dreary waste;
But winds to ships injurious spring by night,
And how shall we escape a dreadful death
If, chance, a sudden gust from South arise
Or stormy West, that dash in pieces oft
The vessel, even in the Gods' despight?
Prepare we rather now, as night enjoins,
340 Our evening fare beside the sable bark,
In which at peep of day we may again
Launch forth secure into the boundless flood.
He ceas'd, whom all applauded. Then I knew
That sorrow by the will of adverse heav'n
Approach'd, and in wing'd accents thus replied.

---

[56] They passed the line through a pipe of horn, to secure it against the fishes' bite.

I suffer force, Eurylochus! and yield
O'er-ruled by numbers. Come, then, swear ye all
A solemn oath, that should we find an herd
Or num'rous flock, none here shall either sheep
350 Or bullock slay, by appetite profane
Seduced, but shall the viands eat content
Which from immortal Circe we received.
I spake; they readily a solemn oath
Sware all, and when their oath was fully sworn,
Within a creek where a fresh fountain rose
They moor'd the bark, and, issuing, began
Brisk preparation of their evening cheer.
But when nor hunger now nor thirst remain'd
Unsated, recollecting, then, their friends
360 By Scylla seized and at her cave devour'd,
They mourn'd, nor ceased to mourn them, till they slept.
The night's third portion come, when now the stars
Had travers'd the mid-sky, cloud-gath'rer Jove
Call'd forth a vehement wind with tempest charged,
Menacing earth and sea with pitchy clouds
Tremendous, and the night fell dark from heav'n.
But when Aurora, daughter of the day,
Look'd rosy forth, we haled, drawn inland more,
Our bark into a grot, where nymphs were wont
370 Graceful to tread the dance, or to repose.
Convening there my friends, I thus began.
My friends! food fails us not, but bread is yet
And wine on board. Abstain we from the herds,
Lest harm ensue; for ye behold the flocks
And herds of a most potent God, the Sun!
Whose eye and watchful ear none may elude.
So saying, I sway'd the gen'rous minds of all.
A month complete the South wind ceaseless blew,
Nor other wind blew next, save East and South,
380 Yet they, while neither food nor rosy wine
Fail'd them, the herds harm'd not, through fear to die.
But, our provisions failing, they employed
Whole days in search of food, snaring with hooks
Birds, fishes, of what kind soe'er they might.
By famine urged. I solitary roam'd
Meantime the isle, seeking by pray'r to move
Some God to shew us a deliv'rance thence.
When, roving thus the isle, I had at length
Left all my crew remote, laving my hands
390 Where shelter warm I found from the rude blast,
I supplicated ev'ry Pow'r above;
But they my pray'rs answer'd with slumbers soft
Shed o'er my eyes, and with pernicious art
Eurylochus, the while, my friends harangued.
My friends! afflicted as ye are, yet hear
A fellow-suff'rer. Death, however caused,
Abhorrence moves in miserable man,
But death by famine is a fate of all
Most to be fear'd. Come-let us hither drive
400 And sacrifice to the Immortal Pow'rs
The best of all the oxen of the Sun,
Resolving thus-that soon as we shall reach
Our native Ithaca, we will erect
To bright Hyperion an illustrious fane,
Which with magnificent and num'rous gifts
We will enrich. But should he chuse to sink
Our vessel, for his stately beeves incensed,

And should, with him, all heav'n conspire our death,
I rather had with open mouth, at once,
410 Meeting the billows, perish, than by slow
And pining waste here in this desert isle.
So spake Eurylochus, whom all approved.
Then, driving all the fattest of the herd
Few paces only, (for the sacred beeves
Grazed rarely distant from the bark) they stood
Compassing them around, and, grasping each
Green foliage newly pluck'd from saplings tall,
(For barley none in all our bark remain'd)
Worshipp'd the Gods in pray'r. Pray'r made, they slew
And flay'd them, and the thighs with double fat
421 Investing, spread them o'er with slices crude.
No wine had they with which to consecrate
The blazing rites, but with libation poor
Of water hallow'd the interior parts.
Now, when the thighs were burnt, and each had shared
His portion of the maw, and when the rest
All-slash'd and scored hung roasting at the fire,
Sleep, in that moment, suddenly my eyes
Forsaking, to the shore I bent my way.
430 But ere the station of our bark I reach'd,
The sav'ry steam greeted me. At the scent
I wept aloud, and to the Gods exclaim'd.
Oh Jupiter, and all ye Pow'rs above!
With cruel sleep and fatal ye have lull'd
My cares to rest, such horrible offence
Meantime my rash companions have devised.
Then, flew long-stoled Lampetia to the Sun
At once with tidings of his slaughter'd beeves,
And he, incensed, the Immortals thus address'd.
440 Jove, and ye everlasting Pow'rs divine!
Avenge me instant on the crew profane
Of Laertiades; Ulysses' friends
Have dared to slay my beeves, which I with joy
Beheld, both when I climb'd the starry heav'ns,
And when to earth I sloped my "westring wheels,"
But if they yield me not amercement due
And honourable for my loss, to Hell
I will descend and give the ghosts my beams.
Then, thus the cloud-assembler God replied.
450 Sun! shine thou still on the Immortal Pow'rs,
And on the teeming earth, frail man's abode.
My candent bolts can in a moment reach
And split their flying bark in the mid-sea.
These things Calypso told me, taught, herself,
By herald Hermes, as she oft affirm'd.
But when, descending to the shore, I reach'd
At length my bark, with aspect stern and tone
I reprimanded them, yet no redress
Could frame, or remedy-the beeves were dead.
460 Soon follow'd signs portentous sent from heav'n.
The skins all crept, and on the spits the flesh
Both roast and raw bellow'd, as with the voice
Of living beeves. Thus my devoted friends
Driving the fattest oxen of the Sun,
Feasted six days entire; but when the sev'nth
By mandate of Saturnian Jove appeared,
The storm then ceased to rage, and we, again
Embarking, launch'd our galley, rear'd the mast,
And gave our unfurl'd canvas to the wind.

470 The island left afar, and other land
Appearing none, but sky alone and sea,
Right o'er the hollow bark Saturnian Jove
Hung a cærulean cloud, dark'ning the Deep.
Not long my vessel ran, for, blowing wild,
Now came shrill Zephyrus; a stormy gust
Snapp'd sheer the shrouds on both sides; backward fell
The mast, and with loose tackle strew'd the hold;
Striking the pilot in the stern, it crush'd
His scull together; he a diver's plunge
480 Made downward, and his noble spirit fled.
Meantime, Jove thund'ring, hurl'd into the ship
His bolts; she, smitten by the fires of Jove,
Quaked all her length; with sulphur fill'd she reek'd,
And o'er her sides headlong my people plunged
Like sea-mews, interdicted by that stroke
Of wrath divine to hope their country more.
But I, the vessel still paced to and fro,
Till, fever'd by the boist'rous waves, her sides
Forsook the keel now left to float alone.
490 Snapp'd where it join'd the keel the mast had fall'n,
But fell encircled with a leathern brace,
Which it retain'd; binding with this the mast
And keel together, on them both I sat,
Borne helpless onward by the dreadful gale.
And now the West subsided, and the South
Arose instead, with mis'ry charged for me,
That I might measure back my course again
To dire Charybdis. All night long I drove,
And when the sun arose, at Scylla's rock
500 Once more, and at Charybdis' gulph arrived.

It was the time when she absorb'd profound
The briny flood, but by a wave upborne
I seized the branches fast of the wild-fig.[57]
To which, bat-like, I clung; yet where to fix
My foot secure found not, or where to ascend,
For distant lay the roots, and distant shot
The largest arms erect into the air,
O'ershadowing all Charybdis; therefore hard
I clench'd the boughs, till she disgorg'd again
510 Both keel and mast. Not undesired by me
They came, though late; for at what hour the judge,
After decision made of num'rous strifes[58]
Between young candidates for honour, leaves
The forum for refreshment' sake at home,
Then was it that the mast and keel emerged.
Deliver'd to a voluntary fall,
Fast by those beams I dash'd into the flood,
And seated on them both, with oary palms
Impell'd them; nor the Sire of Gods and men
520 Permitted Scylla to discern me more,
Else had I perish'd by her fangs at last.
Nine days I floated thence, and, on the tenth
Dark night, the Gods convey'd me to the isle
Ogygia, habitation of divine
Calypso, by whose hospitable aid
And assiduity, my strength revived.
But wherefore this? ye have already learn'd
That hist'ry, thou and thy illustrious spouse;
I told it yesterday, and hate a tale
530 Once amply told, then, needless, traced again.

---

[57] See line 120.

[58] He had therefore held by the fig-tree from sunrise till afternoon.

Book XIII

Ulysses, having finished his narrative, and received additional presents from the Phœacians, embarks; he is conveyed in his sleep to Ithaca, and in his sleep is landed on that island. The ship that carried him is in her return transformed by Neptune to a rock.

Minerva meets him on the shore, enables him to recollect his country, which, till enlightened by her, he believed to be a country strange to him, and they concert together the means of destroying the suitors. The Goddess then repairs to Sparta to call thence Telemachus, and Ulysses, by her aid disguised like a beggar, proceeds towards the cottage of Eumœus.

He ceas'd; the whole assembly silent sat,
Charm'd into ecstacy with his discourse
Throughout the twilight hall. Then, thus the King.
Ulysses, since beneath my brazen dome
Sublime thou hast arrived, like woes, I trust,
Thou shalt not in thy voyage hence sustain
By tempests tost, though much to woe inured.
To you, who daily in my presence quaff
Your princely meed of gen'rous wine and hear
The sacred bard, my pleasure, thus I speak.
10 The robes, wrought gold, and all the other gifts
To this our guest, by the Phæacian Chiefs
Brought hither in the sumptuous coffer lie.
But come-present ye to the stranger, each,
An ample tripod also, with a vase
Of smaller size, for which we will be paid
By public impost; for the charge of all
Excessive were by one alone defray'd.
So spake Alcinoüs, and his counsel pleased;
Then, all retiring, sought repose at home.
20 But when Aurora, daughter of the dawn,
Look'd rosy forth, each hasted to the bark
With his illustrious present, which the might
Of King Alcinoüs, who himself her sides
Ascended, safe beneath the seats bestowed,
Lest it should harm or hinder, while he toil'd
In rowing, some Phæacian of the crew.
The palace of Alcinoüs seeking next,
Together, they prepared a new regale.

For them, in sacrifice, the sacred might[59]
30 Of King Alcinoüs slew an ox to Jove
Saturnian, cloud-girt governor of all.
The thighs with fire prepared, all glad partook
The noble feast; meantime, the bard divine
Sang, sweet Demodocus, the people's joy.
But oft Ulysses to the radiant sun
Turn'd wistful eyes, anxious for his decline,
Nor longer, now, patient of dull delay.
As when some hungry swain whose sable beeves
Have through the fallow dragg'd his pond'rous plow
40 All day, the setting sun views with delight
For supper' sake, which with tir'd feet he seeks,
So welcome to Ulysses' eyes appear'd
The sun-set of that eve; directing, then,
His speech to maritime Phæacia's sons,
But to Alcinoüs chiefly, thus he said.
Alcinoüs, o'er Phæacia's realm supreme!

Libation made, dismiss ye me in peace,
And farewell all! for what I wish'd, I have,
Conductors hence, and honourable gifts
50 With which heav'n prosper me! and may the Gods
Vouchsafe to me, at my return, to find
All safe, my spotless consort and my friends!
May ye, whom here I leave, gladden your wives
And see your children blest, and may the pow'rs
Immortal with all good enrich you all,
And from calamity preserve the land!
He ended, they unanimous, his speech
Applauded loud, and bade dismiss the guest
Who had so wisely spoken and so well.
60 Then thus Alcinoüs to his herald spake.
Pontonoüs! charging high the beaker, bear
To ev'ry guest beneath our roof the wine,
That, pray'r preferr'd to the eternal Sire,
We may dismiss our inmate to his home.
Then, bore Pontonoüs to ev'ry guest
The brimming cup; they, where they sat, perform'd
Libation due; but the illustrious Chief
Ulysses, from his seat arising, placed
A massy goblet in Areta's hand,
70 To whom in accents wing'd, grateful, he said.
Farewell, O Queen, a long farewell, till age
Arrive, and death, the appointed lot of all!
I go; but be this people, and the King
Alcinoüs, and thy progeny, thy joy
Yet many a year beneath this glorious roof!
So saying, the Hero through the palace-gate
Issued, whom, by Alcinoüs' command,
The royal herald to his vessel led.
Three maidens also of Areta's train
80 His steps attended; one, the robe well-bleach'd
And tunic bore; the corded coffer, one;
And food the third, with wine of crimson hue.
Arriving where the galley rode, each gave
Her charge to some brave mariner on board,
And all was safely stow'd. Meantime were spread
Linen and arras on the deck astern,
For his secure repose. And now the Chief
Himself embarking, silent lay'd him down.
Then, ev'ry rower to his bench repair'd;
90 They drew the loosen'd cable from its hold
In the drill'd rock, and, resupine, at once
With lusty strokes upturn'd the flashing waves.
His eye-lids, soon, sleep, falling as a dew,
Closed fast, death's simular, in sight the same.

---

[59] +Hieron menos Alkinooio+.

She, as four harness'd stallions o'er the plain
Shooting together at the scourge's stroke,
Toss high their manes, and rapid scour along,
So mounted she the waves, while dark the flood
Roll'd after her of the resounding Deep.
100 Steady she ran and safe, passing in speed
The falcon, swiftest of the fowls of heav'n;
With such rapidity she cut the waves,
An hero bearing like the Gods above
In wisdom, one familiar long with woe
In fight sustain'd, and on the perilous flood,
Though sleeping now serenely, and resign'd
To sweet oblivion of all sorrow past.
The brightest star of heav'n, precursor chief
Of day-spring, now arose, when at the isle
110 (Her voyage soon perform'd) the bark arrived.
There is a port sacred in Ithaca
To Phorcys, hoary ancient of the Deep,
Form'd by converging shores, prominent both
And both abrupt, which from the spacious bay
Exclude all boist'rous winds; within it, ships
(The port once gain'd) uncabled ride secure.
An olive, at the haven's head, expands
Her branches wide, near to a pleasant cave
Umbrageous, to the nymphs devoted named
120 The Naiads. In that cave beakers of stone
And jars are seen; bees lodge their honey there;
And there, on slender spindles of the rock
The nymphs of rivers weave their wond'rous robes.
Perennial springs water it, and it shows
A twofold entrance; ingress one affords
To mortal man, which Northward looks direct,
But holier is the Southern far; by that
No mortal enters, but the Gods alone.
Familiar with that port before, they push'd
130 The vessel in; she, rapid, plow'd the sands
With half her keel, such rowers urged her on.
Descending from the well-bench'd bark ashore,
They lifted forth Ulysses first, with all
His splendid couch complete, then, lay'd him down
Still wrapt in balmy slumber on the sands.
His treasures, next, by the Phæacian Chiefs
At his departure given him as the meed
Due to his wisdom, at the olive's foot
They heap'd, without the road, lest, while he slept
140 Some passing traveller should rifle them.
Then homeward thence they sped. Nor Ocean's God
His threats forgot denounced against divine
Ulysses, but with Jove thus first advised.
Eternal Sire! I shall no longer share
Respect and reverence among the Gods,
Since, now, Phæacia's mortal race have ceas'd
To honour me, though from myself derived.
It was my purpose, that by many an ill
Harass'd, Ulysses should have reach'd his home,
150 Although to intercept him, whose return
Thyself had promis'd, ne'er was my intent.
But him fast-sleeping swiftly o'er the waves
They have conducted, and have set him down
In Ithaca, with countless gifts enrich'd,
With brass, and tissued raiment, and with gold;
Much treasure! more than he had home convey'd

Even had he arrived with all his share
Allotted to him of the spoils of Troy.
To whom the cloud-assembler God replied.
160 What hast thou spoken, Shaker of the shores,
Wide-ruling Neptune? Fear not; thee the Gods
Will ne'er despise; dangerous were the deed
To cast dishonour on a God by birth
More ancient, and more potent far than they.
But if, profanely rash, a mortal man
Should dare to slight thee, to avenge the wrong
Some future day is ever in thy pow'r.
Accomplish all thy pleasure, thou art free.
Him answer'd, then, the Shaker of the shores.
170 Jove cloud-enthroned! that pleasure I would soon
Perform, as thou hast said, but that I watch
Thy mind continual, fearful to offend.
My purpose is, now to destroy amid
The dreary Deep yon fair Phæacian bark,
Return'd from safe conveyance of her freight;
So shall they waft such wand'rers home no more,
And she shall hide their city, to a rock
Transform'd of mountainous o'ershadowing size.
Him, then, Jove answer'd, gath'rer of the clouds.
180 Perform it, O my brother, and the deed
Thus done, shall best be done-What time the people
Shall from the city her approach descry,
Fix her to stone transform'd, but still in shape
A gallant bark, near to the coast, that all
May wonder, seeing her transform'd to stone
Of size to hide their city from the view.
These words once heard, the Shaker of the shores
Instant to Scheria, maritime abode
Of the Phæacians, went. Arrived, he watch'd.
190 And now the flying bark full near approach'd,
When Neptune, meeting her, with out-spread palm
Depress'd her at a stroke, and she became
Deep-rooted stone. Then Neptune went his way.
Phæacia's ship-ennobled sons meantime
Conferring stood, and thus, in accents wing'd,
Th' amazed spectator to his fellow spake.
Ah! who hath sudden check'd the vessel's course
Homeward? this moment she was all in view.
Thus they, unconscious of the cause, to whom
200 Alcinoüs, instructing them, replied.
Ye Gods! a prophecy now strikes my mind
With force, my father's. He was wont to say-
Neptune resents it, that we safe conduct
Natives of ev'ry region to their home.
He also spake, prophetic, of a day
When a Phæacian gallant bark, return'd
After conveyance of a stranger hence,
Should perish in the dreary Deep, and changed
To a huge mountain, cover all the town.
210 So spake my father, all whose words we see
This day fulfill'd. Thus, therefore, act we all
Unanimous; henceforth no longer bear
The stranger home, when such shall here arrive;
And we will sacrifice, without delay,
Twelve chosen bulls to Neptune, if, perchance,
He will commiserate us, and forbear
To hide our town behind a mountain's height.
He spake, they, terrified, the bulls prepared.

Thus all Phæacia's Senators and Chiefs
220 His altar compassing, in pray'r adored
The Ocean's God. Meantime, Ulysses woke,
Unconscious where; stretch'd on his native soil
He lay, and knew it not, long-time exiled.
For Pallas, progeny of Jove, a cloud
Drew dense around him, that, ere yet agnized
By others, he might wisdom learn from her,
Neither to citizens, nor yet to friends
Reveal'd, nor even to his own espoused,
Till, first, he should avenge complete his wrongs
230 Domestic from those suitors proud sustained.
All objects, therefore, in the Hero's eyes
Seem'd alien, foot-paths long, commodious ports,
Heav'n-climbing rocks, and trees of amplest growth.
Arising, fixt he stood, his native soil
Contemplating, till with expanded palms
Both thighs he smote, and, plaintive, thus began.
Ah me! what mortal race inhabits here?
Rude are they, contumacious and unjust,
Or hospitable, and who fear the Gods?
240 Where now shall I secrete these num'rous stores?
Where wander I, myself? I would that still
Phæacians own'd them, and I had arrived
In the dominions of some other King
Magnanimous, who would have entertain'd
And sent me to my native home secure!
Now, neither know I where to place my wealth,
Nor can I leave it here, lest it become
Another's prey. Alas! Phæacia's Chiefs
Not altogether wise I deem or just,
250 Who have misplaced me in another land,
Promis'd to bear me to the pleasant shores
Of Ithaca, but have not so perform'd.
Jove, guardian of the suppliant's rights, who all
Transgressors marks, and punishes all wrong,
Avenge me on the treach'rous race! — but hold-
I will revise my stores, so shall I know
If they have left me here of aught despoiled.
So saying, he number'd carefully the gold,
The vases, tripods bright, and tissued robes,
260 But nothing miss'd of all. Then he bewail'd
His native isle, with pensive steps and slow
Pacing the border of the billowy flood,
Forlorn; but while he wept, Pallas approach'd,
In form a shepherd stripling, girlish fair
In feature, such as are the sons of Kings;
A sumptuous mantle o'er his shoulders hung
Twice-folded, sandals his nice feet upbore,
And a smooth javelin glitter'd in his hand.
Ulysses, joyful at the sight, his steps
270 Turn'd brisk toward her, whom he thus address'd.
Sweet youth! since thee, of all mankind, I first
Encounter in this land unknown, all hail!
Come not with purposes of harm to me!
These save, and save me also. I prefer
To thee, as to some God, my pray'r, and clasp
Thy knees a suppliant. Say, and tell me true,
What land? what people? who inhabit here?

Is this some isle delightful, or a shore
Of fruitful main-land sloping to the sea?
280 Then Pallas, thus, Goddess cærulean-eyed.
Stranger! thou sure art simple, or hast dwelt
Far distant hence, if of this land thou ask.
It is not, trust me, of so little note,
But known to many, both to those who dwell
Toward the sunrise, and to others placed
Behind it, distant in the dusky West.
Rugged it is, not yielding level course
To the swift steed, and yet no barren spot,
However small, but rich in wheat and wine;
290 Nor wants it rain or fertilising dew,
But pasture green to goats and beeves affords,
Trees of all kinds, and fountains never dry.
Ithaca therefore, stranger, is a name
Known ev'n at Troy, a city, by report,
At no small distance from Achaia's shore.
The Goddess ceased; then, toil-enduring Chief
Ulysses, happy in his native land,
(So taught by Pallas, progeny of Jove)
In accents wing'd her answ'ring, utter'd prompt
300 Not truth, but figments to truth opposite,
For guile, in him, stood never at a pause.

O'er yonder flood, even in spacious Crete[60]
I heard of Ithaca, where now, it seems,
I have, myself, with these my stores arrived;
Not richer stores than, flying thence, I left
To my own children; for from Crete I fled
For slaughter of Orsilochus the swift,
Son of Idomeneus, whom none in speed
Could equal throughout all that spacious isle.
310 His purpose was to plunder me of all
My Trojan spoils, which to obtain, much woe
I had in battle and by storms endured,
For that I would not gratify his Sire,
Fighting beside him in the fields of Troy,
But led a diff'rent band. Him from the field
Returning homeward, with my brazen spear
I smote, in ambush waiting his return
At the road-side, with a confed'rate friend.
Unwonted darkness over all the heav'ns
320 That night prevailed, nor any eye of man
Observed us, but, unseen, I slew the youth.
No sooner, then, with my sharp spear of life
I had bereft him, than I sought a ship
Mann'd by renown'd Phæacians, whom with gifts
Part of my spoils, and by requests, I won.
I bade them land me on the Pylian shore,
Or in fair Elis by th' Epeans ruled,
But they, reluctant, were by violent winds
Driv'n devious thence, for fraud they purposed none.
330 Thus through constraint we here arrived by night,
And with much difficulty push'd the ship
Into safe harbour, nor was mention made
Of food by any, though all needed food,
But, disembark'd in haste, on shore we lay.
I, weary, slept profound, and they my goods
Forth heaving from the bark, beside me placed

---

[60] Homer dates all the fictions of Ulysses from Crete, as if he meant to pass a similar censure on the Cretans to that quoted by St. Paul-+krêtes aei pseusai+.

The treasures on the sea-beach where I slept,
Then, reimbarking, to the populous coast
Steer'd of Sidonia, and me left forlorn.
340 He ceased; then smiled Minerva azure-eyed
And stroaked his cheek, in form a woman now,
Beauteous, majestic, in all elegant arts
Accomplish'd, and with accents wing'd replied.
Who passes thee in artifice well-framed
And in imposture various, need shall find
Of all his policy, although a God.
Canst thou not cease, inventive as thou art
And subtle, from the wiles which thou hast lov'd
Since thou wast infant, and from tricks of speech
350 Delusive, even in thy native land?
But come, dismiss we these ingenious shifts
From our discourse, in which we both excel;
For thou of all men in expedients most
Abound'st and eloquence, and I, throughout
All heav'n have praise for wisdom and for art.
And know'st thou not thine Athenæan aid,
Pallas, Jove's daughter, who in all thy toils
Assist thee and defend? I gave thee pow'r
T' engage the hearts of all Phæacia's sons,
360 And here arrive ev'n now, counsels to frame
Discrete with thee, and to conceal the stores
Giv'n to thee by the rich Phæacian Chiefs
On my suggestion, at thy going thence.
I will inform thee also what distress
And hardship under thy own palace-roof
Thou must endure; which, since constraint enjoins,
Bear patiently, and neither man apprize
Nor woman that thou hast arrived forlorn
And vagabond, but silent undergo
370 What wrongs soever from the hands of men.
To whom Ulysses, ever-wise, replied.
O Goddess! thou art able to elude,
Wherever met, the keenest eye of man,
For thou all shapes assum'st; yet this I know
Certainly, that I ever found thee kind,
Long as Achaia's Heroes fought at Troy;
But when (the lofty tow'rs of Priam laid
In dust) we re-embark'd, and by the will
Of heav'n Achaia's fleet was scatter'd wide,
380 Thenceforth, O daughter wise of Jove, I thee
Saw not, nor thy appearance in my ship
Once mark'd, to rid me of my num'rous woes,
But always bearing in my breast a heart
With anguish riv'n, I roam'd, till by the Gods
Relieved at length, and till with gracious words
Thyself didst in Phæacia's opulent land
Confirm my courage, and becam'st my guide.
But I adjure thee in thy father's name-
O tell me truly, (for I cannot hope
390 That I have reach'd fair Ithaca; I tread
Some other soil, and thou affirm'st it mine
To mock me merely, and deceive) oh say-
Am I in Ithaca? in truth, at home?
Thus then Minerva the cærulean-eyed.
Such caution in thy breast always prevails
Distrustful; but I know thee eloquent,
With wisdom and with ready thought endued,
And cannot leave thee, therefore, thus distress'd

For what man, save Ulysses, new-return'd
400 After long wand'rings, would not pant to see
At once his home, his children, and his wife?
But thou preferr'st neither to know nor ask
Concerning them, till some experience first
Thou make of her whose wasted youth is spent
In barren solitude, and who in tears
Ceaseless her nights and woeful days consumes.
I ne'er was ignorant, but well foreknew
That not till after loss of all thy friends
Thou should'st return; but loth I was to oppose
410 Neptune, my father's brother, sore incensed
For his son's sake deprived of sight by thee.
But, I will give thee proof-come now-survey
These marks of Ithaca, and be convinced.
This is the port of Phorcys, sea-born sage;
That, the huge olive at the haven's head;
Fast by it, thou behold'st the pleasant cove
Umbrageous, to the nymphs devoted named
The Naiads; this the broad-arch'd cavern is
Where thou wast wont to offer to the nymphs
420 Many a whole hecatomb; and yonder stands
The mountain Neritus with forests cloath'd.
So saying, the Goddess scatter'd from before
His eyes all darkness, and he knew the land.
Then felt Ulysses, Hero toil-inured,
Transport unutterable, seeing plain
Once more his native isle. He kiss'd the glebe,
And with uplifted hands the nymphs ador'd.
Nymphs, Naiads, Jove's own daughters! I despair'd
To see you more, whom yet with happy vows
430 I now can hail again. Gifts, as of old,
We will hereafter at your shrines present,
If Jove-born Pallas, huntress of the spoils,
Grant life to me, and manhood to my son.
Then Pallas, blue-eyed progeny of Jove.
Take courage; trouble not thy mind with thoughts
Now needless. Haste-delay not-far within
This hallow'd cave's recess place we at once
Thy precious stores, that they may thine remain,
Then muse together on thy wisest course.
440 So saying, the Goddess enter'd deep the cave
Caliginous, and its secret nooks explored
From side to side; meantime, Ulysses brought
All his stores into it, the gold, the brass,
And robes magnificent, his gifts received
From the Phæacians; safe he lodg'd them all,
And Pallas, daughter of Jove Ægis-arm'd,
Closed fast, herself, the cavern with a stone.
Then, on the consecrated olive's root
Both seated, they in consultation plann'd
450 The deaths of those injurious suitors proud,
And Pallas, blue-eyed Goddess, thus began.
Laertes' noble son, Ulysses! think
By what means likeliest thou shalt assail
Those shameless suitors, who have now controuled
Three years thy family, thy matchless wife
With language amorous and with spousal gifts
Urging importunate; but she, with tears
Watching thy wish'd return, hope gives to all
By messages of promise sent to each,
460 Framing far other purposes the while.

Then answer thus Ulysses wise return'd.
Ah, Agamemnon's miserable fate
Had surely met me in my own abode,
But for thy gracious warning, pow'r divine!
Come then-Devise the means; teach me, thyself,
The way to vengeance, and my soul inspire
With daring fortitude, as when we loos'd
Her radiant frontlet from the brows of Troy.
Would'st thou with equal zeal, O Pallas! aid
470 Thy servant here, I would encounter thrice
An hundred enemies, let me but perceive
Thy dread divinity my prompt ally.
Him answer'd then Pallas cærulean-eyed.
And such I will be; not unmark'd by me,
(Let once our time of enterprize arrive)
Shalt thou assail them. Many, as I judge,
Of those proud suitors who devour thy wealth
Shall leave their brains, then, on thy palace floor.
But come. Behold! I will disguise thee so
480 That none shall know thee! I will parch the skin
On thy fair body; I will cause thee shed
Thy wavy locks; I will enfold thee round
In such a kirtle as the eyes of all
Shall loath to look on; and I will deform
With blurring rheums thy eyes, so vivid erst;
So shall the suitors deem thee, and thy wife,
And thy own son whom thou didst leave at home,
Some sordid wretch obscure. But seek thou first
Thy swine-herd's mansion; he, alike, intends
490 Thy good, and loves, affectionate, thy son
And thy Penelope; thou shalt find the swain
Tending his herd; they feed beneath the rock
Corax, at side of Arethusa's fount,
On acorns dieted, nutritious food
To them, and drinking of the limpid stream.

There waiting, question him of thy concerns,
While I from Sparta praised for women fair
Call home thy son Telemachus, a guest
With Menelaus now, whom to consult
500 In spacious Lacedæmon he is gone,
Anxious to learn if yet his father lives.
To whom Ulysses, ever-wise, replied.
And why, alas! all-knowing as thou art,
Him left'st thou ignorant? was it that he,
He also, wand'ring wide the barren Deep,
Might suffer woe, while these devour his wealth?
Him answer'd then Pallas cærulean-eyed.
Grieve thou not much for him. I sent him forth
Myself, that there arrived, he might acquire
510 Honour and fame. No suff'rings finds he there,
But in Atrides' palace safe resides,
Enjoying all abundance. Him, in truth,
The suitors watch close ambush'd on the Deep,
Intent to slay him ere he reach his home,
But shall not as I judge, till of themselves
The earth hide some who make thee, now, a prey.
So saying, the Goddess touch'd him with a wand.
At once o'er all his agile limbs she parch'd
The polish'd skin; she wither'd to the root
520 His wavy locks; and cloath'd him with the hide
Deform'd of wrinkled age; she charged with rheums
His eyes before so vivid, and a cloak
And kirtle gave him, tatter'd, both, and foul,
And smutch'd with smoak; then, casting over all
An huge old deer-skin bald, with a long staff
She furnish'd him, and with a wallet patch'd
On all sides, dangling by a twisted thong.
Thus all their plan adjusted, diff'rent ways
They took, and she, seeking Ulysses' son,
530 To Lacedæmon's spacious realm repair'd.

Book XIV

Ulysses arriving at the house of Eumæus, is hospitably entertained, and spends the night there.

Leaving the haven-side, he turn'd his steps
Into a rugged path, which over hills
Mantled with trees led him to the abode
By Pallas mention'd of his noble friend[61]
The swineherd, who of all Ulysses' train
Watch'd with most diligence his rural stores.
Him sitting in the vestibule he found
Of his own airy lodge commodious, built
Amidst a level lawn. That structure neat
Eumæus, in the absence of his Lord,
10 Had raised, himself, with stones from quarries hewn,
Unaided by Laertes or the Queen.
With tangled thorns he fenced it safe around,
And with contiguous stakes riv'n from the trunks
Of solid oak black-grain'd hemm'd it without.
Twelve penns he made within, all side by side,
Lairs for his swine, and fast-immured in each
Lay fifty pregnant females on the floor.
The males all slept without, less num'rous far,
Thinn'd by the princely wooers at their feasts
2 °Continual, for to them he ever sent
The fattest of his saginated charge.
Three hundred, still, and sixty brawns remained.
Four mastiffs in adjoining kennels lay,
Resembling wild-beasts nourish'd at the board
Of the illustrious steward of the styes.
Himself sat fitting sandals to his feet,
Carved from a stain'd ox-hide. Four hinds he kept,
Now busied here and there; three in the penns
Were occupied; meantime, the fourth had sought
30 The city, whither, for the suitors' use,
With no good will, but by constraint, he drove
A boar, that, sacrificing to the Gods,
Th' imperious guests might on his flesh regale.
Soon as those clamorous watch-dogs the approach
Saw of Ulysses, baying loud, they ran
Toward him; he, as ever, well-advised,
Squatted, and let his staff fall from his hand.
Yet foul indignity he had endured
Ev'n there, at his own farm, but that the swain,
40 Following his dogs in haste, sprang through the porch
To his assistance, letting fall the hide.
With chiding voice and vollied stones he soon
Drove them apart, and thus his Lord bespake.
Old man! one moment more, and these my dogs
Had, past doubt, worried thee, who should'st have proved,
So slain, a source of obloquy to me.
But other pangs the Gods, and other woes
To me have giv'n, who here lamenting sit
My godlike master, and his fatted swine

50 Nourish for others' use, while he, perchance,
A wand'rer in some foreign city, seeks
Fit sustenance, and none obtains, if still
Indeed he live, and view the light of day.
But, old friend! follow me into the house,
That thou, at least, with plenteous food refresh'd,
And cheer'd with wine sufficient, may'st disclose
Both who thou art, and all that thou hast borne.
So saying, the gen'rous swineherd introduced
Ulysses, and thick bundles spread of twigs
60 Beneath him, cover'd with the shaggy skin
Of a wild goat, of which he made his couch
Easy and large; the Hero, so received,
Rejoiced, and thus his gratitude express'd.
Jove grant thee and the Gods above, my host,
For such beneficence thy chief desire!
To whom, Eumæus, thou didst thus reply.
My guest! I should offend, treating with scorn
The stranger, though a poorer should arrive
Than ev'n thyself; for all the poor that are,
70 And all the strangers are the care of Jove.
Little, and with good will, is all that lies
Within my scope; no man can much expect
From servants living in continual fear
Under young masters; for the Gods, no doubt,
Have intercepted my own Lord's return,
From whom great kindness I had, else, received,
With such a recompense as servants gain
From gen'rous masters, house and competence,
And lovely wife from many a wooer won,
80 Whose industry should have requited well
His goodness, with such blessing from the Gods
As now attends me in my present charge.
Much had I, therefore, prosper'd, had my Lord
Grown old at home; but he hath died-I would
That the whole house of Helen, one and all,
Might perish too, for she hath many slain
Who, like my master, went glory to win
For Agamemnon in the fields of Troy.
So saying, he girdled, quick, his tunic close,
90 And, issuing, sought the styes; thence bringing two
Of the imprison'd herd, he slaughter'd both,
Singed them, and slash'd and spitted them, and placed
The whole well-roasted banquet, spits and all,
Reeking before Ulysses; last, with flour
He sprinkled them, and filling with rich wine
His ivy goblet, to his master sat
Opposite, whom inviting thus he said.
Now, eat, my guest! such as a servant may
I set before thee, neither large of growth

---

[61] +Dios hyphorbos+.-The swineherd's was therefore in those days, and in that country, an occupation honourable as well as useful. Barnes deems the epithet +dios+ significant of his noble birth. Vide Clarke in loco.

100 Nor fat; the fatted-those the suitors eat,
Fearless of heav'n, and pitiless of man.
Yet deeds unjust as theirs the blessed Gods
Love not; they honour equity and right.
Even an hostile band when they invade
A foreign shore, which by consent of Jove
They plunder, and with laden ships depart,
Even they with terrours quake of wrath divine.
But these are wiser; these must sure have learn'd
From some true oracle my master's death,
110 Who neither deign with decency to woo,
Nor yet to seek their homes, but boldly waste
His substance, shameless, now, and sparing nought.
Jove ne'er hath giv'n us yet the night or day
When with a single victim, or with two
They would content them, and his empty jars
Witness how fast the squand'rers use his wine.
Time was, when he was rich indeed; such wealth
No Hero own'd on yonder continent,
Nor yet in Ithaca; no twenty Chiefs
12 °Could match with all their treasures his alone;
I tell thee their amount. Twelve herds of his
The mainland graze;[62] as many flocks of sheep;
As many droves of swine; and hirelings there
And servants of his own seed for his use,
As many num'rous flocks of goats; his goats,
(Not fewer than eleven num'rous flocks)
Here also graze the margin of his fields
Under the eye of servants well-approved,
And ev'ry servant, ev'ry day, brings home
130 The goat, of all his flock largest and best.
But as for me, I have these swine in charge,
Of which, selected with exactest care
From all the herd, I send the prime to them.
He ceas'd, meantime Ulysses ate and drank
Voracious, meditating, mute, the death
Of those proud suitors. His repast, at length,
Concluded, and his appetite suffic'd,
Eumæus gave him, charged with wine, the cup
From which he drank himself; he, glad, received
140 The boon, and in wing'd accents thus began.
My friend, and who was he, wealthy and brave
As thou describ'st the Chief, who purchased thee?
Thou say'st he perish'd for the glory-sake
Of Agamemnon. Name him; I, perchance,
May have beheld the Hero. None can say
But Jove and the inhabitants of heav'n
That I ne'er saw him, and may not impart
News of him; I have roam'd through many a clime.
To whom the noble swineherd thus replied.
150 Alas, old man! no trav'ler's tale of him
Will gain his consort's credence, or his son's;
For wand'rers, wanting entertainment, forge
Falsehoods for bread, and wilfully deceive.
No wand'rer lands in Ithaca, but he seeks
With feign'd intelligence my mistress' ear;
She welcomes all, and while she questions each
Minutely, from her lids lets fall the tear
Affectionate, as well beseems a wife

Whose mate hath perish'd in a distant land.
160 Thou could'st thyself, no doubt, my hoary friend!
(Would any furnish thee with decent vest
And mantle) fabricate a tale with ease;
Yet sure it is that dogs and fowls, long since,
His skin have stript, or fishes of the Deep
Have eaten him, and on some distant shore
Whelm'd in deep sands his mould'ring bones are laid.
So hath he perish'd; whence, to all his friends,
But chiefly to myself, sorrow of heart;
For such another Lord, gentle as he,
170 Wherever sought, I have no hope to find,
Though I should wander even to the house
Of my own father. Neither yearns my heart
So feelingly (though that desiring too)
To see once more my parents and my home,
As to behold Ulysses yet again.
Ah stranger; absent as he is, his name
Fills me with rev'rence, for he lov'd me much,
Cared for me much, and, though we meet no more,
Holds still an elder brother's part in me.
180 Him answer'd, then, the Hero toil-inured.
My friend! since his return, in thy account,
Is an event impossible, and thy mind
Always incredulous that hope rejects,
I shall not slightly speak, but with an oath-
Ulysses comes again; and I demand
No more, than that the boon such news deserves,
Be giv'n me soon as he shall reach his home.
Then give me vest and mantle fit to wear,
Which, ere that hour, much as I need them both,
190 I neither ask, nor will accept from thee.
For him whom poverty can force aside
From truth-I hate him as the gates of hell.
Be Jove, of all in heav'n, my witness first,
Then, this thy hospitable board, and, last,
The household Gods of the illustrious Chief
Himself, Ulysses, to whose gates I go,
That all my words shall surely be fulfill'd.
In this same year Ulysses shall arrive,
Ere, this month closed, another month succeed,
200 He shall return, and punish all who dare
Insult his consort and his noble son.
To whom Eumæus, thou didst thus reply.
Old friend! that boon thou wilt ne'er earn from me;
Ulysses comes no more. But thou thy wine
Drink quietly, and let us find, at length,
Some other theme; recall not this again
To my remembrance, for my soul is grieved
Oft as reminded of my honour'd Lord.
Let the oath rest, and let Ulysses come
210 Ev'n as myself, and as Penelope,
And as his ancient father, and his son
Godlike Telemachus, all wish he may.
Ay-there I feel again-nor cease to mourn
His son Telemachus; who, when the Gods
Had giv'n him growth like a young plant, and I
Well hoped that nought inferior he should prove
In person or in mind to his own sire,

---

[62] It may be proper to suggest that Ulysses was lord of part of the continent opposite to Ithaca-viz.-of the peninsula Nericus or Leuca, which afterward became an island, and is now called Santa Maura. F.

Hath lost, through influence human or divine,
I know not how, his sober intellect,
220 And after tidings of his sire is gone
To far-famed Pylus; his return, meantime,
In ambush hidden the proud suitors wait,
That the whole house may perish of renown'd
Arcesias, named in Ithaca no more.
But whether he have fallen or 'scaped, let him
Rest also, whom Saturnian Jove protect!
But come, my ancient guest! now let me learn
Thy own afflictions; answer me in truth.
Who, and whence art thou? in what city born?
230 Where dwell thy parents; in what kind of ship
Cam'st thou? the mariners, why brought they thee
To Ithaca? and of what land are they?
For, that on foot thou found'st us not, is sure.
Him answer'd, then, Ulysses, ever-wise.
I will with truth resolve thee; and if here
Within thy cottage sitting, we had wine
And food for many a day, and business none
But to regale at ease while others toiled,
I could exhaust the year complete, my woes
240 Rehearsing, nor, at last, rehearse entire
My sorrows by the will of heav'n sustained.
I boast me sprung from ancestry renown'd
In spacious Crete; son of a wealthy sire,
Who other sons train'd num'rous in his house,
Born of his wedded wife; but he begat
Me on his purchased concubine, whom yet
Dear as his other sons in wedlock born
Castor Hylacides esteem'd and lov'd,
For him I boast my father. Him in Crete,
250 While yet he liv'd, all reverenc'd as a God,
So rich, so prosp'rous, and so blest was he
With sons of highest praise. But death, the doom
Of all, him bore to Pluto's drear abode,
And his illustrious sons among themselves
Portion'd his goods by lot; to me, indeed,
They gave a dwelling, and but little more,
Yet, for my virtuous qualities, I won
A wealthy bride, for I was neither vain
Nor base, forlorn as thou perceiv'st me now.
260 But thou canst guess, I judge, viewing the straw
What once was in the ear. Ah! I have borne
Much tribulation; heap'd and heavy woes.
Courage and phalanx-breaking might had I
From Mars and Pallas; at what time I drew,
(Planning some dread exploit) an ambush forth
Of our most valiant Chiefs, no boding fears
Of death seized *me* , but foremost far of all
I sprang to fight, and pierced the flying foe.
Such was I once in arms. But household toils
270 Sustain'd for children's sake, and carking cares
T' enrich a family, were not for me.
My pleasures were the gallant bark, the din
Of battle, the smooth spear and glitt'ring shaft,
Objects of dread to others, but which me
The Gods disposed to love and to enjoy.
Thus diff'rent minds are diff'rently amused;
For ere Achaia's fleet had sailed to Troy,
Nine times was I commander of an host
Embark'd against a foreign foe, and found

280 In all those enterprizes great success.
From the whole booty, first, what pleased me most
Chusing, and sharing also much by lot
I rapidly grew rich, and had thenceforth
Among the Cretans rev'rence and respect.
But when loud-thund'ring Jove that voyage dire
Ordain'd, which loos'd the knees of many a Greek,
Then, to Idomeneus and me they gave
The charge of all their fleet, which how to avoid
We found not, so importunate the cry
290 Of the whole host impell'd us to the task.
There fought we nine long years, and in the tenth
(Priam's proud city pillag'd) steer'd again
Our galleys homeward, which the Gods dispersed.
Then was it that deep-planning Jove devised
For me much evil. One short month, no more,
I gave to joys domestic, in my wife
Happy, and in my babes, and in my wealth,
When the desire seiz'd me with sev'ral ships
Well-rigg'd, and furnish'd all with gallant crews,
300 To sail for Ægypt; nine I fitted forth,
To which stout mariners assembled fast.
Six days the chosen partners of my voyage
Feasted, to whom I num'rous victims gave
For sacrifice, and for their own regale.
Embarking on the sev'nth from spacious Crete,
Before a clear breeze prosp'rous from the North
We glided easily along, as down
A river's stream; nor one of all my ships
Damage incurr'd, but healthy and at ease
310 We sat, while gales well-managed urged us on.
The fifth day thence, smooth-flowing Nile we reach'd,
And safe I moor'd in the Ægyptian stream.
Then, charging all my mariners to keep
Strict watch for preservation of the ships,
I order'd spies into the hill-tops; but they
Under the impulse of a spirit rash
And hot for quarrel, the well-cultur'd fields
Pillaged of the Ægyptians, captive led
Their wives and little ones, and slew the men.
320 Soon was the city alarm'd, and at the cry
Down came the citizens, by dawn of day,
With horse and foot, and with the gleam of arms
Filling the plain. Then Jove with panic dread
Struck all my people; none found courage more
To stand, for mischiefs swarm'd on ev'ry side.
There, num'rous by the glittering spear we fell
Slaughter'd, while others they conducted thence
Alive to servitude. But Jove himself
My bosom with this thought inspired, (I would
330 That, dying, I had first fulfill'd my fate
In Ægypt, for new woes were yet to come!)
Loosing my brazen casque, and slipping off
My buckler, there I left them on the field,
Then cast my spear away, and seeking, next,
The chariot of the sov'reign, clasp'd his knees,
And kiss'd them. He, by my submission moved,
Deliver'd me, and to his chariot-seat
Raising, convey'd me weeping to his home.
With many an ashen spear his warriors sought
340 To slay me, (for they now grew fiery wroth)
But he, through fear of hospitable Jove,

Chief punisher of wrong, saved me alive.
Sev'n years I there abode, and much amass'd
Among the Ægyptians, gifted by them all;
But, in the eighth revolving year, arrived
A shrewd Phoenician, in all fraud adept,
Hungry, and who had num'rous harm'd before,
By whom I also was cajoled, and lured
T' attend him to Phoenicia, where his house
350 And his possessions lay; there I abode
A year complete his inmate; but (the days
And months accomplish'd of the rolling year,
And the new seasons ent'ring on their course)
To Lybia then, on board his bark, by wiles
He won me with him, partner of the freight
Profess'd, but destin'd secretly to sale,
That he might profit largely by my price.
Not unsuspicious, yet constrain'd to go,
With this man I embark'd. A cloudless gale
360 Propitious blowing from the North, our ship
Ran right before it through the middle sea,
In the offing over Crete; but adverse Jove
Destruction plann'd for them and death the while.
For, Crete now left afar, and other land
Appearing none, but sky alone and sea,
Right o'er the hollow bark Saturnian Jove
A cloud cærulean hung, dark'ning the Deep.
Then, thund'ring oft, he hurl'd into the bark
His bolts; she smitten by the fires of Jove,
370 Quaked all her length; with sulphur fill'd she reek'd,
And, o'er her sides precipitated, plunged
Like gulls the crew, forbidden by that stroke
Of wrath divine to hope their country more.
But Jove himself, when I had cast away
All hope of life, conducted to my arms
The strong tall mast, that I might yet escape.
Around that beam I clung, driving before
The stormy blast. Nine days complete I drove,
And, on the tenth dark night, the rolling flood
380 Immense convey'd me to Thesprotia's shore.
There me the Hero Phidon, gen'rous King
Of the Thesprotians, freely entertained;
For his own son discov'ring me with toil
Exhausted and with cold, raised me, and thence
Led me humanely to his father's house,
Who cherish'd me, and gave me fresh attire.
There heard I of Ulysses, whom himself
Had entertain'd, he said, on his return
To his own land; he shew'd me also gold,
390 Brass, and bright steel elab'rate, whatsoe'er
Ulysses had amass'd, a store to feed
A less illustrious family than his
To the tenth generation, so immense
His treasures in the royal palace lay.
Himself, he said, was to Dodona gone,
There, from the tow'ring oaks of Jove to ask
Counsel divine, if openly to land
(After long absence) in his opulent realm
Of Ithaca, be best, or in disguise.
400 To me the monarch swore, in his own hall
Pouring libation, that the ship was launch'd,
And the crew ready for his conduct home.
But me he first dismiss'd, for, as it chanced,

A ship lay there of the Thesprotians, bound
To green Dulichium's isle. He bade the crew
Bear me to King Acastus with all speed;
But them far other thoughts pleased more, and thoughts
Of harm to me, that I might yet be plunged
In deeper gulphs of woe than I had known.
410 For, when the billow-cleaving bark had left
The land remote, framing, combined, a plot
Against my liberty, they stripp'd my vest
And mantle, and this tatter'd raiment foul
Gave me instead, which thy own eyes behold.
At even-tide reaching the cultur'd coast
Of Ithaca, they left me bound on board
With tackle of the bark, and quitting ship
Themselves, made hasty supper on the shore.
But me, meantime, the Gods easily loos'd
420 By their own pow'r, when, with wrapper vile
Around my brows, sliding into the sea
At the ship's stern, I lay'd me on the flood.
With both hands oaring thence my course, I swam
Till past all ken of theirs; then landing where
Thick covert of luxuriant trees I mark'd,
Close couchant down I lay; they mutt'ring loud,
Paced to and fro, but deeming farther search
Unprofitable, soon embark'd again.
Thus baffling all their search with ease, the Gods
43 °Conceal'd and led me thence to the abode
Of a wise man, dooming me still to live.
To whom, Eumæus, thou didst thus reply,
Alas! my most compassionable guest!
Thou hast much moved me by this tale minute
Of thy sad wand'rings and thy num'rous woes.
But, speaking of Ulysses, thou hast pass'd
All credence; I at least can give thee none.
Why, noble as thou art, should'st thou invent
Palpable falsehoods? as for the return
440 Of my regretted Lord, myself I know
That had he not been hated by the Gods
Unanimous, he had in battle died
At Troy, or (that long doubtful war, at last,
Concluded,) in his people's arms at home.
Then universal Greece had raised his tomb,
And he had even for his son atchiev'd
Immortal glory; but alas! by beaks
Of harpies torn, unseemly sight, he lies.
Here is my home the while; I never seek
450 The city, unless summon'd by discrete
Penelope to listen to the news
Brought by some stranger, whencesoe'er arrived.
Then, all, alike inquisitive, attend,
Both who regret the absence of our King,
And who rejoice gratuitous to gorge
His property; but as for me, no joy
Find I in list'ning after such reports,
Since an Ætolian cozen'd me, who found
(After long wand'ring over various lands
460 A fugitive for blood) my lone retreat.
Him warm I welcom'd, and with open arms
Receiv'd, who bold affirm'd that he had seen
My master with Idomeneus at Crete
His ships refitting shatter'd by a storm,
And that in summer with his godlike band

He would return, bringing great riches home,
Or else in autumn. And thou ancient guest
Forlorn! since thee the Gods have hither led,
Seek not to gratify me with untruths
470 And to deceive me, since for no such cause
I shall respect or love thee, but alone
By pity influenced, and the fear of Jove.
To whom Ulysses, ever-wise, replied.
Thou hast, in truth, a most incredulous mind,
Whom even with an oath I have not moved,
Or aught persuaded. Come then—let us make
In terms express a cov'nant, and the Gods
Who hold Olympus, witness to us both!
If thy own Lord at this thy house arrive,
480 Thou shalt dismiss me decently attired
In vest and mantle, that I may repair
Hence to Dulichium, whither I would go.
But, if thy Lord come not, then, gath'ring all
Thy servants, headlong hurl me from a rock,
That other mendicants may fear to lie.
To whom the generous swineherd in return.
Yes, stranger! doubtless I should high renown
Obtain for virtue among men, both now
And in all future times, if, having first
490 Invited thee, and at my board regaled,
I, next, should slay thee; then my pray'rs would mount,
Past question, swiftly to Saturnian Jove.
But the hour calls to supper, and, ere long,
The partners of my toils will come prepared
To spread the board with no unsav'ry cheer.
Thus they conferr'd. And now the swains arrived,
Driving their charge, which fast they soon enclosed
Within their customary penns, and loud
The hubbub was of swine prison'd within.
500 Then call'd the master to his rustic train.
Bring ye the best, that we may set him forth
Before my friend from foreign climes arrived,
With whom ourselves will also feast, who find
The bright-tusk'd multitude a painful charge,
While others, at no cost of theirs, consume
Day after day, the profit of our toils.
So saying, his wood for fuel he prepared,
And dragging thither a well-fatted brawn
Of the fifth year his servants held him fast
510 At the hearth-side. Nor failed the master swain
T' adore the Gods, (for wise and good was he)
But consecration of the victim, first,
Himself performing, cast into the fire
The forehead bristles of the tusky boar,
Then pray'd to all above, that, safe, at length,
Ulysses might regain his native home.
Then lifting an huge shive that lay beside
The fire, he smote the boar, and dead he fell,
Next, piercing him, and scorching close his hair,
520 They carv'd him quickly, and Eumæus spread
Thin slices crude taken from ev'ry limb

O'er all his fat, then other slices cast,
Sprinkling them first with meal, into the fire.
The rest they slash'd and scored, and roasted well,
And placed it, heap'd together, on the board.
Then rose the good Eumæus to his task
Of distribution, for he understood
The hospitable entertainer's part.
Sev'n-fold partition of the banquet made,
530 He gave, with previous pray'r, to Maia's son[63]
And to the nymphs one portion of the whole,
Then served his present guests, honouring first
Ulysses with the boar's perpetual chine;
By that distinction just his master's heart
He gratified, and thus the Hero spake.
Eumæus! be thou as belov'd of Jove
As thou art dear to me, whom, though attired
So coarsely, thou hast served with such respect!
To whom, Eumæus, thou didst thus reply.
540 Eat, noble stranger! and refreshment take
Such as thou may'st; God[64] gives, and God denies
At his own will, for He is Lord of all.
He said, and to the everlasting Gods
The firstlings sacrificed of all, then made
Libation, and the cup placed in the hands
Of city-spoiler Laertiades
Sitting beside his own allotted share.
Meantime, Mesaulius bread dispensed to all,
Whom, in the absence of his Lord, himself
550 Eumæus had from Taphian traders bought
With his own proper goods, at no expence
Either to old Laertes or the Queen.
And now, all stretch'd their hands toward the feast
Reeking before them, and when hunger none
Felt more or thirst, Mesaulius clear'd the board.
Then, fed to full satiety, in haste
Each sought his couch. Black came a moonless night,
And Jove all night descended fast in show'rs,
With howlings of the ever wat'ry West.
560 Ulysses, at that sound, for trial sake
Of his good host, if putting off his cloak
He would accommodate him, or require
That service for him at some other hand,
Addressing thus the family, began.
Hear now, Eumæus, and ye other swains
His fellow-lab'rers! I shall somewhat boast,
By wine befool'd, which forces ev'n the wise
To carol loud, to titter and to dance,
And words to utter, oft, better suppress'd.
570 But since I have begun, I shall proceed,
Prating my fill. Ah might those days return
With all the youth and strength that I enjoy'd,
When in close ambush, once, at Troy we lay!
Ulysses, Menelaus, and myself
Their chosen coadjutor, led the band.
Approaching to the city's lofty wall

---

[63] Mercury.

[64] +Theos+-without a relative, and consequently signifying GOD in the abstract, is not unfrequently found in Homer, though fearing to give offence to serious minds unacquainted with the original, I have not always given it that force in the translation. But here, the sentiment is such as fixes the sense intended by the author with a precision that leaves no option. It is observable too, that +dynatai gar apanta+-is an ascription of power such as the poet never makes to his Jupiter.

Through the thick bushes and the reeds that gird
The bulwarks, down we lay flat in the marsh,
Under our arms, then Boreas blowing loud,
580 A rueful night came on, frosty and charged
With snow that blanch'd us thick as morning rime,
And ev'ry shield with ice was crystall'd o'er.
The rest with cloaks and vests well cover'd, slept
Beneath their bucklers; I alone my cloak,
Improvident, had left behind, no thought
Conceiving of a season so severe;
Shield and belt, therefore, and nought else had I.
The night, at last, nigh spent, and all the stars
Declining in their course, with elbow thrust
590 Against Ulysses' side I roused the Chief,
And thus address'd him ever prompt to hear.
Laertes' noble son, for wiles renown'd!
I freeze to death. Help me, or I am lost.
No cloak have I; some evil dæmon, sure,
Beguil'd me of all prudence, that I came
Thus sparely clad; I shall, I must expire.
So I; he, ready as he was in arms
And counsel both, the remedy at once
Devised, and thus, low-whisp'ring, answer'd me.
600 Hush! lest perchance some other hear-He said,
And leaning on his elbow, spake aloud.
My friends! all hear-a monitory dream
Hath reach'd me, for we lie far from the ships.
Haste, therefore, one of you, with my request
To Agamemnon, Atreus' son, our Chief,
That he would reinforce us from the camp.
He spake, and at the word, Andræmon's son
Thoas arose, who, casting off his cloak,
Ran thence toward the ships, and folded warm
610 Within it, there lay I till dawn appear'd.
Oh for the vigour of such youth again!
Then, some good peasant here, either for love
Or for respect, would cloak a man like me,

Whom, now, thus sordid in attire ye scorn.
To whom, Eumæus, thou didst thus reply.
My ancient guest! I cannot but approve
Thy narrative, nor hast thou utter'd aught
Unseemly, or that needs excuse. No want
Of raiment, therefore, or of aught beside
620 Needful to solace penury like thine,
Shall harm thee here; yet, at the peep of dawn
Gird thy own tatters to thy loins again;
For *we* have no great store of cloaks to boast,
Or change of vests, but singly one for each.
But when Ulysses' son shall once arrive,
He will himself with vest and mantle both
Cloath thee, and send thee whither most thou would'st.
So saying, he rose, and nearer made his couch
To the hearth-side, spreading it thick with skins
630 Of sheep and goats; then lay the Hero down,
O'er whom a shaggy mantle large he threw,
Which ofttimes served him with a change, when rough
The winter's blast and terrible arose.
So was Ulysses bedded, and the youths
Slept all beside him; but the master-swain
Chose not his place of rest so far remote
From his rude charge, but to the outer court
With his nocturnal furniture, repair'd,
Gladd'ning Ulysses' heart that one so true
640 In his own absence kept his rural stores.
Athwart his sturdy shoulders, first, he flung
His faulchion keen, then wrapp'd him in a cloak
Thick-woven, winter-proof; he lifted, next,
The skin of a well-thriven goat, in bulk
Surpassing others, and his javelin took
Sharp-pointed, with which dogs he drove and men.
Thus arm'd, he sought his wonted couch beneath
A hollow rock where the herd slept, secure
From the sharp current of the Northern blast.
650

Book XV

Telemachus, admonished by Minerva, takes leave of Menelaus, but ere he sails, is accosted by Theoclymenos, a prophet of Argos, whom at his earnest request he takes on board. In the meantime Eumæus relates to Ulysses the means by which he came to Ithaca. Telemachus arriving there, gives orders for the return of his bark to the city, and repairs himself to Eumæus.

Meantime to Lacedæmon's spacious vale
Minerva went, that she might summon thence
Ulysses' glorious son to his own home.
Arrived, she found Telemachus reposed
And Nestor's son beneath the vestibule
Of Menelaus, mighty Chief; she saw
Pisistratus in bands of gentle sleep
Fast-bound, but not Telemachus; his mind
No rest enjoy'd, by filial cares disturb'd
Amid the silent night, when, drawing near
10 To his couch side, the Goddess thus began.
Thou canst no longer prudently remain
A wand'rer here, Telemachus! thy home
Abandon'd, and those haughty suitors left
Within thy walls; fear lest, partition made
Of thy possessions, they devour the whole,
And in the end thy voyage bootless prove.
Delay not; from brave Menelaus ask
Dismission hence, that thou may'st find at home
Thy spotless mother, whom her brethren urge
20 And her own father even now to wed
Eurymachus, in gifts and in amount
Of proffer'd dow'r superior to them all.
Some treasure, else, shall haply from thy house
Be taken, such as thou wilt grudge to spare.
For well thou know'st how woman is disposed;
Her whole anxiety is to encrease
His substance whom she weds; no care hath she
Of her first children, or remembers more
The buried husband of her virgin choice.
30 Returning then, to her of all thy train
Whom thou shalt most approve, the charge commit
Of thy concerns domestic, till the Gods
Themselves shall guide thee to a noble wife.
Hear also this, and mark it. In the frith
Samos the rude, and Ithaca between,
The chief of all her suitors thy return
In vigilant ambush wait, with strong desire
To slay thee, ere thou reach thy native shore,
But shall not, as I judge, till the earth hide
40 Many a lewd reveller at thy expence.
Yet, steer thy galley from those isles afar,
And voyage make by night; some guardian God
Shall save thee, and shall send thee prosp'rous gales.
Then, soon as thou attain'st the nearest shore
Of Ithaca, dispatching to the town
Thy bark with all thy people, seek at once
The swineherd; for Eumæus is thy friend.
There sleep, and send him forth into the town
With tidings to Penelope, that safe
50 Thou art restored from Pylus home again.
She said, and sought th' Olympian heights sublime.

Then, with his heel shaking him, he awoke
The son of Nestor, whom he thus address'd.
Rise, Nestor's son, Pisistratus! lead forth
The steeds, and yoke them. We must now depart.
To whom the son of Nestor thus replied.
Telemachus! what haste soe'er we feel,
We can by no means prudently attempt
To drive by night, and soon it will be dawn.
60 Stay, therefore, till the Hero, Atreus' son,
Spear-practis'd Menelaus shall his gifts
Place in the chariot, and with kind farewell
Dismiss thee; for the guest in mem'ry holds
Through life, the host who treats him as a friend.
Scarce had he spoken, when the golden dawn
Appearing, Menelaus, from the side
Of beauteous Helen ris'n, their bed approach'd,
Whose coming when Telemachus perceived,
Cloathing himself hastily in his vest
70 Magnificent, and o'er his shoulders broad
Casting his graceful mantle, at the door
He met the Hero, whom he thus address'd.
Atrides, Menelaus, Chief renown'd!
Dismiss me hence to Ithaca again,
My native isle, for I desire to go.
Him answer'd Menelaus famed in arms.
Telemachus! I will not long delay
Thy wish'd return. I disapprove alike
The host whose assiduity extreme
80 Distresses, and whose negligence offends;
The middle course is best; alike we err,
Him thrusting forth whose wish is to remain,
And hind'ring the impatient to depart.
This only is true kindness-To regale
The present guest, and speed him when he would.
Yet stay, till thou shalt see my splendid gifts
Placed in thy chariot, and till I command
My women from our present stores to spread
The table with a plentiful repast.
90 For both the honour of the guest demands,
And his convenience also, that he eat
Sufficient, ent'ring on a length of road.
But if through Hellas thou wilt take thy way
And traverse Argos, I will, then, myself
Attend thee; thou shalt journey with my steeds
Beneath thy yoke, and I will be thy guide
To many a city, whence we shall not go
Ungratified, but shall in each receive
Some gift at least, tripod, or charger bright,
100 Or golden chalice, or a pair of mules.
To whom Telemachus, discrete, replied.
Atrides, Menelaus, Chief renown'd!
I would at once depart, (for guardian none

Of my possessions have I left behind)
Lest, while I seek my father, I be lost
Myself, or lose what I should grudge to spare.
Which when the valiant Menelaus heard,
He bade his spouse and maidens spread the board
At once with remnants of the last regale.
110 Then Eteoneus came, Boetheus' son
Newly aris'n, for nigh at hand he dwelt,
Whom Menelaus bade kindle the fire
By which to dress their food, and he obey'd.
He next, himself his fragrant chamber sought,
Not sole, but by his spouse and by his son
Attended, Megapenthes. There arrived
Where all his treasures lay, Atrides, first,
Took forth, himself, a goblet, then consign'd
To his son's hand an argent beaker bright.
120 Meantime, beside her coffers Helen stood
Where lay her variegated robes, fair works
Of her own hand. Producing one, in size
And in magnificence the chief, a star
For splendour, and the lowest placed of all,
Loveliest of her sex, she bore it thence.
Then, all proceeding through the house, they sought
Telemachus again, whom reaching, thus
The Hero of the golden locks began.
May Jove the Thunderer, dread Juno's mate,
130 Grant thee, Telemachus! such voyage home
As thy own heart desires! accept from all
My stores selected as the richest far
And noblest gift for finish'd beauty-This.
I give thee wrought elaborate a cup,
Itself all silver, bound with lip of gold.
It is the work of Vulcan, which to me
The Hero Phædimus imparted, King
Of the Sidonians, when, on my return,
Beneath his roof I lodg'd. I make it thine.
140 So saying, the Hero, Atreus' son, the cup
Placed in his hands, and Megapenthes set
Before him, next, the argent beaker bright;
But lovely Helen drawing nigh, the robe
Presented to him, whom she thus address'd.
I also give thee, oh my son, a gift,
Which seeing, thou shalt think on her whose hands
Wrought it; a present on thy nuptial day
For thy fair spouse; meantime, repose it safe
In thy own mother's keeping. Now, farewell!
150 Prosp'rous and happy be thy voyage home!
She ceas'd, and gave it to him, who the gift
Accepted glad, and in the chariot-chest
Pisistratus the Hero all disposed,
Admiring them the while. They, following, next,
The Hero Menelaus to his hall
Each on his couch or on his throne reposed.
A maiden, then, with golden ewer charged
And silver bowl, pour'd water on their hands,
And spread the polish'd table, which with food
160 Various, selected from her present stores,
The mistress of the household charge supplied.
Boetheus' son stood carver, and to each
His portion gave, while Megapenthes, son
Of glorious Menelaus, serv'd the cup.
Then, all with outstretch'd hands the feast assail'd,

And when nor hunger more nor thirst of wine
They felt, Telemachus and Nestor's son
Yoked the swift steeds, and, taking each his seat
In the resplendent chariot, drove at once
170 Right through the sounding portico abroad.
But Menelaus, Hero amber-hair'd,
A golden cup bearing with richest wine
Replete in his right hand, follow'd them forth,
That not without libation first perform'd
They might depart; he stood before the steeds,
And drinking first, thus, courteous, them bespake.
Health to you both, young friends! and from my lips
Like greeting bear to Nestor, royal Chief,
For he was ever as a father kind
180 To me, while the Achaians warr'd at Troy.
To whom Telemachus discrete replied.
And doubtless, so we will; at our return
We will report to him, illustrious Prince!
Thy ev'ry word. And oh, I would to heav'n
That reaching Ithaca, I might at home
Ulysses hail as sure, as I shall hence
Depart, with all benevolence by thee
Treated, and rich in many a noble gift.
While thus he spake, on his right hand appear'd
190 An eagle; in his talons pounced he bore
A white-plumed goose domestic, newly ta'en
From the house-court. Ran females all and males
Clamorous after him; but he the steeds
Approaching on the right, sprang into air.
That sight rejoicing and with hearts reviv'd
They view'd, and thus Pisistratus his speech
Amid them all to Menelaus turn'd.
Now, Menelaus, think, illustrious Chief!
If us, this omen, or thyself regard.
200 While warlike Menelaus musing stood
What answer fit to frame, Helen meantime,
His spouse long-stoled preventing him, began.
Hear me; for I will answer as the Gods
Teach me, and as I think shall come to pass.
As he, descending from his place of birth
The mountains, caught our pamper'd goose away,
So shall Ulysses, after many woes
And wand'rings to his home restored, avenge
His wrongs, or even now is at his home
210 For all those suitors sowing seeds of woe.
To whom Telemachus, discrete, replied.
Oh grant it Jove, Juno's high-thund'ring mate!
So will I, there arrived, with vow and pray'r
Thee worship, as thou wert, thyself, divine.
He said, and lash'd the coursers; fiery they
And fleet, sprang through the city to the plain.
All day the yoke on either side they shook,
Journeying swift; and now the setting sun
To gloomy evening had resign'd the roads,
220 When they to Pheræ came, and in the house
Of good Diocles slept, their lib'ral host,
Whose sire Orsilochus from Alpheus sprang.
But when Aurora, daughter of the Dawn,
Look'd rosy from the East, yoking their steeds,
They in the sumptuous chariot sat again.
Forth through the vestibule they drove, and through
The sounding portico, when Nestor's son

Plied brisk the scourge, and willing flew the steeds.
Thus whirl'd along, soon they approach'd the gates
230 Of Pylus, when Telemachus, his speech
Turning to his companion, thus began.
How, son of Nestor! shall I win from thee
Not promise only, but performance kind
Of my request? we are not bound alone
To friendship by the friendship of our sires,
But by equality of years, and this
Our journey shall unite us still the more.
Bear me not, I intreat thee, noble friend!
Beyond the ship, but drop me at her side,
240 Lest ancient Nestor, though against my will,
Detain me in his palace through desire
To feast me, for I dread the least delay.
He spake; then mused Pisistratus how best
He might effect the wishes of his friend,
And thus at length resolved; turning his steeds
With sudden deviation to the shore
He sought the bark, and placing in the stern
Both gold and raiment, the illustrious gifts
Of Menelaus, thus, in accents wing'd
250 With ardour, urged Telemachus away.
Dispatch, embark, summon thy crew on board,
Ere my arrival notice give of thine
To the old King; for vehement I know
His temper, neither will he let thee hence,
But, hasting hither, will himself enforce
Thy longer stay, that thou may'st not depart
Ungifted; nought will fire his anger more.
So saying, he to the Pylian city urged
His steeds bright-maned, and at the palace-gate
260 Arrived of Nestor speedily; meantime
Telemachus exhorted thus his crew.
My gallant friends! set all your tackle, climb
The sable bark, for I would now return.
He spake; they heard him gladly, and at once
All fill'd the benches. While his voyage he
Thus expedited, and beside the stern
To Pallas sacrifice perform'd and pray'd,
A stranger, born remote, who had escaped
From Argos, fugitive for blood, a seer
270 And of Melampus' progeny, approach'd.
Melampus, in old time, in Pylus dwelt,
Mother of flocks, alike for wealth renown'd
And the magnificence of his abode.
He, flying from the far-famed Pylian King,
The mighty Neleus[65], migrated at length
Into another land, whose wealth, the while,
Neleus by force possess'd a year complete.
Meantime, Melampus in the house endured
Of Phylacus imprisonment and woe,
280 And burn'd with wrath for Neleus' daughter sake
By fell Erynnis kindled in his heart.
But, 'scaping death, he drove the lowing beeves

From Phylace to Pylus, well avenged
His num'rous injuries at Neleus' hands
Sustain'd, and gave into his brother's arms
King Neleus' daughter fair, the promis'd bride.
To Argos steed-renown'd he journey'd next,
There destin'd to inhabit and to rule
Multitudes of Achaians. In that land
290 He married, built a palace, and became
Father of two brave sons, Antiphates
And Mantius; to Antiphates was born
The brave Oïcleus; from Oïcleus sprang
Amphiaraüs, demagogue renown'd,
Whom with all tenderness, and as a friend
Alike the Thund'rer and Apollo prized;
Yet reach'd he not the bounds of hoary age.
But by his mercenary consort's arts[66]
Persuaded, met his destiny at Thebes.
300 He 'gat Alcmæon and Amphilocus.
Mantius was also father of two sons,
Clytus and Polyphides. Clytus pass'd
From earth to heav'n, and dwells among the Gods,
Stol'n by Aurora for his beauty's sake.
But (brave Amphiaraüs once deceased)
Phoebus exalted Polyphides far
Above all others in the prophet's part.
He, anger'd by his father, roam'd away
To Hyperesia, where he dwelt renown'd
310 Throughout all lands the oracle of all.
His son, named Theoclymenus, was he
Who now approach'd; he found Telemachus
Libation off'ring in his bark, and pray'r,
And in wing'd accents ardent him address'd.
Ah, friend! since sacrificing in this place
I find thee, by these sacred rites and those
Whom thou ador'st, and by thy own dear life,
And by the lives of these thy mariners
I beg true answer; hide not what I ask.
320 Who art thou? whence? where born? and sprung from whom?
To whom Telemachus, discrete, replied.
I will inform thee, stranger! and will solve
Thy questions with much truth. I am by birth
Ithacan, and Ulysses was my sire.
But he hath perish'd by a woeful death,
And I, believing it, with these have plow'd
The ocean hither, int'rested to learn
A father's fate long absent from his home.
Then answer'd godlike Theoclymenus.
330 I also am a wand'rer, having slain
A man of my own tribe; brethren and friends
Num'rous had he in Argos steed-renown'd,
And pow'rful are the Achaians dwelling there.
From them, through terrour of impending death,
I fly, a banish'd man henceforth for ever.
Ah save a suppliant fugitive! lest death
O'ertake me, for I doubt not their pursuit.

---

[65] Iphyclus the son of Phylacus had seized and detained cattle belonging to Neleus; Neleus ordered his nephew Melampus to recover them, and as security for his obedience seized on a considerable part of his possessions. Melampus attempted the service, failed, and was cast into prison; but at length escaping, accomplished his errand, vanquished Neleus in battle, and carried off his daughter Pero, whom Neleus had promised to the brother of Melampus, but had afterward refused her.

[66] His wife Eryphyle, bribed by Polynices, persuaded him, though aware that death awaited him at that city, to go to Thebes, where he fell accordingly.

Whom thus Telemachus answer'd discrete.
I shall not, be assured, since thou desir'st
340 To join me, chace thee from my bark away.
Follow me, therefore, and with us partake,
In Ithaca, what best the land affords.
So saying, he at the stranger's hand received
His spear, which on the deck he lay'd, then climb'd
Himself the bark, and, seated in the stern,
At his own side placed Theoclymenus.
They cast the hawsers loose; then with loud voice
Telemachus exhorted all to hand
The tackle, whom the sailors prompt obey'd.
350 The tall mast heaving, in its socket deep
They lodg'd it, and its cordage braced secure,
Then, straining at the halyards, hoised the sail.
Fair wind, and blowing fresh through æther pure
Minerva sent them, that the bark might run
Her nimblest course through all the briny way.
Now sank the sun, and dusky ev'ning dimm'd
The waves, when, driven by propitious Jove,
His bark stood right for Pheræ; thence she stretch'd
To sacred Elis where the Epeans rule,
360 And through the sharp Echinades he next
Steer'd her, uncertain whether fate ordain'd
His life or death, surprizal or escape.
Meantime Ulysses and the swineherd ate
Their cottage-mess, and the assistant swains
Theirs also; and when hunger now and thirst
Had ceased in all, Ulysses thus began,
Proving the swineherd, whether friendly still,
And anxious for his good, he would intreat
His stay, or thence hasten him to the town.
370 Eumæus, and all ye his servants, hear!
It is my purpose, lest I wear thee out,
Thee and thy friends, to seek at early dawn
The city, there to beg-But give me first
Needful instructions, and a trusty guide
Who may conduct me thither; there my task
Must be to roam the streets; some hand humane
Perchance shall give me a small pittance there,
A little bread, and a few drops to drink.
Ulysses' palace I shall also seek,
380 And to discrete Penelope report
My tidings; neither shall I fail to mix
With those imperious suitors, who, themselves
Full-fed, may spare perhaps some boon to me.
Me shall they find, in whatsoe'er they wish
Their ready servitor, for (understand
And mark me well) the herald of the skies,
Hermes, from whom all actions of mankind
Their grace receive and polish, is my friend,
So that in menial offices I fear
390 No rival, whether I be called to heap
The hearth with fuel, or dry wood to cleave,
To roast, to carve, or to distribute wine,
As oft the poor are wont who serve the great.
To whom, Eumæus! at those words displeased,
Thou didst reply. Gods! how could such a thought
Possess thee, stranger? surely thy resolve
Is altogether fixt to perish there,

If thou indeed hast purposed with that throng
To mix, whose riot and outrageous acts
400 Of violence echo through the vault of heav'n.
None, such as thou, serve *them* ; their servitors
Are youths well-cloak'd, well-vested; sleek their heads,
And smug their countenances; such alone
Are their attendants, and the polish'd boards
Groan overcharg'd with bread, with flesh, with wine.
Rest here content; for neither me nor these
Thou weariest aught, and when Ulysses' son
Shall come, he will with vest and mantle fair
Cloath thee, and send thee whither most thou would'st.
410 To whom Ulysses, toil-inured.
I wish thee, O Eumæus! dear to Jove
As thou art dear to me, for this reprieve
Vouchsafed me kind, from wand'ring and from woe!
No worse condition is of mortal man
Than his who wanders; for the poor man, driv'n
By woe and by misfortune homeless forth,
A thousand mis'ries, day by day, endures.
Since thou detain'st me, then, and bidd'st me wait
His coming, tell me if the father still
420 Of famed Ulysses live, whom, going hence,
He left so nearly on the verge of life?
And lives his mother? or have both deceased
Already, and descended to the shades?
To whom the master swineherd thus replied.
I will inform thee, and with strictest truth,
Of all that thou hast ask'd. Laertes lives,
But supplication off'ring to the Gods
Ceaseless, to free him from a weary life,
So deeply his long-absent son he mourns,
430 And the dear consort of his early youth,
Whose death is his chief sorrow, and hath brought
Old age on him, or ere its date arrived.
She died of sorrow for her glorious son,
And died deplorably;[67] may never friend
Of mine, or benefactor die as she!
While yet she liv'd, dejected as she was,
I found it yet some solace to converse
With her, who rear'd me in my childish days,
Together with her lovely youngest-born
440 The Princess Ctimena; for side by side
We grew, and I, scarce honour'd less than she.
But soon as our delightful prime we both
Attain'd, to Samos her they sent, a bride,
And were requited with rich dow'r; but me
Cloath'd handsomely with tunic and with vest,
And with fair sandals furnish'd, to the field
She order'd forth, yet loved me still the more.
I miss her kindness now; but gracious heav'n
Prospers the work on which I here attend;
450 Hence have I food, and hence I drink, and hence
Refresh, sometimes, a worthy guest like thee.
But kindness none experience I, or can,
From fair Penelope (my mistress now)
In word or action, so is the house curs'd
With that lewd throng. Glad would the servants be
Might they approach their mistress, and receive
Advice from her; glad too to eat and drink,

---

[67] She is said to have hanged herself.

And somewhat bear each to his rural home,
For perquisites are ev'ry servant's joy.
460 Then answer thus, Ulysses wise return'd.
Alas! good swain, Eumæus, how remote
From friends and country wast thou forced to roam
Ev'n in thy infancy! But tell me true.
The city where thy parents dwelt, did foes
Pillage it? or did else some hostile band
Surprizing thee alone, on herd or flock
Attendant, bear thee with them o'er the Deep,
And sell thee at this Hero's house, who pay'd
Doubtless for *thee* no sordid price or small?
470 To whom the master swineherd in reply.
Stranger! since thou art curious to be told
My story, silent listen, and thy wine
At leisure quaff. The nights are longest now,
And such as time for sleep afford, and time
For pleasant conf'rence; neither were it good
That thou should'st to thy couch before thy hour,
Since even sleep is hurtful, in excess.
Whoever here is weary, and desires
Early repose, let him depart to rest,
480 And, at the peep of day, when he hath fed
Sufficiently, drive forth my master's herd;
But we with wine and a well-furnish'd board
Supplied, will solace mutually derive
From recollection of our sufferings past;
For who hath much endured, and wander'd far,
Finds the recital ev'n of sorrow sweet.
Now hear thy question satisfied; attend!
There is an island (thou hast heard, perchance,
Of such an isle) named Syria;[68] it is placed
490 Above Ortigia, and a dial owns[69]
True to the tropic changes of the year.
No great extent she boasts, yet is she rich
In cattle and in flocks, in wheat and wine.
No famine knows that people, or disease
Noisome, of all that elsewhere seize the race
Of miserable man; but when old age
Steals on the citizens, Apollo, arm'd
With silver bow and bright Diana come,
Whose gentle shafts dismiss them soon to rest.
500 Two cities share between them all the isle,
And both were subject to my father's sway
Ctesius Ormenides, a godlike Chief.
It chanced that from Phoenicia, famed for skill
In arts marine, a vessel thither came
By sharpers mann'd, and laden deep with toys.
Now, in my father's family abode
A fair Phoenician, tall, full-sized, and skill'd
In works of elegance, whom they beguiled.
While she wash'd linen on the beach, beside
510 The ship, a certain mariner of those
Seduced her; for all women, ev'n the wise
And sober, feeble prove by love assail'd.

Who was she, he enquired, and whence? nor she
Scrupled to tell at once her father's home.
I am of Sidon,[70] famous for her works
In brass and steel; daughter of Arybas,
Who rolls in affluence; Taphian pirates thence
Stole me returning from the field, from whom
This Chief procured me at no little cost.
520 Then answer thus her paramour return'd.
Wilt thou not hence to Sidon in our ship,
That thou may'st once more visit the abode
Of thy own wealthy parents, and themselves?
For still they live, and still are wealthy deem'd.
To whom the woman. Even that might be,
Would ye, ye seamen, by a solemn oath
Assure me of a safe conveyance home.
Then sware the mariners as she required,
And, when their oath was ended, thus again
530 The woman of Phoenicia them bespake.
Now, silence! no man, henceforth, of you all
Accost me, though he meet me on the road,
Or at yon fountain; lest some tattler run
With tidings home to my old master's ear,
Who, with suspicion touch'd, may *me* confine
In cruel bonds, and death contrive for *you* .
But be ye close; purchase your stores in haste;
And when your vessel shall be freighted full,
Quick send me notice, for I mean to bring
540 What gold soever opportune I find,
And will my passage cheerfully defray
With still another moveable. I nurse
The good man's son, an urchin shrewd, of age
To scamper at my side; him will I bring,
Whom at some foreign market ye shall prove
Saleable at what price soe'er ye will.
So saying, she to my father's house return'd.
They, there abiding the whole year, their ship
With purchased goods freighted of ev'ry kind,
550 And when, her lading now complete, she lay
For sea prepared, their messenger arrived
To summon down the woman to the shore.
A mariner of theirs, subtle and shrewd,
Then, ent'ring at my father's gate, produced
A splendid collar, gold with amber strung.
My mother (then at home) with all her maids
Handling and gazing on it with delight,
Proposed to purchase it, and he the nod
Significant, gave unobserv'd, the while,
560 To the Phoenician woman, and return'd.
She, thus informed, leading me by the hand
Went forth, and finding in the vestibule
The cups and tables which my father's guests
Had used, (but they were to the forum gone
For converse with their friends assembled there)
Convey'd three cups into her bosom-folds,
And bore them off, whom I a thoughtless child

---

[68] Not improbably the isthmus of Syracuse, an island, perhaps, or peninsula at that period, or at least imagined to be such by Homer. The birth of Diana gave fame to Ortygia. F.

[69] +Hothi tropai êelioio+-The Translator has rendered the passage according to that interpretation of it to which several of the best expositors incline. Nothing can be so absurd as to suppose that Homer, so correct in his geography, could mean to place a Mediterranean island under the Tropic.

[70] A principal city of Phoenicia.

Accompanied, at the decline of day,
When dusky evening had embrown'd the shore.
570 We, stepping nimbly on, soon reach'd the port
Renown'd, where that Phoenician vessel lay.
They shipp'd us both, and all embarking cleav'd
Their liquid road, by favourable gales,
Jove's gift, impell'd. Six days we day and night
Continual sailed, but when Saturnian Jove
Now bade the sev'nth bright morn illume the skies,
Then, shaft-arm'd Dian struck the woman dead.
At once she pitch'd headlong into the bilge
Like a sea-coot, whence heaving her again,
580 The seamen gave her to be fishes' food,
And I survived to mourn her. But the winds
And rolling billows them bore to the coast
Of Ithaca, where with his proper goods
Laertes bought me. By such means it chanced
That e'er I saw the isle in which I dwell.
To whom Ulysses, glorious Chief, replied.
Eumæus! thou hast moved me much, thy woes
Enumerating thus at large. But Jove
Hath neighbour'd all thy evil with this good,
590 That after num'rous sorrows thou hast reach'd
The house of a kind master, at whose hands
Thy sustenance is sure, and here thou lead'st
A tranquil life; but I have late arrived,
City after city of the world explored.
Thus mutual they conferr'd, nor leisure found
Save for short sleep, by morning soon surprized.
Meantime the comrades of Telemachus
Approaching land, cast loose the sail, and lower'd
Alert the mast, then oar'd the vessel in.
600 The anchors heav'd aground,[71] and hawsers tied
Secure, themselves, forth-issuing on the shore,
Breakfast prepared, and charged their cups with wine.
When neither hunger now, nor thirst remained
Unsatisfied, Telemachus began.
Push ye the sable bark without delay
Home to the city. I will to the field
Among my shepherds, and, (my rural works
Survey'd,) at eve will to the town return.
To-morrow will I set before you wine
610 And plenteous viands, wages of your toil.
To whom the godlike Theoclymenus.
Whither must I, my son? who, of the Chiefs
Of rugged Ithaca, shall harbour me?
Shall I to thine and to thy mother's house?
Then thus Telemachus, discrete, replied.
I would invite thee to proceed at once
To our abode, since nought should fail thee there
Of kind reception, but it were a course
Now not adviseable; for I must myself,
620 Be absent, neither would my mother's eyes

Behold thee, so unfrequent she appears
Before the suitors, shunning whom, she sits
Weaving continual at the palace-top.
But I will name to thee another Chief
Whom thou may'st seek, Eurymachus, the son
Renown'd of prudent Polybus, whom all
The people here reverence as a God.
Far noblest of them all is he, and seeks
More ardent than his rivals far, to wed
630 My mother, and to fill my father's throne.
But, He who dwells above, Jove only knows
If some disastrous day be not ordain'd
For them, or ere those nuptials shall arrive.
While thus he spake, at his right hand appear'd,
Messenger of Apollo, on full wing,
A falcon; in his pounces clench'd he bore
A dove, which rending, down he pour'd her plumes
Between the galley and Telemachus.
Then, calling him apart, the prophet lock'd
640 His hand in his, and thus explain'd the sign.
Not undirected by the Gods his flight
On our right hand, Telemachus! this hawk
Hath wing'd propitious; soon as I perceived
I knew him ominous-In all the isle
No family of a more royal note
Than yours is found, and yours shall still prevail.
Whom thus Telemachus answer'd discrete.
Grant heav'n, my guest! that this good word of thine
Fail not, and soon thou shalt such bounty share
650 And friendship at my hands, that, at first sight,
Whoe'er shall meet thee shall pronounce thee blest.
Then, to Piræus thus, his friend approved.
Piræus, son of Clytius! (for of all
My followers to the shore of Pylus, none
More prompt than thou hath my desires perform'd)
Now also to thy own abode conduct
This stranger, whom with hospitable care
Cherish and honour till myself arrive.
To whom Piræus answer'd, spear-renown'd.
660 Telemachus! however long thy stay,
Punctual I will attend him, and no want
Of hospitality shall he find with me.
So saying, he climb'd the ship, then bade the crew
Embarking also, cast the hawsers loose,
And each, obedient, to his bench repair'd.
Meantime Telemachus his sandals bound,
And lifted from the deck his glitt'ring spear.
Then, as Telemachus had bidden them,
Son of divine Ulysses, casting loose
670 The hawsers, forth they push'd into the Deep
And sought the city, while with nimble pace
Proceeding thence, Telemachus attain'd
The cottage soon where good Eumæus slept,
The swineherd, faithful to his num'rous charge.

---

[71] The anchors were lodged on the shore, not plunged as ours.

Book XVI

Telemachus dispatches Eumæus to the city to inform Penelope of his safe return from Pylus; during his absence, Ulysses makes himself known to his son. The suitors, having watched for Telemachus in vain, arrive again at Ithaca.

It was the hour of dawn, when in the cot
Kindling fresh fire, Ulysses and his friend
Noble Eumæus dress'd their morning fare,
And sent the herdsmen with the swine abroad.
Seeing Telemachus, the watchful dogs
Bark'd not, but fawn'd around him. At that sight,
And at the sound of feet which now approach'd,
Ulysses in wing'd accents thus remark'd.
Eumæus! certain, either friend of thine
Is nigh at hand, or one whom well thou know'st;
10 Thy dogs bark not, but fawn on his approach
Obsequious, and the sound of feet I hear.
Scarce had he ceased, when his own son himself
Stood in the vestibule. Upsprang at once
Eumæus wonder-struck, and from his hand
Let fall the cups with which he was employ'd
Mingling rich wine; to his young Lord he ran,
His forehead kiss'd, kiss'd his bright-beaming eyes
And both his hands, weeping profuse the while,
As when a father folds in his embrace
20 Arrived from foreign lands in the tenth year
His darling son, the offspring of his age,
His only one, for whom he long hath mourn'd,
So kiss'd the noble peasant o'er and o'er
Godlike Telemachus, as from death escaped,
And in wing'd accents plaintive thus began.
Light of my eyes, thou com'st; it is thyself,
Sweetest Telemachus! I had no hope
To see thee more, once told that o'er the Deep
Thou hadst departed for the Pylian coast.
30 Enter, my precious son; that I may sooth
My soul with sight of thee from far arrived,
For seldom thou thy feeders and thy farm
Visitest, in the city custom'd much
To make abode, that thou may'st witness there
The manners of those hungry suitors proud.
To whom Telemachus, discrete, replied.
It will be so. There is great need, my friend!
But here, for thy sake, have I now arrived,
That I may look on thee, and from thy lips
40 Learn if my mother still reside at home,
Or have become spouse of some other Chief,
Leaving untenanted Ulysses' bed
To be by noisome spiders webb'd around.
To whom the master swineherd in return.
Not so, she, patient still as ever, dwells
Beneath thy roof, but all her cheerless days
Despairing wastes, and all her nights in tears.
So saying, Eumæus at his hand received
His brazen lance, and o'er the step of stone
50 Enter'd Telemachus, to whom his sire
Relinquish'd, soon as he appear'd, his seat,
But him Telemachus forbidding, said-

Guest, keep thy seat; our cottage will afford
Some other, which Eumæus will provide.
He ceased, and he, returning at the word,
Reposed again; then good Eumæus spread
Green twigs beneath, which, cover'd with a fleece,
Supplied Ulysses' offspring with a seat.
He, next, disposed his dishes on the board
60 With relicts charged of yesterday; with bread,
Alert, he heap'd the baskets; with rich wine
His ivy cup replenish'd; and a seat
Took opposite to his illustrious Lord
Ulysses. They toward the plenteous feast
Stretch'd forth their hands, (and hunger now and thirst
Both satisfied) Telemachus, his speech
Addressing to their gen'rous host, began.
Whence is this guest, my father? How convey'd
Came he to Ithaca? What country boast
70 The mariners with whom he here arrived?
For, that on foot he found us not, is sure.
To whom Eumæus, thou didst thus reply.
I will with truth answer thee, O my son!
He boasts him sprung from ancestry renown'd
In spacious Crete, and hath the cities seen
Of various lands, by fate ordain'd to roam.
Ev'n now, from a Thesprotian ship escaped,
He reach'd my cottage-but he is thy own;
I yield him to thee; treat him as thou wilt;
80 He is thy suppliant, and depends on thee.
Then thus, Telemachus, discrete, replied.
Thy words, Eumæus, pain my very soul.
For what security can I afford
To any in my house? myself am young,
Nor yet of strength sufficient to repel
An offer'd insult, and my mother's mind
In doubtful balance hangs, if, still with me
An inmate, she shall manage my concerns,
Attentive only to her absent Lord
90 And her own good report, or shall espouse
The noblest of her wooers, and the best
Entitled by the splendour of his gifts.
But I will give him, since I find him lodg'd
A guest beneath thy roof, tunic and cloak,
Sword double-edged, and sandals for his feet,
With convoy to the country of his choice.
Still, if it please thee, keep him here thy guest,
And I will send him raiment, with supplies
Of all sorts, lest he burthen thee and thine.
100 But where the suitors come, there shall not he
With my consent, nor stand exposed to pride
And petulance like theirs, lest by some sneer
They wound him, and through him, wound also me;
For little is it that the boldest can
Against so many; numbers will prevail.

Him answer'd then Ulysses toil-inured.
Oh amiable and good! since even I
Am free to answer thee, I will avow
My heart within me torn by what I hear
110 Of those injurious suitors, who the house
Infest of one noble as thou appear'st.
But say-submittest thou to their controul
Willingly, or because the people, sway'd
By some response oracular, incline
Against thee? Thou hast brothers, it may chance,
Slow to assist thee-for a brother's aid
Is of importance in whatever cause.
For oh that I had youth as I have will,
Or that renown'd Ulysses were my sire,
120 Or that himself might wander home again.
Whereof hope yet remains! then might I lose
My head, that moment, by an alien's hand,
If I would fail, ent'ring Ulysses' gate,
To be the bane and mischief of them all.
But if alone to multitudes opposed
I should perchance be foiled; nobler it were
With my own people, under my own roof
To perish, than to witness evermore
Their unexampled deeds, guests shoved aside,
130 Maidens dragg'd forcibly from room to room,
Casks emptied of their rich contents, and them
Indulging glutt'nous appetite day by day
Enormous, without measure, without end.
To whom, Telemachus, discrete, replied.
Stranger! thy questions shall from me receive
True answer. Enmity or hatred none
Subsists the people and myself between,
Nor have I brothers to accuse, whose aid
Is of importance in whatever cause,
140 For Jove hath from of old with single heirs
Our house supplied; Arcesias none begat
Except Laertes, and Laertes none
Except Ulysses, and Ulysses me
Left here his only one, and unenjoy'd.
Thence comes it that our palace swarms with foes;
For all the rulers of the neighbour isles,
Samos, Dulichium, and the forest-crown'd
Zacynthus, others also rulers here
In craggy Ithaca, my mother seek
150 In marriage, and my household stores consume.
But neither she those nuptial rites abhorr'd
Refuses absolute, nor yet consents
To end them; they my patrimony waste
Meantime, and will destroy me also soon,
As I expect, but heav'n disposes all.
Eumæus! haste, my father! bear with speed
News to Penelope that I am safe,
And have arrived from Pylus; I will wait
Till thou return; and well beware that none
Hear thee beside, for I have many foes.
To whom Eumæus, thou didst thus reply.
It is enough. I understand. Thou speak'st
To one intelligent. But say beside,
Shall I not also, as I go, inform
Distress'd Laertes? who while yet he mourn'd
Ulysses only, could o'ersee the works,
And dieted among his menials oft

As hunger prompted him, but now, they say,
Since thy departure to the Pylian shore,
170 He neither eats as he was wont, nor drinks,
Nor oversees his hinds, but sighing sits
And weeping, wasted even to the bone.
Him then Telemachus answer'd discrete.
Hard though it be, yet to his tears and sighs
Him leave we now. We cannot what we would.
For, were the ordering of all events
Referr'd to our own choice, our first desire
Should be to see my father's glad return.
But once thy tidings told, wander not thou
180 In quest of Him, but hither speed again.
Rather request my mother that she send
Her household's governess without delay
Privately to him; she shall best inform
The ancient King that I have safe arrived.
He said, and urged him forth, who binding on
His sandals, to the city bent his way.
Nor went Eumæus from his home unmark'd
By Pallas, who in semblance of a fair
Damsel, accomplish'd in domestic arts,
190 Approaching to the cottage' entrance, stood
Opposite, by Ulysses plain discern'd,
But to his son invisible; for the Gods
Appear not manifest alike to all.
The mastiffs saw her also, and with tone
Querulous hid themselves, yet bark'd they not.
She beckon'd him abroad. Ulysses saw
The sign, and, issuing through the outer court,
Approach'd her, whom the Goddess thus bespake.
Laertes' progeny, for wiles renown'd!
200 Disclose thyself to thy own son, that, death
Concerting and destruction to your foes,
Ye may the royal city seek, nor long
Shall ye my presence there desire in vain,
For I am ardent to begin the fight.
Minerva spake, and with her rod of gold
Touch'd him; his mantle, first, and vest she made
Pure as new-blanch'd; dilating, next, his form,
She gave dimensions ampler to his limbs;
Swarthy again his manly hue became,
210 Round his full face, and black his bushy chin.
The change perform'd, Minerva disappear'd,
And the illustrious Hero turn'd again
Into the cottage; wonder at that sight
Seiz'd on Telemachus; askance he look'd,
Awe-struck, not unsuspicious of a God,
And in wing'd accents eager thus began.
Thou art no longer, whom I lately saw,
Nor are thy cloaths, nor is thy port the same.
Thou art a God, I know, and dwell'st in heav'n.
220 Oh, smile on us, that we may yield thee rites
Acceptable, and present thee golden gifts
Elaborate; ah spare us, Pow'r divine!
To whom Ulysses, Hero toil-inured.
I am no God. Why deem'st thou me divine?
I am thy father, for whose sake thou lead'st
A life of woe, by violence oppress'd.
So saying, he kiss'd his son, while from his cheeks
Tears trickled, tears till then, perforce restrained.
Telemachus, (for he believed him not

230 His father yet) thus, wond'ring, spake again.
My father, said'st thou? no. Thou art not He,
But some Divinity beguiles my soul
With mock'ries to afflict me still the more;
For never mortal man could so have wrought
By his own pow'r; some interposing God
Alone could render thee both young and old,
For old thou wast of late, and foully clad,
But wear'st the semblance, now, of those in heav'n!
To whom Ulysses, ever-wise, replied.
240 Telemachus! it is not well, my son!
That thou should'st greet thy father with a face
Of wild astonishment, and stand aghast.
Ulysses, save myself, none comes, be sure.
Such as thou seest, after ten thousand woes
Which I have borne, I visit once again
My native country in the twentieth year.
This wonder Athenæan Pallas wrought,
She cloath'd me even with what form she would,
For so she can. Now poor I seem and old,
250 Now young again, and clad in fresh attire.
The Gods who dwell in yonder heav'n, with ease
Dignify or debase a mortal man.
So saying, he sat. Then threw Telemachus
His arms around his father's neck, and wept.
Desire intense of lamentation seized
On both; soft murmurs utt'ring, each indulged
His grief, more frequent wailing than the bird,
(Eagle, or hook-nail'd vulture) from whose nest
Some swain hath stol'n her yet unfeather'd young.
260 So from their eyelids they big drops distill'd
Of tend'rest grief, nor had the setting sun
Cessation of their weeping seen, had not
Telemachus his father thus address'd.
What ship convey'd thee to thy native shore,
My father! and what country boast the crew?
For, that on foot thou not arriv'dst, is sure.
Then thus divine Ulysses toil-inured.
My son! I will explicit all relate.
Conducted by Phæacia's maritime sons
270 I came, a race accustom'd to convey
Strangers who visit them across the Deep.
Me, o'er the billows in a rapid bark
Borne sleeping, on the shores of Ithaca
They lay'd; rich gifts they gave me also, brass,
Gold in full bags, and beautiful attire,
Which, warn'd from heav'n, I have in caves conceal'd.
By Pallas prompted, hither I repair'd
That we might plan the slaughter of our foes,
Whose numbers tell me now, that I may know
280 How pow'rful, certainly, and who they are,
And consultation with my dauntless heart
May hold, if we be able to contend
Ourselves with all, or must have aid beside.
Then, answer thus his son, discrete, return'd.
My father! thy renown hath ever rung
In thy son's ears, and by report thy force
In arms, and wisdom I have oft been told.
But terribly thou speak'st; amazement-fixt
I hear; can two a multitude oppose,
290 And valiant warriors all? for neither ten
Are they, nor twenty, but more num'rous far.

Learn, now, their numbers. Fifty youths and two
Came from Dulichium; they are chosen men,
And six attendants follow in their train;
From Samos twenty youths and four arrive,
Zacynthus also of Achaia's sons
Sends twenty more, and our own island adds,
Herself, her twelve chief rulers; Medon, too,
Is there the herald, and the bard divine,
300 With other two, intendants of the board.
Should we within the palace, we alone,
Assail them all, I fear lest thy revenge
Unpleasant to thyself and deadly prove,
Frustrating thy return. But recollect-
Think, if thou canst, on whose confed'rate arm
Strenuous on our behalf we may rely.
To him replied his patient father bold.
I will inform thee. Mark. Weigh well my words.
Will Pallas and the everlasting Sire
310 Alone suffice? or need we other aids?
Then answer thus Telemachus return'd.
Good friends indeed are they whom thou hast named,
Though throned above the clouds; for their controul
Is universal both in earth and heav'n.
To whom Ulysses, toil-worn Chief renown'd.
Not long will they from battle stand aloof,
When once, within my palace, in the strength
Of Mars, to sharp decision we shall urge
The suitors. But thyself at early dawn
320 Our mansion seek, that thou may'st mingle there
With that imperious throng; me in due time
Eumæus to the city shall conduct,
In form a miserable beggar old.
But should they with dishonourable scorn
Insult me, thou unmov'd my wrongs endure,
And should they even drag me by the feet
Abroad, or smite me with the spear, thy wrath
Refraining, gently counsel them to cease
From such extravagance; but well I know
330 That cease they will not, for their hour is come.
And mark me well; treasure what now I say
Deep in thy soul. When Pallas shall, herself,
Suggest the measure, then, shaking my brows,
I will admonish thee; thou, at the sign,
Remove what arms soever in the hall
Remain, and in the upper palace safe
Dispose them; should the suitors, missing them,
Perchance interrogate thee, then reply
Gently-I have removed them from the smoke;
340 For they appear no more the arms which erst
Ulysses, going hence to Ilium, left,
But smirch'd and sullied by the breath of fire.
This weightier reason (thou shalt also say)
Jove taught me; lest, intoxicate with wine,
Ye should assault each other in your brawls,
Shaming both feast and courtship; for the view
Itself of arms incites to their abuse.
Yet leave two faulchions for ourselves alone,
Two spears, two bucklers, which with sudden force
350 Impetuous we will seize, and Jove all-wise
Their valour shall, and Pallas, steal away.
This word store also in remembrance deep-
If mine in truth thou art, and of my blood,

Then, of Ulysses to his home returned
Let none hear news from thee, no, not my sire
Laertes, nor Eumæus, nor of all
The menials any, or ev'n Penelope,
That thou and I, alone, may search the drift
Of our domestic women, and may prove
360 Our serving-men, who honours and reveres
And who contemns us both, but chiefly thee
So gracious and so worthy to be loved.
Him then thus answer'd his illustrious son.
Trust me, my father! thou shalt soon be taught
That I am not of drowsy mind obtuse.
But this I think not likely to avail
Or thee or me; ponder it yet again;
For tedious were the task, farm after farm
To visit of those servants, proving each,
370 And the proud suitors merciless devour
Meantime thy substance, nor abstain from aught.
Learn, if thou wilt, (and I that course myself
Advise) who slights thee of the female train,
And who is guiltless; but I would not try
From house to house the men, far better proved
Hereafter, if in truth by signs from heav'n
Inform'd, thou hast been taught the will of Jove.
Thus they conferr'd. The gallant bark, meantime,
Reach'd Ithaca, which from the Pylian shore
380 Had brought Telemachus with all his band.
Within the many-fathom'd port arrived
His lusty followers haled her far aground,
Then carried thence their arms, but to the house
Of Clytius the illustrious gifts convey'd.
Next to the royal mansion they dispatch'd
An herald charg'd with tidings to the Queen,
That her Telemachus had reach'd the cot
Of good Eumæus, and the bark had sent
Home to the city; lest the matchless dame
390 Should still deplore the absence of her son.
They, then, the herald and the swineherd, each
Bearing like message to his mistress, met,
And at the palace of the godlike Chief
Arriving, compass'd by the female throng
Inquisitive, the herald thus began.
Thy son, O Queen! is safe; ev'n now return'd.
Then, drawing nigh to her, Eumæus told
His message also from her son received,
And, his commission punctually discharged,
400 Leaving the palace, sought his home again.
Grief seized and anguish, at those tidings, all
The suitors; issuing forth, on the outside
Of the high wall they sat, before the gate,
When Polybus' son, Eurymachus, began.
My friends! his arduous task, this voyage, deem'd
By us impossible, in our despight
Telemachus hath atchieved. Haste! launch we forth
A sable bark, our best, which let us man
With mariners expert, who, rowing forth
410 Swiftly, shall summon our companions home.
Scarce had he said, when turning where he sat,
Amphinomus beheld a bark arrived
Just then in port; he saw them furling sail,
And seated with their oars in hand; he laugh'd
Through pleasure at that sight, and thus he spake.

Our message may be spared. Lo! they arrive.
Either some God inform'd them, or they saw,
Themselves, the vessel of Telemachus
Too swiftly passing to be reach'd by theirs.
420 He spake; they, rising, hasted to the shore.
Alert they drew the sable bark aground,
And by his servant each his arms dispatch'd
To his own home. Then, all, to council those
Assembling, neither elder of the land
Nor youth allow'd to join them, and the rest
Eupithes' son, Antinoüs, thus bespake.
Ah! how the Gods have rescued him! all day
Perch'd on the airy mountain-top, our spies
Successive watch'd; and, when the sun declined,
430 We never slept on shore, but all night long
Till sacred dawn arose, plow'd the abyss,
Hoping Telemachus, that we might seize
And slay him, whom some Deity hath led,
In our despight, safe to his home again.
But frame we yet again means to destroy
Telemachus; ah-let not Him escape!
For end of this our task, while he survives,
None shall be found, such prudence he displays
And wisdom, neither are the people now
440 Unanimous our friends as heretofore.
Come, then-prevent him, ere he call the Greeks
To council; for he will not long delay,
But will be angry, doubtless, and will tell
Amid them all, how we in vain devised
His death, a deed which they will scarce applaud,
But will, perhaps, punish and drive us forth
From our own country to a distant land.-
Prevent him, therefore, quickly; in the field
Slay him, or on the road; so shall his wealth
450 And his possessions on ourselves devolve
Which we will share equally, but his house
Shall be the Queen's, and his whom she shall wed.
Yet, if not so inclined, ye rather chuse
That he should live and occupy entire
His patrimony, then, no longer, here
Assembled, let us revel at his cost,
But let us all with spousal gifts produced
From our respective treasures, woo the Queen,
Leaving her in full freedom to espouse
460 Who proffers most, and whom the fates ordain.
He ceased; the assembly silent sat and mute.
Then rose Amphinomus amid them all,
Offspring renown'd of Nisus, son, himself,
Of King Aretias. He had thither led
The suitor train who from the pleasant isle
Corn-clad of green Dulichium had arrived,
And by his speech pleased far beyond them all
Penelope, for he was just and wise,
And thus, well-counselling the rest, began.
470 Not I, my friends! far be the thought from me
To slay Telemachus! it were a deed
Momentous, terrible, to slay a prince.
First, therefore, let us counsel ask of heav'n,
And if Jove's oracle that course approve,
I will encourage you, and will myself
Be active in his death; but if the Gods
Forbid it, then, by my advice, forbear.

So spake Amphinomus, whom all approved.
Arising then, into Ulysses' house
480 They went, where each his splendid seat resumed.
A novel purpose occupied, meantime,
Penelope; she purposed to appear
Before her suitors, whose design to slay
Telemachus she had from Medon learn'd,
The herald, for his ear had caught the sound.
Toward the hall with her attendant train
She moved, and when, most graceful of her sex,
Where sat the suitors she arrived, between
The columns standing of the stately dome,
490 And covering with her white veil's lucid folds
Her features, to Antinoüs thus she spake.
Antinoüs, proud, contentious, evermore
To mischief prone! the people deem thee wise
Past thy compeers, and in all grace of speech
Pre-eminent, but such wast never thou.
Inhuman! why is it thy dark design
To slay Telemachus? and why with scorn
Rejectest thou the suppliant's pray'r,[72] which Jove
Himself hath witness'd? Plots please not the Gods.
500 Know'st not that thy own father refuge found
Here, when he fled before the people's wrath
Whom he had irritated by a wrong
Which, with a band of Taphian robbers joined,
He offer'd to the Thesprots, our allies?
They would have torn his heart, and would have laid
All his delights and his possessions waste,
But my Ulysses slaked the furious heat
Of their revenge, whom thou requitest now
Wasting his goods, soliciting his wife,
510 Slaying his son, and filling me with woe.
But cease, I charge thee, and bid cease the rest.
To whom the son of Polybus replied,
Eurymachus.-Icarius' daughter wise!
Take courage, fair Penelope, and chace
These fears unreasonable from thy mind!
The man lives not, nor shall, who while I live,
And faculty of sight retain, shall harm
Telemachus, thy son. For thus I say,
And thus will I perform; his blood shall stream
520 A sable current from my lance's point
That moment; for the city-waster Chief

Ulysses, oft, me placing on his knees,
Hath fill'd my infant grasp with sav'ry food,
And giv'n me ruddy wine. I, therefore, hold
Telemachus of all men most my friend,
Nor hath he death to fear from hand of ours.
Yet, if the Gods shall doom him, die he must.
So he encouraged her, who yet, himself,
Plotted his death. She, re-ascending, sought
530 Her stately chamber, and, arriving there,
Deplored with tears her long-regretted Lord
Till Athenæan Pallas azure-eyed
Dews of soft slumber o'er her lids diffused.
And now, at even-tide, Eumæus reach'd
Ulysses and his son. A yearling swine
Just slain they skilfully for food prepared,
When Pallas, drawing nigh, smote with her wand
Ulysses, at the stroke rend'ring him old,
And his apparel sordid as before,
540 Lest, knowing him, the swain at once should seek
Penelope, and let the secret forth.
Then foremost him Telemachus address'd.
Noble Eumæus! thou art come; what news
Bring'st from the city? Have the warrior band
Of suitors, hopeless of their ambush, reach'd
The port again, or wait they still for me?
To whom Eumæus, thou didst thus reply.
No time for such enquiry, nor to range,
Curious, the streets had I, but anxious wish'd
550 To make my message known, and to return.
But, as it chanced, a nimble herald sent
From thy companions, met me on the way,
Who reach'd thy mother first. Yet this I know,
For this I saw. Passing above the town
Where they have piled a way-side hill of stones
To Mercury, I beheld a gallant bark
Ent'ring the port; a bark she was of ours,
The crew were num'rous, and I mark'd her deepLaden
with shields and spears of double edge.
560 Theirs I conjectured her, and could no more.
He spake, and by Eumæus unperceived,
Telemachus his father eyed and smiled.
Their task accomplish'd, and the table spread,
They ate, nor any his due portion miss'd,
And hunger, now, and thirst both sated, all
To rest repair'd, and took the gift of sleep.

---

[72] Alluding probably to entreaties made to him at some former time by herself and Telemachus, that he would not harm them. Clarke.

Book XVII

Telemachus returns to the city, and relates to his mother the principal passages of his voyage; Ulysses, conducted by Eumæus, arrives there also, and enters among the suitors, having been known only by his old dog Argus, who dies at his feet. The curiosity of Penelope being excited by the account which Eumæus gives her of Ulysses, she orders him immediately into her presence, but Ulysses postpones the interview till evening, when the suitors having left the palace, there shall be no danger of interruption. Eumæus returns to his cottage.

Now look'd Aurora from the East abroad,
When the illustrious offspring of divine
Ulysses bound his sandals to his feet;
He seiz'd his sturdy spear match'd to his gripe,
And to the city meditating quick
Departure now, the swineherd thus bespake.
Father! I seek the city, to convince
My mother of my safe return, whose tears,
I judge, and lamentation shall not cease
Till her own eyes behold me. But I lay
10 On thee this charge. Into the city lead,
Thyself, this hapless guest, that he may beg
Provision there, a morsel and a drop
From such as may, perchance, vouchsafe the boon.
I cannot, vext and harass'd as I am,
Feed all, and should the stranger take offence,
The worse for him. Plain truth is my delight.
To whom Ulysses, ever-wise, replied.
Nor is it my desire to be detained.
Better the mendicant in cities seeks
20 His dole, vouchsafe it whosoever may,
Than in the villages. I am not young,
Nor longer of an age that well accords
With rural tasks, nor could I all perform
That it might please a master to command.
Go then, and when I shall have warm'd my limbs
Before the hearth, and when the risen sun
Shall somewhat chase the cold, thy servant's task
Shall be to guide me thither, as thou bidd'st,
For this is a vile garb; the frosty air
30 Of morning would benumb me thus attired,
And, as ye say, the city is remote.
He ended, and Telemachus in haste
Set forth, his thoughts all teeming as he went
With dire revenge. Soon in the palace-courts
Arriving, he reclined his spear against
A column, and proceeded to the hall.
Him Euryclea, first, his nurse, perceived,
While on the variegated seats she spread
Their fleecy cov'ring; swift with tearful eyes
40 She flew to him, and the whole female train
Of brave Ulysses swarm'd around his son,
Clasping him, and his forehead and his neck
Kissing affectionate; then came, herself,
As golden Venus or Diana fair,
Forth from her chamber to her son's embrace,
The chaste Penelope; with tears she threw
Her arms around him, his bright-beaming eyes
And forehead kiss'd, and with a murmur'd plaint
Maternal, in wing'd accents thus began.
50 Thou hast return'd, light of my eyes! my son!

My lov'd Telemachus! I had no hope
To see thee more when once thou hadst embark'd
For Pylus, privily, and with no consent
From me obtain'd, news seeking of thy sire.
But haste; unfold. Declare what thou hast seen.
To whom Telemachus, discrete, replied.
Ah mother! let my sorrows rest, nor me
From death so lately 'scaped afflict anew,
But, bathed and habited in fresh attire,
60 With all the maidens of thy train ascend
To thy superior chamber, there to vow
A perfect hecatomb to all the Gods,
When Jove shall have avenged our num'rous wrongs.
I seek the forum, there to introduce
A guest, my follower from the Pylian shore,
Whom sending forward with my noble band,
I bade Piræus to his own abode
Lead him, and with all kindness entertain
The stranger, till I should myself arrive.
70 He spake, nor flew his words useless away.
She, bathed and habited in fresh attire,
Vow'd a full hecatomb to all the Gods,
Would Jove but recompense her num'rous wrongs.
Then, spear in hand, went forth her son, two dogs
Fleet-footed following him. O'er all his form
Pallas diffused a dignity divine,
And ev'ry eye gazed on him as he pass'd.
The suitors throng'd him round, joy on their lips
And welcome, but deep mischief in their hearts.
80 He, shunning all that crowd, chose to himself
A seat, where Mentor sat, and Antiphus,
And Halytherses, long his father's friends
Sincere, who of his voyage much enquired.
Then drew Piræus nigh, leading his guest
Toward the forum; nor Telemachus
Stood long aloof, but greeted his approach,
And was accosted by Piræus thus.
Sir! send thy menial women to bring home
The precious charge committed to my care,
90 Thy gifts at Menelaus' hands received.
To whom Telemachus, discrete, replied.
Piræus! wait; for I not yet foresee
The upshot. Should these haughty ones effect
My death, clandestine, under my own roof,
And parcel my inheritance by lot,
I rather wish those treasures thine, than theirs.
But should I with success plan for them all
A bloody death, then, wing'd with joy, thyself
Bring home those presents to thy joyful friend.
100 So saying, he led the anxious stranger thence
Into the royal mansion, where arrived,

Each cast his mantle on a couch or throne,
And plung'd his feet into a polish'd bath.
There wash'd and lubricated with smooth oils,
From the attendant maidens each received
Tunic and shaggy mantle. Thus attired,
Forth from the baths they stepp'd, and sat again.
A maiden, next, with golden ewer charged,
And silver bowl, pour'd water on their hands,
110 And spread the polish'd table, which with food
Of all kinds, remnants of the last regale,
The mistress of the household charge supplied.
Meantime, beside a column of the dome
His mother, on a couch reclining, twirl'd
Her slender threads. They to the furnish'd board
Stretch'd forth their hands, and, hunger now and thirst
Both satisfied, Penelope began.
Telemachus! I will ascend again,
And will repose me on my woeful bed;
120 For such it hath been, and with tears of mine
Ceaseless bedew'd, e'er since Ulysses went
With Atreus' sons to Troy. For not a word
Thou would'st vouchsafe me till our haughty guests
Had occupied the house again, of all
That thou hast heard (if aught indeed thou hast)
Of thy long-absent father's wish'd return.
Her answer'd then Telemachus discrete.
Mother, at thy request I will with truth
Relate the whole. At Pylus shore arrived
130 We Nestor found, Chief of the Pylian race.
Receiving me in his august abode,
He entertain'd me with such welcome kind
As a glad father shews to his own son
Long-lost and newly found; so Nestor me,
And his illustrious offspring, entertain'd,
But yet assured me that he nought had heard
From mortal lips of my magnanimous sire,
Whether alive or dead; with his own steeds
He sent me, and with splendid chariot thence
140 To spear-famed Menelaus, Atreus' son.
There saw I Helen, by the Gods' decree
Auth'ress of trouble both to Greece and Troy.
The Hero Menelaus then enquired
What cause had urged me to the pleasant vale
Of Lacedæmon; plainly I rehearsed
The occasion, and the Hero thus replied.
Ye Gods! they are ambitious of the bed
Of a brave man, however base themselves.
But, as it chances when the hart hath laid
150 Her fawns new-yean'd and sucklings yet, to rest
In some resistless lion's den, she roams,
Meantime, the hills, and in the grassy vales
Feeds heedless, but the lion to his lair
Returning soon, both her and hers destroys,
So shall thy father, brave Ulysses, them.
Jove! Pallas! and Apollo! oh that such
As erst in well-built Lesbos, where he strove
With Philomelides, whom wrestling, flat
He threw, when all Achaia's sons rejoiced,
160 Ulysses, now, might mingle with his foes!

Short life and bitter nuptials should be theirs,
But thy enquiries neither indirect
Will I evade, nor give thee false reply,
But all that from the Ancient of the Deep[73]
I have received will utter, hiding nought.
The God declared that he had seen thy sire
In a lone island, sorrowing, and detain'd
An inmate in the grotto of the nymph
Calypso, wanting also means by which
170 To reach the country of his birth again,
For neither gallant barks nor friends had he
To speed his passage o'er the boundless waves.
So Menelaus spake, the spear-renown'd.
My errand thus accomplish'd, I return'd-
And by the Gods with gales propitious blest,
Was wafted swiftly to my native shore.
He spake, and tumult in his mother's heart
So speaking, raised. Consolatory, next,
The godlike Theoclymenus began.
18 °Consort revered of Laertiades!
Little the Spartan knew, but list to me,
For I will plainly prophesy and sure.
Be Jove of all in heav'n my witness first,
Then this thy hospitable board, and, last,
The household Gods of the illustrious Chief

Ulysses, at whose hearth I have arrived,[74]
That, even now, within his native isle
Ulysses somewhere sits, or creeps obscure,
Witness of these enormities, and seeds
190 Sowing of dire destruction for his foes;
So sure an augury, while on the deck
Reclining of the gallant bark, I saw,
And with loud voice proclaim'd it to thy son.
Him answer'd then Penelope discrete.
Grant heav'n, my guest, that this good word of thine
Fail not! then shalt thou soon such bounty share
And friendship at my hands, that at first sight
Whoe'er shall meet thee shall pronounce thee blest.
Thus they conferr'd. Meantime the suitors hurl'd
200 The quoit and lance on the smooth area spread
Before Ulysses' gate, the custom'd scene
Of their contentions, sports, and clamours rude.
But when the hour of supper now approach'd,
And from the pastures on all sides the sheep
Came with their wonted drivers, Medon then
(For he of all the heralds pleas'd them most,
And waited at the board) them thus address'd.
Enough of play, young princes! ent'ring now
The house, prepare we sedulous our feast,
210 Since in well-timed refreshment harm is none.
He spake, whose admonition pleas'd. At once
All, rising, sought the palace; there arrived,
Each cast his mantle off, which on his throne
Or couch he spread, then, brisk, to slaughter fell
Of many a victim; sheep and goats and brawns
They slew, all fatted, and a pastur'd ox,
Hast'ning the banquet; nor with less dispatch
Ulysses and Eumæus now prepared

---

[73] Proteus.

[74] The hearth was the altar on which the lares or household-gods were worshipped.

To seek the town, when thus the swain began.
220 My guest! since thy fixt purpose is to seek
This day the city as my master bade,
Though I, in truth, much rather wish thee here
A keeper of our herds, yet, through respect
And rev'rence of his orders, whose reproof
I dread, for masters seldom gently chide,
I would be gone. Arise, let us depart,
For day already is far-spent, and soon
The air of even-tide will chill thee more.
To whom Ulysses, ever-wise, replied.
230 It is enough. I understand. Thou speak'st
To one intelligent. Let us depart,
And lead, thyself, the way; but give me, first,
(If thou have one already hewn) a staff
To lean on, for ye have described the road
Rugged, and ofttimes dang'rous to the foot.
So saying, his tatter'd wallet o'er his back
He cast, suspended by a leathern twist,
Eumæus gratified him with a staff,
And forth they went, leaving the cottage kept
240 By dogs and swains. He city-ward his King
Led on, in form a squalid beggar old,
Halting, and in unseemly garb attired.
But when, slow-travelling the craggy way,
They now approach'd the town, and had attain'd
The marble fountain deep, which with its streams
Pellucid all the citizens supplied,
(Ithacus had that fountain framed of old
With Neritus and Polyctor, over which
A grove of water-nourish'd alders hung
25 °Circular on all sides, while cold the rill
Ran from the rock, on whose tall summit stood
The altar of the nymphs, by all who pass'd
With sacrifice frequented, still, and pray'r)
Melantheus, son of Dolius, at that fount
Met them; the chosen goats of ev'ry flock,
With two assistants, from the field he drove,
The suitors' supper. He, seeing them both,
In surly accent boorish, such as fired
Ulysses with resentment, thus began.
260 Ay-this is well-The villain leads the vile-
Thus evermore the Gods join like to like.
Thou clumsy swineherd, whither would'st conduct
This morsel-hunting mendicant obscene,
Defiler base of banquets? many a post
Shall he rub smooth that props him while he begs
Lean alms, sole object of his low pursuit,
Who ne'er to sword or tripod yet aspired.
Would'st thou afford him to me for a guard
Or sweeper of my stalls, or to supply
270 My kids with leaves, he should on bulkier thewes
Supported stand, though nourish'd but with whey.
But no such useful arts hath he acquired,
Nor likes he work, but rather much to extort
From others food for his unsated maw.
But mark my prophecy, for it is true,
At famed Ulysses' house should he arrive,
His sides shall shatter many a footstool hurl'd
Against them by the offended princes there.
He spake, and drawing nigh, with his rais'd foot,
280 Insolent as he was and brutish, smote

Ulysses' haunch, yet shook not from his path
The firm-set Chief, who, doubtful, mused awhile
Whether to rush on him, and with his staff
To slay him, or uplifting him on high,
Downward to dash him headlong; but his wrath
Restraining, calm he suffer'd the affront.
Him then Eumæus with indignant look
Rebuking, rais'd his hands, and fervent pray'd.
Nymphs of the fountains, progeny of Jove!
290 If e'er Ulysses on your altar burn'd
The thighs of fatted lambs or kidlings, grant
This my request. O let the Hero soon,
Conducted by some Deity, return!
So shall he quell that arrogance which safe
Thou now indulgest, roaming day by day
The city, while bad shepherds mar the flocks.
To whom the goat-herd answer thus return'd
Melantheus. Marvellous! how rare a speech
The subtle cur hath framed! whom I will send
300 Far hence at a convenient time on board
My bark, and sell him at no little gain.
I would, that he who bears the silver bow
As sure might pierce Telemachus this day
In his own house, or that the suitors might,
As that same wand'rer shall return no more!
He said, and them left pacing slow along,
But soon, himself, at his Lord's house arrived;
There ent'ring bold, he with the suitors sat
Opposite to Eurymachus, for him
310 He valued most. The sewers his portion placed
Of meat before him, and the maiden, chief
Directress of the household gave him bread.
And now, Ulysses, with the swain his friend
Approach'd, when, hearing the harmonious lyre,
Both stood, for Phemius had begun his song.
He grasp'd the swineherd's hand, and thus he said.
This house, Eumæus! of Ulysses seems
Passing magnificent, and to be known
With ease for his among a thousand more.
320 One pile supports another, and a wall
Crested with battlements surrounds the court;
Firm, too, the folding doors all force of man
Defy; but num'rous guests, as I perceive,
Now feast within; witness the sav'ry steam
Fast-fuming upward, and the sounding harp,
Divine associate of the festive board.
To whom, Eumæus, thou didst thus reply.
Thou hast well-guess'd; no wonder, thou art quick
On ev'ry theme; but let us well forecast
330 This business. Wilt thou, ent'ring first, thyself,
The splendid mansion, with the suitors mix,
Me leaving here? or shall I lead the way
While thou remain'st behind? yet linger not,
Lest, seeing thee without, some servant strike
Or drive thee hence. Consider which were best.
Him answer'd, then, the patient Hero bold.
It is enough. I understand. Thou speak'st
To one intelligent. Lead thou the way
Me leaving here, for neither stripes nor blows
340 To me are strange. Much exercised with pain
In fight and on the Deep, I have long since
Learn'd patience. Follow, next, what follow may!

But, to suppress the appetite, I deem
Impossible; the stomach is a source
Of ills to man, an avaricious gulph
Destructive, which to satiate, ships are rigg'd,
Seas travers'd, and fierce battles waged remote.
Thus they discoursing stood; Argus the while,
Ulysses' dog, uplifted where he lay
350 His head and ears erect. Ulysses him
Had bred long since, himself, but rarely used,
Departing, first, to Ilium. Him the youths
In other days led frequent to the chace
Of wild goat, hart and hare; but now he lodg'd
A poor old cast-off, of his Lord forlorn,
Where mules and oxen had before the gate
Much ordure left, with which Ulysses' hinds
Should, in due time, manure his spacious fields.
There lay, with dog-devouring vermin foul
360 All over, Argus; soon as he perceived
Long-lost Ulysses nigh, down fell his ears
Clapp'd close, and with his tail glad sign he gave
Of gratulation, impotent to rise
And to approach his master as of old.
Ulysses, noting him, wiped off a tear
Unmark'd, and of Eumæus quick enquired.
I can but wonder seeing such a dog
Thus lodg'd, Eumæus! beautiful in form
He is, past doubt, but whether he hath been
370 As fleet as fair I know not; rather such
Perchance as masters sometimes keep to grace
Their tables, nourish'd more for shew than use.
To whom, Eumæus, thou didst thus reply.
He is the dog of one dead far remote.
But had he now such feat-performing strength
As when Ulysses left him, going hence
To Ilium, in one moment thou shouldst mark,
Astonish'd, his agility and force.
He never in the sylvan deep recess
380 The wild beast saw that 'scaped him, and he track'd
Their steps infallible; but he hath now
No comfort, for (the master dead afar)
The heedless servants care not for his dog.
Domestics, missing once their Lord's controul,
Grow wilful, and refuse their proper tasks;
For whom Jove dooms to servitude, he takes
At once the half of that man's worth away.
He said, and, ent'ring at the portal, join'd
The suitors. Then his destiny released
390 Old Argus, soon as he had lived to see
Ulysses in the twentieth year restored.
Godlike Telemachus, long ere the rest,
Marking the swineherd's entrance, with a nod
Summon'd him to approach. Eumæus cast
His eye around, and seeing vacant there
The seat which the dispenser of the feast
Was wont to occupy while he supplied
The num'rous guests, planted it right before
Telemachus, and at his table sat,
400 On which the herald placed for him his share
Of meat, and from the baskets gave him bread.
Soon after *him*, Ulysses enter'd slow

The palace, like a squalid beggar old,
Staff-propp'd, and in loose tatters foul attired.
Within the portal on the ashen sill
He sat, and, seeming languid, lean'd against
A cypress pillar by the builder's art
Polish'd long since, and planted at the door.
Then took Telemachus a loaf entire
410 Forth from the elegant basket, and of flesh
A portion large as his two hands contained,
And, beck'ning close the swineherd, charged him thus.
These to the stranger; whom advise to ask
Some dole from ev'ry suitor; bashful fear
Ill suits the mendicant by want oppress'd.
He spake; Eumæus went, and where he sat
Arriving, in wing'd accents thus began.
Telemachus, oh stranger, sends thee these,
And counsels thee to importune for more
420 The suitors, one by one; for bashful fear
Ill suits the mendicant by want oppress'd.
To whom Ulysses, ever-wise, replied.
Jove, King of all, grant ev'ry good on earth
To kind Telemachus, and the complete
Accomplishment of all that he desires!
He said, and with both hands outspread, the mess
Receiving as he sat, on his worn bag
Disposed it at his feet. Long as the bard
Chaunted, he ate, and when he ceas'd to eat,
430 Then also ceas'd the bard divine to sing.
And now ensued loud clamour in the hall
And tumult, when Minerva, drawing nigh
To Laertiades, impell'd the Chief
Crusts to collect, or any pittance small
At ev'ry suitor's hand, for trial's sake
Of just and unjust; yet deliv'rance none
From evil she design'd for any there.

From left to right[75] his progress he began
Petitioning, with outstretch'd hands, the throng,
440 As one familiar with the beggar's art.
They, pitying, gave to him, but view'd him still
With wonder, and enquiries mutual made
Who, and whence was he? Then the goat-herd rose
Melanthius, and th' assembly thus address'd.
Hear me, ye suitors of th' illustrious Queen!
This guest, of whom ye ask, I have beheld
Elsewhere; the swineherd brought him; but himself
I know not, neither who nor whence he is.
So he; then thus Antinoüs stern rebuked
450 The swineherd. Ah, notorious as thou art,
Why hast thou shewn this vagabond the way
Into the city? are we not enough
Infested with these troublers of our feasts?
Deem'st it a trifle that such numbers eat
At thy Lord's cost, and hast thou, therefore, led
This fellow hither, found we know not where?
To whom, Eumæus, thou didst thus reply.
Antinoüs! though of high degree, thou speak'st
Not wisely. What man to another's house
460 Repairs to invite him to a feast, unless
He be of those who by profession serve
The public, prophet, healer of disease,

---

75 That he might begin auspiciously. Wine was served in the same direction. F.

Ingenious artist, or some bard divine
Whose music may exhilarate the guests?
These, and such only, are in ev'ry land
Call'd to the banquet; none invites the poor,
Who much consume, and no requital yield.
But thou of all the suitors roughly treat'st
Ulysses' servants most, and chiefly me;
470 Yet thee I heed not, while the virtuous Queen
Dwells in this palace, and her godlike son.
To whom Telemachus, discrete, replied.
Peace! answer not verbose a man like him.
Antinoüs hath a tongue accustom'd much
To tauntings, and promotes them in the rest.
Then, turning to Antinoüs, quick he said-
Antinoüs! as a father for his son
Takes thought, so thou for me, who bidd'st me chase
The stranger harshly hence; but God forbid![76]
480 Impart to him. I grudge not, but myself
Exhort thee to it; neither, in this cause,
Fear thou the Queen, or in the least regard
Whatever menial throughout all the house
Of famed Ulysses. Ah! within thy breast
Dwells no such thought; thou lov'st not to impart
To others, but to gratify thyself.
To whom Antinoüs answer thus return'd.
High-soaring and intemp'rate in thy speech
How hast thou said, Telemachus? Would all
490 As much bestow on him, he should not seek
Admittance here again three months to come.
So saying, he seized the stool which, banqueting,
He press'd with his nice feet, and from beneath
The table forth advanced it into view.
The rest all gave to him, with bread and flesh
Filling his wallet, and Ulysses, now,
Returning to his threshold, there to taste
The bounty of the Greeks, paused in his way
Beside Antinoüs, whom he thus address'd.
500 Kind sir! vouchsafe to me! for thou appear'st
Not least, but greatest of the Achaians here,
And hast a kingly look. It might become
Thee therefore above others to bestow,
So should I praise thee wheresoe'er I roam.
I also lived the happy owner once
Of such a stately mansion, and have giv'n
To num'rous wand'rers (whencesoe'er they came)
All that they needed; I was also served
By many, and enjoy'd all that denotes
510 The envied owner opulent and blest.
But Jove (for so it pleas'd him) hath reduced
My all to nothing, prompting me, in league
With rovers of the Deep, to sail afar
To Ægypt, for my sure destruction there.
Within th' Ægyptian stream my barks well-oar'd
I station'd, and, enjoining strict my friends
To watch them close-attendant at their side,
Commanded spies into the hill-tops; but they,
Under the impulse of a spirit rash
520 And hot for quarrel, the well-cultur'd fields
Pillaged of the Ægyptians, captive led
Their wives and little-ones, and slew the men.

Ere long, the loud alarm their city reach'd.
Down came the citizens, by dawn of day,
With horse and foot and with the gleam of arms
Filling the plain. Then Jove with panic dread
Struck all my people; none found courage more
To stand, for mischiefs swarm'd on ev'ry side.
There, num'rous by the glitt'ring spear we fell
530 Slaughter'd, while others they conducted thence
Alive to servitude; but me they gave
To Dmetor, King in Cyprus, Jasus' son;
He entertained me liberally, and thence
This land I reach'd, but poor and woe-begone.
Then answer thus Antinoüs harsh return'd.
What dæmon introduced this nuisance here,
This troubler of our feast? stand yonder, keep
Due distance from my table, or expect
To see an Ægypt and a Cyprus worse
540 Than those, bold mendicant and void of shame!
Thou hauntest each, and, inconsid'rate, each
Gives to thee, because gifts at other's cost
Are cheap, and, plentifully serv'd themselves,
They squander, heedless, viands not their own.
To whom Ulysses while he slow retired.
Gods! how illib'ral with that specious form!
Thou wouldst not grant the poor a grain of salt
From thy own board, who at another's fed
So nobly, canst thou not spare a crust to me.
550 He spake; then raged Antinoüs still the more,
And in wing'd accents, louring, thus replied.
Take such dismission now as thou deserv'st,
Opprobrious! hast thou dared to scoff at me?
So saying, he seized his stool, and on the joint
Of his right shoulder smote him; firm as rock
He stood, by no such force to be displaced,
But silent shook his brows, and dreadful deeds
Of vengeance ruminating, sought again
His seat the threshold, where his bag full-charged
560 He grounded, and the suitors thus address'd.
Hear now, ye suitors of the matchless Queen,
My bosom's dictates. Trivial is the harm,
Scarce felt, if, fighting for his own, his sheep
Perchance, or beeves, a man receive a blow.
But me Antinoüs struck for that I ask'd
Food from him merely to appease the pangs
Of hunger, source of num'rous ills to man.
If then the poor man have a God t' avenge
His wrongs, I pray to him that death may seize
570 Antinoüs, ere his nuptial hour arrive!
To whom Antinoüs answer thus return'd,
Son of Eupithes. Either seated there
Or going hence, eat, stranger, and be still;
Lest for thy insolence, by hand or foot
We drag thee forth, and thou be flay'd alive.
He ceased, whom all indignant heard, and thus
Ev'n his own proud companions censured him.
Antinoüs! thou didst not well to smite
The wretched vagabond. O thou art doom'd

---

[76] Here again +Theos+ occurs in the abstract.

580 For ever, if there be a God in heav'n;[77]
For, in similitude of strangers oft,
The Gods, who can with ease all shapes assume,
Repair to populous cities, where they mark
The outrageous and the righteous deeds of men.
So they, for whose reproof he little cared.
But in his heart Telemachus that blow
Resented, anguish-torn, yet not a tear
He shed, but silent shook his brows, and mused
Terrible things. Penelope, meantime,
590 Told of the wand'rer so abused beneath
Her roof, among her maidens thus exclaim'd.
So may Apollo, glorious archer, smite
Thee also. Then Eurynome replied,
Oh might our pray'rs prevail, none of them all
Should see bright-charioted Aurora more.
Her answer'd then Penelope discrete.
Nurse! they are odious all, for that alike
All teem with mischief; but Antinoüs' looks
Remind me ever of the gloom of death.
600 A stranger hath arrived who, begging, roams
The house, (for so his penury enjoins)
The rest have giv'n him, and have fill'd his bag
With viands, but Antinoüs hath bruised
His shoulder with a footstool hurl'd at him.
While thus the Queen conversing with her train
In her own chamber sat, Ulysses made
Plenteous repast. Then, calling to her side
Eumæus, thus she signified her will.
Eumæus, noble friend! bid now approach
610 Yon stranger. I would speak with him, and ask
If he has seen Ulysses, or have heard
Tidings, perchance, of the afflicted Chief,
For much a wand'rer by his garb he seems.
To whom, Eumæus, thou didst thus reply.
Were those Achaians silent, thou shouldst hear,
O Queen! a tale that would console thy heart.
Three nights I housed him, and within my cot
Three days detain'd him, (for his ship he left
A fugitive, and came direct to me)
620 But half untold his hist'ry still remains.
As when his eye one fixes on a bard
From heav'n instructed in such themes as charm
The ear of mortals, ever as he sings
The people press, insatiable, to hear,
So, in my cottage, seated at my side,
That stranger with his tale enchanted me.
Laertes, he affirms, hath been his guest
Erewhile in Crete, where Minos' race resides,
And thence he hath arrived, after great loss,
630 A suppliant to the very earth abased;
He adds, that in Thesprotia's neighbour realm
He of Ulysses heard, both that he lives,
And that he comes laden with riches home.
To whom Penelope, discrete, replied.
Haste; call him. I would hear, myself, his tale.

Meantime, let these, or in the palace gate
Sport jocular, or here; their hearts are light,
For their possessions are secure; *their* wine
None drinks, or eats *their* viands, save their own,
640 While my abode, day after day, themselves
Haunting, my beeves and sheep and fatted goats
Slay for the banquet, and my casks exhaust
Extravagant, whence endless waste ensues;
For no such friend as was Ulysses once
Have I to expel the mischief. But might he
Revisit once his native shores again,
Then, aided by his son, he should avenge,
Incontinent, the wrongs which now I mourn.
Then sneezed Telemachus with sudden force,
650 That all the palace rang; his mother laugh'd,
And in wing'd accents thus the swain bespake.
Haste-bid him hither-hear'st thou not the sneeze
Propitious of my son? oh might it prove
A presage of inevitable death
To all these revellers! may none escape!
Now mark me well. Should the event his tale
Confirm, at my own hands he shall receive
Mantle and tunic both for his reward.
She spake; he went, and where Ulysses sat
660 Arriving, in wing'd accents thus began.
Penelope, my venerable friend!
Calls thee, the mother of Telemachus.
Oppress'd by num'rous troubles, she desires
To ask thee tidings of her absent Lord.
And should the event verify thy report,
Thy meed shall be (a boon which much thou need'st)
Tunic and mantle; but she gives no more;
Thy sustenance thou must, as now, obtain,[78]
Begging it at their hands who chuse to give.
670 Then thus Ulysses, Hero toil-inured.
Eumæus! readily I can relate
Truth, and truth only, to the prudent Queen
Icarius' daughter; for of him I know
Much, and have suff'red sorrows like his own.
But dread I feel of this imperious throng
Perverse, whose riot and outrageous acts
Of violence echo through the vault of heav'n.
And, even now, when for no fault of mine
Yon suitor struck me as I pass'd, and fill'd
680 My flesh with pain, neither Telemachus
Nor any interposed to stay his arm.
Now, therefore, let Penelope, although
Impatient, till the sun descend postpone
Her questions; then she may enquire secure
When comes her husband, and may nearer place
My seat to the hearth-side, for thinly clad
Thou know'st I am, whose aid I first implored.
He ceas'd; at whose reply Eumæus sought
Again the Queen, but ere he yet had pass'd
690 The threshold, thus she greeted his return.
Com'st thou alone, Eumæus? why delays

---

[77] +Ei dê pou tis epouranios theos esi+

Eustathius, and Clarke after him, understand an aposiopesis here, as if the speaker meant to say-what if there should be? or-suppose there should be? But the sentence seems to fall in better with what follows interpreted as above, and it is a sense of the passage not unwarranted by the opinion of other commentators. See Schaufelbergerus.

[78] This seems added by Eumæus to cut off from Ulysses the hope that might otherwise tempt him to use fiction.

The invited wand'rer? dreads he other harm?
Or sees he aught that with a bashful awe
Fills him? the bashful poor are poor indeed.
To whom, Eumæus, thou didst thus reply.
He hath well spoken; none who would decline
The rudeness of this contumelious throng
Could answer otherwise; thee he entreats
To wait till sun-set, and that course, O Queen,
700 Thou shalt thyself far more commodious find,
To hold thy conf'rence with the guest, alone.
Then answer thus Penelope return'd.
The stranger, I perceive, is not unwise,
Whoe'er he be, for on the earth are none
Proud, insolent, and profligate as these.
So spake the Queen. Then (all his message told)
The good Eumæus to the suitors went
Again, and with his head inclined toward
Telemachus, lest others should his words
710 Witness, in accents wing'd him thus address'd.

Friend and kind master! I return to keep
My herds, and to attend my rural charge,
Whence we are both sustain'd. Keep thou, meantime,
All here with vigilance, but chiefly watch
For thy own good, and save *thyself* from harm;
For num'rous here brood mischief, whom the Gods
Exterminate, ere yet their plots prevail!
To whom Telemachus, discrete, replied.
So be it, father! and (thy evening-mess
720 Eaten) depart; to-morrow come again,
Bringing fair victims hither; I will keep,
I and the Gods, meantime, all here secure.
He ended; then resumed once more the swain
His polish'd seat, and, both with wine and food
Now satiate, to his charge return'd, the court
Leaving and all the palace throng'd with guests;
They (for it now was evening) all alike
Turn'd jovial to the song and to the dance.

Book XVIII

The beggar Irus arrives at the palace; a combat takes place between him and Ulysses, in which Irus is by one blow vanquished. Penelope appears to the suitors, and having reminded them of the presents which she had a right to expect from them, receives a gift from each. Eurymachus, provoked by a speech of Ulysses, flings a footstool at him, which knocks down the cup-bearer; a general tumult is the consequence, which continues, till by the advice of Telemachus, seconded by Amphinomus, the suitors retire to their respective homes.

Now came a public mendicant, a man
Accustom'd, seeking alms, to roam the streets
Of Ithaca; one never sated yet
With food or drink; yet muscle had he none,
Or strength of limb, though giant-built in show.
Arnæus was the name which at his birth
His mother gave him, but the youthful band
Of suitors, whom as messenger he served,
All named him Irus. He, arriving, sought
To drive Ulysses forth from his own home,
10 And in rough accents rude him thus rebuked.
Forth from the porch, old man! lest by the foot
I drag thee quickly forth. Seest not how all
Wink on me, and by signs give me command
To drag thee hence? nor is it aught but shame
That checks me. Yet arise, lest soon with fists
Thou force me to adjust our diff'rence.
To whom Ulysses, low'ring dark, replied.
Peace, fellow! neither word nor deed of mine
Wrongs thee, nor feel I envy at the boon,
20 However plentiful, which thou receiv'st.
The sill may hold us both; thou dost not well
To envy others; thou appear'st like me
A vagrant; plenty is the gift of heav'n.
But urge me not to trial of our fists,
Lest thou provoke me, and I stain with blood
Thy bosom and thy lips, old as I am.
So, my attendance should to-morrow prove
More tranquil here; for thou should'st leave, I judge,
Ulysses' mansion, never to return.
30 Then answer'd Irus, kindling with disdain.
Gods! with what volubility of speech
The table-hunter prates, like an old hag
Collied with chimney-smutch! but ah beware!
For I intend thee mischief, and to dash
With both hands ev'ry grinder from thy gums,
As men untooth a pig pilf'ring the corn.
Come-gird thee, that all here may view the strife-
But how wilt thou oppose one young as I?
Thus on the threshold of the lofty gate
40 They, wrangling, chafed each other, whose dispute
The high-born youth Antinoüs mark'd; he laugh'd
Delighted, and the suitors thus address'd.
Oh friends! no pastime ever yet occurr'd
Pleasant as this which, now, the Gods themselves
Afford us. Irus and the stranger brawl
As they would box. Haste-let us urge them on.
He said; at once loud-laughing all arose;
The ill-clad disputants they round about
Encompass'd, and Antinoüs thus began.
50 Attend ye noble suitors to my voice.

Two paunches lie of goats here on the fire,
Which fill'd with fat and blood we set apart
For supper; he who conquers, and in force
Superior proves, shall freely take the paunch
Which he prefers, and shall with us thenceforth
Feast always; neither will we here admit
Poor man beside to beg at our repasts.
He spake, whom all approved; next, artful Chief
Ulysses thus, dissembling, them address'd.
60 Princes! unequal is the strife between
A young man and an old with mis'ry worn;
But hunger, always counsellor of ill,
Me moves to fight, that many a bruise received,
I may be foil'd at last. Now swear ye all
A solemn oath, that none, for Irus' sake
Shall, interposing, smite me with his fist
Clandestine, forcing me to yield the prize.
He ceas'd, and, as he bade, all present swore
A solemn oath; then thus, amid them all
70 Standing, Telemachus majestic spake.
Guest! if thy courage and thy manly mind
Prompt thee to banish this man hence, no force
Fear thou beside, for who smites thee, shall find
Yet other foes to cope with; I am here
In the host's office, and the royal Chiefs
Eurymachus and Antinoüs, alike
Discrete, accord unanimous with me.
He ceas'd, whom all approved. Then, with his rags
Ulysses braced for decency his loins
80 Around, but gave to view his brawny thighs
Proportion'd fair, and stripp'd his shoulders broad,
His chest and arms robust; while, at his side,
Dilating more the Hero's limbs and more
Minerva stood; the assembly with fixt eyes
Astonish'd gazed on him, and, looking full
On his next friend, a suitor thus remark'd.
Irus shall be in Irus found no more.
He hath pull'd evil on himself. What thewes
And what a haunch the senior's tatters hid!
90 So he-meantime in Irus' heart arose
Horrible tumult; yet, his loins by force
Girding, the servants dragg'd him to the fight
Pale, and his flesh all quiv'ring as he came;
Whose terrors thus Antinoüs sharp rebuked.
Now, wherefore liv'st, and why wast ever born
Thou mountain-mass of earth! if such dismay
Shake thee at thought of combat with a man
Ancient as he, and worn with many woes?
But mark, I threaten not in vain; should he
100 O'ercome thee, and in force superior prove,
To Echetus thou go'st; my sable bark

Shall waft thee to Epirus, where he reigns
Enemy of mankind; of nose and ears
He shall despoil thee with his ruthless steel,
And tearing by the roots the parts away[79]
That mark thy sex, shall cast them to the dogs.
He said; *His* limbs new terrors at that sound
Shook under him; into the middle space
They led him, and each raised his hands on high.
110 Then doubtful stood Ulysses toil-inured,
Whether to strike him lifeless to the earth
At once, or fell him with a managed blow.
To smite with managed force at length he chose
As wisest, lest, betray'd by his own strength,
He should be known. With elevated fists
Both stood; him Irus on the shoulder struck,
But he his adversary on the neck
Pash'd close beneath his ear; he split the bones,
And blood in sable streams ran from his mouth.
120 With many an hideous yell he dropp'd, his teeth
Chatter'd, and with his heels he drumm'd the ground.
The wooers, at that sight, lifting their hands
In glad surprize, laugh'd all their breath away.
Then, through the vestibule, and right across
The court, Ulysses dragg'd him by the foot
Into the portico, where propping him
Against the wall, and giving him his staff,
In accents wing'd he bade him thus farewell.
There seated now, dogs drive and swine away,
130 Nor claim (thyself so base) supreme controul
O'er other guests and mendicants, lest harm
Reach thee, hereafter, heavier still than this.
So saying, his tatter'd wallet o'er his back
He threw suspended by its leathern twist,
And tow'rd the threshold turning, sat again,
They laughing ceaseless still, the palace-door
Re-enter'd, and him, courteous, thus bespake.
Jove, and all Jove's assessors in the skies
Vouchsafe thee, stranger, whatsoe'er it be,
140 Thy heart's desire! who hast our ears reliev'd
From that insatiate beggar's irksome tone.
Soon to Epirus he shall go dispatch'd
To Echetus the King, pest of mankind.
So they, to whose propitious words the Chief
Listen'd delighted. Then Antinoüs placed
The paunch before him, and Amphinomus
Two loaves, selected from the rest; he fill'd
A goblet also, drank to him, and said,
My father, hail! O stranger, be thy lot
150 Hereafter blest, though adverse now and hard!
To whom Ulysses, ever-wise, replied.
To me, Amphinomus, endued thou seem'st
With much discretion, who art also son
Of such a sire, whose fair report I know,
Dulichian Nysus, opulent and good.
Fame speaks thee his, and thou appear'st a man
Judicious; hear me, therefore; mark me well.
Earth nourishes, of all that breathe or creep,

No creature weak as man; for while the Gods
160 Grant him prosperity and health, no fear
Hath he, or thought, that he shall ever mourn;
But when the Gods with evils unforeseen
Smite him, he bears them with a grudging mind;
For such as the complexion of his lot
By the appointment of the Sire of all,
Such is the colour of the mind of man.
I, too, have been familiar in my day
With wealth and ease, but I was then self-will'd,
And many wrong'd, embolden'd by the thought
170 Of my own father's and my brethren's pow'r.
Let no man, therefore, be unjust, but each
Use modestly what gift soe'er of heav'n.
So do not these. These ever bent I see
On deeds injurious, the possessions large
Consuming, and dishonouring the wife
Of one, who will not, as I judge, remain
Long absent from his home, but is, perchance,
Ev'n at the door. Thee, therefore, may the Gods
Steal hence in time! ah, meet not his return
180 To his own country! for they will not part,
(He and the suitors) without blood, I think,
If once he enter at these gates again!
He ended, and, libation pouring, quaff'd
The generous juice, then in the prince's hand
Replaced the cup; he, pensive, and his head
Inclining low, pass'd from him; for his heart
Forboded ill; yet 'scaped not even he,
But in the snare of Pallas caught, his life
To the heroic arm and spear resign'd
190 Of brave Telemachus. Reaching, at length,
The seat whence he had ris'n, he sat again.
Minerva then, Goddess, cærulean-eyed,
Prompted Icarius' daughter to appear
Before the suitors; so to expose the more
Their drift iniquitous, and that herself
More bright than ever in her husband's eyes
Might shine, and in her son's. Much mirth she feign'd,[80]
And, bursting into laughter, thus began.
I wish, Eurynome! (who never felt
200 That wish till now) though I detest them all,
To appear before the suitors, in whose ears
I will admonish, for his good, my son,
Not to associate with that lawless crew
Too much, who speak him fair, but foul intend.
Then answer thus Eurynome return'd.
My daughter! wisely hast thou said and well.
Go! bathe thee and anoint thy face, then give
To thy dear son such counsel as thou wilt
Without reserve; but shew not there thy cheeks
210 Sullied with tears, for profit none accrues
From grief like thine, that never knows a change.
And he is now bearded, and hath attained
That age which thou wast wont with warmest pray'r
To implore the Gods that he might live to see.
Her answer'd then Penelope discrete.

---

[79] Tradition says that Echetus, for a love-affair, condemned his daughter to lose her eyes, and to grind iron barley-grains, while her lover was doomed to suffer what Antinoüs threatens to Irus. F.

[80] This seems the sort of laughter intended by the word +Achreion+.

Persuade not me, though studious of my good,
To bathe, Eurynome! or to anoint
My face with oil; for all my charms the Gods
Inhabitants of Olympus then destroy'd,
220 When he, embarking, left me. Go, command
Hippodamia and Autonöe
That they attend me to the hall, and wait
Beside me there; for decency forbids
That I should enter to the men, alone.
She ceas'd, and through the house the ancient dame
Hasted to summon whom she had enjoin'd.
But Pallas, Goddess of the azure eyes,
Diffused, meantime, the kindly dew of sleep
Around Icarius' daughter; on her couch
230 Reclining, soon as she reclin'd, she dozed,
And yielded to soft slumber all her frame.
Then, that the suitors might admire her more,
The glorious Goddess cloath'd her, as she lay,
With beauty of the skies; her lovely face
She with ambrosia purified, with such
As Cytherea chaplet-crown'd employs
Herself, when in the eye-ensnaring dance
She joins the Graces; to a statelier height
Beneath her touch, and ampler size she grew,
240 And fairer than the elephantine bone
Fresh from the carver's hand. These gifts conferr'd
Divine, the awful Deity retired.
And now, loud-prattling as they came, arrived
Her handmaids; sleep forsook her at the sound,
She wiped away a tear, and thus she said.
Me gentle sleep, sad mourner as I am,
Hath here involved. O would that by a death
As gentle chaste Diana would herself
This moment set me free, that I might waste
250 My life no longer in heart-felt regret
Of a lamented husband's various worth
And virtue, for in Greece no Peer had he!
She said, and through her chambers' stately door
Issuing, descended; neither went she sole,
But with those two fair menials of her train.
Arriving, most majestic of her sex,
In presence of the num'rous guests, beneath
The portal of the stately dome she stood
Between her maidens, with her lucid veil
260 Mantling her lovely cheeks. Then, ev'ry knee
Trembled, and ev'ry heart with am'rous heat
Dissolv'd, her charms all coveting alike,
While to Telemachus her son she spake.
Telemachus! thou art no longer wise
As once thou wast, and even when a child.
For thriven as thou art, and at full size
Arrived of man, so fair proportion'd, too,
That ev'n a stranger, looking on thy growth
And beauty, would pronounce thee nobly born,
270 Yet is thy intellect still immature.
For what is this? why suffer'st thou a guest
To be abused in thy own palace? how?
Know'st not that if the stranger seated here
Endure vexation, the disgrace is thine?
Her answer'd, then, Telemachus discrete.

I blame thee not, my mother, that thou feel'st
Thine anger moved; yet want I not a mind
Able to mark and to discern between
Evil and good, child as I lately was,
280 Although I find not promptitude of thought
Sufficient always, overaw'd and check'd
By such a multitude, all bent alike
On mischief, of whom none takes part with me.
But Irus and the stranger have not fought,
Urged by the suitors, and the stranger prov'd
Victorious; yes-heav'n knows how much I wish
That, (in the palace some, some in the court)
The suitors all sat vanquish'd, with their heads
Depending low, and with enfeebled limbs,
290 Even as that same Irus, while I speak,
With chin on bosom propp'd at the hall-gate
Sits drunkard-like, incapable to stand
Erect, or to regain his proper home.
So they; and now addressing to the Queen
His speech, Eurymachus thus interposed.
O daughter of Icarius! could all eyes
Throughout Iäsian Argos[81] view thy charms,
Discrete Penelope! more suitors still
Assembling in thy courts would banquet here
300 From morn to eve; for thou surpassest far
In beauty, stature, worth, all womankind.
To whom replied Penelope discrete.
The Gods, Eurymachus! reduced to nought
My virtue, beauty, stature, when the Greeks,
Whom my Ulysses follow'd, sail'd to Troy.
Could he, returning, my domestic charge
Himself intend, far better would my fame
Be so secured, and wider far diffused.
But I am wretched now, such storms the Gods
310 Of woe have sent me. When he left his home,
Clasping my wrist with his right hand, he said.
My love! for I imagine not that all
The warrior Greeks shall safe from Troy return,
Since fame reports the Trojans brave in fight,
Skill'd in the spear, mighty to draw the bow,
And nimble vaulters to the backs of steeds
High-mettled, which to speediest issue bring
The dreadful struggle of all-wasting war-
I know not, therefore, whether heav'n intend
320 My safe return, or I must perish there.
But manage thou at home. Cherish, as now,
While I am absent, or more dearly still
My parents, and what time our son thou seest
Mature, then wed; wed even whom thou wilt,
And hence to a new home.-Such were his words,
All which shall full accomplishment ere long
Receive. The day is near, when hapless I,
Lost to all comfort by the will of Jove,
Must meet the nuptials that my soul abhors.
330 But this thought now afflicts me, and my mind
Continual haunts. Such was not heretofore
The suitors' custom'd practice; all who chose
To engage in competition for a wife
Well-qualitied and well-endow'd, produced
From their own herds and fatted flocks a feast

---

[81] From Iäsus, once King of Peloponnesus.

For the bride's friends, and splendid presents made,
But never ate as ye, at others' cost.
She ceased; then brave Ulysses toil-inured
Rejoiced that, soothing them, she sought to draw
340 From each some gift, although on other views,
And more important far, himself intent.
Then thus Antinoüs, Eupithes' son.
Icarius' daughter wise! only accept
Such gifts as we shall bring, for gifts demand
That grace, nor can be decently refused;
But to our rural labours, or elsewhere
Depart not we, till first thy choice be made
Of the Achaian, chief in thy esteem.
Antinoüs spake, whose answer all approved.
350 Then each dispatch'd his herald who should bring
His master's gift. Antinoüs' herald, first
A mantle of surpassing beauty brought,
Wide, various, with no fewer clasps adorn'd
Than twelve, all golden, and to ev'ry clasp
Was fitted opposite its eye exact.
Next, to Eurymachus his herald bore
A necklace of wrought gold, with amber rich
Bestudded, ev'ry bead bright as a sun.
Two servants for Eurydamas produced
360 Ear-pendants fashion'd with laborious art,
Broad, triple-gemm'd, of brilliant light profuse.
The herald of Polyctor's son, the prince
Pisander, brought a collar to his Lord,
A sumptuous ornament. Each Greecian gave,
And each a gift dissimilar from all.
Then, loveliest of her sex, turning away,
She sought her chamber, whom her maidens fair
Attended, charged with those illustrious gifts.
Then turn'd, they all to dance and pleasant song
370 Joyous, expecting the approach of ev'n.
Ere long the dusky evening came, and them
Found sporting still. Then, placing in the hall
Three hearths that should illumine wide the house,
They compass'd them around with fuel-wood
Long-season'd and new-split, mingling the sticks
With torches. The attendant women watch'd
And fed those fires by turns, to whom, himself,
Their unknown Sov'reign thus his speech address'd.
Ye maidens of the long-regretted Chief
380 Ulysses! to the inner-courts retire,
And to your virtuous Queen, that following there
Your sev'ral tasks, spinning and combing wool,
Ye may amuse her; I, meantime, for these
Will furnish light, and should they chuse to stay
Till golden morn appear, they shall not tire
My patience aught, for I can much endure.
He said; they, titt'ring, on each other gazed.
But one, Melantho with the blooming cheeks,
Rebuked him rudely. Dolius was her sire,
390 But by Penelope she had been reared
With care maternal, and in infant years
Supplied with many a toy; yet even she
Felt not her mistress' sorrows in her heart,
But, of Eurymachus enamour'd, oft
His lewd embraces met; she, with sharp speech
Reproachful, to Ulysses thus replied.
Why-what a brainsick vagabond art thou!

Who neither wilt to the smith's forge retire
For sleep, nor to the public portico,
400 But here remaining, with audacious prate
Disturb'st this num'rous company, restrain'd
By no respect or fear; either thou art
With wine intoxicated, or, perchance,
Art always fool, and therefore babblest now.
Say, art thou drunk with joy that thou hast foiled
The beggar Irus? Tremble, lest a man
Stronger than Irus suddenly arise,
Who on thy temples pelting thee with blows
Far heavier than his, shall drive thee hence
410 With many a bruise, and foul with thy own blood.
To whom Ulysses, frowning stern, replied.
Snarler! Telemachus shall be inform'd
This moment of thy eloquent harangue,
That he may hew thee for it, limb from limb.
So saying, he scared the women; back they flew
Into the house, but each with falt'ring knees
Through dread, for they believ'd his threats sincere.
He, then illumin'd by the triple blaze,
Watch'd close the lights, busy from hearth to hearth,
420 But in his soul, meantime, far other thoughts
Revolved, tremendous, not conceived in vain.
Nor Pallas (that they might exasp'rate more
Laertes' son) permitted to abstain
From heart-corroding bitterness of speech
Those suitors proud, of whom Eurymachus,
Offspring of Polybus, while thus he jeer'd
Ulysses, set the others in a roar.
Hear me, ye suitors of the illustrious Queen!
I shall promulge my thought. This man, methinks,
430 Not unconducted by the Gods, hath reach'd
Ulysses' mansion, for to me the light
Of yonder torches altogether seems
His own, an emanation from his head,
Which not the smallest growth of hair obscures.
He ended; and the city-waster Chief
Himself accosted next. Art thou disposed
To serve me, friend! would I afford thee hire,
A labourer at my farm? thou shalt not want
Sufficient wages; thou may'st there collect
440 Stones for my fences, and may'st plant my oaks,
For which I would supply thee all the year
With food, and cloaths, and sandals for thy feet.
But thou hast learn'd less creditable arts,
Nor hast a will to work, preferring much
By beggary from others to extort
Wherewith to feed thy never-sated maw.
Then answer, thus, Ulysses wise return'd.
Forbear, Eurymachus; for were we match'd
In work against each other, thou and I,
450 Mowing in spring-time, when the days are long,
I with my well-bent sickle in my hand,
Thou arm'd with one as keen, for trial sake
Of our ability to toil unfed
Till night, grass still sufficing for the proof.-
Or if, again, it were our task to drive
Yoked oxen of the noblest breed, sleek-hair'd,
Big-limb'd, both batten'd to the full with grass,
Their age and aptitude for work the same
Not soon to be fatigued, and were the field

460 In size four acres, with a glebe through which
The share might smoothly slide, then should'st thou see
How strait my furrow should be cut and true.-
Or should Saturnian Jove this day excite
Here, battle, or elsewhere, and were I arm'd
With two bright spears and with a shield, and bore
A brazen casque well-fitted to my brows,
Me, then, thou should'st perceive mingling in fight
Amid the foremost Chiefs, nor with the crime
Of idle beggary should'st upbraid me more.
470 But thou art much a railer, one whose heart
Pity moves not, and seem'st a mighty man
And valiant to thyself, only because
Thou herd'st with few, and those of little worth.
But should Ulysses come, at his own isle
Again arrived, wide as these portals are,
To thee, at once, too narrow they should seem
To shoot thee forth with speed enough abroad.
He ceased-then tenfold indignation fired
Eurymachus; he furrow'd deep his brow
480 With frowns, and in wing'd accents thus replied.
Wretch, I shall roughly handle thee anon,
Who thus with fluent prate presumptuous dar'st
Disturb this num'rous company, restrain'd
By no respect or fear. Either thou art
With wine intoxicated, or, perchance,
Art always fool, and therefore babblest now;
Or thou art frantic haply with delight
That thou hast foil'd yon vagabond obscure.
So saying, he seized a stool; but to the knees
490 Ulysses flew of the Dulichian Prince
Amphinomus, and sat, fearing incensed
Eurymachus; he on his better hand
Smote full the cup-bearer; on the hall-floor
Loud rang the fallen beaker, and himself
Lay on his back clamouring in the dust.
Strait through the dusky hall tumult ensued

Among the suitors, of whom thus, a youth,
With eyes directed to the next, exclaim'd.
Would that this rambling stranger had elsewhere
500 Perish'd, or ever he had here arrived,
Then no such uproar had he caused as this!
This doth the beggar; he it is for whom
We wrangle thus, and may despair of peace
Or pleasure more; now look for strife alone.
Then in the midst Telemachus upstood
Majestic, and the suitors thus bespake.
Sirs! ye are mad, and can no longer eat
Or drink in peace; some dæmon troubles you.
But since ye all have feasted, to your homes
510 Go now, and, at your pleasure, to your beds;
Soonest were best, but I thrust no man hence.
He ceased; they gnawing stood their lips, aghast
With wonder that Telemachus in his speech
Such boldness used. Then rose Amphinomus,
Brave son of Nisus offspring of the King
Aretus, and the assembly thus address'd.
My friends! let none with contradiction thwart
And rude reply words rational and just;
Assault no more the stranger, nor of all
520 The servants of renown'd Ulysses here
Harm any. Come. Let the cup-bearer fill
To all, that due libation made, to rest
We may repair at home, leaving the Prince
To accommodate beneath his father's roof
The stranger, for he is the Prince's guest.
He ended, whose advice none disapproved.
The Hero Mulius then, Dulichian-born,
And herald of Amphinomus, the cup
Filling, dispensed it, as he stood, to all;
530 They, pouring forth to the Immortals, quaff'd
The luscious bev'rage, and when each had made
Libation, and such measure as he would
Of wine had drunk, then all to rest retired.

Book XIX

Ulysses and Telemachus remove the arms from the hall to an upper-chamber. The Hero then confers with Penelope, to whom he gives a fictitious narrative of his adventures. Euryclea, while bathing Ulysses, discovers him by a scar on his knee, but he prevents her communication of that discovery to Penelope.

They went, but left the noble Chief behind
In his own house, contriving by the aid
Of Pallas, the destruction of them all,
And thus, in accents wing'd, again he said.
My son! we must remove and safe dispose
All these my well-forged implements of war;
And should the suitors, missing them, enquire
Where are they? thou shalt answer smoothly thus-
I have convey'd them from the reach of smoke,
For they appear no more the same which erst
10 Ulysses, going hence to Ilium, left,
So smirch'd and sullied by the breath of fire.
This weightier reason (thou shalt also say)
Some God suggested to me, — lest, inflamed
With wine, ye wound each other in your brawls,
Shaming both feast and courtship; for the view
Itself of arms incites to their abuse.
He ceased, and, in obedience to his will,
Calling the ancient Euryclea forth,
His nurse, Telemachus enjoin'd her thus.
20 Go-shut the women in; make fast the doors
Of their apartment, while I safe dispose
Elsewhere, my father's implements of war,
Which, during his long absence, here have stood
Till smoke hath sullied them. For I have been
An infant hitherto, but, wiser grown,
Would now remove them from the breath of fire.
Then thus the gentle matron in return.
Yes truly-and I wish that now, at length,
Thou would'st assert the privilege of thy years,
30 My son, thyself assuming charge of all,
Both house and stores; but who shall bear the light?
Since they, it seems, who would, are all forbidden.
To whom Telemachus discrete replied.
This guest; for no man, from my table fed,
Come whence he may; shall be an idler here.
He ended, nor his words flew wing'd away,
But Euryclea bolted every door.
Then, starting to the task, Ulysses caught,
And his illustrious son, the weapons thence,
40 Helmet, and bossy shield, and pointed spear,
While Pallas from a golden lamp illumed
The dusky way before them. At that sight
Alarm'd, the Prince his father thus address'd.
Whence-whence is this, my father? I behold
A prodigy! the walls of the whole house,
The arches, fir-tree beams, and pillars tall
Shine in my view, as with the blaze of fire!
Some Pow'r celestial, doubtless, is within.
To whom Ulysses, ever-wise, replied.
50 Soft! ask no questions. Give no vent to thought,
Such is the custom of the Pow'rs divine.

Hence, thou, to bed. I stay, that I may yet
Both in thy mother and her maidens move
More curiosity; yes-she with tears
Shall question me of all that I have seen.
He ended, and the Prince, at his command,
Guided by flaming torches, sought the couch
Where he was wont to sleep, and there he slept
On that night also, waiting the approach
60 Of sacred dawn. Thus was Ulysses left
Alone, and planning sat in solitude,
By Pallas' aid, the slaughter of his foes.
At length, Diana-like, or like herself,
All golden Venus, (her apartment left)
Enter'd Penelope. Beside the hearth
Her women planted her accustom'd seat
With silver wreathed and ivory. That throne
Icmalius made, artist renown'd, and join'd
A footstool to its splendid frame beneath,
70 Which ever with an ample fleece they spread.
There sat discrete Penelope; then came
Her beautiful attendants from within,
Who cleared the litter'd bread, the board, and cups
From which the insolent companions drank.
They also raked the embers from the hearths
Now dim, and with fresh billets piled them high,
Both for illumination and for warmth.
Then yet again Melantho with rude speech
Opprobrious, thus, assail'd Ulysses' ear.
80 Guest-wilt thou trouble us throughout the night
Ranging the house? and linger'st thou a spy
Watching the women? Hence-get thee abroad
Glad of such fare as thou hast found, or soon
With torches beaten we will thrust thee forth.
To whom Ulysses, frowning stern, replied.
Petulant woman! wherefore thus incensed
Inveigh'st thou against me? is it because
I am not sleek? because my garb is mean?
Because I beg? thanks to necessity-
90 I would not else. But such as I appear,
Such all who beg and all who wander are.
I also lived the happy owner once
Of such a stately mansion, and have giv'n
To num'rous wand'rers, whencesoe'er they came,
All that they needed; I was also served
By many, and enjoy'd all that denotes
The envied owner opulent and blest.
But Jove (for so it pleas'd him) hath reduced
My all to nothing. Therefore well beware
100 Thou also, mistress, lest a day arrive
When all these charms by which thou shin'st among
Thy sister-menials, fade; fear, too, lest her
Thou should'st perchance irritate, whom thou serv'st,

And lest Ulysses come, of whose return
Hope yet survives; but even though the Chief
Have perish'd, as ye think, and comes no more,
Consider yet his son, how bright the gifts
Shine of Apollo in the illustrious Prince
Telemachus; no woman, unobserved
110 By him, can now commit a trespass here;
His days of heedless infancy are past.
He ended, whom Penelope discrete
O'erhearing, her attendant sharp rebuked.
Shameless, audacious woman! known to me
Is thy great wickedness, which with thy life
Thou shalt atone; for thou wast well aware,
(Hearing it from myself) that I design'd
To ask this stranger of my absent Lord,
For whose dear sake I never cease to mourn.
120 Then to her household's governess she said.
Bring now a seat, and spread it with a fleece,
Eurynome! that, undisturb'd, the guest
May hear and answer all that I shall ask.
She ended. Then the matron brought in haste
A polish'd seat, and spread it with a fleece,
On which the toil-accustom'd Hero sat,
And thus the chaste Penelope began.
Stranger! my first enquiry shall be this-
Who art thou? whence? where born? and sprung from whom?
130 Then answer thus Ulysses, wise, return'd.
O Queen! uncensurable by the lips
Of mortal man! thy glory climbs the skies
Unrivall'd, like the praise of some great King
Who o'er a num'rous people and renown'd
Presiding like a Deity, maintains
Justice and truth. The earth, under his sway,
Her produce yields abundantly; the trees
Fruit-laden bend; the lusty flocks bring forth;
The Ocean teems with finny swarms beneath
140 His just controul, and all the land is blest.
Me therefore, question of what else thou wilt
In thy own palace, but forbear to ask
From whom I sprang, and of my native land,
Lest thou, reminding me of those sad themes,
Augment my woes; for I have much endured;
Nor were it seemly, in another's house,
To pass the hours in sorrow and in tears,
Wearisome when indulg'd with no regard
To time or place; thy train (perchance thyself)
150 Would blame me, and I should reproach incur
As one tear-deluged through excess of wine.
Him answer'd then Penelope discrete.
The immortal Gods, O stranger, then destroy'd
My form, my grace, my beauty, when the Greeks
Whom my Ulysses follow'd, sail'd to Troy.
Could he, returning, my domestic charge
Himself intend, far better would my fame
Be so secured, and wider far diffused.
But I am wretched now, such storms of woe
160 The Gods have sent me; for as many Chiefs
As hold dominion in the neighbour isles
Samos, Dulichium, and the forest-crown'd
Zacynthus; others, also, rulers here
In pleasant Ithaca, me, loth to wed,
Woo ceaseless, and my household stores consume.

I therefore, neither guest nor suppliant heed,
Nor public herald more, but with regret
Of my Ulysses wear my soul away.
They, meantime, press my nuptials, which by art
170 I still procrastinate. Some God the thought
Suggested to me, to commence a robe
Of amplest measure and of subtlest woof,
Laborious task; which done, I thus address'd them.
Princes, my suitors! since the noble Chief
Ulysses is no more, enforce not now
My nuptials; wait till I shall finish first
A fun'ral robe (lest all my threads be marr'd)
Which for the ancient Hero I prepare
Laertes, looking for the mournful hour
180 When fate shall snatch him to eternal rest.
Else, I the censure dread of all my sex,
Should he, so wealthy, want at last a shroud.
Such was my speech; they, unsuspicious all,
With my request complied. Thenceforth, all day
I wove the ample web, and, by the aid
Of torches, ravell'd it again at night.
Three years by artifice I thus their suit
Eluded safe; but when the fourth arrived,
And the same season after many moons
190 And fleeting days return'd, passing my train
Who had neglected to release the dogs,
They came, surprized and reprimanded me.
Thus, through necessity, not choice, at last
I have perform'd it, in my own despight.
But no escape from marriage now remains,
Nor other subterfuge for me; meantime
My parents urge my nuptials, and my son
(Of age to note it) with disgust observes
His wealth consumed; for he is now become
200 Adult, and abler than myself to rule
The house, a Prince distinguish'd by the Gods,
Yet, stranger, after all, speak thy descent;
Say whence thou art; for not of fabulous birth
Art thou, nor from the oak, nor from the rock.
Her answer'd then Ulysses, ever-wise.
O spouse revered of Laertiades!
Resolv'st thou still to learn from whom I sprang?
Learn then; but know that thou shalt much augment
My present grief, natural to a man
210 Who hath, like me, long exiled from his home
Through various cities of the sons of men
Wander'd remote, and num'rous woes endured.
Yet, though it pain me, I will tell thee all.
There is a land amid the sable flood
Call'd Crete; fair, fruitful, circled by the sea.
Num'rous are her inhabitants, a race
Not to be summ'd, and ninety towns she boasts.
Diverse their language is; Achaians some,
And some indigenous are; Cydonians there,
22 °Crest-shaking Dorians, and Pelasgians dwell.
One city in extent the rest exceeds,
Cnossus; the city in which Minos reign'd,
Who, ever at a nine years' close, conferr'd
With Jove himself; from him my father sprang
The brave Deucalion; for Deucalion's sons
Were two, myself and King Idomeneus.
To Ilium he, on board his gallant barks,

Follow'd the Atridæ. I, the youngest-born,
By my illustrious name, Æthon, am known,
230 But he ranks foremost both in worth and years.
There I beheld Ulysses, and within
My walls receiv'd him; for a violent wind
Had driv'n him from Malea (while he sought
The shores of Troy) to Crete. The storm his barks
Bore into the Amnisus, for the cave
Of Ilythia known, a dang'rous port,
And which with difficulty he attain'd.
He, landing, instant to the city went,
Seeking Idomeneus; his friend of old,
240 As he affirm'd, and one whom much he lov'd.
But *he* was far remote, ten days advanced,
Perhaps eleven, on his course to Troy.
Him, therefore, I conducted to my home,
Where hospitably, and with kindest care
I entertain'd him, (for I wanted nought)
And for himself procured and for his band,-
By public contribution, corn, and wine,
And beeves for food, that all might be sufficed.
Twelve days his noble Greecians there abode,
250 Port-lock'd by Boreas blowing with a force
Resistless even on the land, some God
So roused his fury; but the thirteenth day
The wind all fell, and they embark'd again.
With many a fiction specious, as he sat,
He thus her ear amused; she at the sound
Melting, with fluent tears her cheeks bedew'd;
And as the snow by Zephyrus diffused,
Melts on the mountain tops, when Eurus breathes,
And fills the channels of the running streams,
260 So melted she, and down her lovely cheeks
Pour'd fast the tears, him mourning as remote
Who sat beside her. Soft compassion touch'd
Ulysses of his consort's silent woe;
His eyes as they had been of steel or horn,
Moved not, yet artful, he suppress'd his tears,
And she, at length with overflowing grief
Satiate, replied, and thus enquired again.
Now, stranger, I shall prove thee, as I judge,
If thou, indeed, hast entertain'd in Crete
270 My spouse and his brave followers, as thou say'st.
Describe his raiment and himself; his own
Appearance, and the appearance of his friends.
Then her Ulysses answer'd, ever-wise.
Hard is the task, O Queen! (so long a time
Hath since elaps'd) to tell thee. Twenty years
Have pass'd since he forsook my native isle,
Yet, from my best remembrance, I will give
A likeness of him, such as now I may.
A double cloak, thick-piled, Moeonian dyed,
280 The noble Chief had on; two fast'nings held
The golden clasp, and it display'd in front
A well-wrought pattern with much art design'd.
An hound between his fore-feet holding fast
A dappled fawn, gaped eager on his prey.
All wonder'd, seeing, how in lifeless gold
Express'd, the dog with open mouth her throat
Attempted still, and how the fawn with hoofs
Thrust trembling forward, struggled to escape.
That glorious mantle much I noticed, soft

290 To touch, as the dried garlick's glossy film;
Such was the smoothness of it, and it shone
Sun-bright; full many a maiden, trust me, view'd
The splendid texture with admiring eyes.
But mark me now; deep treasure in thy mind
This word. I know not if Ulysses wore
That cloak at home, or whether of his train
Some warrior gave it to him on his way,
Or else some host of his; for many loved
Ulysses, and with him might few compare.
300 I gave to him, myself, a brazen sword,
A purple cloak magnificent, and vest
Of royal length, and when he sought his bark,
With princely pomp dismiss'd him from the shore.
An herald also waited on the Chief,
Somewhat his Senior; him I next describe.
His back was bunch'd, his visage swarthy, curl'd
His poll, and he was named Eurybates;
A man whom most of all his followers far
Ulysses honour'd, for their minds were one.
310 He ceased; she recognising all the proofs
Distinctly by Ulysses named, was moved
Still more to weep, till with o'erflowing grief
Satiate, at length she answer'd him again.
Henceforth, O stranger, thou who hadst before
My pity, shalt my rev'rence share and love,
I folded for him (with these hands) the cloak
Which thou describ'st, produced it when he went,
And gave it to him; I that splendid clasp
Attach'd to it myself, more to adorn
320 My honour'd Lord, whom to his native land
Return'd secure I shall receive no more.
In such an evil hour Ulysses went
To that bad city never to be named.
To whom Ulysses, ever-wise, replied.
Consort revered of Laertiades!
No longer let anxiety impair
Thy beauteous form, nor any grief consume
Thy spirits more for thy Ulysses' sake.
And yet I blame thee not; a wife deprived
330 Of her first mate to whom she had produced
Fair fruit of mutual love, would mourn his loss,
Although he were inferior far to thine,
Whom fame affirms the semblance of the Gods.
But cease to mourn. Hear me. I will relate
A faithful tale, nor will from thee withhold
Such tidings of Ulysses living still,
And of his safe return, as I have heard
Lately, in yon neighb'ring opulent land
Of the Thesprotians. He returns enrich'd
340 With many precious stores from those obtain'd
Whom he hath visited; but he hath lost,
Departing from Thrinacia's isle, his bark
And all his lov'd companions in the Deep,
For Jove was adverse to him, and the Sun,
Whose beeves his followers slew. They perish'd all
Amid the billowy flood; but Him, the keel
Bestriding of his bark, the waves at length
Cast forth on the Phæacian's land, a race
Allied to heav'n, who rev'renced like a God
350 Thy husband, honour'd him with num'rous gifts,
And willing were to have convey'd him home.

Ulysses, therefore, had attained long since
His native shore, but that he deem'd it best
To travel far, that he might still amass
More wealth; so much Ulysses all mankind
Excels in policy, and hath no peer.
This information from Thesprotia's King
I gain'd, from Phidon; to myself he swore,
Libation off'ring under his own roof,
360 That both the bark was launch'd, and the stout crew
Prepared, that should conduct him to his home.
But me he first dismiss'd; for, as it chanced,
A ship lay there of the Thesprotians, bound
To corn-enrich'd Dulichium. All the wealth
He shew'd me by the Chief amass'd, a store
To feed the house of yet another Prince
To the tenth generation; so immense
His treasures were within that palace lodg'd.
Himself he said was to Dodona gone,
37 °Counsel to ask from the oracular oaks
Sublime of Jove, how safest he might seek,
After long exile thence, his native land,
If openly were best, or in disguise.
Thus, therefore, he is safe, and at his home
Well-nigh arrived, nor shall his country long
Want him. I swear it with a solemn oath.
First Jove be witness, King and Lord of all!
Next these domestic Gods of the renown'd
Ulysses, in whose royal house I sit,
380 That thou shalt see my saying all fulfill'd.
Ulysses shall this self-same year return,
This self-same month, ere yet the next begin.
Him answer'd then Penelope discrete.
Grant heav'n, my guest, that this good word of thine
Fail not! then, soon shalt thou such bounty share
And friendship at my hands, that, at first sight,
Whoe'er shall meet thee shall pronounce thee blest.
But ah! my soul forebodes how it will prove;
Neither Ulysses will return, nor thou
390 Receive safe conduct hence; for we have here
None, such as once Ulysses was, to rule
His household with authority, and to send
With honourable convoy to his home
The worthy guest, or to regale him here.
Give him the bath, my maidens; spread his couch
With linen soft, with fleecy gaberdines[82]
And rugs of splendid hue, that he may lie
Waiting, well-warm'd, the golden morn's return.
Attend him also at the peep of day
400 With bath and unction, that, his seat resumed
Here in the palace, he may be prepared
For breakfast with Telemachus; and woe
To him who shall presume to incommode
Or cause him pain; that man shall be cashier'd
Hence instant, burn his anger as it may.
For how, my honour'd inmate! shalt thou learn
That I in wisdom oeconomic aught
Pass other women, if unbathed, unoiled,
Ill-clad, thou sojourn here? man's life is short,
410 Whoso is cruel, and to cruel arts
Addict, on him all men, while yet he lives,

Call plagues and curses down, and after death
Scorn and proverbial mock'ries hunt his name.
But men, humane themselves, and giv'n by choice
To offices humane, from land to land
Are rumour'd honourably by their guests,
And ev'ry tongue is busy in their praise.
Her answer'd then, Ulysses, ever-wise.
Consort revered of Laertiades!
420 Warm gaberdines and rugs of splendid hue
To me have odious been, since first the sight
Of Crete's snow-mantled mountain-tops I lost,
Sweeping the billows with extended oars.
No; I will pass, as I am wont to pass
The sleepless night; for on a sordid couch
Outstretch'd, full many a night have I reposed
Till golden-charioted Aurora dawn'd.
Nor me the foot-bath pleases more; my foot
Shall none of all thy ministring maidens touch,
430 Unless there be some ancient matron grave
Among them, who hath pangs of heart endured
Num'rous, and keen as I have felt myself;
Her I refuse not. She may touch my feet.
Him answer'd then prudent Penelope.
Dear guest! for of all trav'llers here arrived
From distant regions, I have none received
Discrete as thou, or whom I more have lov'd,
So just thy matter is, and with such grace
Express'd. I have an ancient maiden grave,
440 The nurse who at my hapless husband's birth
Receiv'd him in her arms, and with kind care
Maternal rear'd him; she shall wash thy feet,
Although decrepid. Euryclea, rise!
Wash one coeval with thy Lord; for such
The feet and hands, it may be, are become
Of my Ulysses now; since man beset
With sorrow once, soon wrinkled grows and old.
She said, then Euryclea with both hands
Cov'ring her face, in tepid tears profuse
450 Dissolved, and thus in mournful strains began.
Alas! my son, trouble for thy dear sake
Distracts me. Jove surely of all mankind
Thee hated most, though ever in thy heart
Devoutly giv'n; for never mortal man
So many thighs of fatted victims burn'd,
And chosen hecatombs produced as thou
To Jove the Thund'rer, him entreating still
That he would grant thee a serene old age,
And to instruct, thyself, thy glorious son.
460 Yet thus the God requites thee, cutting off
All hope of thy return-oh ancient sir!
Him too, perchance, where'er he sits a guest
Beneath some foreign roof, the women taunt,
As all these shameless ones have taunted thee,
Fearing whose mock'ry thou forbidd'st their hands
This office, which Icarius' daughter wise
To me enjoins, and which I, glad perform.
Yes, I will wash thy feet; both for her sake
And for thy own, — for sight of thee hath raised
470 A tempest in my mind. Hear now the cause!
Full many a guest forlorn we entertain,

---

[82] A gaberdine is a shaggy cloak of coarse but warm materials. Such always make part of Homer's bed-furniture.

But never any have I seen, whose size,
The fashion of whose foot and pitch of voice,
Such likeness of Ulysses show'd, as thine.
To whom Ulysses, ever-shrewd, replied.
Such close similitude, O ancient dame!
As thou observ'st between thy Lord and me,
All, who have seen us both, have ever found.
He said; then taking the resplendent vase
480 Allotted always to that use, she first
Infused cold water largely, then, the warm.
Ulysses (for beside the hearth he sat)
Turn'd quick his face into the shade, alarm'd
Lest, handling him, she should at once remark
His scar, and all his stratagem unveil.
She then, approaching, minister'd the bath
To her own King, and at first touch discern'd
That token, by a bright-tusk'd boar of old
Impress'd, what time he to Parnassus went
490 To visit there Autolycus and his sons,
His mother's noble sire, who all mankind

In furtive arts and fraudful oaths excell'd.[83]
For such endowments he by gift receiv'd
From Hermes' self, to whom the thighs of kids
He offer'd and of lambs, and, in return,
The watchful Hermes never left his side.
Autolycus arriving in the isle
Of pleasant Ithaca, the new-born son
Of his own daughter found, whom on his knees
500 At close of supper Euryclea placed,
And thus the royal visitant address'd.
Thyself, Autolycus! devise a name
For thy own daughter's son, by num'rous pray'rs
Of thine and fervent, from the Gods obtained.
Then answer thus Autolycus return'd.
My daughter and my daughter's spouse! the name
Which I shall give your boy, that let him bear.
Since after provocation and offence
To numbers giv'n of either sex, I come,

51 °Call him Ulysses;[84] and when, grown mature,
He shall Parnassus visit, the abode
Magnificent in which his mother dwelt,
And where my treasures lie, from my own stores
I will enrich and send him joyful home.
Ulysses, therefore, that he might obtain
Those princely gifts, went thither. Him arrived,
With right-hand gratulation and with words
Of welcome kind, Autolycus received,
Nor less his offspring; but the mother most
520 Of his own mother clung around his neck,
Amphithea; she with many a fervent kiss
His forehead press'd, and his bright-beaming eyes.
Then bade Autolycus his noble sons
Set forth a banquet. They, at his command,
Led in a fatted ox of the fifth year,
Which slaying first, they spread him carved abroad,
Then scored his flesh, transfixed it with the spits,

And roasting all with culinary skill
Exact, gave each his portion. Thus they sat
530 Feasting all day, and till the sun declined,
But when the sun declined, and darkness fell,
Each sought his couch, and took the gift of sleep.
Then, soon as day-spring's daughter rosy-palm'd
Aurora look'd abroad, forth went the hounds,
And, with the hounds Ulysses, and the youths,
Sons of Autolycus, to chase the boar.
Arrived at the Parnassian mount, they climb'd
His bushy sides, and to his airy heights
Ere long attain'd. It was the pleasant hour
540 When from the gently-swelling flood profound
The sun, emerging, first smote on the fields.
The hunters reach'd the valley; foremost ran,
Questing, the hounds; behind them, swift, the sons
Came of Autolycus, with whom advanced
The illustrious Prince Ulysses, pressing close
The hounds, and brandishing his massy spear.
There, hid in thickest shades, lay an huge boar.
That covert neither rough winds blowing moist
Could penetrate, nor could the noon-day sun
550 Smite through it, or fast-falling show'rs pervade,
So thick it was, and underneath the ground
With litter of dry foliage strew'd profuse.
Hunters and dogs approaching him, his ear
The sound of feet perceived; upridging high
His bristly back and glaring fire, he sprang
Forth from the shrubs, and in defiance stood
Near and right opposite. Ulysses, first,
Rush'd on him, elevating his long spear
Ardent to wound him; but, preventing quick
560 His foe, the boar gash'd him above the knee.
Much flesh, assailing him oblique, he tore
With his rude tusk, but to the Hero's bone
Pierced not; Ulysses *his* right shoulder reach'd;
And with a deadly thrust impell'd the point
Of his bright spear through him and far beyond.
Loud yell'd the boar, sank in the dust, and died.
Around Ulysses, then, the busy sons
Throng'd of Autolycus; expert they braced
The wound of the illustrious hunter bold,
570 With incantation staunched the sable blood,
And sought in haste their father's house again,
Whence, heal'd and gratified with splendid gifts
They sent him soon rejoicing to his home,
Themselves rejoicing also. Glad their son
His parents saw again, and of the scar
Enquired, where giv'n, and how? He told them all,
How to Parnassus with his friends he went,
Sons of Autolycus to hunt, and how
A boar had gash'd him with his iv'ry tusk.
580 That scar, while chafing him with open palms,
The matron knew; she left his foot to fall;
Down dropp'd his leg into the vase; the brass
Rang, and o'ertilted by the sudden shock,
Poured forth the water, flooding wide the floor.

---

[83] Homer's morals seem to allow to a good man dissimulation, and even an ambiguous oath, should they be necessary to save him from a villain. Thus in Book XX. Telemachus swears by Zeus, that he does not hinder his mother from marrying whom she pleases of the wooers, though at the same time he is plotting their destruction with his father. F.

[84] In the Greek +ODYSSEUS+ from the verb +odyssô+-Irascor, *I am angry*.

Her spirit joy at once and sorrow seized;
Tears fill'd her eyes; her intercepted voice
Died in her throat; but to Ulysses' beard
Her hand advancing, thus, at length, she spake.
Thou art himself, Ulysses. Oh my son!
590 Dear to me, and my master as thou art,
I knew thee not, till I had touch'd the scar.
She said, and to Penelope her eyes
Directed, all impatient to declare
Her own Ulysses even then at home.
But she, nor eye nor ear for aught that pass'd
Had then, her fixt attention so entire
Minerva had engaged. Then, darting forth
His arms, the Hero with his right-hand close
Compress'd her throat, and nearer to himself
600 Drawing her with his left, thus caution'd her.
Why would'st thou ruin me? Thou gav'st me milk
Thyself from thy own breast. See me return'd
After long suff'rings, in the twentieth year,
To my own land. But since (some God the thought
Suggesting to thee) thou hast learn'd the truth,
Silence! lest others learn it from thy lips.
For this I say, nor shall the threat be vain;
If God vouchsafe to me to overcome
The haughty suitors, when I shall inflict
610 Death on the other women of my house,
Although my nurse, thyself shalt also die.
Him answer'd Euryclea then, discrete.
My son! oh how could so severe a word
Escape thy lips? my fortitude of mind
Thou know'st, and even now shalt prove me firm
As iron, secret as the stubborn rock.
But hear and mark me well. Should'st thou prevail,
Assisted by a Pow'r divine, to slay
The haughty suitors, I will then, myself,
620 Give thee to know of all the female train
Who have dishonour'd thee, and who respect.
To whom Ulysses, ever-wise, replied.
My nurse, it were superfluous; spare thy tongue
That needless task. I can distinguish well
Myself, between them, and shall know them all;
But hold thy peace. Hush! leave it with the Gods.
So he; then went the ancient matron forth,
That she might serve him with a second bath,
For the whole first was spilt. Thus, laved at length,
630 And smooth'd with oil, Ulysses nearer pull'd
His seat toward the glowing hearth to enjoy
More warmth, and drew his tatters o'er the scar.
Then, prudent, thus Penelope began.
One question, stranger, I shall yet propound,
Though brief, for soon the hour of soft repose
Grateful to all, and even to the sad
Whom gentle sleep forsakes not, will arrive.
But heav'n to me immeasurable woe
Assigns, — whose sole delight is to consume
640 My days in sighs, while here retired I sit,
Watching my maidens' labours and my own;
But (night return'd, and all to bed retired)

I press mine also, yet with deep regret
And anguish lacerated, even there.
As when at spring's first entrance, her sweet song
The azure-crested nightingale renews,
Daughter of Pandarus; within the grove's
Thick foliage perch'd, she pours her echoing voice
Now deep, now clear, still varying the strain
650 With which she mourns her Itylus, her son

By royal Zethus, whom she, erring, slew,[85]
So also I, by soul-distressing doubts
Toss'd ever, muse if I shall here remain
A faithful guardian of my son's affairs,
My husband's bed respecting, and not less
My own fair fame, or whether I shall him
Of all my suitors follow to his home
Who noblest seems, and offers richest dow'r.
My son while he was infant yet, and own'd
660 An infant's mind, could never give consent
That I should wed and leave him; but at length,
Since he hath reached the stature of a man,
He wishes my departure hence, the waste
Viewing indignant by the suitors made.
But I have dream'd. Hear, and expound my dream.
My geese are twenty, which within my walls
I feed with sodden wheat; they serve to amuse
Sometimes my sorrow. From the mountains came
An eagle, huge, hook-beak'd, brake all their necks,
670 And slew them; scatter'd on the palace-floor
They lay, and he soar'd swift into the skies.
Dream only as it was, I wept aloud,
Till all my maidens, gather'd by my voice,
Arriving, found me weeping still, and still
Complaining, that the eagle had at once
Slain all my geese. But, to the palace-roof
Stooping again, he sat, and with a voice
Of human sound, forbad my tears, and said-
Courage! O daughter of the far-renown'd
680 Icarius! no vain dream thou hast beheld,
But, in thy sleep, a truth. The slaughter'd geese
Denote thy suitors. I who have appear'd
An eagle in thy sight, am yet indeed
Thy husband, who have now, at last, return'd,
Death, horrid death designing for them all.
He said; then waking at the voice, I cast
An anxious look around, and saw my geese
Beside their tray, all feeding as before.
Her then Ulysses answer'd, ever-wise.
690 O Queen! it is not possible to miss
Thy dream's plain import, since Ulysses' self
Hath told thee the event; thy suitors all
Must perish; not one suitor shall escape.
To whom Penelope discrete replied.
Dreams are inexplicable, O my guest!
And oft-times mere delusions that receive
No just accomplishment. There are two gates
Through which the fleeting phantoms pass; of horn
Is one, and one of ivory.[86] Such dreams

---

[85] She intended to slay the son of her husband's brother Amphion, incited to it by the envy of his wife, who had six children, while herself had only two, but through mistake she slew her own son Itylus, and for her punishment was transformed by Jupiter into a nightingale.

[86] The difference of the two substances may perhaps serve to account for the preference given in this case to the gate of horn; horn being

700 As through the thin-leaf'd iv'ry portal come
Sooth, but perform not, utt'ring empty sounds;
But such as through the polish'd horn escape,
If, haply seen by any mortal eye,
Prove faithful witnesses, and are fulfill'd.
But through those gates my wond'rous dream, I think,
Came not; thrice welcome were it else to me
And to my son. Now mark my words; attend.
This is the hated morn that from the house
Removes me of Ulysses. I shall fix,
710 This day, the rings for trial to them all
Of archership; Ulysses' custom was

To plant twelve spikes, all regular arranged[87]
Like galley-props, and crested with a ring,
Then standing far remote, true in his aim
He with his whizzing shaft would thrid them all.
This is the contest in which now I mean
To prove the suitors; him, who with most ease
Shall bend the bow, and shoot through all the rings,
I follow, this dear mansion of my youth
720 Leaving, so fair, so fill'd with ev'ry good,
Though still to love it even in my dreams.
Her answer'd then Ulysses, ever-wise.
Consort revered of Laertiades!

Postpone not this contention, but appoint
Forthwith the trial; for Ulysses here
Will sure arrive, ere they, (his polish'd bow
Long tamp'ring) shall prevail to stretch the nerve,
And speed the arrow through the iron rings.
To whom Penelope replied discrete.
730 Would'st thou with thy sweet converse, O my guest!
Here sooth me still, sleep ne'er should influence
These eyes the while; but always to resist
Sleep's pow'r is not for man, to whom the Gods
Each circumstance of his condition here
Fix universally. Myself will seek
My own apartment at the palace-top,
And there will lay me down on my sad couch,
For such it hath been, and with tears of mine
Ceaseless bedew'd, e'er since Ulysses went
740 To that bad city, never to be named.
There will I sleep; but sleep thou here below,
Either, thyself, preparing on the ground
Thy couch, or on a couch by these prepared.
So saying, she to her splendid chamber thence
Retired, not sole, but by her female train
Attended; there arrived, she wept her spouse,
Her lov'd Ulysses, till Minerva dropp'd
The balm of slumber on her weary lids.

---

transparent, and as such emblematical of truth, while ivory, from its whiteness, promises light, but is, in fact, opaque. F.

[87] The translation here is somewhat pleonastic for the sake of perspicuity; the original is clear in itself, but not to us who have no such practice. Twelve stakes were fixt in the earth, each having a ring at the top; the order in which they stood was so exact, that an arrow sent with an even hand through the first ring, would pass them all.

Book XX

Ulysses, doubting whether he shall destroy or not the women servants who commit lewdness with the suitors, resolves at length to spare them for the present. He asks an omen from Jupiter, and that he would grant him also to hear some propitious words from the lips of one in the family. His petitions are both answered. Preparation is made for the feast. Whilst the suitors sit at table, Pallas smites them with a horrid frenzy. Theoclymenus, observing the strange effects of it, prophesies their destruction, and they deride his prophecy.

But in the vestibule the Hero lay
On a bull's-hide undress'd, o'er which he spread
The fleece of many a sheep slain by the Greeks,
And, cover'd by the household's governess
With a wide cloak, composed himself to rest.
Yet slept he not, but meditating lay
Woe to his enemies. Meantime, the train
Of women, wonted to the suitors' arms,
Issuing all mirth and laughter, in his soul
A tempest raised of doubts, whether at once
10 To slay, or to permit them yet to give
Their lusty paramours one last embrace.
As growls the mastiff standing on the start
For battle, if a stranger's foot approach
Her cubs new-whelp'd-so growl'd Ulysses' heart,
While wonder fill'd him at their impious deeds.
But, smiting on his breast, thus he reproved
The mutinous inhabitant within.
Heart! bear it. Worse than this thou didst endure
When, uncontroulable by force of man,
20 The Cyclops thy illustrious friends devour'd.
Thy patience then fail'd not, till prudence found
Deliv'rance for thee on the brink of fate.
So disciplined the Hero his own heart,
Which, tractable, endured the rigorous curb,
And patient; yet he turn'd from side to side.
As when some hungry swain turns oft a maw
Unctuous and sav'ry on the burning coals,
Quick expediting his desired repast,
So he from side to side roll'd, pond'ring deep
30 How likeliest with success he might assail
Those shameless suitors; one to many opposed.
Then, sudden from the skies descending, came
Minerva in a female form; her stand
Above his head she took, and thus she spake.
Why sleep'st thou not, unhappiest of mankind?
Thou art at home; here dwells thy wife, and here
Thy son; a son, whom all might wish their own.
Then her Ulysses answer'd, ever-wise.
O Goddess! true is all that thou hast said,
40 But, not without anxiety, I muse
How, single as I am, I shall assail
Those shameless suitors who frequent my courts
Daily; and always their whole multitude.
This weightier theme I meditate beside;
Should I, with Jove's concurrence and with thine
Prevail to slay them, how shall I escape,

Myself, at last?[88] oh Goddess, weigh it well.
Him answer'd then Pallas cærulean-eyed.
Oh faithless man! a man will in his friend
5 °Confide, though mortal, and in valour less
And wisdom than himself; but I who keep
Thee in all difficulties, am divine.
I tell thee plainly. Were we hemm'd around
By fifty troops of shouting warriors bent
To slay thee, thou should'st yet securely drive
The flocks away and cattle of them all.
But yield to sleep's soft influence; for to lie
All night thus watchful, is, itself, distress.
Fear not. Deliv'rance waits, not far remote.
60 So saying, she o'er Ulysses' eyes diffused
Soft slumbers, and when sleep that sooths the mind
And nerves the limbs afresh had seized him once,
To the Olympian summit swift return'd.
But his chaste spouse awoke; she weeping sat
On her soft couch, and, noblest of her sex,
Satiate at length with tears, her pray'r address'd
First to Diana of the Pow'rs above.
Diana, awful progeny of Jove!
I would that with a shaft this moment sped
70 Into my bosom, thou would'st here conclude
My mournful life! or, oh that, as it flies,
Snatching me through the pathless air, a storm
Would whelm me deep in Ocean's restless tide!
So, when the Gods their parents had destroy'd,
Storms suddenly the beauteous daughters snatch'd[89]
Of Pandarus away; them left forlorn
Venus with curds, with honey and with wine
Fed duly; Juno gave them to surpass
All women in the charms of face and mind,
80 With graceful stature eminent the chaste
Diana bless'd them, and in works of art
Illustrious, Pallas taught them to excel.
But when the foam-sprung Goddess to the skies
A suitress went on their behalf, to obtain
Blest nuptials for them from the Thund'rer Jove,
(For Jove the happiness, himself, appoints,
And the unhappiness of all below)
Meantime, the Harpies ravishing away
Those virgins, gave them to the Furies Three,
90 That they might serve them. O that me the Gods
Inhabiting Olympus so would hide
From human eyes for ever, or bright-hair'd
Diana pierce me with a shaft, that while

---

[88] That is, how shall I escape the vengeance of their kindred?
[89] Aedon, Cleothera, Merope.

Ulysses yet engages all my thoughts,
My days concluded, I might 'scape the pain
Of gratifying some inferior Chief!
This is supportable, when (all the day
To sorrow giv'n) the mourner sleeps at night;
For sleep, when it hath once the eyelids veil'd,
100 All reminiscence blots of all alike,
Both good and ill; but me the Gods afflict
Not seldom ev'n in dreams, and at my side,
This night again, one lay resembling him;
Such as my own Ulysses when he join'd
Achaia's warriors; my exulting heart
No airy dream believed it, but a truth.
While thus she spake, in orient gold enthroned
Came forth the morn; Ulysses, as she wept,
Heard plain her lamentation; him that sound
110 Alarm'd; he thought her present, and himself
Known to her. Gath'ring hastily the cloak
His cov'ring, and the fleeces, them he placed
Together on a throne within the hall,
But bore the bull's-hide forth into the air.
Then, lifting high his hands to Jove, he pray'd.
Eternal Sire! if over moist and dry
Ye have with good-will sped me to my home
After much suff'ring, grant me from the lips
Of some domestic now awake, to hear
120 Words of propitious omen, and thyself
Vouchsafe me still some other sign abroad.
Such pray'r he made, and Jove omniscient heard.
Sudden he thunder'd from the radiant heights
Olympian; glad, Ulysses heard the sound.
A woman, next, a labourer at the mill
Hard by, where all the palace-mills were wrought,
Gave him the omen of propitious sound.
Twelve maidens, day by day, toil'd at the mills,
Meal grinding, some, of barley, some, of wheat,
130 Marrow of man.[90] The rest (their portion ground)
All slept; she only from her task as yet
Ceas'd not, for she was feeblest of them all;
She rested on her mill, and thus pronounced
The happy omen by her Lord desired.
Jove, Father, Governor of heav'n and earth!
Loud thou hast thunder'd from the starry skies
By no cloud veil'd; a sign propitious, giv'n
To whom I know not; but oh grant the pray'r
Of a poor bond-woman! appoint their feast
140 This day, the last that in Ulysses' house
The suitors shall enjoy, for whom I drudge,
With aching heart and trembling knees their meal
Grinding continual. Feast they here no more!
She ended, and the list'ning Chief received
With equal joy both signs; for well he hoped
That he should punish soon those guilty men.
And now the other maidens in the hall
Assembling, kindled on the hearth again
Th' unwearied blaze; then, godlike from his couch
150 Arose Telemachus, and, fresh-attired,
Athwart his shoulders his bright faulchion slung,

Bound his fair sandals to his feet, and took
His sturdy spear pointed with glitt'ring brass;
Advancing to the portal, there he stood,
And Euryclea thus, his nurse, bespake.
Nurse! have ye with respectful notice serv'd
Our guest? or hath he found a sordid couch
E'en where he might? for, prudent though she be,
My mother, inattentive oft, the worse
160 Treats kindly, and the better sends away.
Whom Euryclea answer'd, thus, discrete.
Blame not, my son! who merits not thy blame.
The guest sat drinking till he would no more,
And ate, till, question'd, he replied-Enough.
But when the hour of sleep call'd him to rest,
She gave commandment to her female train
To spread his couch. Yet he, like one forlorn,
And, through despair, indiff'rent to himself,
Both bed and rugs refused, and in the porch
170 On skins of sheep and on an undress'd hide
Reposed, where we threw cov'ring over him.
She ceas'd, and, grasping his bright-headed spear,
Forth went the Prince attended, as he went,
By his fleet hounds; to the assembled Greeks
In council with majestic gait he moved,
And Euryclea, daughter wise of Ops,
Pisenor's son, call'd to the serving-maids.
Haste ye! be diligent! sweep the palace-floor
And sprinkle it; then give the sumptuous seats
180 Their purple coverings. Let others cleanse
With sponges all the tables, wash and rince
The beakers well, and goblets rich-emboss'd;
Run others to the fountain, and bring thence
Water with speed. The suitors will not long
Be absent, but will early come to-day,

For this day is a public festival.[91]
So she; whom all, obedient, heard; forth went
Together, twenty to the crystal fount,
While in their sev'ral provinces the rest
190 Bestirr'd them brisk at home. Then enter'd all
The suitors, and began cleaving the wood.
Meantime, the women from the fountain came,
Whom soon the swine-herd follow'd, driving three
His fattest brawns; them in the spacious court
He feeding left, and to Ulysses' side
Approaching, courteously bespake the Chief.
Guest! look the Greecians on thee with respect
At length, or still disdainful as before?
Then, answer thus Ulysses wise return'd.
200 Yes-and I would that vengeance from the Gods
Might pay their insolence, who in a house
Not theirs, dominion exercise, and plan
Unseemly projects, shameless as they are!
Thus they conferr'd; and now Melanthius came
The goat-herd, driving, with the aid of two
His fellow-swains, the fattest of his goats
To feast the suitors. In the sounding porch
The goats he tied, then, drawing near, in terms
Reproachful thus assail'd Ulysses' ear.

---

[90] +muelon andrôn+.

[91] The new moon.

210 How, stranger? persever'st thou, begging, still
To vex the suitors? wilt thou not depart?
Scarce shall we settle this dispute, I judge,
Till we have tasted each the other's fist;
Thou art unreasonable thus to beg
Here always-have the Greeks no feasts beside?
He spake, to whom Ulysses answer none
Return'd, but shook his brows, and, silent, framed
Terrible purposes. Then, third, approach'd
Chief o'er the herds, Philoetius; fatted goats
220 He for the suitors brought, with which he drove
An heifer; (ferry-men had pass'd them o'er,
Carriers of all who on their coast arrive)
He tied them in the sounding porch, then stood
Beside the swine-herd, to whom thus he said.
Who is this guest, Eumæus, here arrived
So lately? from what nation hath he come?
What parentage and country boasts the man?
I pity him, whose figure seems to speak
Royalty in him. Heav'n will surely plunge
230 The race of common wand'rers deep in woe,
If thus it destine even Kings to mourn.
He ceas'd; and, with his right hand, drawing nigh,
Welcom'd Ulysses, whom he thus bespake.
Hail venerable guest! and be thy lot
Prosp'rous at least hereafter, who art held
At present in the bonds of num'rous ills.
Thou, Jupiter, of all the Gods, art most
Severe, and spar'st not to inflict distress
Even on creatures from thyself derived.[92]
240 I had no sooner mark'd thee, than my eyes
Swam, and the sweat gush'd from me at the thought
Of dear Ulysses; for if yet he live
And see the sun, such tatters, I suppose,
He wears, a wand'rer among human-kind.
But if already with the dead he dwell
In Pluto's drear abode, oh then, alas
For kind Ulysses! who consign'd to me,
While yet a boy, his Cephalenian herds,
And they have now encreas'd to such a store
250 Innumerable of broad-fronted beeves,
As only care like mine could have produced.
These, by command of others, I transport
For their regale, who neither heed his son,
Nor tremble at the anger of the Gods,
But long have wish'd ardently to divide
And share the substance of our absent Lord.
Me, therefore, this thought occupies, and haunts
My mind not seldom; while the heir survives
It were no small offence to drive his herds
260 Afar, and migrate to a foreign land;
Yet here to dwell, suff'ring oppressive wrongs
While I attend another's beeves, appears
Still less supportable; and I had fled,
And I had served some other mighty Chief
Long since, (for patience fails me to endure
My present lot) but that I cherish still
Some hope of my ill-fated Lord's return,

To rid his palace of those lawless guests.
To whom Ulysses, ever-wise, replied.
270 Herdsman! since neither void of sense thou seem'st,
Nor yet dishonest, but myself am sure
That thou art owner of a mind discrete,
Hear therefore, for I swear! bold I attest
Jove and this hospitable board, and these
The Lares[93] of the noble Chief, whose hearth
Protects me now, that, ere thy going hence,
Ulysses surely shall have reach'd his home,
And thou shalt see him, if thou wilt, thyself,
Slaying the suitors who now lord it here.
280 Him answer'd then the keeper of his beeves.
Oh stranger! would but the Saturnian King
Perform that word, thou should'st be taught (thyself
Eye-witness of it) what an arm is mine.
Eumæus also ev'ry power of heav'n
Entreated, that Ulysses might possess
His home again. Thus mutual they conferr'd.
Meantime, in conf'rence close the suitors plann'd
Death for Telemachus; but while they sat
Consulting, on their left the bird of Jove
290 An eagle soar'd, grasping a tim'rous dove.
Then, thus, Amphinomus the rest bespake.
Oh friends! our consultation how to slay
Telemachus, will never smoothly run
To its effect; but let us to the feast.
So spake Amphinomus, whose counsel pleased.
Then, all into the royal house repaired,
And on the thrones and couches throwing off
Their mantles, slew the fatted goats, the brawns,
The sheep full-sized, and heifer of the herd.
300 The roasted entrails first they shared, then fill'd
The beakers, and the swine-herd placed the cups,
Philoetius, chief intendant of the beeves,
Served all with baskets elegant of bread,
While all their cups Melanthius charged with wine,
And they assail'd at once the ready feast.
Meantime Telemachus, with forecast shrewd,
Fast by the marble threshold, but within
The spacious hall his father placed, to whom
A sordid seat he gave and scanty board.
310 A portion of the entrails, next, he set
Before him, fill'd a golden goblet high,
And thus, in presence of them all, began.
There seated now, drink as the suitors drink.
I will, myself, their biting taunts forbid,
And violence. This edifice is mine,
Not public property; my father first
Possess'd it, and my right from him descends.
Suitors! controul your tongues, nor with your hands
Offend, lest contest fierce and war ensue.
320 He ceas'd: they gnawing, sat, their lips, aghast
With wonder that Telemachus in his speech
Such boldness used. Then spake Eupithes' son,
Antinoüs, and the assembly thus address'd.
Let pass, ye Greeks! the language of the Prince,
Harsh as it is, and big with threats to us.

---

[92] He is often called-+patêr andrôn te theôn te+.

[93] Household Gods who presided over the hearth.

Had Jove permitted, his orations here,
Although thus eloquent, ere now had ceased.
So spake Antinoüs, whom Ulysses' son
Heard unconcern'd. And now the heralds came
330 In solemn pomp, conducting through the streets
A sacred hecatomb, when in the grove
Umbrageous of Apollo, King shaft-arm'd,
The assembled Greecians met. The sav'ry roast
Finish'd, and from the spits withdrawn, each shared
His portion of the noble feast, and such
As they enjoy'd themselves the attendants placed
Before Ulysses, for the Hero's son
Himself, Telemachus, had so enjoined.
But Pallas (that they might exasp'rate more
340 Ulysses) suffer'd not the suitor Chiefs
To banquet, guiltless of heart-piercing scoffs
Malign. There was a certain suitor named
Ctesippus, born in Samos; base of mind
Was he and profligate, but, in the wealth
Confiding of his father, woo'd the wife
Of long-exiled Ulysses. From his seat
The haughty suitors thus that man address'd.
Ye noble suitors, I would speak; attend!
The guest is served; he hath already shared
350 Equal with us; nor less the laws demand
Of hospitality; for neither just
It were nor decent, that a guest, received
Here by Telemachus, should be denied
His portion of the feast. Come then-myself
Will give to him, that he may also give
To her who laved him in the bath, or else
To whatsoever menial here he will.
So saying, he from a basket near at hand
Heav'd an ox-foot, and with a vig'rous arm
360 Hurl'd it. Ulysses gently bow'd his head,
Shunning the blow, but gratified his just
Resentment with a broad sardonic smile[94]
Of dread significance. He smote the wall.
Then thus Telemachus rebuked the deed.
Ctesippus, thou art fortunate; the bone
Struck not the stranger, for he shun'd the blow;
Else, I had surely thrust my glitt'ring lance
Right through thee; then, no hymenæal rites
Of thine should have employ'd thy father here,
370 But thy funereal. No man therefore treat
Me with indignity within these walls,
For though of late a child, I can discern
Now, and distinguish between good and ill.
Suffice it that we patiently endure
To be spectators daily of our sheep
Slaughter'd, our bread consumed, our stores of wine
Wasted; for what can one to all opposed?
Come then-persist no longer in offence
And hostile hate of me; or if ye wish
380 To slay me, pause not. It were better far
To die, and I had rather much be slain,
Than thus to witness your atrocious deeds
Day after day; to see our guests abused,

With blows insulted, and the women dragg'd
With a licentious violence obscene
From side to side of all this fair abode.
He said, and all sat silent, till at length
Thus Agelaüs spake, Diastor's son.
My friends! let none with contradiction thwart
390 And rude reply, words rational and just;
Assault no more the stranger, nor of all
The servants of renown'd Ulysses here
Harm any. My advice, both to the Queen
And to Telemachus, shall gentle be,
May it but please them. While the hope survived
Within your bosoms of the safe return
Of wise Ulysses to his native isle,
So long good reason was that she should use
Delay, and hold our wooing in suspence;
400 For had Ulysses come, that course had proved
Wisest and best; but that he comes no more
Appears, now, manifest. Thou, therefore, Prince!
Seeking thy mother, counsel her to wed
The noblest, and who offers richest dow'r,
That thou, for thy peculiar, may'st enjoy
Thy own inheritance in peace and ease,
And she, departing, find another home.
To whom Telemachus, discrete, replied.
I swear by Jove, and by my father's woes,
410 Who either hath deceased far from his home,
Or lives a wand'rer, that I interpose
No hindrance to her nuptials. Let her wed
Who offers most, and even whom she will.
But to dismiss her rudely were a deed
Unfilial-That I dare not-God forbid!
So spake Telemachus. Then Pallas struck
The suitors with delirium; wide they stretch'd
Their jaws with unspontaneous laughter loud;
Their meat dripp'd blood; tears fill'd their eyes, and dire
Presages of approaching woe, their hearts.

421 Then thus the prophet Theoclymenus.[95]
Ah miserable men! what curse is this
That takes you now? night wraps itself around
Your faces, bodies, limbs; the palace shakes
With peals of groans-and oh, what floods ye weep!
I see the walls and arches dappled thick
With gore; the vestibule is throng'd, the court
On all sides throng'd with apparitions grim
Of slaughter'd men sinking into the gloom
430 Of Erebus; the sun is blotted out
From heav'n, and midnight whelms you premature.
He said, they, hearing, laugh'd; and thus the son
Of Polybus, Eurymachus replied.
This wand'rer from a distant shore hath left
His wits behind. Hoa there! conduct him hence
Into the forum; since he dreams it night
Already, teach him there that it is day.
Then answer'd godlike Theoclymenus.
I have no need, Eurymachus, of guides
440 To lead me hence, for I have eyes and ears,
The use of both my feet, and of a mind

---

[94] A smile of displeasure.

[95] Who had sought refuge in the ship of Telemachus when he left Sparta, and came with him to Ithaca.

In no respect irrational or wild.
These shall conduct me forth, for well I know
That evil threatens you, such, too, as none
Shall 'scape of all the suitors, whose delight
Is to insult the unoffending guest
Received beneath this hospitable roof.
He said, and, issuing from the palace, sought
Piræus' house, who gladly welcom'd him.
450 Then all the suitors on each other cast
A look significant, and, to provoke
Telemachus the more, fleer'd at his guests.
Of whom a youth thus, insolent began.
No living wight, Telemachus, had e'er
Guests such as thine. Witness, we know not who,
This hungry vagabond, whose means of life
Are none, and who hath neither skill nor force
To earn them, a mere burthen on the ground.

Witness the other also, who upstarts
460 A prophet suddenly. Take my advice;
I counsel wisely; send them both on board
Some gallant bark to Sicily for sale;
Thus shall they somewhat profit thee at last.
So spake the suitors, whom Telemachus
Heard unconcern'd, and, silent, look'd and look'd
Toward his father, watching still the time
When he should punish that licentious throng.
Meantime, Icarius' daughter, who had placed
Her splendid seat opposite, heard distinct
470 Their taunting speeches. They, with noisy mirth,
Feasted deliciously, for they had slain
Many a fat victim; but a sadder feast
Than, soon, the Goddess and the warrior Chief
Should furnish for them, none shall ever share.
Of which their crimes had furnish'd first the cause.

Book XXI

Penelope proposes to the suitors a contest with the bow, herself the prize. They prove unable to bend the bow; when Ulysses having with some difficulty possessed himself of it, manages it with the utmost ease, and dispatches his arrow through twelve rings erected for the trial.

Minerva, now, Goddess cærulean-eyed,
Prompted Icarius' daughter, the discrete
Penelope, with bow and rings to prove
Her suitors in Ulysses' courts, a game
Terrible in conclusion to them all.
First, taking in her hand the brazen key
Well-forged, and fitted with an iv'ry grasp,
Attended by the women of her train
She sought her inmost chamber, the recess
In which she kept the treasures of her Lord,
10 His brass, his gold, and steel elaborate.
Here lay his stubborn bow, and quiver fill'd
With num'rous shafts, a fatal store. That bow
He had received and quiver from the hand
Of godlike Iphitus Eurytides,

Whom, in Messenia,[96] in the house he met
Of brave Orsilochus. Ulysses came
Demanding payment of arrearage due
From all that land; for a Messenian fleet
Had borne from Ithaca three hundred sheep,
20 With all their shepherds; for which cause, ere yet
Adult, he voyaged to that distant shore,
Deputed by his sire, and by the Chiefs
Of Ithaca, to make the just demand.
But Iphitus had thither come to seek
Twelve mares and twelve mule colts which he had lost,
A search that cost him soon a bloody death.
For, coming to the house of Hercules
The valiant task-performing son of Jove,
He perish'd there, slain by his cruel host
30 Who, heedless of heav'n's wrath, and of the rights
Of his own board, first fed, then slaughter'd him;
For in *his* house the mares and colts were hidden.
He, therefore, occupied in that concern,
Meeting Ulysses there, gave him the bow
Which, erst, huge Eurytus had borne, and which
Himself had from his dying sire received.
Ulysses, in return, on him bestowed
A spear and sword, pledges of future love
And hospitality; but never more
40 They met each other at the friendly board,
For, ere that hour arrived, the son of Jove
Slew his own guest, the godlike Iphitus.
Thus came the bow into Ulysses' hands,
Which, never in his gallant barks he bore
To battle with him, (though he used it oft
In times of peace) but left it safely stored

At home, a dear memorial of his friend.
Soon as, divinest of her sex, arrived
At that same chamber, with her foot she press'd
50 The oaken threshold bright, on which the hand
Of no mean architect had stretch'd the line,
Who had erected also on each side
The posts on which the splendid portals hung,
She loos'd the ring and brace, then introduced

The key, and aiming at them from without,[97]
Struck back the bolts. The portals, at that stroke,
Sent forth a tone deep as the pastur'd bull's,
And flew wide open. She, ascending, next,
The elevated floor on which the chests
60 That held her own fragrant apparel stood,
With lifted hand aloft took down the bow
In its embroider'd bow-case safe enclosed.
Then, sitting there, she lay'd it on her knees,
Weeping aloud, and drew it from the case.
Thus weeping over it long time she sat,
Till satiate, at the last, with grief and tears,
Descending by the palace steps she sought
Again the haughty suitors, with the bow
Elastic, and the quiver in her hand
70 Replete with pointed shafts, a deadly store.
Her maidens, as she went, bore after her
A coffer fill'd with prizes by her Lord,
Much brass and steel; and when at length she came,
Loveliest of women, where the suitors sat,
Between the pillars of the stately dome
Pausing, before her beauteous face she held
Her lucid veil, and by two matrons chaste
Supported, the assembly thus address'd.
Ye noble suitors hear, who rudely haunt
80 This palace of a Chief long absent hence,
Whose substance ye have now long time consumed,
Nor palliative have yet contrived, or could,
Save your ambition to make me a bride-
Attend this game to which I call you forth.
Now suitors! prove yourselves with this huge bow
Of wide-renown'd Ulysses; he who draws
Easiest the bow, and who his arrow sends
Through twice six rings, he takes me to his home,
And I must leave this mansion of my youth
90 Plenteous, magnificent, which, doubtless, oft
I shall remember even in my dreams.
So saying, she bade Eumæus lay the bow
Before them, and the twice six rings of steel.

---

[96] A province of Laconia.

[97] The reader will of course observe, that the whole of this process implies a sort of mechanism very different from that with which we are acquainted.-The translation, I believe, is exact.

He wept, received them, and obey'd; nor wept
The herdsman less, seeing the bow which erst
His Lord had occupied; when at their tears
Indignant, thus, Antinoüs began.
Ye rural drones, whose purblind eyes see not
Beyond the present hour, egregious fools!
100 Why weeping trouble ye the Queen, too much
Before afflicted for her husband lost?
Either partake the banquet silently,
Or else go weep abroad, leaving the bow,
That stubborn test, to us; for none, I judge,
None here shall bend this polish'd bow with ease,
Since in this whole assembly I discern
None like Ulysses, whom myself have seen
And recollect, though I was then a boy.
He said, but in his heart, meantime, the hope
11 °Cherish'd, that he should bend, himself, the bow,
And pass the rings; yet was he destin'd first
Of all that company to taste the steel
Of brave Ulysses' shaft, whom in that house
He had so oft dishonour'd, and had urged
So oft all others to the like offence.
Amidst them, then, the sacred might arose
Of young Telemachus, who thus began.
Saturnian Jove questionless hath deprived
Me of all reason. My own mother, fam'd
120 For wisdom as she is, makes known to all
Her purpose to abandon this abode
And follow a new mate, while, heedless, I
Trifle and laugh as I were still a child.
But come, ye suitors! since the prize is such,
A woman like to whom none can be found
This day in all Achaia; on the shores
Of sacred Pylus; in the cities proud
Of Argos or Mycenæ; or even here
In Ithaca; or yet within the walls
130 Of black Epirus; and since this yourselves
Know also, wherefore should I speak her praise?
Come then, delay not, waste not time in vain
Excuses, turn not from the proof, but bend
The bow, that thus the issue may be known.
I also will, myself, that task essay;
And should I bend the bow, and pass the rings,
Then shall not my illustrious mother leave
Her son forlorn, forsaking this abode
To follow a new spouse, while I remain
140 Disconsolate, although of age to bear,
Successful as my sire, the prize away.
So saying, he started from his seat, cast off
His purple cloak, and lay'd his sword aside,
Then fix'd, himself, the rings, furrowing the earth
By line, and op'ning one long trench for all,
And stamping close the glebe. Amazement seized
All present, seeing with how prompt a skill
He executed, though untaught, his task.
Then, hasting to the portal, there he stood.
150 Thrice, struggling, he essay'd to bend the bow,
And thrice desisted, hoping still to draw

The bow-string home, and shoot through all the rings.[98]
And now the fourth time striving with full force
He had prevail'd to string it, but his sire
Forbad his eager efforts by a sign.
Then thus the royal youth to all around-
Gods! either I shall prove of little force
Hereafter, and for manly feats unapt,
Or I am yet too young, and have not strength
160 To quell the aggressor's contumely. But come-
(For ye have strength surpassing mine) try ye
The bow, and bring this contest to an end.
He ceas'd, and set the bow down on the floor,
Reclining it against the shaven pannels smooth
That lined the wall; the arrow next he placed,
Leaning against the bow's bright-polish'd horn,
And to the seat, whence he had ris'n, return'd.
Then thus Eupithes' son, Antinoüs spake.

My friends! come forth successive from the right,[99]
170 Where he who ministers the cup begins.
So spake Antinoüs, and his counsel pleased.
Then, first, Leiodes, Oenop's son, arose.
He was their soothsayer, and ever sat
Beside the beaker, inmost of them all.
To him alone, of all, licentious deeds
Were odious, and, with indignation fired,
He witness'd the excesses of the rest.
He then took foremost up the shaft and bow,
And, station'd at the portal, strove to bend
180 But bent it not, fatiguing, first, his hands
Delicate and uncustom'd to the toil.
He ceased, and the assembly thus bespake.
My friends, I speed not; let another try;
For many Princes shall this bow of life
Bereave, since death more eligible seems,
Far more, than loss of her, for whom we meet
Continual here, expecting still the prize.
Some suitor, haply, at this moment, hopes
That he shall wed whom long he hath desired,
190 Ulysses' wife, Penelope; let him
Essay the bow, and, trial made, address
His spousal offers to some other fair
Among the long-stoled Princesses of Greece,
This Princess leaving his, whose proffer'd gifts
Shall please her most, and whom the Fates ordain.
He said, and set the bow down on the floor,
Reclining it against the shaven pannels smooth
That lined the wall; the arrow, next, he placed,
Leaning against the bow's bright-polish'd horn,
200 And to the seat whence he had ris'n return'd.
Then him Antinoüs, angry, thus reproved.
What word, Leiodes, grating to our ears
Hath scap'd thy lips? I hear it with disdain.
Shall this bow fatal prove to many a Prince,
Because thou hast, thyself, too feeble proved
To bend it? no. Thou wast not born to bend
The unpliant bow, or to direct the shaft,
But here are nobler who shall soon prevail.

---

[98] This first attempt of Telemachus and the suitors was not an attempt to shoot, but to lodge the bow-string on the opposite horn, the bow having been released at one end, and slackened while it was laid by.

[99] Antinoüs prescribes to them this manner of rising to the trial for the good omen's sake, the left-hand being held unpropitious.

He said, and to Melanthius gave command,
210 The goat-herd. Hence, Melanthius, kindle fire;
Beside it place, with fleeces spread, a form
Of length commodious; from within procure
A large round cake of suet next, with which
When we have chafed and suppled the tough bow
Before the fire, we will again essay
To bend it, and decide the doubtful strife.
He ended, and Melanthius, kindling fire
Beside it placed, with fleeces spread, a form
Of length commodious; next, he brought a cake
220 Ample and round of suet from within,
With which they chafed the bow, then tried again
To bend, but bent it not; superior strength
To theirs that task required. Yet two, the rest
In force surpassing, made no trial yet,
Antinoüs, and Eurymachus the brave.
Then went the herdsman and the swine-herd forth
Together; after whom, the glorious Chief
Himself the house left also, and when all
Without the court had met, with gentle speech
230 Ulysses, then, the faithful pair address'd.
Herdsman! and thou, Eumæus! shall I keep
A certain secret close, or shall I speak
Outright? my spirit prompts me, and I will.
What welcome should Ulysses at your hands
Receive, arriving suddenly at home,
Some God his guide; would ye the suitors aid,
Or would ye aid Ulysses? answer true.
Then thus the chief intendant of his herds.
Would Jove but grant me my desire, to see
240 Once more the Hero, and would some kind Pow'r,
Restore him, I would shew thee soon an arm
Strenuous to serve him, and a dauntless heart.
Eumæus, also, fervently implored
The Gods in pray'r, that they would render back
Ulysses to his home. He, then, convinced
Of their unfeigning honesty, began.
Behold him! I am he myself, arrived
After long suff'rings in the twentieth year!
I know how welcome to yourselves alone
250 Of all my train I come, for I have heard
None others praying for my safe return.
I therefore tell you truth; should heav'n subdue
The suitors under me, ye shall receive
Each at my hands a bride, with lands and house
Near to my own, and ye shall be thenceforth
Dear friends and brothers of the Prince my son.
Lo! also this indisputable proof
That ye may know and trust me. View it here.
It is the scar which in Parnassus erst
260 (Where with the sons I hunted of renown'd
Autolycus) I from a boar received.
So saying, he stripp'd his tatters, and unveil'd
The whole broad scar; then, soon as they had seen
And surely recognized the mark, each cast
His arms around Ulysses, wept, embraced
And press'd him to his bosom, kissing oft
His brows and shoulders, who as oft their hands
And foreheads kiss'd, nor had the setting sun

Beheld them satisfied, but that himself
270 Ulysses thus admonished them, and said.
Cease now from tears, lest any, coming forth,
Mark and report them to our foes within.
Now, to the hall again, but one by one,
Not all at once, I foremost, then yourselves,
And this shall be the sign. Full well I know
That, all unanimous, they will oppose
Deliv'ry of the bow and shafts to me;
But thou, (proceeding with it to my seat)
Eumæus, noble friend! shalt give the bow
280 Into my grasp; then bid the women close
The massy doors, and should they hear a groan
Or other noise made by the Princes shut
Within the hall, let none set step abroad,
But all work silent. Be the palace-door
Thy charge, my good Philoetius! key it fast
Without a moment's pause, and fix the brace.[100]
He ended, and, returning to the hall,
Resumed his seat; nor stay'd his servants long
Without, but follow'd their illustrious Lord.
290 Eurymachus was busily employ'd
Turning the bow, and chafing it before
The sprightly blaze, but, after all, could find
No pow'r to bend it. Disappointment wrung
A groan from his proud heart, and thus he said.
Alas! not only for myself I grieve,
But grieve for all. Nor, though I mourn the loss
Of such a bride, mourn I that loss alone,
(For lovely Greecians may be found no few
In Ithaca, and in the neighbour isles)
300 But should we so inferior prove at last
To brave Ulysses, that no force of ours
Can bend his bow, we are for ever shamed.
To whom Antinoüs, thus, Eupithes' son.
Not so; (as even thou art well-assured
Thyself, Eurymachus!) but Phoebus claims
This day his own. Who then, on such a day,
Would strive to bend it? Let it rather rest.
And should we leave the rings where now they stand,
I trust that none ent'ring Ulysses' house
310 Will dare displace them. Cup-bearer, attend!
Serve all with wine, that, first, libation made,
We may religiously lay down the bow.
Command ye too Melanthius, that he drive
Hither the fairest goats of all his flocks
At dawn of day, that burning first, the thighs
To the ethereal archer, we may make
New trial, and decide, at length, the strife.
So spake Antinoüs, and his counsel pleased.
The heralds, then, pour'd water on their hands,
320 While youths crown'd high the goblets which they bore
From right to left, distributing to all.
When each had made libation, and had drunk
Till well suffic'd, then, artful to effect
His shrewd designs, Ulysses thus began.
Hear, O ye suitors of the illustrious Queen,
My bosom's dictates. But I shall entreat
Chiefly Eurymachus and the godlike youth
Antinoüs, whose advice is wisely giv'n.

---

[100] The +desmos+ seems to have been a strap designed to close the only aperture by which the bolt could be displaced, and the door opened.

Tamper no longer with the bow, but leave
330 The matter with the Gods, who shall decide
The strife to-morrow, fav'ring whom they will.
Meantime, grant *me* the polish'd bow, that I
May trial make among you of my force,
If I retain it still in like degree
As erst, or whether wand'ring and defect
Of nourishment have worn it all away.
He said, whom they with indignation heard
Extreme, alarm'd lest he should bend the bow,
And sternly thus Antinoüs replied.
340 Desperate vagabond! ah wretch deprived
Of reason utterly! art not content?
Esteem'st it not distinction proud enough
To feast with us the nobles of the land?
None robs thee of thy share, thou witnessest
Our whole discourse, which, save thyself alone,
No needy vagrant is allow'd to hear.
Thou art befool'd by wine, as many have been,
Wide-throated drinkers, unrestrain'd by rule.
Wine in the mansion of the mighty Chief
350 Pirithoüs, made the valiant Centaur mad
Eurytion, at the Lapithæan feast.[101]
He drank to drunkenness, and being drunk,
Committed great enormities beneath
Pirithoüs' roof, and such as fill'd with rage
The Hero-guests; who therefore by his feet
Dragg'd him right through the vestibule, amerced
Of nose and ears, and he departed thence
Provoked to frenzy by that foul disgrace,
Whence war between the human kind arose
360 And the bold Centaurs-but he first incurred
By his ebriety that mulct severe.
Great evil, also, if thou bend the bow,
To thee I prophesy; for thou shalt find
Advocate or protector none in all
This people, but we will dispatch thee hence
Incontinent on board a sable bark
To Echetus, the scourge of human kind,
From whom is no escape. Drink then in peace,
And contest shun with younger men than thou.
370 Him answer'd, then, Penelope discrete.
Antinoüs! neither seemly were the deed
Nor just, to maim or harm whatever guest
Whom here arrived Telemachus receives.
Canst thou expect, that should he even prove
Stronger than ye, and bend the massy bow,
He will conduct me hence to his own home,
And make me his own bride? No such design
His heart conceives, or hope; nor let a dread
So vain the mind of any overcloud
380 Who banquets here, since it dishonours me.
So she; to whom Eurymachus reply'd,
Offspring of Polybus. O matchless Queen!
Icarius' prudent daughter! none suspects
That thou wilt wed with him; a mate so mean
Should ill become thee; but we fear the tongues
Of either sex, lest some Achaian say
Hereafter, (one inferior far to us)

Ah! how unworthy are they to compare
With him whose wife they seek! to bend his bow
390 Pass'd all their pow'r, yet this poor vagabond,
Arriving from what country none can tell,
Bent it with ease, and shot through all the rings.
So will they speak, and so shall we be shamed.
Then answer, thus, Penelope return'd.
No fair report, Eurymachus, attends
Their names or can, who, riotous as ye,
The house dishonour, and consume the wealth
Of such a Chief. Why shame ye thus *yourselves*?
The guest is of athletic frame, well form'd,
400 And large of limb; he boasts him also sprung
From noble ancestry. Come then-consent-
Give him the bow, that we may see the proof;
For thus I say, and thus will I perform;
Sure as he bends it, and Apollo gives
To him that glory, tunic fair and cloak
Shall be his meed from me, a javelin keen
To guard him against men and dogs, a sword
Of double edge, and sandals for his feet,
And I will send him whither most he would.
410 Her answer'd then prudent Telemachus.
Mother-the bow is mine; and, save myself,
No Greek hath right to give it, or refuse.
None who in rock-bound Ithaca possess
Dominion, none in the steed-pastured isles
Of Elis, if I chose to make the bow
His own for ever, should that choice controul.
But thou into the house repairing, ply
Spindle and loom, thy province, and enjoin
Diligence to thy maidens; for the bow
420 Is man's concern alone, and shall be mine
Especially, since I am master here.
She heard astonish'd, and the prudent speech
Reposing of her son deep in her heart,
Withdrew; then mounting with her female train
To her superior chamber, there she wept
Her lost Ulysses, till Minerva bathed
With balmy dews of sleep her weary lids.
And now the noble swine-herd bore the bow
Toward Ulysses, but with one voice all
430 The suitors, clamorous, reproved the deed,
Of whom a youth, thus, insolent exclaim'd.
Thou clumsy swine-herd, whither bear'st the bow,
Delirious wretch? the hounds that thou hast train'd
Shall eat thee at thy solitary home
Ere long, let but Apollo prove, at last,
Propitious to us, and the Pow'rs of heav'n.
So they, whom hearing he replaced the bow
Where erst it stood, terrified at the sound
Of such loud menaces; on the other side
440 Telemachus as loud assail'd his ear.
Friend! forward with the bow; or soon repent
That thou obey'dst the many. I will else
With huge stones drive thee, younger as I am,
Back to the field. My strength surpasses thine.
I would to heav'n that I in force excell'd
As far, and prowess, every suitor here!

---

[101] When Pirithoüs, one of the Lapithæ, married Hippodamia, daughter of Adrastus, he invited the Centaurs to the wedding. The Centaurs, intoxicated with wine, attempted to ravish the wives of the Lapithæ, who in resentment of that insult, slew them.

So would I soon give rude dismission hence
To some, who live but to imagine harm.
He ceased, whose words the suitors laughing heard.
450 And, for their sake, in part their wrath resign'd
Against Telemachus; then through the hall
Eumæus bore, and to Ulysses' hand
Consign'd the bow; next, summoning abroad
The ancient nurse, he gave her thus in charge.
It is the pleasure of Telemachus,
Sage Euryclea! that thou key secure
The doors; and should you hear, perchance, a groan
Or other noise made by the Princes shut
Within the hall, let none look, curious, forth,
460 But each in quietness pursue her work.
So he; nor flew his words useless away,
But she, incontinent, shut fast the doors.
Then, noiseless, sprang Philoetius forth, who closed
The portals also of the palace-court.
A ship-rope of Ægyptian reed, it chanced,
Lay in the vestibule; with that he braced
The doors securely, and re-entring fill'd
Again his seat, but watchful, eyed his Lord.
He, now, assaying with his hand the bow,
470 Made curious trial of it ev'ry way,
And turn'd it on all sides, lest haply worms
Had in its master's absence drill'd the horn.
Then thus a suitor to his next remark'd.
He hath an eye, methinks, exactly skill'd
In bows, and steals them; or perhaps, at home,
Hath such himself, or feels a strong desire
To make them; so inquisitive the rogue
Adept in mischief, shifts it to and fro!
To whom another, insolent, replied.
480 I wish him like prosperity in all
His efforts, as attends his effort made
On this same bow, which he shall never bend.
So they; but when the wary Hero wise

Had made his hand familiar with the bow
Poising it and examining-at once-
As when in harp and song adept, a bard
Unlab'ring strains the chord to a new lyre,
The twisted entrails of a sheep below
With fingers nice inserting, and above,
490 With such facility Ulysses bent
His own huge bow, and with his right hand play'd
The nerve, which in its quick vibration sang
Clear as the swallow's voice. Keen anguish seized
The suitors, wan grew ev'ry cheek, and Jove
Gave him his rolling thunder for a sign.
That omen, granted to him by the son
Of wily Saturn, with delight he heard.
He took a shaft that at the table-side
Lay ready drawn; but in his quiver's womb
500 The rest yet slept, by those Achaians proud
To be, ere long, experienced. True he lodg'd
The arrow on the centre of the bow,
And, occupying still his seat, drew home
Nerve and notch'd arrow-head; with stedfast sight
He aimed and sent it; right through all the rings
From first to last the steel-charged weapon flew
Issuing beyond, and to his son he spake.
Thou need'st not blush, young Prince, to have received
A guest like me; neither my arrow swerved,
510 Nor labour'd I long time to draw the bow;
My strength is unimpair'd, not such as these
In scorn affirm it. But the waning day

Calls us to supper, after which succeeds[102]
Jocund variety, the song, the harp,
With all that heightens and adorns the feast.
He said, and with his brows gave him the sign.
At once the son of the illustrious Chief
Slung his keen faulchion, grasp'd his spear, and stood
Arm'd bright for battle at his father's side.
520

---

[102] This is an instance of the +Sardanion mala toion+ mentioned in Book XX.; such as, perhaps, could not be easily paralleled. I question if there be a passage, either in ancient or modern tragedy, so truly terrible as this seeming levity of Ulysses, in the moment when he was going to begin the slaughter.

Book XXII

Ulysses, with some little assistance from Telemachus, Eumæus and Philoetius, slays all the suitors, and twelve of the female servants who had allowed themselves an illicit intercourse with them, are hanged. Melanthius also is punished with miserable mutilation.

Then, girding up his rags, Ulysses sprang
With bow and full-charged quiver to the door;
Loose on the broad stone at his feet he pour'd
His arrows, and the suitors, thus, bespake.
This prize, though difficult, hath been atchieved.
Now for another mark which never man
Struck yet, but I will strike it if I may,
And if Apollo make that glory mine.
He said, and at Antinoüs aimed direct
A bitter shaft; he, purposing to drink,
10 Both hands advanced toward the golden cup
Twin-ear'd, nor aught suspected death so nigh.
For who, at the full banquet, could suspect
That any single guest, however brave,
Should plan his death, and execute the blow?
Yet him Ulysses with an arrow pierced
Full in the throat, and through his neck behind
Started the glitt'ring point. Aslant he droop'd;
Down fell the goblet, through his nostrils flew
The spouted blood, and spurning with his foot
20 The board, he spread his viands in the dust.
Confusion, when they saw Antinoüs fall'n,
Seized all the suitors; from the thrones they sprang,
Flew ev'ry way, and on all sides explored
The palace-walls, but neither sturdy lance
As erst, nor buckler could they there discern,
Then, furious, to Ulysses thus they spake.
Thy arrow, stranger, was ill-aimed; a man
Is no just mark. Thou never shalt dispute
Prize more. Inevitable death is thine.
30 For thou hast slain a Prince noblest of all
In Ithaca, and shalt be vultures' food.
Various their judgments were, but none believed
That he had slain him wittingly, nor saw
Th' infatuate men fate hov'ring o'er them all.
Then thus Ulysses, louring dark, replied.
O dogs! not fearing aught my safe return
From Ilium, ye have shorn my substance close,
Lain with my women forcibly, and sought,
While yet I lived, to make my consort yours,
40 Heedless of the inhabitants of heav'n
Alike, and of the just revenge of man.
But death is on the wing; death for you all.
He said; their cheeks all faded at the sound,
And each with sharpen'd eyes search'd ev'ry nook
For an escape from his impending doom,
Till thus, alone, Eurymachus replied.
If thou indeed art he, the mighty Chief
Of Ithaca return'd, thou hast rehears'd
With truth the crimes committed by the Greeks
50 Frequent, both in thy house and in thy field.
But he, already, who was cause of all,
Lies slain, Antinoüs; he thy palace fill'd
With outrage, not solicitous so much

To win the fair Penelope, but thoughts
Far diff'rent framing, which Saturnian Jove
Hath baffled all; to rule, himself, supreme
In noble Ithaca, when he had kill'd
By an insidious stratagem thy son.
But he is slain. Now therefore, spare thy own,
60 Thy people; public reparation due
Shall sure be thine, and to appease thy wrath
For all the waste that, eating, drinking here
We have committed, we will yield thee, each,
Full twenty beeves, gold paying thee beside
And brass, till joy shall fill thee at the sight,
However just thine anger was before.
To whom Ulysses, frowning stern, replied,
Eurymachus, would ye contribute each
His whole inheritance, and other sums
70 Still add beside, ye should not, even so,
These hands of mine bribe to abstain from blood,
Till ev'ry suitor suffer for his wrong.
Ye have your choice. Fight with me, or escape
(Whoever may) the terrours of his fate,
But ye all perish, if my thought be true.
He ended, they with trembling knees and hearts
All heard, whom thus Eurymachus address'd.
To your defence, my friends! for respite none
Will he to his victorious hands afford,
80 But, arm'd with bow and quiver, will dispatch
Shafts from the door till he have slain us all.
Therefore to arms-draw each his sword-oppose
The tables to his shafts, and all at once
Rush on him; that, dislodging him at least
From portal and from threshold, we may give
The city on all sides a loud alarm,
So shall this archer soon have shot his last.
Thus saying, he drew his brazen faulchion keen
Of double edge, and with a dreadful cry
90 Sprang on him; but Ulysses with a shaft
In that same moment through his bosom driv'n
Transfix'd his liver, and down dropp'd his sword.
He, staggering around his table, fell
Convolv'd in agonies, and overturn'd
Both food and wine; his forehead smote the floor;
Woe fill'd his heart, and spurning with his heels
His vacant seat, he shook it till he died.
Then, with his faulchion drawn, Amphinomus
Advanced to drive Ulysses from the door,
100 And fierce was his assault; but, from behind,
Telemachus between his shoulders fix'd
A brazen lance, and urged it through his breast.
Full on his front, with hideous sound, he fell.
Leaving the weapon planted in his spine
Back flew Telemachus, lest, had he stood
Drawing it forth, some enemy, perchance,
Should either pierce him with a sudden thrust

Oblique, or hew him with a downright edge.
Swift, therefore, to his father's side he ran,
110 Whom reaching, in wing'd accents thus he said.
My father! I will now bring thee a shield,
An helmet, and two spears; I will enclose
Myself in armour also, and will give
Both to the herdsmen and Eumæus arms
Expedient now, and needful for us all.
To whom Ulysses, ever-wise, replied.
Run; fetch them, while I yet have arrows left,
Lest, single, I be justled from the door.
He said, and, at his word, forth went the Prince,
120 Seeking the chamber where he had secured
The armour. Thence he took four shields, eight spears,
With four hair-crested helmets, charged with which
He hasted to his father's side again,
And, arming first himself, furnish'd with arms
His two attendants. Then, all clad alike
In splendid brass, beside the dauntless Chief
Ulysses, his auxiliars firm they stood.
He, while a single arrow unemploy'd
Lay at his foot, right-aiming, ever pierced
130 Some suitor through, and heaps on heaps they fell.
But when his arrows fail'd the royal Chief,
His bow reclining at the portal's side
Against the palace-wall, he slung, himself,
A four-fold buckler on his arm, he fix'd
A casque whose crest wav'd awful o'er his brows
On his illustrious head, and fill'd his gripe
With two stout spears, well-headed both, with brass.

There was a certain postern in the wall[103]
At the gate-side, the customary pass
140 Into a narrow street, but barr'd secure.
Ulysses bade his faithful swine-herd watch
That egress, station'd near it, for it own'd
One sole approach; then Agelaüs loud
Exhorting all the suitors, thus exclaim'd.
Oh friends, will none, ascending to the door
Of yonder postern, summon to our aid
The populace, and spread a wide alarm?
So shall this archer soon have shot his last.
To whom the keeper of the goats replied
150 Melanthius. Agelaüs! Prince renown'd!

That may not be. The postern and the gate[104]
Neighbour too near each other, and to force
The narrow egress were a vain attempt;
One valiant man might thence repulse us all.
But come-myself will furnish you with arms
Fetch'd from above; for there, as I suppose,
(And not elsewhere) Ulysses and his son
Have hidden them, and there they shall be found.
So spake Melanthius, and, ascending, sought
160 Ulysses' chambers through the winding stairs
And gall'ries of the house. Twelve bucklers thence
He took, as many spears, and helmets bright
As many, shagg'd with hair, then swift return'd
And gave them to his friends. Trembled the heart

Of brave Ulysses, and his knees, at sight
Of his opposers putting armour on,
And shaking each his spear; arduous indeed
Now seem'd his task, and in wing'd accents brief
Thus to his son Telemachus he spake.
170 Either some woman of our train contrives
Hard battle for us, furnishing with arms
The suitors, or Melanthius arms them all.
Him answer'd then Telemachus discrete.
Father, this fault was mine, and be it charged
On none beside; I left the chamber-door
Unbarr'd, which, more attentive than myself,
Their spy perceived. But haste, Eumæus, shut
The chamber-door, observing well, the while,
If any women of our train have done
180 This deed, or whether, as I more suspect,
Melanthius, Dolius' son, have giv'n them arms.
Thus mutual they conferr'd; meantime, again
Melanthius to the chamber flew in quest
Of other arms. Eumæus, as he went,
Mark'd him, and to Ulysses' thus he spake.
Laertes' noble son, for wiles renown'd!
Behold, the traytor, whom ourselves supposed,
Seeks yet again the chamber! Tell me plain,
Shall I, should I superior prove in force,
190 Slay him, or shall I drag him thence to thee,
That he may suffer at thy hands the doom
Due to his treasons perpetrated oft
Against thee, here, even in thy own house?
Then answer thus Ulysses shrewd return'd.
I, with Telemachus, will here immew
The lordly suitors close, rage as they may.
Ye two, the while, bind fast Melanthius' hands
And feet behind his back, then cast him bound
Into the chamber, and (the door secured)
200 Pass underneath his arms a double chain,
And by a pillar's top weigh him aloft
Till he approach the rafters, there to endure,
Living long time, the mis'ries he hath earned.
He spake; they prompt obey'd; together both
They sought the chamber, whom the wretch within
Heard not, exploring ev'ry nook for arms.
They watching stood the door, from which, at length,
Forth came Melanthius, bearing in one hand
A casque, and in the other a broad shield
210 Time-worn and chapp'd with drought, which in his youth
Warlike Laertes had been wont to bear.
Long time neglected it had lain, till age
Had loosed the sutures of its bands. At once
Both, springing on him, seized and drew him in
Forcibly by his locks, then cast him down
Prone on the pavement, trembling at his fate.
With painful stricture of the cord his hands
They bound and feet together at his back,
As their illustrious master had enjoined,
220 Then weigh'd him with a double chain aloft
By a tall pillar to the palace-roof,

---

[103] If the ancients found it difficult to ascertain clearly the situation of this +ortothyrê+, well may we. The Translator has given it the position which to him appeared most probable.-There seem to have been two of these posterns, one leading to a part from which the town might be alarmed, the other to the chamber to which Telemachus went for armour. There was one, perhaps, on each side of the portal, and they appear to have been at some height above the floor.

[104] At which Ulysses stood.

And thus, deriding him, Eumæus spake.
Now, good Melanthius, on that fleecy bed
Reclined, as well befits thee, thou wilt watch
All night, nor when the golden dawn forsakes
The ocean stream, will she escape thine eye,
But thou wilt duly to the palace drive
The fattest goats, a banquet for thy friends.
So saying, he left him in his dreadful sling.
230 Then, arming both, and barring fast the door,
They sought brave Laertiades again.
And now, courageous at the portal stood
Those four, by numbers in the interior house
Opposed of adversaries fierce in arms,
When Pallas, in the form and with the voice
Approach'd of Mentor, whom Laertes' son
Beheld, and joyful at the sight, exclaim'd.
Help, Mentor! help—now recollect a friend
And benefactor, born when thou wast born.
240 So he, not unsuspicious that he saw
Pallas, the heroine of heav'n. Meantime
The suitors fill'd with menaces the dome,
And Agelaüs, first, Damastor's son,
In accents harsh rebuked the Goddess thus.
Beware, oh Mentor! that he lure thee not
To oppose the suitors and to aid himself,
For thus will we. Ulysses and his son
Both slain, in vengeance of thy purpos'd deeds
Against us, we will slay *thee* next, and thou
250 With thy own head shalt satisfy the wrong.
Your force thus quell'd in battle, all thy wealth
Whether in house or field, mingled with his,
We will confiscate, neither will we leave
Or son of thine, or daughter in thy house
Alive, nor shall thy virtuous consort more
Within the walls of Ithaca be seen.
He ended, and his words with wrath inflamed
Minerva's heart the more; incensed, she turn'd
Towards Ulysses, whom she thus reproved.
260 Thou neither own'st the courage nor the force,
Ulysses, now, which nine whole years thou showd'st
At Ilium, waging battle obstinate
For high-born Helen, and in horrid fight
Destroying multitudes, till thy advice
At last lay'd Priam's bulwark'd city low.
Why, in possession of thy proper home
And substance, mourn'st thou want of pow'r t'oppose
The suitors? Stand beside me, mark my deeds,
And thou shalt own Mentor Alcimides
270 A valiant friend, and mindful of thy love.
She spake; nor made she victory as yet
Entire his own, proving the valour, first,
Both of the sire and of his glorious son,
But, springing in a swallow's form aloft,
Perch'd on a rafter of the splendid roof.
Then, Agelaüs animated loud
The suitors, whom Eurynomus also roused,
Amphimedon, and Demoptolemus,
And Polyctorides, Pisander named,
280 And Polybus the brave; for noblest far
Of all the suitor-chiefs who now survived
And fought for life were these. The bow had quell'd

And shafts, in quick succession sent, the rest.
Then Agelaüs, thus, harangued them all.
We soon shall tame, O friends, this warrior's might,
Whom Mentor, after all his airy vaunts
Hath left, and at the portal now remain
Themselves alone. Dismiss not therefore, all,
Your spears together, but with six alone
290 Assail them first; Jove willing, we shall pierce
Ulysses, and subduing him, shall slay
With ease the rest; their force is safely scorn'd.
He ceas'd; and, as he bade, six hurl'd the spear
Together; but Minerva gave them all
A devious flight; one struck a column, one
The planks of the broad portal, and a third[105]
Flung right his ashen beam pond'rous with brass
Against the wall. Then (ev'ry suitor's spear
Eluded) thus Ulysses gave the word—
300 Now friends! I counsel you that ye dismiss
Your spears at *them*, who, not content with past
Enormities, thirst also for our blood.
He said, and with unerring aim, all threw
Their glitt'ring spears. Ulysses on the ground
Stretch'd Demoptolemus; Euryades
Fell by Telemachus; the swine-herd slew
Elatus; and the keeper of the beeves
Pisander; in one moment all alike
Lay grinding with their teeth the dusty floor.
310 Back flew the suitors to the farthest wall,
On whom those valiant four advancing, each
Recover'd, quick, his weapon from the dead.
Then hurl'd the desp'rate suitors yet again
Their glitt'ring spears, but Pallas gave to each
A frustrate course; one struck a column, one
The planks of the broad portal, and a third
Flung full his ashen beam against the wall.
Yet pierced Amphimedon the Prince's wrist,
But slightly, a skin-wound, and o'er his shield
32 °Ctesippus reach'd the shoulder of the good
Eumæus, but his glancing weapon swift
O'erflew the mark, and fell. And now the four,
Ulysses, dauntless Hero, and his friends
All hurl'd their spears together in return,
Himself Ulysses, city-waster Chief,
Wounded Eurydamas; Ulysses' son
Amphimedon; the swine-herd Polybus;
And in his breast the keeper of the beeves
Ctesippus, glorying over whom, he cried.
330 Oh son of Polytherses! whose delight
Hath been to taunt and jeer, never again
Boast foolishly, but to the Gods commit
Thy tongue, since they are mightier far than thou.
Take this—a compensation for thy pledge
Of hospitality, the huge ox-hoof,
Which while he roam'd the palace, begging alms,
Ulysses at thy bounteous hand received.
So gloried he; then, grasping still his spear,
Ulysses pierced Damastor's son, and, next,
340 Telemachus, enforcing his long beam
Sheer through his bowels and his back, transpierced
Leiocritus, he prostrate smote the floor.
Then, Pallas from the lofty roof held forth

---

105 The deviation of three only is described, which must be understood, therefore, as instances of the ill success of all.

Her host-confounding Ægis o'er their heads,
With'ring their souls with fear. They through the hall
Fled, scatter'd as an herd, which rapid-wing'd
The gad-fly dissipates, infester fell
Of beeves, when vernal suns shine hot and long.

But, as when bow-beak'd vultures crooked-claw'd[106]
350 Stoop from the mountains on the smaller fowl;
Terrified at the toils that spread the plain
The flocks take wing, they, darting from above,
Strike, seize, and slay, resistance or escape
Is none, the fowler's heart leaps with delight,
So they, pursuing through the spacious hall
The suitors, smote them on all sides, their heads
Sounded beneath the sword, with hideous groans
The palace rang, and the floor foamed with blood.
Then flew Leiodes to Ulysses' knees,
360 Which clasping, in wing'd accents thus he cried.
I clasp thy knees, Ulysses! oh respect
My suit, and spare me! Never have I word
Injurious spoken, or injurious deed
Attempted 'gainst the women of thy house,
But others, so transgressing, oft forbad.
Yet they abstain'd not, and a dreadful fate
Due to their wickedness have, therefore, found.
But I, their soothsayer alone, must fall,
Though unoffending; such is the return
370 By mortals made for benefits received!
To whom Ulysses, louring dark, replied.
Is that thy boast? Hast thou indeed for these
The seer's high office fill'd? Then, doubtless, oft
Thy pray'r hath been that distant far might prove
The day delectable of my return,
And that my consort might thy own become
To bear thee children; wherefore thee I doom
To a dire death which thou shalt not avoid.
So saying, he caught the faulchion from the floor
380 Which Agelaüs had let fall, and smote
Leiodes, while he kneel'd, athwart his neck
So suddenly, that ere his tongue had ceased
To plead for life, his head was in the dust.
But Phemius, son of Terpius, bard divine,
Who, through compulsion, with his song regaled
The suitors, a like dreadful death escaped.
Fast by the postern, harp in hand, he stood,
Doubtful if, issuing, he should take his seat
Beside the altar of Hercæan Jove,[107]
390 Where oft Ulysses offer'd, and his sire,
Fat thighs of beeves, or whether he should haste,
An earnest suppliant, to embrace his knees,
That course, at length, most pleased him; then, between
The beaker and an argent-studded throne
He grounded his sweet lyre, and seizing fast
The Hero's knees, him, suppliant, thus address'd.
I clasp thy knees, Ulysses! oh respect
My suit, and spare me. Thou shalt not escape
Regret thyself hereafter, if thou slay
400 Me, charmer of the woes of Gods and men.

Self-taught am I, and treasure in my mind
Themes of all argument from heav'n inspired,
And I can sing to thee as to a God.
Ah, then, behead me not. Put ev'n the wish
Far from thee! for thy own beloved son
Can witness, that not drawn by choice, or driv'n
By stress of want, resorting to thine house
I have regaled these revellers so oft,
But under force of mightier far than I.
410 So he; whose words soon as the sacred might
Heard of Telemachus, approaching quick
His father, thus, humane, he interposed.
Hold, harm not with the vengeful faulchion's edge
This blameless man; and we will also spare
Medon the herald, who hath ever been
A watchful guardian of my boyish years,
Unless Philoetius have already slain him,
Or else Eumæus, or thyself, perchance,
Unconscious, in the tumult of our foes.
420 He spake, whom Medon hearing (for he lay
Beneath a throne, and in a new-stript hide
Enfolded, trembling with the dread of death)
Sprang from his hiding-place, and casting off
The skin, flew to Telemachus, embraced
His knees, and in wing'd accents thus exclaim'd.
Prince! I am here-oh, pity me! repress
Thine own, and pacify thy father's wrath,
That he destroy not me, through fierce revenge
Of their iniquities who have consumed
430 His wealth, and, in their folly scorn'd his son.
To whom Ulysses, ever-wise, replied,
Smiling complacent. Fear not; my own son
Hath pleaded for thee. Therefore (taught thyself
That truth) teach others the superior worth
Of benefits with injuries compared.
But go ye forth, thou and the sacred bard,
That ye may sit distant in yonder court
From all this carnage, while I give command,
Myself, concerning it, to those within.
440 He ceas'd; they going forth, took each his seat
Beside Jove's altar, but with careful looks
Suspicious, dreading without cease the sword.
Meantime Ulysses search'd his hall, in quest
Of living foes, if any still survived
Unpunish'd; but he found them all alike
Welt'ring in dust and blood; num'rous they lay
Like fishes when they strew the sinuous shore
Of Ocean, from the grey gulph drawn aground
In nets of many a mesh; they on the sands
450 Lie spread, athirst for the salt wave, till hot
The gazing sun dries all their life away;
So lay the suitors heap'd, and thus at length
The prudent Chief gave order to his son.
Telemachus! bid Euryclea come
Quickly, the nurse, to whom I would impart
The purpose which now occupies me most.
He said; obedient to his sire, the Prince

---

[106] In this simile we seem to have a curious account of the ancient manner of fowling. The nets (for +nephea+ is used in that sense by Aristophanes) were spread on a plain; on an adjoining rising ground were stationed they who had charge of the vultures (such Homer calls them) which were trained to the sport. The alarm being given to the birds below, the vultures were loosed, when if any of them escaped their talons, the nets were ready to enclose them. *See* Eustathius Dacier. Clarke.

[107] So called because he was worshipped within the +Erkos+ or wall that surrounded the court.

Smote on the door, and summon'd loud the nurse.
Arise thou ancient governess of all
460 Our female menials, and come forth; attend
My father; he hath somewhat for thine ear.
So he; nor flew his words useless away,
For, throwing wide the portal, forth she came,
And, by Telemachus conducted, found
Ere long Ulysses amid all the slain,
With blood defiled and dust; dread he appear'd
As from the pastur'd ox newly-devoured
The lion stalking back; his ample chest
With gory drops and his broad cheeks are hung,
470 Tremendous spectacle! such seem'd the Chief,
Blood-stain'd all over. She, the carnage spread
On all sides seeing, and the pools of blood,
Felt impulse forcible to publish loud
That wond'rous triumph; but her Lord repress'd
The shout of rapture ere it burst abroad,
And in wing'd accents thus his will enforced.
Silent exult, O ancient matron dear!
Shout not, be still. Unholy is the voice
Of loud thanksgiving over slaughter'd men.
480 Their own atrocious deeds and the Gods' will
Have slain all these; for whether noble guest
Arrived or base, they scoff'd at all alike,
And for their wickedness have, therefore, died.
But say; of my domestic women, who
Have scorn'd me, and whom find'st thou innocent?
To whom good Euryclea thus replied.
My son! I will declare the truth; thou keep'st
Female domestics fifty in thy house,
Whom we have made intelligent to comb
490 The fleece, and to perform whatever task.
Of these, twice six have overpass'd the bounds
Of modesty, respecting neither me,
Nor yet the Queen; and thy own son, adult
So lately, no permission had from her
To regulate the women of her train.
But I am gone, I fly with what hath pass'd
To the Queen's ear, who nought suspects, so sound
She sleeps, by some divinity composed.
Then answer, thus, Ulysses wise returned.
500 Hush, and disturb her not. Go. Summon first
Those wantons, who have long deserved to die.
He ceas'd; then issued forth the ancient dame
To summon those bad women, and, meantime,
Calling his son, Philoetius, and Eumæus,
Ulysses in wing'd accents thus began.
Bestir ye, and remove the dead; command
Those women also to your help; then cleanse
With bibulous sponges and with water all
The seats and tables; when ye shall have thus
510 Set all in order, lead those women forth,
And in the centre of the spacious court,
Between the scull'ry and the outer-wall
Smite them with your broad faulchions till they lose
In death the mem'ry of their secret loves
Indulged with wretches lawless as themselves.
He ended, and the damsels came at once
All forth, lamenting, and with tepid tears
Show'ring the ground; with mutual labour, first,
Bearing the bodies forth into the court,

520 They lodged them in the portico; meantime
Ulysses, stern, enjoin'd them haste, and, urged
By sad necessity, they bore all out.
With sponges and with water, next, they cleansed
The thrones and tables, while Telemachus
Beesom'd the floor, Eumæus in that work
Aiding him and the keeper of the beeves,
And those twelve damsels bearing forth the soil.
Thus, order giv'n to all within, they, next,
Led forth the women, whom they shut between
530 The scull'ry and the outer-wall in close
Durance, from which no pris'ner could escape,
And thus Telemachus discrete began.
An honourable death is not for these
By my advice, who have so often heap'd
Reproach on mine and on my mother's head,
And held lewd commerce with the suitor-train.
He said, and noosing a strong galley-rope
To an huge column, led the cord around
The spacious dome, suspended so aloft
540 That none with quiv'ring feet might reach the floor.
As when a flight of doves ent'ring the copse,
Or broad-wing'd thrushes, strike against the net
Within, ill rest, entangled, there they find,
So they, suspended by the neck, expired
All in one line together. Death abhorr'd!
With restless feet awhile they beat the air,
Then ceas'd. And now through vestibule and hall
They led Melanthius forth. With ruthless steel
They pared away his ears and nose, pluck'd forth
550 His parts of shame, destin'd to feed the dogs,
And, still indignant, lopp'd his hands and feet.
Then, laving each his feet and hands, they sought
Again Ulysses; all their work was done,
And thus the Chief to Euryclea spake.
Bring blast-averting sulphur, nurse, bring fire!
That I may fumigate my walls; then bid
Penelope with her attendants down,
And summon all the women of her train.
But Euryclea, thus, his nurse, replied.
560 My son! thou hast well said; yet will I first
Serve thee with vest and mantle. Stand not here
In thy own palace cloath'd with tatters foul
And beggarly-she will abhor the sight.
Then answer thus Ulysses wise return'd.
Not so. Bring fire for fumigation first.
He said; nor Euryclea his lov'd nurse
Longer delay'd, but sulphur brought and fire,
When he with purifying steams, himself,
Visited ev'ry part, the banquet-room,
570 The vestibule, the court. Ranging meantime
His house magnificent, the matron call'd
The women to attend their Lord in haste,
And they attended, bearing each a torch.
Then gather'd they around him all, sincere
Welcoming his return; with close embrace
Enfolding him, each kiss'd his brows, and each
His shoulders, and his hands lock'd fast in hers.
He, irresistible the impulse felt
To sigh and weep, well recognizing all.
580

Book XXIII

Ulysses with some difficulty, convinces Penelope of his identity, who at length, overcome by force of evidence, receives him to her arms with transport. He entertains her with a recital of his adventures, and in his narration the principal events of the poem are recapitulated. In the morning, Ulysses, Telemachus, the herdsman and the swine-herd depart into the country.

And now, with exultation loud the nurse
Again ascended, eager to apprize
The Queen of her Ulysses' safe return;
Joy braced her knees, with nimbleness of youth
She stepp'd, and at her ear, her thus bespake.
Arise, Penelope! dear daughter, see
With thy own eyes thy daily wish fulfill'd.
Ulysses is arrived; hath reach'd at last
His native home, and all those suitors proud
10 Hath slaughter'd, who his family distress'd,
His substance wasted, and controul'd his son.
To whom Penelope discrete replied.
Dear nurse! the Gods have surely ta'en away
Thy judgment; they transform the wise to fools,
And fools conduct to wisdom, and have marr'd
Thy intellect, who wast discrete before.
Why wilt thou mock me, wretched as I am,
With tales extravagant? and why disturb
Those slumbers sweet that seal'd so fast mine eyes?
For such sweet slumbers have I never known
20 Since my Ulysses on his voyage sail'd
To that bad city never to be named.
Down instant to thy place again-begone-
For had another of my maidens dared
Disturb my sleep with tidings wild as these,
I had dismiss'd her down into the house
More roughly; but thine age excuses *thee* .
To whom the venerable matron thus.
I mock thee not, my child; no-he is come-
Himself, Ulysses, even as I say,
30 That stranger, object of the scorn of all.
Telemachus well knew his sire arrived,
But prudently conceal'd the tidings, so
To insure the more the suitors' punishment.
So Euryclea she transported heard,
And springing from the bed, wrapp'd in her arms
The ancient woman shedding tears of joy,
And in wing'd accents ardent thus replied.
Ah then, dear nurse inform me! tell me true!
Hath he indeed arriv'd as thou declar'st?
40 How dared he to assail alone that band
Of shameless ones, for ever swarming here?
Then Euryclea, thus, matron belov'd.
I nothing saw or knew; but only heard
Groans of the wounded; in th' interior house
We trembling sat, and ev'ry door was fast.
Thus all remain'd till by his father sent,
Thy own son call'd me forth. Going, I found
Ulysses compass'd by the slaughter'd dead.
They cover'd wide the pavement, heaps on heaps.
50 It would have cheer'd thy heart to have beheld
Thy husband lion-like with crimson stains

Of slaughter and of dust all dappled o'er;
Heap'd in the portal, at this moment, lie
Their bodies, and he fumigates, meantime,
The house with sulphur and with flames of fire,
And hath, himself, sent me to bid thee down.
Follow me, then, that ye may give your hearts
To gladness, both, for ye have much endured;
But the event, so long your soul's desire,
60 Is come; himself hath to his household Gods
Alive return'd, thee and his son he finds
Unharm'd and at your home, nor hath he left
Unpunish'd one of all his enemies.
Her answer'd, then, Penelope discrete.
Ah dearest nurse! indulge not to excess
This dang'rous triumph. Thou art well apprized
How welcome his appearance here would prove
To all, but chief, to me, and to his son,
Fruit of our love. But these things are not so;
70 Some God, resentful of their evil deeds,
And of their biting contumely severe,
Hath slain those proud; for whether noble guest
Arrived or base, alike they scoff'd at all,
And for their wickedness have therefore died.
But my Ulysses distant far, I know,
From Greece hath perish'd, and returns no more.
To whom thus Euryclea, nurse belov'd.
What word my daughter had escaped thy lips,
Who thus affirm'st thy husband, now within
80 And at his own hearth-side, for ever lost?
Canst thou be thus incredulous? Hear again-
I give thee yet proof past dispute, his scar
Imprinted by a wild-boar's iv'ry tusk.
Laving him I remark'd it, and desired,
Myself, to tell thee, but he, ever-wise,
Compressing with both hands my lips, forbad.
Come, follow me. My life shall be the pledge.
If I deceive thee, kill me as thou wilt.
To whom Penelope, discrete, replied.
90 Ah, dearest nurse, sagacious as thou art,
Thou little know'st to scan the counsels wise
Of the eternal Gods. But let us seek
My son, however, that I may behold
The suitors dead, and him by whom they died.
So saying, she left her chamber, musing much
In her descent, whether to interrogate
Her Lord apart, or whether to imprint,
At once, his hands with kisses and his brows.
O'erpassing light the portal-step of stone
100 She enter'd. He sat opposite, illumed
By the hearth's sprightly blaze, and close before
A pillar of the dome, waiting with eyes
Downcast, till viewing him, his noble spouse

Should speak to him; but she sat silent long,
Her faculties in mute amazement held.
By turns she riveted her eyes on his,
And, seeing him so foul attired, by turns
She recognized him not; then spake her son
Telemachus, and her silence thus reprov'd.
110 My mother! ah my hapless and my most
Obdurate mother! wherefore thus aloof
Shunn'st thou my father, neither at his side
Sitting affectionate, nor utt'ring word?
Another wife lives not who could endure
Such distance from her husband new-return'd
To his own country in the twentieth year,
After much hardship; but thy heart is still
As ever, less impressible than stone,
To whom Penelope, discrete, replied.
120 I am all wonder, O my son; my soul
Is stunn'd within me; pow'r to speak to him
Or to interrogate him have I none,
Or ev'n to look on him; but if indeed
He be Ulysses, and have reach'd his home,
I shall believe it soon, by proof convinced
Of signs known only to himself and me.
She said; then smiled the Hero toil-inured,
And in wing'd accents thus spake to his son.
Leave thou, Telemachus, thy mother here
130 To sift and prove me; she will know me soon
More certainly; she sees me ill-attired
And squalid now; therefore she shews me scorn,
And no belief hath yet that I am he.
But we have need, thou and myself, of deep
Deliberation. If a man have slain
One only citizen, who leaves behind
Few interested to avenge his death,
Yet, flying, he forsakes both friends and home;
But we have slain the noblest Princes far
140 Of Ithaca, on whom our city most
Depended; therefore, I advise thee, think!
Him, prudent, then answer'd Telemachus.
Be that thy care, my father! for report
Proclaims *thee* shrewdest of mankind, with whom
In ingenuity may none compare.
Lead thou; to follow thee shall be our part
With prompt alacrity; nor shall, I judge,
Courage be wanting to our utmost force.
Thus then replied Ulysses, ever-wise.
150 To me the safest counsel and the best
Seems this. First wash yourselves, and put ye on
Your tunics; bid ye, next, the maidens take
Their best attire, and let the bard divine
Harping melodious play a sportive dance,
That, whether passenger or neighbour near,
All may imagine nuptials held within.
So shall not loud report that we have slain
All those, alarm the city, till we gain
Our woods and fields, where, once arriv'd, such plans
160 We will devise, as Jove shall deign to inspire.
He spake, and all, obedient, in the bath

First laved themselves, then put their tunics on;
The damsels also dress'd, and the sweet bard,
Harping melodious, kindled strong desire
In all, of jocund song and graceful dance.
The palace under all its vaulted roof
Remurmur'd to the feet of sportive youths
And cinctured maidens, while no few abroad,
Hearing such revelry within, remark'd-
170 The Queen with many wooers, weds at last.
Ah fickle and unworthy fair! too frail
Always to keep inviolate the house
Of her first Lord, and wait for his return.
So spake the people; but they little knew
What had befall'n. Eurynome, meantime,
With bath and unction serv'd the illustrious Chief
Ulysses, and he saw himself attired
Royally once again in his own house.
Then, Pallas over all his features shed
180 Superior beauty, dignified his form
With added amplitude, and pour'd his curls
Like hyacinthine flow'rs down from his brows.
As when some artist by Minerva made
And Vulcan, wise to execute all tasks
Ingenious, borders silver with a wreath
Of gold, accomplishing a graceful work,
Such grace the Goddess o'er his ample chest
Copious diffused, and o'er his manly brows.
He, godlike, stepping from the bath, resumed
190 His former seat magnificent, and sat
Opposite to the Queen, to whom he said.
Penelope! the Gods to thee have giv'n
Of all thy sex, the most obdurate heart.
Another wife lives not who could endure
Such distance from her husband new-return'd
To his own country in the twentieth year,
After such hardship. But prepare me, nurse,
A bed, for solitary I must sleep,
Since she is iron, and feels not for me.
200 Him answer'd then prudent Penelope.
I neither magnify thee, sir! nor yet
Depreciate thee, nor is my wonder such
As hurries me at once into thy arms,
Though my remembrance perfectly retains,
Such as he was, Ulysses, when he sail'd
On board his bark from Ithaca-Go, nurse,
Prepare his bed, but not within the walls
Of his own chamber built with his own hands.
Spread it without, and spread it well with warm
210 Mantles, with fleeces, and with richest rugs.
So spake she, proving him,[108] and not untouch'd
With anger at that word, thus he replied.
Penelope, that order grates my ear.
Who hath displaced my bed? The task were hard
E'en to an artist; other than a God
None might with ease remove it; as for man,
It might defy the stoutest in his prime
Of youth, to heave it to a different spot.
For in that bed elaborate, a sign,

---

[108] The proof consisted in this-that the bed being attached to the stump of an olive tree still rooted, was immovable, and Ulysses having made it himself, no person present, he must needs be apprized of the impossibility of her orders, if he were indeed Ulysses; accordingly, this demonstration of his identity satisfies all her scruples.

220 A special sign consists; I was myself
The artificer; I fashion'd it alone.
Within the court a leafy olive grew
Lofty, luxuriant, pillar-like in girth.
Around this tree I built, with massy stones
Cemented close, my chamber, roof'd it o'er,
And hung the glutinated portals on.
I lopp'd the ample foliage and the boughs,
And sev'ring near the root its solid bole,
Smooth'd all the rugged stump with skilful hand,
230 And wrought it to a pedestal well squared
And modell'd by the line. I wimbled, next,
The frame throughout, and from the olive-stump
Beginning, fashion'd the whole bed above
Till all was finish'd, plated o'er with gold,
With silver, and with ivory, and beneath
Close interlaced with purple cordage strong.
Such sign I give thee. But if still it stand
Unmoved, or if some other, sev'ring sheer
The olive from its bottom, have displaced
240 My bed-that matter is best known to thee.
He ceas'd; she, conscious of the sign so plain
Giv'n by Ulysses, heard with flutt'ring heart
And fault'ring knees that proof. Weeping she ran
Direct toward him, threw her arms around
The Hero, kiss'd his forehead, and replied.
Ah my Ulysses! pardon me-frown not-
Thou, who at other times hast ever shewn
Superior wisdom! all our griefs have flow'd
From the Gods' will; they envied us the bliss
250 Of undivided union sweet enjoy'd
Through life, from early youth to latest age.
No. Be not angry now; pardon the fault
That I embraced thee not as soon as seen,
For horror hath not ceased to overwhelm
My soul, lest some false alien should, perchance,
Beguile me, for our house draws num'rous such.
Jove's daughter, Argive Helen, ne'er had given
Free entertainment to a stranger's love,
Had she foreknown that the heroic sons
260 Of Greece would bring her to her home again.
But heav'n incited her to that offence,
Who never, else, had even in her thought
Harbour'd the foul enormity, from which
Originated even our distress.
But now, since evident thou hast described
Our bed, which never mortal yet beheld,
Ourselves except and Actoris my own
Attendant, giv'n me when I left my home
By good Icarius, and who kept the door,
270 Though hard to be convinced, at last I yield.
So saying, she awaken'd in his soul
Pity and grief; and folding in his arms
His blameless consort beautiful, he wept.
Welcome as land appears to those who swim,
Whose gallant bark Neptune with rolling waves
And stormy winds hath sunk in the wide sea,
A mariner or two, perchance, escape
The foamy flood, and, swimming, reach the land,
Weary indeed, and with incrusted brine

280 All rough, but oh, how glad to climb the coast!
So welcome in her eyes Ulysses seem'd,
Around whose neck winding her snowy arms,
She clung as she would loose him never more.
Thus had they wept till rosy-finger'd morn
Had found them weeping, but Minerva check'd
Night's almost finish'd course, and held, meantime,
The golden dawn close pris'ner in the Deep,
Forbidding her to lead her coursers forth,
Lampus and Phaëton that furnish light
290 To all the earth, and join them to the yoke.
Then thus, Ulysses to Penelope.
My love; we have not yet attain'd the close
Of all our sufferings, but unmeasured toil
Arduous remains, which I must still atchieve.
For so the spirit of the Theban seer
Inform'd me, on that day, when to enquire
Of mine and of my people's safe return
I journey'd down to Pluto's drear abode.
But let us hence to bed, there to enjoy
300 Tranquil repose. My love, make no delay.
Him answer'd then prudent Penelope.
Thou shalt to bed at whatsoever time
Thy soul desires, since the immortal Gods
Give thee to me and to thy home again.
But, thou hast spoken from the seer of Thebes
Of arduous toils yet unperform'd; declare
What toils? Thou wilt disclose them, as I judge,
Hereafter, and why not disclose them now?
To whom Ulysses, ever-wise, replied.
310 Ah conversant with woe! why would'st thou learn
That tale? but I will tell it thee at large.
Thou wilt not hear with joy, nor shall myself
With joy rehearse it; for he bade me seek
City after city, bearing, as I go,
A shapely oar, till I shall find, at length,
A people who the sea know not, nor eat
Food salted; they trim galley crimson-prow'd
Have ne'er beheld, nor yet smooth-shaven oar
With which the vessel wing'd scuds o'er the waves.
320 He gave me also this authentic sign,
Which I will tell thee. In what place soe'er
I chance to meet a trav'ler who shall name

The oar on my broad shoulder borne, a van;[109]
He bade me, planting it on the same spot,
Worship the King of Ocean with a bull,
A ram, and a lascivious boar, then seek
My home again, and sacrifice at home
An hecatomb to the immortal Gods
Inhabitants of the expanse above.
330 So shall I die, at length, the gentlest death
Remote from Ocean; it shall find me late,
In soft serenity of age, the Chief
Of a blest people.-Thus he prophesied.
Him answer'd then Penelope discrete.
If heav'n appoint thee in old age a lot
More tranquil, hope thence springs of thy escape
Some future day from all thy threaten'd woes.
Such was their mutual conf'rence sweet; meantime
Eurynome and Euryclea dress'd

---

[109] See the note on the same passage, Book XI.

340 Their bed by light of the clear torch, and when
Dispatchful they had spread it broad and deep,
The ancient nurse to her own bed retired.
Then came Eurynome, to whom in trust
The chambers appertain'd, and with a torch
Conducted them to rest; she introduced
The happy pair, and went; transported they
To rites connubial intermitted long,

And now recover'd, gave themselves again.[110]
Meantime, the Prince, the herdsman, and the good
350 Eumæus, giving rest each to his feet,
Ceased from the dance; they made the women cease
Also, and to their sev'ral chambers all
Within the twilight edifice repair'd.
At length, with conjugal endearment both
Satiate, Ulysses tasted and his spouse
The sweets of mutual converse. She rehearsed,
Noblest of women, all her num'rous woes
Beneath that roof sustain'd, while she beheld
The profligacy of the suitor-throng,
360 Who in their wooing had consumed his herds
And fatted flocks, and drawn his vessels dry;
While brave Ulysses, in his turn, to her
Related his successes and escapes,
And his afflictions also; he told her all;
She listen'd charm'd, nor slumber on his eyes
Fell once, or ere he had rehearsed the whole.
Beginning, he discoursed, how, at the first
He conquer'd in Ciconia, and thence reach'd
The fruitful shores of the Lotophagi;
370 The Cyclops' deeds he told her next, and how
He well avenged on him his slaughter'd friends
Whom, pitiless, the monster had devour'd.
How to the isle of Æolus he came,
Who welcom'd him and safe dismiss'd him thence,
Although not destin'd to regain so soon
His native land; for o'er the fishy deep
Loud tempests snatch'd him sighing back again.
How, also at Telepylus he arrived,
Town of the Læstrygonians, who destroyed
380 His ships with all their mariners, his own
Except, who in his sable bark escaped.
Of guileful Circe too he spake, deep-skill'd
In various artifice, and how he reach'd
With sails and oars the squalid realms of death,
Desirous to consult the prophet there
Theban Tiresias, and how there he view'd
All his companions, and the mother bland
Who bare him, nourisher of his infant years.
How, next he heard the Sirens in one strain
390 All chiming sweet, and how he reach'd the rocks
Erratic, Scylla and Charybdis dire,
Which none secure from injury may pass.
Then, how the partners of his voyage slew

The Sun's own beeves, and how the Thund'rer Jove
Hurl'd down his smoky bolts into his bark,
Depriving him at once of all his crew,
Whose dreadful fate he yet, himself, escaped.
How to Ogygia's isle he came, where dwelt
The nymph Calypso, who, enamour'd, wish'd
400 To espouse him, and within her spacious grot
Detain'd, and fed, and promis'd him a life
Exempt for ever from the sap of age,
But him moved not. How, also, he arrived
After much toil, on the Phæacian coast,
Where ev'ry heart revered him as a God,
And whence, enriching him with brass and gold,
And costly raiment first, they sent him home.
At this last word, oblivious slumber sweet
Fell on him, dissipating all his cares.
410 Meantime, Minerva, Goddess azure-eyed,
On other thoughts intent, soon as she deem'd
Ulysses with connubial joys sufficed,
And with sweet sleep, at once from Ocean rous'd
The golden-axled chariot of the morn
To illumine earth. Then from his fleecy couch
The Hero sprang, and thus his spouse enjoined.
Oh consort dear! already we have striv'n
Against our lot, till wearied with the toil,
My painful absence, thou with ceaseless tears
420 Deploring, and myself in deep distress
Withheld reluctant from my native shores
By Jove and by the other pow'rs of heav'n.
But since we have in this delightful bed
Met once again, watch thou and keep secure
All my domestic treasures, and ere long
I will replace my num'rous sheep destroy'd
By those imperious suitors, and the Greeks
Shall add yet others till my folds be fill'd.
But to the woodlands go I now-to see
430 My noble father, who for my sake mourns
Continual; as for thee, my love, although
I know thee wise, I give thee thus in charge.
The sun no sooner shall ascend, than fame
Shall wide divulge the deed that I have done,
Slaying the suitors under my own roof.
Thou, therefore, with thy maidens, sit retired
In thy own chamber at the palace-top,
Nor question ask, nor, curious, look abroad.
He said, and cov'ring with his radiant arms
440 His shoulders, called Telemachus; he roused
Eumæus and the herdsman too, and bade
All take their martial weapons in their hand.
Not disobedient they, as he enjoin'd,
Put armour on, and issued from the gates
Ulysses at their head. The earth was now
Enlighten'd, but Minerva them in haste
Led forth into the fields, unseen by all.

---

[110] Aristophanes the grammarian and Aristarchus chose that the Odyssey should end here; but the story is not properly concluded till the tumult occasioned by the slaughter of so many Princes being composed, Ulysses finds himself once more in peaceful possession of his country.

Book XXIV

Mercury conducts the souls of the suitors down to Ades. Ulysses discovers himself to Laertes, and quells, by the aid of Minerva, an insurrection of the people resenting the death of the suitors.

And now Cyllenian Hermes summon'd forth
The spirits of the suitors; waving wide
The golden wand of pow'r to seal all eyes
In slumber, and to ope them wide again,
He drove them gibb'ring down into the shades,[111]
As when the bats within some hallow'd cave
Flit squeaking all around, for if but one
Fall from the rock, the rest all follow him,
In such connexion mutual they adhere,
So, after bounteous Mercury, the ghosts,
10 Troop'd downward gibb'ring all the dreary way.
The Ocean's flood and the Leucadian rock,
The Sun's gate also and the land of Dreams
They pass'd, whence, next, into the meads they came
Of Asphodel, by shadowy forms possess'd,
Simulars of the dead. They found the souls
Of brave Pelides there, and of his friend
Patroclus, of Antilochus renown'd,
And of the mightier Ajax, for his form
And bulk (Achilles sole except) of all
20 The sons of the Achaians most admired.
These waited on Achilles. Then, appear'd
The mournful ghost of Agamemnon, son
Of Atreus, compass'd by the ghosts of all
Who shared his fate beneath Ægisthus' roof,
And him the ghost of Peleus' son bespake.
Atrides! of all Heroes we esteem'd
Thee dearest to the Gods, for that thy sway
Extended over such a glorious host
At Ilium, scene of sorrow to the Greeks.
30 But Fate, whose ruthless force none may escape
Of all who breathe, pursued thee from the first.
Thou should'st have perish'd full of honour, full
Of royalty, at Troy; so all the Greeks
Had rais'd thy tomb, and thou hadst then bequeath'd
Great glory to thy son; but Fate ordain'd
A death, oh how deplorable! for thee.
To whom Atrides' spirit thus replied.
Blest son of Peleus, semblance of the Gods,
At Ilium, far from Argos, fall'n! for whom
4 °Contending, many a Trojan, many a Chief
Of Greece died also, while in eddies whelm'd
Of dust thy vastness spread the plain,[112] nor thee
The chariot aught or steed could int'rest more!
All day we waged the battle, nor at last

Desisted, but for tempests sent from Jove.
At length we bore into the Greecian fleet
Thy body from the field; there, first, we cleansed
With tepid baths and oil'd thy shapely corse,
Then placed thee on thy bier, while many a Greek
50 Around thee wept, and shore his locks for thee.
Thy mother, also, hearing of thy death
With her immortal nymphs from the abyss
Arose and came; terrible was the sound
On the salt flood; a panic seized the Greeks,
And ev'ry warrior had return'd on board
That moment, had not Nestor, ancient Chief,
Illumed by long experience, interposed,
His counsels, ever wisest, wisest proved
Then also, and he thus address'd the host.
60 Sons of Achaia; fly not; stay, ye Greeks!
Thetis arrives with her immortal nymphs
From the abyss, to visit her dead son.
So he; and, by his admonition stay'd,
The Greeks fled not. Then, all around thee stood
The daughters of the Ancient of the Deep,
Mourning disconsolate; with heav'nly robes
They clothed thy corse, and all the Muses nine
Deplored thee in full choir with sweetest tones
Responsive, nor one Greecian hadst thou seen
70 Dry-eyed, such grief the Muses moved in all.
Full sev'nteen days we, day and night, deplored
Thy death, both Gods in heav'n and men below,
But, on the eighteenth day, we gave thy corse
Its burning, and fat sheep around thee slew
Num'rous, with many a pastur'd ox moon-horn'd.
We burn'd thee clothed in vesture of the Gods,
With honey and with oil feeding the flames
Abundant, while Achaia's Heroes arm'd,
Both horse and foot, encompassing thy pile,
8 °Clash'd on their shields, and deaf'ning was the din.
But when the fires of Vulcan had at length
Consumed thee, at the dawn we stored thy bones
In unguent and in undiluted wine;
For Thetis gave to us a golden vase
Twin-ear'd, which she profess'd to have received
From Bacchus, work divine of Vulcan's hand.
Within that vase, Achilles, treasured lie
Thine and the bones of thy departed friend
Patroclus, but a sep'rate urn we gave
90 To those of brave Antilochus, who most

---

[111] +Trizousai-tetriguiai+-the ghosts
Did squeak and gibber in the Roman streets.
SHAKSPEARE.

[112] — Behemoth, biggest born of earth,
Upheav'd his vastness.
MILTON.

Of all thy friends at Ilium shared thy love
And thy respect, thy friend Patroclus slain.
Around both urns we piled a noble tomb,
(We warriors of the sacred Argive host)
On a tall promontory shooting far
Into the spacious Hellespont, that all
Who live, and who shall yet be born, may view
Thy record, even from the distant waves.
Then, by permission from the Gods obtain'd,
100 To the Achaian Chiefs in circus met
Thetis appointed games. I have beheld
The burial rites of many an Hero bold,
When, on the death of some great Chief, the youths
Girding their loins anticipate the prize,
But sight of those with wonder fill'd me most,
So glorious past all others were the games
By silver-footed Thetis giv'n for thee,
For thou wast ever favour'd of the Gods.
Thus, hast thou not, Achilles! although dead,
110 Foregone thy glory, but thy fair report
Is universal among all mankind;
But, as for me, what recompense had I,
My warfare closed? for whom, at my return,
Jove framed such dire destruction by the hands
Of fell Ægisthus and my murth'ress wife.
Thus, mutual, they conferr'd; meantime approach'd,
Swift messenger of heav'n, the Argicide,
Conducting thither all the shades of those
Slain by Ulysses. At that sight amazed
120 Both moved toward them. Agamemnon's shade
Knew well Amphimedon, for he had been
Erewhile his father's guest in Ithaca,
And thus the spirit of Atreus' son began.
Amphimedon! by what disastrous chance,
Cooevals as ye seem, and of an air
Distinguish'd all, descend ye to the Deeps?
For not the chosen youths of a whole town
Should form a nobler band. Perish'd ye sunk
Amid vast billows and rude tempests raised
130 By Neptune's pow'r? or on dry land through force
Of hostile multitudes, while cutting off
Beeves from the herd, or driving flocks away?
Or fighting for your city and your wives?
Resolve me? I was once a guest of yours.
Remember'st not what time at your abode
With godlike Menelaus I arrived,
That we might win Ulysses with his fleet
To follow us to Troy? scarce we prevail'd
At last to gain the city-waster Chief,
140 And, after all, consumed a whole month more
The wide sea traversing from side to side.
To whom the spirit of Amphimedon.
Illustrious Agamemnon, King of men!
All this I bear in mind, and will rehearse
The manner of our most disastrous end.
Believing brave Ulysses lost, we woo'd
Meantime his wife; she our detested suit
Would neither ratify nor yet refuse,
But, planning for us a tremendous death,
150 This novel stratagem, at last, devised.
Beginning, in her own recess, a web
Of slend'rest thread, and of a length and breadth

Unusual, thus the suitors she address'd.
Princes, my suitors! since the noble Chief
Ulysses is no more, enforce not yet
My nuptials; wait till I shall finish first
A fun'ral robe (lest all my threads decay)
Which for the ancient Hero I prepare,
Laertes, looking for the mournful hour
160 When fate shall snatch him to eternal rest;
Else, I the censure dread of all my sex,
Should he so wealthy, want at last a shroud.
So spake the Queen; we, unsuspicious all,
With her request complied. Thenceforth, all day
She wove the ample web, and by the aid
Of torches ravell'd it again at night.
Three years she thus by artifice our suit
Eluded safe, but when the fourth arrived,
And the same season, after many moons
170 And fleeting days, return'd, a damsel then
Of her attendants, conscious of the fraud,
Reveal'd it, and we found her pulling loose
The splendid web. Thus, through constraint, at length,
She finish'd it, and in her own despight.
But when the Queen produced, at length, her work
Finish'd, new-blanch'd, bright as the sun or moon,
Then came Ulysses, by some adverse God
Conducted, to a cottage on the verge
Of his own fields, in which his swine-herd dwells;
180 There also the illustrious Hero's son
Arrived soon after, in his sable bark
From sandy Pylus borne; they, plotting both
A dreadful death for all the suitors, sought
Our glorious city, but Ulysses last,
And first Telemachus. The father came
Conducted by his swine-herd, and attired
In tatters foul; a mendicant he seem'd,
Time-worn, and halted on a staff. So clad,
And ent'ring on the sudden, he escaped
190 All knowledge even of our eldest there,
And we reviled and smote him; he although
Beneath his own roof smitten and reproach'd,
With patience suffer'd it awhile, but roused
By inspiration of Jove Ægis-arm'd
At length, in concert with his son convey'd
To his own chamber his resplendent arms,
There lodg'd them safe, and barr'd the massy doors
Then, in his subtlety he bade the Queen
A contest institute with bow and rings
200 Between the hapless suitors, whence ensued
Slaughter to all. No suitor there had pow'r
To overcome the stubborn bow that mock'd
All our attempts; and when the weapon huge
At length was offer'd to Ulysses' hands,
With clamour'd menaces we bade the swain
Withhold it from him, plead he as he might;
Telemachus alone with loud command,
Bade give it him, and the illustrious Chief
Receiving in his hand the bow, with ease
210 Bent it, and sped a shaft through all the rings.
Then, springing to the portal steps, he pour'd
The arrows forth, peer'd terrible around,
Pierced King Antinoüs, and, aiming sure
His deadly darts, pierced others after him,

Till in one common carnage heap'd we lay.
Some God, as plain appear'd, vouchsafed them aid,
Such ardour urged them, and with such dispatch
They slew us on all sides; hideous were heard
The groans of dying men fell'd to the earth
220 With head-strokes rude, and the floor swam with blood.
Such, royal Agamemnon! was the fate
By which we perish'd, all whose bodies lie
Unburied still, and in Ulysses' house,
For tidings none have yet our friends alarm'd
And kindred, who might cleanse from sable gore
Our clotted wounds, and mourn us on the bier,
Which are the rightful privilege of the dead.
Him answer'd, then, the shade of Atreus' son.
Oh happy offspring of Laertes! shrewd
230 Ulysses! matchless valour thou hast shewn
Recov'ring thus thy wife; nor less appears
The virtue of Icarius' daughter wise,
The chaste Penelope, so faithful found
To her Ulysses, husband of her youth.
His glory, by superior merit earn'd,
Shall never die, and the immortal Gods
Shall make Penelope a theme of song
Delightful in the ears of all mankind.
Not such was Clytemnestra, daughter vile
240 Of Tyndarus; she shed her husband's blood,
And shall be chronicled in song a wife
Of hateful memory, by whose offence
Even the virtuous of her sex are shamed.
Thus they, beneath the vaulted roof obscure
Of Pluto's house, conferring mutual stood.
Meantime, descending from the city-gates,
Ulysses, by his son and by his swains
Follow'd, arrived at the delightful farm
Which old Laertes had with strenuous toil
250 Himself long since acquired. There stood his house
Encompass'd by a bow'r in which the hinds
Who served and pleased him, ate, and sat, and slept.
An ancient woman, a Sicilian, dwelt
There also, who in that sequester'd spot
Attended diligent her aged Lord.
Then thus Ulysses to his followers spake.
Haste now, and, ent'ring, slay ye of the swine
The best for our regale; myself, the while,
Will prove my father, if his eye hath still
260 Discernment of me, or if absence long
Have worn the knowledge of me from his mind.
He said, and gave into his servants' care
His arms; they swift proceeded to the house,
And to the fruitful grove himself as swift
To prove his father. Down he went at once
Into the spacious garden-plot, but found
Nor Dolius there, nor any of his sons
Or servants; they were occupied elsewhere,
And, with the ancient hind himself, employ'd
27 °Collecting thorns with which to fence the grove.
In that umbrageous spot he found alone
Laertes, with his hoe clearing a plant;
Sordid his tunic was, with many a patch
Mended unseemly; leathern were his greaves,
Thong-tied and also patch'd, a frail defence
Against sharp thorns, while gloves secured his hands

From briar-points, and on his head he bore
A goat-skin casque, nourishing hopeless woe.
No sooner then the Hero toil-inured
280 Saw him age-worn and wretched, than he paused
Beneath a lofty pear-tree's shade to weep.
There standing much he mused, whether, at once,
Kissing and clasping in his arms his sire,
To tell him all, by what means he had reach'd
His native country, or to prove him first.
At length, he chose as his best course, with words
Of seeming strangeness to accost his ear,
And, with that purpose, moved direct toward him.
He, stooping low, loosen'd the earth around
290 A garden-plant, when his illustrious son
Now, standing close beside him, thus began.
Old sir! thou art no novice in these toils
Of culture, but thy garden thrives; I mark
In all thy ground no plant, fig, olive, vine,
Pear-tree or flow'r-bed suff'ring through neglect.
But let it not offend thee if I say
That thou neglect'st thyself, at the same time
Oppress'd with age, sun-parch'd and ill-attired.
Not for thy inactivity, methinks,
300 Thy master slights thee thus, nor speaks thy form
Or thy surpassing stature servile aught
In thee, but thou resemblest more a King.
Yes-thou resemblest one who, bathed and fed,
Should softly sleep; such is the claim of age.
But tell me true-for whom labourest thou,
And whose this garden? answer me beside,
For I would learn; have I indeed arrived
In Ithaca, as one whom here I met
Ev'n now assured me, but who seem'd a man
310 Not overwise, refusing both to hear
My questions, and to answer when I ask'd
Concerning one in other days my guest
And friend, if he have still his being here,
Or have deceas'd and journey'd to the shades.
For I will tell thee; therefore mark. Long since
A stranger reach'd my house in my own land,
Whom I with hospitality receiv'd,
Nor ever sojourn'd foreigner with me
Whom I lov'd more. He was by birth, he said,
320 Ithacan, and Laertes claim'd his sire,
Son of Arcesias. Introducing him
Beneath my roof, I entertain'd him well,
And proved by gifts his welcome at my board.
I gave him seven talents of wrought gold,
A goblet, argent all, with flow'rs emboss'd,
Twelve single cloaks, twelve carpets, mantles twelve
Of brightest lustre, with as many vests,
And added four fair damsels, whom he chose
Himself, well born and well accomplish'd all.
330 Then thus his ancient sire weeping replied.
Stranger! thou hast in truth attain'd the isle
Of thy enquiry, but it is possess'd
By a rude race, and lawless. Vain, alas!
Were all thy num'rous gifts; yet hadst thou found
Him living here in Ithaca, with gifts
Reciprocated he had sent thee hence,
Requiting honourably in his turn
Thy hospitality. But give me quick

Answer and true. How many have been the years
340 Since thy reception of that hapless guest
My son? for mine, my own dear son was he.
But him, far distant both from friends and home,
Either the fishes of the unknown Deep
Have eaten, or wild beasts and fowls of prey,
Nor I, or she who bare him, was ordain'd
To bathe his shrouded body with our tears,
Nor his chaste wife, well-dow'r'd Penelope
To close her husband's eyes, and to deplore
His doom, which is the privilege of the dead.
350 But tell me also thou, for I would learn,
Who art thou? whence? where born? and sprung from whom?
The bark in which thou and thy godlike friends
Arrived, where is she anchor'd on our coast?
Or cam'st thou only passenger on board
Another's bark, who landed thee and went?
To whom Ulysses, ever-wise, replied.
I will with all simplicity relate
What thou hast ask'd. Of Alybas am I,
Where in much state I dwell, son of the rich
360 Apheidas royal Polypemon's son,
And I am named Eperitus; by storms
Driven from Sicily I have arrived,
And yonder, on the margin of the field
That skirts your city, I have moor'd my bark.
Five years have pass'd since thy Ulysses left,
Unhappy Chief! my country; yet the birds
At his departure hovered on the right,
And in that sign rejoicing, I dismiss'd
Him thence rejoicing also, for we hoped
370 To mix in social intercourse again,
And to exchange once more pledges of love.
He spake; then sorrow as a sable cloud
Involved Laertes; gath'ring with both hands
The dust, he pour'd it on his rev'rend head
With many a piteous groan. Ulysses' heart
Commotion felt, and his stretch'd nostrils throbb'd
With agony close-pent, while fixt he eyed
His father; with a sudden force he sprang
Toward him, clasp'd, and kiss'd him, and exclaim'd.
380 My father! I am he. Thou seest thy son
Absent these twenty years at last return'd.
But bid thy sorrow cease; suspend henceforth
All lamentation; for I tell thee true,
(And the occasion bids me briefly tell thee)
I have slain all the suitors at my home,
And all their taunts and injuries avenged.
Then answer thus Laertes quick return'd.
If thou hast come again, and art indeed
My son Ulysses, give me then the proof
390 Indubitable, that I may believe.
To whom Ulysses, ever-wise, replied.
View, first, the scar which with his iv'ry tusk
A wild boar gave me, when at thy command
And at my mother's, to Autolycus
Her father, on Parnassus, I repair'd
Seeking the gifts which, while a guest of yours,
He promis'd should be mine. Accept beside

This proof. I will enum'rate all the trees
Which, walking with thee in this cultured spot
400 (Boy then) I begg'd, and thou confirm'dst my own.
We paced between them, and thou mad'st me learn
The name of each. Thou gav'st me thirteen pears,[113]
Ten apples, thirty figs, and fifty ranks
Didst promise me of vines, their alleys all
Corn-cropp'd between. There, oft as sent from Jove
The influences of the year descend,
Grapes of all hues and flavours clust'ring hang.
He said; Laertes, conscious of the proofs
Indubitable by Ulysses giv'n,
410 With fault'ring knees and fault'ring heart both arms
Around him threw. The Hero toil-inured
Drew to his bosom close his fainting sire,
Who, breath recov'ring, and his scatter'd pow'rs
Of intellect, at length thus spake aloud.
Ye Gods! oh then your residence is still
On the Olympian heights, if punishment
At last hath seized on those flagitious men.
But terrour shakes me, lest, incensed, ere long
All Ithaca flock hither, and dispatch
420 Swift messengers with these dread tidings charged
To ev'ry Cephallenian state around.
Him answer'd then Ulysses ever-wise.
Courage! fear nought, but let us to the house
Beside the garden, whither I have sent
Telemachus, the herdsman, and the good
Eumæus to prepare us quick repast.
So they conferr'd, and to Laertes' house
Pass'd on together; there arrived, they found
Those three preparing now their plenteous feast,
430 And mingling sable wine; then, by the hands
Of his Sicilian matron, the old King
Was bathed, anointed, and attired afresh,
And Pallas, drawing nigh, dilated more
His limbs, and gave his whole majestic form
Encrease of amplitude. He left the bath.
His son, amazed as he had seen a God
Alighted newly from the skies, exclaim'd.
My father! doubtless some immortal Pow'r
Hath clothed thy form with dignity divine.
440 Then thus replied his venerable sire.
Jove! Pallas! Phoebus! oh that I possess'd
Such vigour now, as when in arms I took
Nericus, continental city fair,
With my brave Cephallenians! oh that such
And arm'd as then, I yesterday had stood
Beside thee in thy palace, combating
Those suitors proud, then had I strew'd the floor
With num'rous slain, to thy exceeding joy.
Such was their conference; and now, the task
450 Of preparation ended, and the feast
Set forth, on couches and on thrones they sat,
And, ranged in order due, took each his share.
Then, ancient Dolius, and with him, his sons
Arrived toil-worn, by the Sicilian dame
Summon'd, their cat'ress, and their father's kind
Attendant ever in his eve of life.

---

[113] The fruit is here used for the tree that bore it, as it is in the Greek; the Latins used the same mode of expression, neither is it uncommon in our own language.

They, seeing and recalling soon to mind
Ulysses, in the middle mansion stood
Wond'ring, when thus Ulysses with a voice
460 Of some reproof, but gentle, them bespake.
Old servant, sit and eat, banishing fear
And mute amazement; for, although provoked
By appetite, we have long time abstain'd,
Expecting ev'ry moment thy return.
He said; then Dolius with expanded arms
Sprang right toward Ulysses, seized his hand,
Kiss'd it, and in wing'd accents thus replied.
Oh master ever dear! since thee the Gods
Themselves in answer to our warm desires,
470 Have, unexpectedly, at length restored,
Hail, and be happy, and heav'n make thee such!
But say, and truly; knows the prudent Queen
Already thy return, or shall we send
Ourselves an herald with the joyful news?
To whom Ulysses, ever-wise, replied.
My ancient friend, thou may'st release thy mind
From that solicitude; she knows it well.
So he; then Dolius to his glossy seat
Return'd, and all his sons gath'ring around
480 Ulysses, welcom'd him and grasp'd his hand,
Then sat beside their father; thus beneath
Laertes' roof they, joyful, took repast.
But Fame with rapid haste the city roam'd
In ev'ry part, promulging in all ears
The suitors' horrid fate. No sooner heard
The multitude that tale, than one and all
Groaning they met and murmuring before
Ulysses' gates. Bringing the bodies forth,
They buried each his friend, but gave the dead
490 Of other cities to be ferried home
By fishermen on board their rapid barks.
All hasted then to council; sorrow wrung
Their hearts, and, the assembly now convened,
Arising first Eupithes spake, for grief
Sat heavy on his soul, grief for the loss
Of his Antinoüs by Ulysses slain
Foremost of all, whom mourning, thus he said.
My friends! no trivial fruits the Greecians reap
Of this man's doings. *Those* he took with him
500 On board his barks, a num'rous train and bold,
Then lost his barks, lost all his num'rous train,
And *these* , our noblest, slew at his return.
Come therefore-ere he yet escape by flight
To Pylus or to noble Elis, realm
Of the Epeans, follow him; else shame
Attends us and indelible reproach.
If we avenge not on these men the blood
Of our own sons and brothers, farewell then
All that makes life desirable; my wish
510 Henceforth shall be to mingle with the shades.
Oh then pursue and seize them ere they fly.
Thus he with tears, and pity moved in all.
Then, Medon and the sacred bard whom sleep
Had lately left, arriving from the house
Of Laertiades, approach'd; amid
The throng they stood; all wonder'd seeing them,
And Medon, prudent senior, thus began.
Hear me, my countrymen! Ulysses plann'd

With no disapprobation of the Gods
520 The deed that ye deplore. I saw, myself,
A Pow'r immortal at the Hero's side,
In semblance just of Mentor; now the God,
In front apparent, led him on, and now,
From side to side of all the palace, urged
To flight the suitors; heaps on heaps they fell.
He said; then terrour wan seiz'd ev'ry cheek,
And Halitherses, Hero old, the son
Of Mastor, who alone among them all
Knew past, and future, prudent, thus began.
530 Now, O ye men of Ithaca! my words
Attentive hear! by your own fault, my friends,
This deed hath been perform'd; for when myself
And noble Mentor counsell'd you to check
The sin and folly of your sons, ye would not.
Great was their wickedness, and flagrant wrong
They wrought, the wealth devouring and the wife
Dishonouring of an illustrious Chief
Whom they deem'd destined never to return.
But hear my counsel. Go not, lest ye draw
540 Disaster down and woe on your own heads.
He ended; then with boist'rous roar (although
Part kept their seats) upsprang the multitude,
For Halitherses pleased them not, they chose
Eupithes' counsel rather; all at once
To arms they flew, and clad in dazzling brass
Before the city form'd their dense array.
Leader infatuate at their head appear'd
Eupithes, hoping to avenge his son
Antinoüs, but was himself ordain'd
550 To meet his doom, and to return no more.
Then thus Minerva to Saturnian Jove.
Oh father! son of Saturn! Jove supreme!
Declare the purpose hidden in thy breast.
Wilt thou that this hostility proceed,
Or wilt thou grant them amity again?
To whom the cloud-assembler God replied.
Why asks my daughter? didst thou not design
Thyself, that brave Ulysses coming home
Should slay those profligates? act as thou wilt,
560 But thus I counsel, since the noble Chief
Hath slain the suitors, now let peace ensue
Oath-bound, and reign Ulysses evermore!
The slaughter of their brethren and their sons
To strike from their remembrance, shall be ours.
Let mutual amity, as at the first,
Unite them, and let wealth and peace abound.
So saying, he animated to her task
Minerva prompt before, and from the heights
Olympian down to Ithaca she flew.
570 Meantime Ulysses (for their hunger now
And thirst were sated) thus address'd his hinds.
Look ye abroad, lest haply they approach.
He said, and at his word, forth went a son
Of Dolius; at the gate he stood, and thence
Beholding all that multitude at hand,
In accents wing'd thus to Ulysses spake.
They come-they are already arrived-arm all!
Then, all arising, put their armour on,
Ulysses with his three, and the six sons
580 Of Dolius; Dolius also with the rest,

Arm'd and Laertes, although silver-hair'd,
Warriors perforce. When all were clad alike
In radiant armour, throwing wide the gates
They sallied, and Ulysses led the way.
Then Jove's own daughter Pallas, in the form
And with the voice of Mentor, came in view,
Whom seeing Laertiades rejoiced,
And thus Telemachus, his son, bespake.
Now, oh my son! thou shalt observe, untold
590 By me, where fight the bravest. Oh shame not
Thine ancestry, who have in all the earth
Proof given of valour in all ages past.
To whom Telemachus, discrete, replied.
My father! if thou wish that spectacle,
Thou shalt behold thy son, as thou hast said,
In nought dishonouring his noble race.
Then was Laertes joyful, and exclaim'd,
What sun hath ris'n to-day?[114] oh blessed Gods!
My son and grandson emulous dispute
600 The prize of glory, and my soul exults.
He ended, and Minerva drawing nigh
To the old King, thus counsell'd him. Oh friend
Whom most I love, son of Arcesias! pray'r
Preferring to the virgin azure-eyed,
And to her father Jove, delay not, shake
Thy lance in air, and give it instant flight.
So saying, the Goddess nerved his arm anew.
He sought in pray'r the daughter dread of Jove,
And, brandishing it, hurl'd his lance; it struck

610 Eupithes, pierced his helmet brazen-cheek'd
That stay'd it not, but forth it sprang beyond,
And with loud clangor of his arms he fell.
Then flew Ulysses and his noble son
With faulchion and with spear of double edge
To the assault, and of them all had left
None living, none had to his home return'd,
But that Jove's virgin daughter with a voice
Of loud authority thus quell'd them all.
Peace, O ye men of Ithaca! while yet
620 The field remains undeluged with your blood.
So she, and fear at once paled ev'ry cheek.
All trembled at the voice divine; their arms
Escaping from the grasp fell to the earth,
And, covetous of longer life, each fled
Back to the city. Then Ulysses sent
His voice abroad, and with an eagle's force
Sprang on the people; but Saturnian Jove,
Cast down, incontinent, his smouldring bolt
At Pallas' feet, and thus the Goddess spake.
630 Laertes' noble son, for wiles renown'd!
Forbear; abstain from slaughter; lest thyself
Incur the anger of high thund'ring Jove.
So Pallas, whom Ulysses, glad, obey'd.
Then faithful covenants of peace between
Both sides ensued, ratified in the sight
Of Pallas progeny of Jove, who seem'd,
In voice and form, the Mentor known to all.

END OF THE ODYSSEY

---

114 +Tis nu moi hêmerê hêde?+-So Cicero, who seems to translate it-Proh dii immortales! Quis hic illuxit dies! See Clarke in loco.

NOTES

NOTE I

Bk. x. l.
101–106 (Hom. x. l.
81–86).-It is held now that this passage should be explained by the supposition that the Homeric bards had heard tales of northern latitudes, where, in summer-time, the darkness was so short that evening was followed almost at once by morning. Thus the herdsman coming home in the twilight at one day's close might meet and hail the shepherd who was starting betimes for the next day's work.
Line
86 in the Greek ought probably to be translated, "For the paths of night and day are close together," *i.e.* , the entrance of day follows hard on the entrance of night.

NOTE II

Bk. xi. l.
162,
163 (Hom. xi. l.
134,
135).-
+thanatos de toi ex halos autôi
ablêchros mala toios eleusetai+.
Others translate, "And from the sea shall thy own death come," suggesting that Ulysses after all was lost at sea. This is the rendering followed by Tennyson in his poem "Ulysses" (and see Dante, *Inferno* , Canto xxvi.). It is a more natural translation of the Greek, and gives a far more wonderful vista for the close of the Wanderer's life.

NOTE III

Bk. xix. l.
712 (Hom. xix. l.
573).-The word +pelekeas+, for which Cowper gives as a paraphrase "spikes, crested with a ring," elsewhere means *axes* , and ought so to be translated here. For since Cowper's day an axe-head of the Mycenæan period has been discovered *with the blade pierced* so as to form a hole through which an arrow could pass. (See Tsountas and Manatt, *The Mycenæan Age* .) Axes of this type were not known to Cowper, and hence the hypothesis in his text. He realised correctly the essential conditions of the feat proposed: the axes must have been set up, one behind the other, in the way he suggested for his ringed stakes.

NOTE IV

Bk. xxii. l.
139–162 (Hom. xxii. l.
126–143).-How Melanthius got out of the hall remains a puzzle. Cowper assumes a second postern, but there is no evidence for this, and l.
139 ff. (l.
126 ff. in the Greek) suggest rather strongly that there was only *one* . Unfortunately, the crucial word +rhôges+ which occurs in the line describing Melanthius' exit is not found elsewhere. "He went up," the poet says, "through the +rhôges+ of the hall." Merry suggests that "he scrambled up to the loopholes that were pierced in the wall." Others suppose that there was a ladder at the inner end of the hall leading to the upper story, and on through passages to the armoury.
In l.
141 (l.
128 in the Greek) the word translated "street" by Cowper is usually rendered "corridor."
F. M. S.

140

Made in the USA
Columbia, SC
08 August 2018